UNIVERSITY OF CAMBRIDGE
RESEARCH CENTRE FOR ENGLISH
AND APPLIED LINGUISTICS
ENGLISH FACULTY BUILDING
9 WEST ROAD, CAMBRIDGE CB3 9DP

Genitive Variation in English

Topics in English Linguistics 42

Editors

Elizabeth Closs Traugott
Bernd Kortmann

Mouton de Gruyter
Berlin · New York

Genitive Variation in English

Conceptual Factors in Synchronic and Diachronic Studies

by

Anette Rosenbach

Mouton de Gruyter
Berlin · New York 2002

Mouton de Gruyter (formerly Mouton, The Hague)
is a Division of Walter de Gruyter GmbH & Co. KG, Berlin.

♾ Printed on acid-free paper which falls within the guidelines
of the ANSI to ensure permanence and durability.

Die Deutsche Bibliothek − *CIP-Einheitsaufnahme*

Rosenbach, Anette:
Genitive variation in English : conceptual factors in synchronic
and diachronic studies / by Anette Rosenbach. − Berlin ; New
York : Mouton de Gruyter, 2002
   (Topics in English linguistics ; 42)
   ISBN 3-11-017370-0

Cover design: Christopher Schneider, Berlin.
Printed in Germany.

Acknowledgements

These acknowledgements must necessarily fail to do justice to the many scholars, colleagues, and friends who have contributed in one way or the other to the present study. I will nonetheless attempt to express my gratitude especially to the following people:

I am grateful to Keith Brown, Tania Kuteva, Albert Ortmann, Martina Penke, Dieter Stein, Barbara Stiebels, Letizia Vezzosi, Dieter Wunderlich, and Richard Young for taking their time and discussing, at the various stages of gestation, my work with me. Thanks also to the members of the linguistic research colloquia of the "Philosophische Fakultät" and the Department of General Linguistics in Düsseldorf for giving me the opportunity to discuss my ongoing work with them. Cynthia Allen kindly commented on some earlier work on the historical data included here. I am also indebted to Roger Lass for indulging into an enlightening discussion on his conception of language change, which inspired parts of my final conclusion in chapter 9, and for various other challenging discussions. Even if not always agreeing with all these people (and they with me), I benefitted greatly from these discussions, and they kept me and my work going.

I cannot directly thank the many, largely anonymous British and American volunteers who participated in this study; instead let me express my gratitude towards those people who helped me dig these people up, particularly: Keith Brown, Sabine Buchheister, Susan Dostert, Fred Eckman, Kerrie Elston-Güttler, Elly van Gelderen, Antje Hartmann, Verena Jung, and Richard Young.

Susan Dostert is to be credited for taking the effort of eliminating the worst flaws in the English language, and Monika Schmid generously offered (and provided!) efficient help when I was going crazy formatting this book.

For her ever-willing, patient and most helpful advice, particularly with the experimental design and the statistical analysis I owe a very special thanks to Martina Penke.

Elizabeth Traugott as General Editor provided very valuable and constructive comments and advice; besides she kindly reminded me at the final stages in the production of this work that there is life after the book – and made me finish it.

Letizia Vezzosi brought me to 'the genitives', shared ideas and work with me for the historical data, helped to inspire the present study and became a good friend. I am deeply indebted to her and Dieter Stein for inviting me into this joint research project in the first place.

Last but not least, eternal gratitude to Robert for constantly encouraging me in this work, supporting me in every conceivable way and continuing to be patient until the very last day – nothing without him.

Düsseldorf, April 2002   Anette Rosenbach

Table of contents

List of abbreviations

BrE	British English
EModE	early Modern English
ModE	Modern English
OE	Old English
PrdE	Present-day English
DP	determiner phrase
NP	noun phrase
FLOB	The Freiburg-LOB Corpus of British English
FROWN	The Freiburg Brown Corpus of American English
LOB	The Lancaster-Oslo/Bergen Corpus
OT	Optimality Theory
VO	Verb-Object
OV	Object-Verb
[±a]	[±animate] possessor
[±t]	[±topical] possessor
[±p]	[±prototypical] possessive relation
of	*of*-genitive
POSS *'s*	possessive *'s*
's	s-genitive
n.s.	not significant
p	probability
χ^2	chi-square

Chapter 1
Introduction

How can an investigation of the English genitive variation, i.e. the variation between constructions such as *the girl's eyes* (= *s*-genitive) and *the eyes of the girl* (= *of*-genitive) contribute to our understanding of language, and how does the present study link to what we already know about it?

The question of what governs the choice between these two genitive constructions is not a new one and has been addressed by a number of empirical studies, which try to identify the various factors that favor one or the other genitive construction by calculating the frequency with which these constructions occur in corpora (see e.g. Jahr Sorheim 1980; Jucker 1993; Leech, Francis, and Xu 1994; Raab-Fischer 1995; Anschutz 1997; Hundt 1997, 1998). We can learn two important things from these corpus studies:

(1) Numerous factors conspire when choosing between the *s*-genitive and the *of*-genitive, such as e.g. phonological, morphological, semantic, pragmatic, syntactic and stylistic factors (see particularly Altenberg 1982).

(2) Contrary to the common belief that today the *s*-genitive is generally restricted to animate possessors while the *of*-genitive is preferred with inanimate possessors, these studies show that the *s*-genitive does in fact occur with inanimate possessors (cf. Jahr Sorheim 1980; Jucker 1993; Leech, Francis, and Xu 1994; Anschutz 1997) and is even on the increase in this context in Present-day English (cf. e.g. Raab-Fischer 1995; Hundt 1997, 1998). This extension of the *s*-genitive to inanimate possessors is, however, restricted to certain noun classes, such as temporal nouns (e.g. **today's** *weather*) or geographical nouns (e.g. **Germany's** *chancellor*).

In contrast to most empirical research on the genitive variation so far, the present study does not only set out to *describe* how the two genitive constructions are distributed but also tries to account for *why* the distribution of the *s*-genitive and the *of*-genitive is the way it is. In so doing, the theoretical orientation taken is essentially functionalist in nature. A user-based (psycholinguistic) approach to grammatical variation and change is introduced, in which cognitive pressures are taken to underlie language use. These cognitive pressures are derived from the conceptual factors investigated, i.e. animacy, topicality, and possessive relation. It is well-known from the literature that these factors influence language usage in general and the choice of the *s*-genitive in particular (see e.g. Hawkins 1981; Deane 1987; Taylor 1996; Anschutz 1997, to name but a few). In this study these factors are linked to user-optimal principles that allow for predictions as to which genitive variant is the optimal and therefore the more likely one for the speaker in a given context.

To test these predictions, a methodological tool is used not previously employed in the investigation of the English genitive variation, i.e. an experimental study. An experimental design helps to restrict the analysis to those contexts where there is a real choice between the two constructions, as e.g. *the boy's mother* versus *the mother of the boy*, but not e.g. *a king of honor* versus **an honor's king*. Moreover, given the multitude of factors that govern the choice between the *s*-genitive and the *of*-genitive, in an experimental design certain factors can be focused upon, while other factors known to influence the genitive variation as well can be controlled to a large extent. It is not the goal of this study to present a wholesale analysis of just *any* possible factors affecting the genitive variation but to investigate in a detailed way the effects of some selected conceptual factors, i.e. animacy, topicality, and possessive relation. These factors are, however, known to interact highly in practice and thus are not independent of each other: topics are often animate, and the prototypical possessor is human. Therefore, it is very difficult indeed to tell whether in *John's father* it is (a) the animacy of the possessor, and/or (b) the high topicality/ referentiality of the possessor, and/or (c) the (very prototypical) kin relation expressed, that induces the *s*-genitive. In an experimental design the effects of these factors can be kept apart by deliberately choosing (and testing) examples where these factors do *not* go together. In this way, it is then also possible to weigh the strength of these three factors when choosing a genitive construction, thus allowing for an evaluation of their relative importance.

The results of this experimental study, conducted with British and American speakers of English, indicate that

(i)   the *s*-genitive is indeed favored in those contexts regarded as the (user-) optimal ones, i.e. with an animate and topical possessor, and in a prototypical possessive relation,

(ii)   the relative importance of the three factors is: animacy > topicality > possessive relation,

(iii) the *s*-genitive is currently increasing in Present-day English, particularly with inanimate possessors, and this increase is more advanced in American than in British English,

(iv) the (still ongoing) extension of the *s*-genitive to inanimate possessors is more productive than so far has been assumed, with common noun possessors (e.g. *the building's door, the chair's frame*) participating in a fairly systematic way in this change.

In a second step, the diachronic development of the genitive variation is looked at, and the results of the experimental study for Present-day English are compared with the results of a corpus analysis from late Middle and early Modern English (1400 – 1630). Traditionally, it has been assumed that the most dramatic changes in the distribution of the two genitive constructions took place in the period between Old English and Middle English, when the synthetic *s*-genitive became increasingly replaced by the analytic *of*-genitive, an assumption, which is largely based on the figures given in an early survey study by Thomas (1931). Otherwise, the only available large-scale diachronic empirical analysis is Altenberg's (1982) case study of the genitive variation in the seventeenth century. The results of these diachronic studies somehow seem to have given rise to the assumption that not much has changed in the distribution of the *s*-genitive and the *of*-genitive ever since the early Modern English period, a view reflected in the following statement by Rissanen (1999: 201) in the early Modern English volume of *The Cambridge History of the English Language (1476-1776)*: "In the sixteenth and seventeenth centuries, the distribution of the *s*-genitive and the *of*-genitive developed roughly to what it is today." It is one of the main empirical findings of this study that this view cannot be maintained. It is shown that counter to the general development of English towards more analyticity, the synthetic *s*-genitive became more productive again (at the expense of the *of*-genitive) in the period from 1400 to 1630, and also how the factors animacy, topicality, and possessive relation participate in this change (cf. also the analyses in Rosenbach and Vezzosi 2000, and Rosenbach, Stein, and Vezzosi 2000). Comparing the diachronic corpus data with the results of the Present-day English experimental study, it is finally argued that the *s*-genitive has extended along a preference structure built upon the hierarchical ordering of the conceptual factors (animacy > topicality > possessive relation) from the fifteenth century to the present day. This preference structure demonstrates how, diachronically, these conceptual factors increasingly motivate the use of the *s*-genitive and how it eventually extends more and more, even to unmotivated contexts (and particularly noticeable is the still ongoing extension to inanimate possessors).

The user-based stance to grammatical variation taken in this study helps to account for the diachronic extension of the *s*-genitive in the following way: Knowing what makes speakers choose one genitive construction rather than the other synchronically, also casts more light on the question of why the *s*-genitive has become more productive again. Accordingly, a diachronic scenario of economically-driven language change is proposed, showing that what is optimal for the speaker synchronically, will also become more frequent diachronically (for such an approach, see also Hawkins 1994 or Haspelmath 1999b, although, as I will argue in the final part of this book, there are also differences in the approaches). In this respect, the present book is a case study on the English genitive variation showing how (a) a user-based (i.e. psycholinguistic) approach to grammatical variation and (b) economically-driven language change go hand in hand.

Apart from the analysis of the genitive variation, structural aspects of the *s*-genitive are important in a number of ways, too, particularly to account for the fact of why the *s*-genitive, after a period of steady decline throughout the Middle English period, should suddenly become more frequent again from late Middle English onwards. For Present-day English, the *s*-genitive is generally analyzed as a construction in which the possessor functions as a determiner (cf. e.g. Huddleston 1984: 233; Quirk et al. 1985: §326-328). There is, however, quite a debate on the theoretical status of the relational marker '*s*, exhibiting both characteristics of an inflection and of a clitic (Carstairs 1987; Zwicky 1987; Plank 1992a, 1995; Taylor 1996; Allen 1997a; Seppänen 1997b). This categorially quite indeterminate nature of possessive '*s* is probably best accounted for when regarding it as a reflection of its history (cf. e.g. Plank 1992a), having changed from a fully-fledged inflection in Old English towards a clitic in Modern English, though not having acquired full clitic status (yet?). Such a development from inflectional affix to clitic would, however, pose one of the rare – and accordingly inconvenient – counter-examples to the presumed unidirectionality in the framework of grammaticalization theory, according to which clitics should turn into affixes but not vice versa, and, accordingly, it has been discussed quite controversially in the literature (e.g. Janda 1980, 2001; Allen 1997a; Tabor and Traugott 1998; Plank 1992a, 1995; Newmeyer 1998: §5; Norde 1998, 2001). Now, interestingly, the transition period for this structural change of possessive '*s*, starting in late Middle English, correlates chronologically precisely with the period in which the *s*-genitive is becoming more frequent again, i.e. from late Middle English onwards. Therefore, this change of the *s*-genitive from an inflectional towards a cliticized construction (having determiner function) will be regarded as the structural precondition for the new productivity of the *s*-genitive. In a nutshell, this means: It is not the old inflectional *s*-genitive that becomes more frequent again but the new clitic *s*-genitive. It is also in the very same period that the *s*-genitive acquires determiner function, a fact which is also important for the empirical findings regarding the genitive variation. As is shown, the contexts to which the *s*-genitive is restricted (i.e. an animate and topical possessor in a prototypical possessive relation) and from which it is eventually expanding from late Middle English onwards are precisely those most compatible with its new (anchoring) function as a determiner. Moreover, it is discussed in which respect both processes of (i) (possible) degrammaticalization as well as (ii) grammaticalization can be observed in the diachronic development of the *s*-genitive, although it has so far mainly been discussed as a possible case of *de*grammaticalization in the literature (cf. e.g. Janda 1980, 2001; Plank 1992a, 1995; Newmeyer 1998: §5.3.4; but see Tabor and Traugott 1998 for arguing that the development of the *s*-genitive towards a clitic is a case of grammaticalization). It is in all these ways that both the historical development of the *s*-genitive (inflection > clitic & determiner) and the genitive variation (*s*-genitive versus *of*-genitive), which, so far, have been largely treated independently of each other in the literature, if not in mutual ignorance, are connected here. An implication following from this is that the *s*-genitive, given its peculiar nature and history, will receive special emphasis throughout, although the genitive variation is at the fore of this study.

In sum, the present study links and contributes to previous research in a number of ways, combining theoretical and empirical aspects of the genitive constructions and connecting the study of their present with their past. It is shown that and how the *s*-genitive extended diachronically (to the present day) in the English language and, pursuing an user-based approach to grammatical variation, also why this extension proceeded in the way it did. The structural change of possessive *'s* turning into a clitic and the *s*-genitive acquiring determiner function is hypothesized to spark off the cognitive pressures underlying the synchronic choice as well as the diachronic increase of the *s*-genitive. And although this study is a case study on a particular type of grammatical variation, i.e. the genitive variation in English, it is hoped that it adds to our understanding of linguistic variation and change in general, i.e. why and when language may change.

This book is organized in the following way: The first four chapters are devoted to settling a series of theoretical and methodological issues involved, laying the foundation for the empirical analysis: A structural-functional analysis of the *s*-genitive and the *of*-genitive is given in chapter 1, and in chapter 2 the genitive alternation is established as a case of grammatical variation. The conceptual factors animacy, topicality, and possessive relation are introduced in chapter 3. Along with the distinction between the concepts of "variation" and "choice", which differ as to where to place the locus of variation (in competence versus performance, and situated within the individual language user, or not), the choice-based approach as underlying the present study is introduced vis-à-vis other theoretical frameworks of variation and change in chapter 4. In chapters 5 and 6 the empirical evidence for the factors animacy, topicality, and possessive relation is expounded. Chapter 5 presents the empirical evidence for Present-day English, i.e. the experimental study conducted with British and American speakers of English. Chapter 6 deals with the diachronic development of the genitive variation, presenting the analysis of the late Middle/early Modern English corpus data and treating the historical development of the *s*-genitive in detail here. In chapter 7 the results from the late Middle/early Modern English corpus analysis are compared with the Present-day English experimental data, and a diachronic scenario of economically-driven language change for the *s*-genitive from late Middle English onwards is proposed. Also, the question of (de)grammaticalization is discussed here. Chapter 8 summarizes the main findings, concluding with some reflection on the conception of grammatical variation and change as it underlies the present study.

Chapter 2
The structure of the *s*-genitive and the *of*-genitive: some theoretical preliminaries

2.1 The constructions

The *s*-genitive and the *of*-genitive are the two major nominal devices in Standard English to express possessive relationships. The terms "*s*-genitive" and "*of*-genitive", respectively, will be used to refer to the whole possessive construction. In a nominal possessive construction two noun phrases (NPs), which will be called "possessor" and "possessum", are linked via a relational marker as illustrated by an example in table 1.

Table 1. Characterization of "possessor", "possessum", and "relational marker"

s-genitive			*of*-genitive		
possessor	relational marker	possessum	possessum	relational marker	possessor
the girl	*'s*	*eyes*	*the eyes*	*of*	*the girl*

Superficially, the two constructions only differ in the respective relational marker (*'s* versus *of*) and in the linear arrangement of possessor and possessum. In the *s*-genitive the possessor precedes the possessum, while following it in the *of*-genitive.

Looking more closely, however, the two constructions differ further structurally. In what follows, the *s*-genitive and the *of*-genitive will be analyzed with regard to two questions:

(1) What is the grammatical nature/status of the relational markers?
(2) What is the nature of the grammatical relation between possessor and possessum?

2.2   The nature of the relational markers

It is quite uncontroversial that the *of* in the *of*-genitive is a preposition. What is much less clear is how to categorize the possessive *'s* (POSS *'s*). Traditionally, it has been treated as a morpheme marking genitive case in English, i.e.as an inflection:

> In nouns (sbs and adjs) ModE distinguishes only two cases, a common case and a genitive, the latter always ending in s with the three phonetic values [z, s, iz] according to the final sound of the stem...
>
> (Jespersen [1949] 1961: 281)

> We shall distinguish between two cases of nouns: the unmarked COMMON CASE (*eg: boy* in the singular, *boys* in the plural) and the marked GENITIVE CASE (*eg: boy's* in the singular, *boys'* in the plural.
>
> (Quirk et al. 1985: §5.112)

> The only remaining case inflection for nouns is the **genitive**.
>
> (Biber et al. 1999: 292)

There is, however, strong evidence which points against a categorization of POSS *'s* as an inflectional ending. I will here summarize the main arguments that have been put forward in the literature.[1]

First, there are constructions (see examples [1] – [7]) in which POSS *'s* attaches to – sometimes quite complex (see [4]) – phrases and not – as should be expected for a nominal inflection – to nominal heads.[2] We can basically distinguish three different types of phrases to which POSS *'s* can attach: "group genitives" ([1]–[4]),[3] conjoined NPs (5) and appositions (6).

(1)   *[the teacher of music]'s room*   (cf. Quirk et al. 1985: §17.119)

(2)   *[the man in the car]'s ears*   (cf. Quirk et al. 1985: §17.119)

(3)   *[Old man what-do-you-call-him]'s house has just been sold.*
                                                 (cf. Quirk et al. 1985: §17.119)

(4)   *It's not mine, it's [a person who went to Cambridge and got a first in engineering]'s.*[4]

(5)   *[Melody and Henry]'s window*[5]   (Roddy Doyle, *A Star Called Henry*, 13)

(6)   *[Elizabeth the Second]'s heir*   (Quirk et al. 1985: §17.119)

Note that group genitives seem to be more widespread in colloquial and dialectal language and are hardly ever found in written language (cf. e.g. Carstairs 1987: 152; Jespersen [1918] 1960: 286, 296-297).

Second, since POSS '*s* attaches to the end of the NP complex and not to the possessor itself, it can also attach to non-nominal elements (7), which also seems to rule it out as a representative of a nominal inflection.

(7)   *people who hurry's ideas*   (Zwicky 1987: 141)

Moreover, as has been pointed out by Plank (1985), who again refers to Jespersen (1960: 332), POSS '*s* does not, in contrast to the plural -*s*, trigger voice alternation (plural: *wives* versus POSS: *wife's*).[6] This indicates that POSS '*s* must be something different than an inflection. Why should one inflection, i.e. the plural -*s*, trigger a phonological process, but another one (POSS '*s*) not? Also, the lack of voice alternation with POSS '*s* is consistent with the word-internality constraint proposed by Plank (1985: 205): "Allomorphy cannot be conditioned across (grammatical) word boundaries". If POSS '*s* marks a grammatical word boundary, it cannot condition allomorphy. Inflections, however, do not mark word boundaries but are parts of words.

Finally, as pointed out by Carstairs (1987), clitics can be distinguished from affixes in that the latter usually exhibit a "higher degree of selection" (152). What he means by this is that affixes are typically fairly selective, resulting in a paradigm consisting of different allomorphs for one affix. In Modern English, however, POSS '*s* is the one and only form left, of course not taking its phonetic allomorphs (/s ~z~ ɪz/) into account.

It also seems odd that the plural inflection has retained some irregular forms (e.g. *oxen, children*) but the alleged genitive inflection has not (cf. Jespersen 1960: 299); as Jespersen (1960: 303) puts it "the *s*-ending only surviving as the fittest". This argument is, however, slightly weakened by dialectal evidence. Seppänen (1997b: 196, 207-208) argues that northern England dialects indeed retain some older *s*-less forms (*Jack wife*); see also Klemola (1997) for reporting evidence of the *Survey of English Dialects* (*SED*) that the *s*-less genitive is a common feature of twentieth-century northern English.

There is further evidence which points against an inflectional interpretation of POSS '*s* and which has not, I believe, been addressed so far in the literature. According to Kiparsky's (1982) theory of lexical morphology and phonology, derivational and inflectional processes are organized in a series of three levels of the lexicon as illustrated in table 2 below. According to this model regular inflection takes (logically) place after compounding, i.e. to the whole compound, which explains why irregular plurals in English can occur within compounds (*mice-infested, teeth marks*) but not regular plurals (**rats-infested, *claws marks*); and see also also Bauer (1988: 134-135) for arguing that (regular) inflection should follow compounding. Likewise, if POSS '*s* were a (regular) inflection, it should not be used in compounds. But this is not the case. There are possessive compounds including POSS '*s*, such as *women's shoes* or *driver's licence*, which indicate that POSS '*s* is attached before compounding takes place. Therefore, POSS '*s* cannot be a regular inflection, at least not within Kiparsky's model.[7]

Table 2.   The level-model of the lexicon (see Kiparsky 1982: 5, adapted and modified)

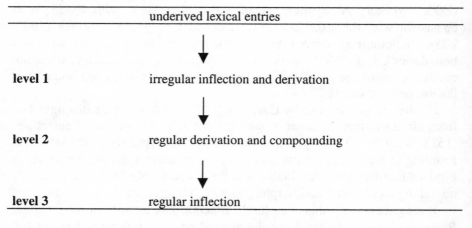

underdived lexical entries
↓
level 1   irregular inflection and derivation
↓
level 2   regular derivation and compounding
↓
level 3   regular inflection

Moreover, in the English example (8a) below the possessive pronoun can have separate scope over *wife* and *mother*, allowing a reading that has two separate referents, i.e. 'my wife' and 'my mother', which is exactly what our cultural knowledge would predict (men usually do not marry their mothers!). In the German example (8b), this is not possible; here *Frau* ('wife') is co-referential with *Mutter* ('mother').[8]

(8)   a.   *my wife and mother*
          b.   * *meine Frau und Mutter*

This indicates that the English possessives seem to have a wider scope than German possessives and may be indirect evidence for the clitic status of POSS '*s*, since clitics usually are syntactically more flexible.

While there seems to be agreement that POSS '*s* is not an inflection in the traditional sense, there is less agreement on what it should be instead. A standard solution is to regard it as a grammatical word, which is structurally/phonologically dependent upon a neighboring word, a clitic (see e.g. Bauer 1988: 99). Yet, on a closer look, POSS '*s* does not fully qualify as a proper clitic, either. For example, POSS '*s* does not have an independent counterpart as other clitics in English do (*'ve* → *have*; *'s* → *has, is*; POSS '*s* → ?). Zwicky's (1987, 1994: 576) main objection against a clitic-analysis of POSS '*s* is the observation that POSS '*s* interacts phonologically with other inflectional /z/ affixes, such as the plural /z/ in (9) or the third person singular /z/ in (10):

(9)   **boys's*

(10)   *anyone who hurries'/ *hurries's ideas*

These morphological haplology effects show that POSS '*s* is sensitive to allomorphy (cf. also Stemberger 1981: 792-793 on POSS '*s* and morphological haplology).[9] Thus, it seems to underlie morphological rules, and not – as should be expected for a genuine clitic – purely syntactic rules, which should be insensitive to allomorphy (for a good summary of Zwicky's argumentation, see also Spencer 1991: 381-383). Therefore, Zwicky (1987, 1994: 576) argues, POSS '*s* should be considered as an inflectional ending which attaches to the end of phrases, and he rejects the analysis of POSS '*s* as a clitic or even a "phrasal affix", a special type of clitic.

To sum up this discussion, POSS '*s* in Present-day English qualifies neither as a genuine inflection nor as a genuine clitic. Depending on whether linguists want to press POSS '*s* into a category or not, two basic approaches to the problem can be observed. One is to relax the requirements for category-membership, such as allowing inflections to attach to phrases, as in Zwicky's (1987) and Seppänen's (1997b) approach. Another one is to admit for the more gradient character of POSS '*s*. This is an approach taken by Plank (1992a), who regards casehood and adpositionhood as complex rather than simple properties and who, based on a set of properties, classifies POSS '*s* into an intermediate category between case and adposition/clitic, thereby avoiding strict categorization (cf. also Plank 1995). Carstairs (1987) suggests that with singular possessors POSS '*s* needs to be analyzed as a clitic, while with regular plural possessors it is an inflectional affix; or more precisely, the '*s* in this case is "the realization of the combination of morphosyntactic properties Plural and Genitive" (Carstairs 1987: 159). Such an analysis would account for the fact that POSS '*s* attaches directly neither to regular plurals ([11a] versus [11b]) nor to the end of phrases if this phrase contains an internal plural ([12a] versus [12b]); examples taken from Carstairs (1987: 160).

(11) a. *my friends' bicycles*
      b. *the children's bicyles*

(12) a. *the soldiers over there's uniforms
      b. *the children over there's uniforms

It is worthwhile mentioning that Taylor (1996: 122-125) makes an interesting connection between the problem of categorizing POSS '*s* into an affix or a clitic and the problem of distinguishing between words and phrases in general, drawing attention to the phenomenon of phrasal compounding in English (examples from Lieber 1988: 204-205, quoted in Taylor 1996: 123):

(13) a. *the [NPCharles and Di] syndrome*
      b. *an [PPoff the rack] dress*
      c. *this [APpleasant to read] book*
      d. *my [VPate too much] headache*
      e. *that [CPwin a Mazda] competition*

In these compounds the first element is always a phrase, which shows that compounding, traditionally a morphological process, can operate over phrases. [10] Although syntactic phrases should not be allowed to enter compounding according to recent morphological theories (see e.g. Spencer 1991: 319), [11] this type of compounding can be found fairly frequently in Modern English, see e.g. examples (14) and (15).

(14)   *these [fantastic-but-true], these [believe-it-or-not-but-it-happened] Tales of the Ferns*   (Graham Swift, *Waterland,* 42)

(15)   *this [sixteen-year-old], [warm-bodied], [stern-eyed], [ten-weeks pregnant], [no-longer-curious] creature* (Graham Swift, *Waterland,* 132)

While the fact that syntactic phrases can enter a morphological process such as compounding is interesting in itself, it is also worthwhile looking at how the end product of such a compounding process, i.e. a phrasal (compound) noun, is inflected. If compounding can cross word boundaries why should inflection not? A good test case in point is plural inflection, the only true nominal inflection left in the English language. Quirk et al. (1985: §5.102) state that, usually, in such cases the last element takes the plural marking, as in *gin-and-tonics* and *forget-me-nots.* [12] If the compound includes a postmodifier or final particle, however, the plural can also be marked on the first element (*commanders-in-chief,* **men**-*of-war*). And, interestingly, there also seem to be cases of variation where the plural can occur either in the first or the last element (*mothers-in-law* versus *mother-in-laws*), with the latter being described as informal. All this indicates that phrasal inflection is not peculiar to the *s*-genitive in English but, at least as far as phrasal nouns are concerned, can also occur with plural marking. [13] And it is, among other things, on these grounds that Seppänen (1997b: 206) as well argues not to "insist on a strict separation of inflectional affixes and clitics on the basis of the word/phrase distinction".[14]

The synchronic similarities between phrasal compounding and the *s*-genitive (as an affix attaching to phrases) pointed out above may have had repercussions – or even played a causal role – in the diachronic development of POSS '*s*, as I will suggest in §7.5 below. There it will be shown that POSS '*s* has gradually changed from a fully-fledged inflectional ending in Old English to a more clitic-like element in Modern English, with the late Middle/early Modern English period representing the crucial transition period in this process. It will be speculated that the 'jump' from a word to a phrasal marker, as witnessed in the development of the *s*-genitive may correlate with – or even be caused by – a very parallel development in the domain of compounding, i.e. a shift from purely word compounding to phrasal compounding. The hybrid category status of ModE POSS '*s* exhibiting both characteristics of an inflection and a clitic as demonstrated throughout this section, can probably be best accounted for when taking a look at its diachronic development. As already argued by Plank (1992a: 19), the apparent difficulties in the classification of ModE POSS '*s* as either a case marker or a clitic seem to have a diachronic reason, with ModE POSS '*s* still exhibiting a categorial transient state. In the present study I will, however, use the term 'clitic' to refer to POSS '*s* to stress that it today behaves quite differently when compared to an inflection in the traditional sense (and as it used to be in Old English; see further §7.5) though still keeping in mind that it does not fully qualify as a clitic, either.

2.3 The nature of the grammatical relation between possessor and possessum

2.3.1 A functional account

Traditionally, the grammatical relations of determination and modification are assigned to the *s*-genitive and the *of*-genitive (see e.g. Quirk et al. 1985: 326-328; Huddleston 1984: 233; 262-264), as illustrated in table 3 below.

Table 3.   Grammatical relations expressed by the *s*-genitive and the *of*-genitive

s-genitive			of-genitive		
possessor	**relation**	**possessum**	**possessum**	**relation**	**possessor**
determiner	determi-nation	head	head	comple-mentation	complement
[the king's]		*daughter*	*the king*		*of England*
[a king's]		*daughter*			
modifier	modifi-cation	head	head	modifi-cation	modifier
a [king's		*daughter]*	*a king*		*of honour*
the [driver's		*seat]*			

In this view, the possessor phrase in the *s*-genitive is primarily understood as a determiner marking the whole possessive NP as definite (see e.g. Huddleston 1984: 253; Lyons, C. 1989, 1999: 23). There are distributional and semantic-pragmatic arguments for this classification. Paradigmatically, the possessor in the *s*-genitive occupies the same slot as other central determiners (16):

(16)   the   daughter
         his   daughter
         John's   daughter
         the king's   daughter

Moreover, it is mutually exclusive with other central determiners (17) below:

(17)   **the [[John's/the king's] daughter]*

Semantically, the possessor in the *s*-genitive marks the whole NP as definite (18 – 19), even if the possessor itself is marked as indefinite as in (19).[15]

(18)   *the king's daughter → the daughter of the king*

(19)   *a king's daughter → the daughter of a king*

Recently, Haspelmath (1999a) has argued that the complementary distribution of article and possessor within the NP is a common cross-linguistic pattern, which is due to the fact that possessed NPs are highly likely to be definite. In his account it is therefore not the structural property of the possessor as a determiner which prohibits co-occurrence with another determiner, but rather semantic-pragmatic reasons connected to the definiteness and the anchoring function of the possessive construction which leads to this syntactic pattern (cf. also §4.4.3 and §7.5.3.1). Since it would be redundant to express definiteness twice within the NP (by the article and by the nature of the possessive construction), the article is left out for economical reasons. And what once used to be a preference only in performance has eventually become grammaticalized in grammar.[16]

Although the possessor in the *s*-genitive functions most often as a determiner, it can also act as a modifier. Note that while in (18) the possessor is a determiner specifying the referent, i.e. *whose* daughter it is (= the king's), in (19) it is a modifier specifying to what denotational class the head noun belongs, i.e. what kind of daughter it is (= a king's). In fact, most *s*-genitives of the latter type (*a king's daughter*) are ambiguous in that the possessor can be interpreted as either a determiner or a modifier. A determiner interpretation is available if *king* is [+referential], i.e. if it is the daughter of an existing king, who is not further specified.[17] Biber et al.'s (1999: 294-295) distinction between "specifying genitives" and "classifying genitives" captures the difference between [+referential] possessors on the one hand and [-referential] possessors on the other hand well.

Table 4.   "Specifying" versus "classifying" *s*-genitives

	specifying genitives	classifying genitives
s-genitive	*the girl's face*	*His hair felt like* [*a bird's nest*]

In its modifier function, i.e. as a classifying genitive, the *s*-genitive is also sometimes referred to as a "possessive compound" (see e.g. Taylor 1996: chapter 11) because it fulfils the criteria for a compound. Note, for example, that in the modifier interpretation (19) has stress on the possessor.[18] Moreover, in the *s*-genitive in modifier relation any further premodification can only modify the possessum, but not the possessor, i.e. it is the daughter that is beautiful (20a) and the license that is old (21a). In contrast, in the determiner reading it is the possessor that is modified by the adjective, i.e. it is the king who is beautiful (20b) and the driver who is old (21b).

(20)   a.   *a beautiful [king's daughter]*
      b.   *[a beautiful king's] daughter*

(21)   a.   *the old [driver's license]*
      b.   *[the old driver's] license*

Table 5 summarizes the main differences between specifying *s*-genitives (= determiner-type) and classifying *s*-genitives (= modifier/compound-type).[19]

Table 5.   Specifying versus classifying *s*-genitives: basic differences

specifying *s*-genitives (determiner type)	classifying *s*- genitives (modifier/compound type)
• possessor = [+referential] • final stress • adjective modifies possessor	• possessor = [-referential] • initial stress • adjective modifies possessum

Note that the very fact that the *s*-genitive, if the possessor is a modifier, can be interpreted as a compound shows how fluid the borderline between words and phrases is in the *s*-genitive. And even if the possessor functions as a determiner, i.e. in specifying genitives, a formally indefinite possessor can be inherently ambiguous between a specifying and a modifying, i.e. compound, reading, since it potentially allows for both a referential and a non-referential interpretation. Moreover, in example (22) below we notice that a specifying genitive (22a) cannot only be interpreted easily as a possessive compound (22b) but also as a non-possessive compound (22c).

(22) a. *[a car's] door*
      b. *the [car's door]*
      c. *the [car door]*

At this point a word on terminology is in order. Noun + noun sequences in English can be both analyzed as (i) prenominal modifiers and (ii) compounds. Analyzing such sequences as nominal premodification presupposes a syntactic construction; as compounds they are treated as one word. There are the usual tests to distinguish between syntactic phrases and compounds, such as semantic unity/transparency (more likely for syntactic phrases), stress alignment (see also above) or orthography (single words such as *seaweed* are more likely to be treated as compounds than written as separate words as in *silk necktie*), though the general consensus seems to be that nominal premodification and compounding form stages on a cline with very fuzzy edges, instead of two clearly distinguishable form classes (for discussions see e.g. Marchand 1969: 20-29; Koziol 1972: 48-49; Huddleston 1984: 259; Biber et al. 1999: §8.3); Bauer (1998: 85) even argues (to my mind very convincingly) "that there is no strong evidence for a distinction between two fundamental types of noun + noun construction" in English. [20] I will in the following use the terms somewhat interchangeably; what is important for the present argumentation is to distinguish noun + noun sequences in which the first part functions as a modifier to the head noun (i.e. both nominal premodifiers and compounds) from specifying genitive constructions in which the possessor functions as a determiner.

There is yet another connection between *s*-genitives and compounds not mentioned so far. Specifying genitives with a clearly referentially definite possessor (as in [23a] below) can easily be transformed into a non-possessive, premodifying construction (as in [23b] below).

(23) a. *I knew from the map that I was not far from **the Steiners' street**.*
        (Patricia Cornwell, *The Body Farm*, 115 [emphasis mine])
     b. *I remembered **the Steiner house** was two down on the left,...*
        (Patricia Cornwell, *The Body Farm*: 116 [emphasis mine])

In both examples *Steiner* is the name of a family, and therefore in both examples this name must be taken to be [+definite] and [+referential]. Also, in both cases it identifies which street (23a) and which house (23b) is meant. In the following examples (24) we can see, parallel to example (23) above, how a phrasal possessor phrase, in which two proper names are conjoined, is alternatively used as a possessive construction (i.e. a specifying genitive) in (24a) and as a premodifying, non-possessive construction in (24b).

(24) a. *Dennett (1983), ..., argues that **Gould and Lewontin's critique** is remarkably similar in logic to...*
        (Pinker and Bloom 1990: 727, fn. 2 [emphasis mine])
     b. *The key point that blunts **the Gould and Lewontin critique of adaptationism** is that...*   (Pinker and Bloom 1990: 709 [emphasis mine])

Note that although (24b) must be regarded as a premodifying construction on structural grounds, the premodifier *Gould and Lewontin* still fulfils an identifying function. The modified head noun *critique* can be taken as a deverbal noun with an open argument slot that needs to be filled, so, strictly speaking, *Gould and Lewontin* serves as an obligatory argument to *critique* rather than an optional modifier. On the other hand, it looks as if the verbal character of *critique* is more present in the possessive construction (24a), somehow allowing more for an activity reading such as 'Gould and Lewontin criticize(d)' and thereby highlighting *Gould and Lewontin* more as individuals, while the premodifying version in (24b) puts more focus on the result of that activity, i.e. the critique, with less activity put on *Gould and Lewontin* but rather emphasizing and classifying the (more stative) meaning of *critique*. Note also, that in Pinker and Bloom's (1990) article, from which this quote is taken, the premodifying variant in (24b) is only used after Gould and Lewontin, or rather their article, have been introduced and already discussed. So a crucial prerequisite for the use of the premodifying construction in such cases seems to be that the proper name, or rather what it stands for, has been previously mentioned and therefore must be regarded as topical.

Taken together, it appears that specifying genitives, in which the possessor functions as a determiner, connect to prenominal modifying constructions (i.e. possessive compounds/classifying genitives, non-possessive compounds and nominal premodifiers) in the following way:

Table 6.   Specifying *s*-genitives and prenominal modifying constructions

specifying *s*-genitives		
[-definite] & ambiguity: [±referential] *a king's daughter, a car's door*		[+definite] [+referential] *[the Steiners'] house*
possessive compounds/ classifying *s*-genitives	(non-possessive) compounds	nominal premodifiers
a [king's daughter] *a [car's door]*	*a/the [car door]*	*the [Steiner house]*

As will be argued in §7.5 below, these links between such prenominal modifying constructions and *s*-genitives may have been important in the diachronic development of POSS '*s* from a word marker (i.e. an inflection) to a phrasal marker (i.e. a clitic).

Similarly to the *s*-genitive, the possessor in the *of*-genitive can relate in two principal ways to the possessum. First, it can be the complement to its head (possessum),[21] expressing one argument (*England*) of a two-place semantic predicate (*king*), (cf. Huddleston 1984: 262) as in (25).

(25)   *the king of England*

Second, it can also serve as a modifier as in (26), where the possessum/head *king* is only a one-place predicate and the possessor *honor* expresses a quality denoted by the possessum.

(26)   *a king of honor*

In both these functions the *of*-genitive differs significantly from the *s*-genitive in determiner function in that the whole possessive construction can be either definite (27a/28a) or indefinite (27b/28b):

(27) a. *the king of England*
     b. *a king of England*

(28) a. *the king of honor*
    b. *a king of honor*

The following table 7 gives an overview of the various types of genitives classified according to the function of the possessor:

Table 7.   Classification: specifying versus classifying genitives

	specifying genitives: [+referential] possessor	classifying genitives: [-referential] possessor
s-genitive	possessor = determiner	possessor = modifier
of-genitive	possessor = complement	possessor = modifier

2.3.2   *A formal account: DP-analysis*

Recently, a radically different analysis of nominal structure has been proposed in formal syntactic approaches, which challenges traditional conceptions of headedness. While the notion of "head of a phrase" has always been reserved for lexical categories (nouns, verbs, adjectives, prepositions), in this recent development within X-Bar syntax, functional elements (such as determiners and complementizer) can function as the head of construction. Accordingly, what previously has been labeled an NP has now been superseded by the notion of a "determiner phrase" (DP), headed by a functional element, i.e. a determiner. The following – very simplified – analysis for the *s*-genitive is taken from Taylor (1996: 140), which again goes back to Radford (1990), and which will suffice here to depict the basic spirit of the analysis. [22]

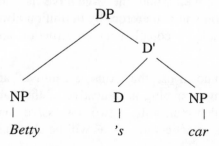

In this analysis, POSS *'s* is a determiner and the head of the whole possessive phrase. The possessor is in SPEC position, and the possessum, which used to be the head in traditional analysis, is now a complement of

POSS '*s*. The Specifier, the possessor, is assigned genitive case by the head, POSS '*s*. Note that this generative notion of (structural) "case" is rather different from the traditional one, where it is exclusively used to refer to morphologically marked case. This analysis acknowledges the determiner function of the *s*-genitive well, i.e. the fact that it marks the whole possessive construction as definite. Since the goal of the present study is not to elaborate on structural aspects of possessive constructions, I will not further follow DP-analysis here, but will continue to use the traditional terminology and analysis introduced in §2.3.1. However, as will become evident in §7.4.3 the question which element of a possessive construction is considered to be the head of construction in linguistic theory will have considerable consequences for typological predictions.

2.4   Terminology revisited

Having presented a structural analysis for the two possessive constructions it seems now that the terms chosen, i.e. *s*-genitive and *of*-genitive are fairly misleading. As argued by Huddleston (1984: 268), calling both constructions "genitives" obscures the fact that

(1)   under traditional terminology (i.e. genitive as a morphological case), only POSS '*s* can possibly be considered a true genitive, but not the periphrastic *of*-construction;

(2)   given (1), there are good reasons to doubt that POSS '*s* is a genuine inflection in the traditional sense;

(3)   there are fundamental syntactic and semantic differences between the two constructions, i.e. while the *s*-genitive is, prototypically, in determiner function and is therefore by definition always definite, the *of*-genitive is usually a complement construction and neutral as to definiteness.

However, I will continue to use the terms "*s*-genitive" and "*of*-genitive" because the parallelism in naming is indicative of their ability to express the same meaning, which makes these two possessive constructions good candidates for morphosyntactic variants, as will be shown in the following chapter.

Chapter 3
Grammatical variation

3.1   The study of variation in linguistics: brief historical outline

For a long time in this century, the study of variation was abandoned in linguistics. [23] Linguists working in the framework of (American) structuralism were interested in language as a system of structured relations, and as true positivists they restricted the scientific investigation of language to observable phenomena. The American structuralists, most notably Bloomfield, maintained that variation (a) cannot be observed and (b) is not structured but random and therefore lies outside linguistic investigation. Within the generative paradigm the main interest was the investigation of the mental capacity, the competence of speakers, which ought to be the same for every individual speaker. To rule out what he considered merely performance factors, such as processing limitations or social factors, from his investigation of competence, Chomsky (1965: 314) postulated the "ideal speaker-listener in a completely homogeneous speech community", a heuristic idealization which, although it does not deny the existence of variation, nonetheless excludes it from linguistic research.

In sharp contrast to the prevailing views on variation at the time, Weinreich, Labov, and Herzog (1968) in their pioneering article claimed that variation is indeed structured and that it therefore can and must be studied by linguists. It was above all Labov, who, starting in the late 1960s, introduced new empirical principles, survey methodology, quantification of data and statistical analysis into linguistics, thereby firmly establishing the study of variation in linguistics. The crucial analytical tool of Labov's variation studies was the notion of the "(socio-)linguistic variable", an abstract term that describes the available set of possible, paradigmatically related candidates (i.e. variants). The various approaches to variation (and change) currently on the linguistic market will be further introduced in chapter 5 below; in this chapter the focus is on establishing the genitive variation as a case of grammatical variation and in so doing also defining and delimiting the scope of the empirical analysis presented in this study.

3.2   Extending the concept of variation to (morpho)syntax

Initially, the study of variation was restricted to phonological variables. As will be shown in this section, the extension of variation studies to the field of morphology and syntax (i.e. "grammatical variation") was and still is problematic for the following reasons. First, it is extremely difficult to define the paradigmatic set of possible morphosyntactic variants, because it is not clear how to define 'sameness' in the fields of morphology and syntax (§3.2.1). Second, morphosyntactic variants are from a methodological point of view more difficult to investigate, particularly in terms of determining obligatory contexts (§3.2.2).

3.2.1   The problem of 'sameness'

What does "variation" mean, and how is it defined? The concept of variation implies the existence of alternating elements, but alternating relative to what? Labov (1972: 271) defined variation as "two ways of saying the same thing". Now, the problem is how to define 'sameness'? For Labov, the variants ought to have the same referential meaning, i.e. they have to be truth-conditionally equivalent. This is a fairly straightforward and easy enough requirement for phonological variables. It does not in any way affect the meaning or truth value of the word *card* whether it is pronounced with the rhotic or non-rhotic variant of postvocalic /r/. Phonological elements can be meaning differentiating at best, but they do not themselves *create* meaning. Linguistic levels above phonology, however, are a completely different matter. Morphological and syntactic elements do by definition carry a meaning. For this reason, the extension of the concept of variation to the level of (morpho)syntax has been an extremely controversial issue. There is a large body of literature debating the question of how to define 'sameness' in the study of syntactic variation (see e.g. Lavandera 1978; Jacobson 1980; Romaine 1984b; Cheshire 1987 and Silva-Corvalán 1986 to name just a few). It seems to depend on the view taken on "syntax" and "meaning" how successful the criterion of 'sameness' can be applied to the study of grammatical variation. In a context-bound definition of syntax, the meaning of an utterance is or will be determined by the context of the utterance, including e.g. the motivations of the interlocutors, their interaction and the organization of information flow (cf. Halliday's interpersonal and textual function).[24] If one adheres to this view, it will probably be impossible to find any two (or more) syntactic constructions which share all contextually determined meanings and motivations, at least not if the notion of syntax is to be taken in its strict sense, i.e. word order. As is well known, e.g. from the concept of "functional sentence perspective" of the Prague School, word order variation by definition reflects communicative demands (see also §4.2.1). The view that two alternating constructions always reflect a difference in meaning was, to give a classic example, vigorously maintained by Bolinger (1977: 1): "... if two ways of saying something differ in their words or their arrangement they will also differ in meaning, .." Including pragmatics in his notion of meaning, Bolinger necessarily proceeds from a context-bound conception of syntax. In a context-free definition of syntax, however, syntactic variants need to be only truth-conditionally equivalent, i.e. they need to convey the same propositional meaning irrespective of any contextual or external factors, comparable to Halliday's ideational function or Chomsky's idea of an underlying deep structure. It is only with such a context-free definition of syntax that 'sameness' in syntactic variation can be defined at all. This is actually the approach taken by Weiner and Labov's (1983) study, where active and passive sentences were taken to have the same underlying meaning. In the same spirit, Jacobson's (1980) criterion of "descriptive synonymy", adopted from Lyons, J. (1977: 242), calls only for identity in the internal sense relations of syntactic variants but not for identity in external reference. Table 8 below summarizes the differences in the definition of 'sameness' in context-free versus context-bound conceptions of syntax.[25]

Table 8. Characterization of 'sameness' within a context-free versus context-bound conception of syntax

characterization of 'sameness' in syntax	
context-free	**context-bound**
• truth conditions	• information flow (e.g. theme/rheme ordering)
• propositional meaning	• motivations/attitudes of interlocutors
• ideational function	• interpersonal & textual function
• deep structure	• 'complete synonymy'
• 'descriptive synonymy'	

3.2.2 Further methodological problems

Apart from the problem of how to define 'sameness' on the (morpho)syntactic level, there appear to be further methodological problems, which make the investigation of syntactic variation a difficult task for the researcher. First, in contrast to phonological variables, it is extremely difficult to define and find all obligatory contexts for the occurrence of syntactic variants. Phonological variants represent a finite and closed set of elements. For phonological variables it is therefore easy to identify the contexts, in which one or the other variant should occur. Taking the variable postvocalic /r/, for example, the obligatory contexts are all postvocalic occurrences of /r/ and the respective variants are rhotic and non-rhotic realizations in this context. Syntax, however, is again a completely different matter, especially, where variation in word order is concerned. Even if we agree on a context-free definition of 'sameness', as proposed in the previous section, there remains the question of how to define and delimit the possible set of candidates.

For illustration, see the following examples taken from Altenberg (1982: 229-230):

(a) *The truck and the bus collided.*
(b) *The bus and the truck collided.*
(c) *The truck collided with the bus.*
(d) *The bus collided with the truck.*

We may say that all the examples have the same propositional meaning, i.e. there is a bus and a truck and the two collide. In this respect, examples (a) to (d) can all be regarded as syntactic variants. Intuitively, however, we feel more inclined to treat (a) and (b) as syntactic variants, while (c) and (d) might form another set of variants. This is probably due to the fact that (a) and (b) are structurally equivalent; (c) and (d) are also structurally equivalent, but not with (a) and (b). So, in addition to the requirement of propositional 'sameness' (or "descriptive synonymy"), in this case we also need a criterion of "structural comparability", which has been proposed by Jacobson (1980) as a further criterion of syntactic variation, though it may well vary from case to case how this is to be defined. Yet, even if we delimit the possible variants to (a) and (b), or (c) and (d) respectively, which kind of constructions are we going to count? All constructions that involve verbs with the same semantic structure as *collide*, or only *collide*-constructions?

Closely connected to this problem is another one, that of frequency. A major methodological tool in the study of variation is the quantification of data. This in turn requires either variants that are relatively frequent, or, if not, huge amounts of data in order to get a satisfactory database. As seen from the discussion above, depending on how much we delimit the set of possible variants, the possibility of finding – and counting! – them will vary considerably. In addition to this, syntactic variants are as such much more infrequent as phonological variants, which are chosen from only a small and fixed set of elements.

To sum up, the extension of the concept of variation to syntax, originally developed and employed in phonology, is highly problematic for the following reasons:

(1) While phonological variants are by definition synonymous, it is not at all clear how 'sameness' in syntax should be defined.
(2) Following from (1), it is extremely difficult to define and delimit the range of obligatory contexts for syntactic variants.
(3) Syntactic variants are by their very nature much less frequent than phonological variants and therefore much more difficult to quantify.

This does not mean, however, that it is impossible to define and investigate syntactic variation. It is just not possible to do it in a straightforward and uniform way. Rather, it seems to depend on which particular constructions are analyzed and under which objectives.

3.3   Establishing the alternation between the *s*-genitive and the *of*-genitive as a case of grammatical variation

In this section, I will first show why and in which cases the alternation between the *s*-genitive and the *of*-genitive can be treated and investigated as a case of morphosyntactic, i.e. grammatical variation, and then go into the methodological implications for investigating the genitive variation.

3.3.1   Why "grammatical" variation?

Before going on to show that and in which respect the genitive alternation can be taken as a case of grammatical variation, let me first address the question of why this variation should indeed be regarded as morphosyntactic in nature. There are, as already indicated in chapter 2 above, basically three main aspects in which the *s*-genitive and the *of*-genitive differ, as illustrated in table 9 below.

Table 9.   Morphosyntactic differences between *s*-genitive and *of*-genitive

morphosyntactic differences	*s*-genitive	*of*-genitive
relational marker	• POSS *'s:* more synthetic	• preposition *of*: more analytic
grammatical function of possessor	• determiner: *[the/a king]'s daughter*	• complement: *the daughter of the/a king*
	• modifier (I): *a [king's daughter]*	• modifier (I): *the daughter of a king*
		• modifier (II): *a king of honor*
word order	• possessor-possessum	• possessum-possessor

First, these two genitive constructions make use of different relational markers to link a possessor to a possessum, i.e. POSS *'s* versus the preposition *of*. As has been shown in §2.2 above, the grammatical nature of POSS *'s* (inflection versus clitic) is not easy to identify; it seems to be best captured as an intermediate category between inflection and clitic. Although no longer a fully-fledged inflection, POSS *'s* does still show traces of inflectional features, and therefore must be regarded as a more synthetic marker in contrast to the analytic, periphrastic *of*. Second, for both the *s*-genitive and the *of*-genitive the same surface form can encode various grammatical functions, which only partly overlap: while the possessor in the *s*-genitive can function as a determiner or a modifier (I), in the *of*-genitive it is either a complement or a modifier (I/II). Third, the *s*-genitive and the *of*-genitive provide two alternative ways of arranging possessor and possessum in linear order; in the *s*-genitive the possessor precedes the possessum, but it follows it in the *of*-genitive.

This brings us directly to the question in which cases there is indeed grammatical *variation* in the sense that the *s*-genitive and the *of*-genitive are in any way interchangeable and can compete.

3.3.2   *Establishing a criterion of 'sameness' for the* s-*genitive and the* of-*genitive*

There are in principle two ways of approaching the question of 'sameness' for the two genitive constructions. Proceeding from a context-free definition of syntax as outlined in §3.2.1 we may first determine what is the underlying, truth-conditional meaning of a possessive construction and then look at the linguistic means by which this is encoded. Although the two elements of a possessive construction, the possessor and the possessum, are usually not seen as thematic roles in the traditional sense, on equal par with notions such as agent, patient or experiencer, we may nonetheless assume that they represent two roles or entities that stand in a relation (possessor – possessed/possessum) to each other. Let us, as a first approximation of the requirement of 'sameness', postulate that all those constructions need to be considered as constituting 'the same' in which there is no doubt as to which element constitutes the possessor and which the possessum. Consider the following cases in which, invariably, *man* is the possessor and *book* is the possessum:

(29) a. *The man has a book.*
      b. *The man owns a book.*
      c. *The man possesses a book.*
      d. *The book belongs to the man.*
      e. *The book is the man's.*

(30) a. *the man's book*
      b. *the book of the man*

We can see from these examples that, when taking a strict onomasiological approach and proceeding from the relation between a possessor and a possessum, both predicative (29) and adnominal possessive constructions (30) must be taken into consideration. For the sake of structural comparability I shall therefore first delimit the range of possible variants for my analysis to constructions of the same structural domain, i.e. the NP, only considering adnominal possessive constructions.

3.3.2.1 Categorical versus choice contexts

Yet, even when restricting the requirement of 'sameness' to the *s*-genitive and the *of*-genitive as the major adnominal devices in English to express possessive relations, there appear to be contexts in which only one possessive construction can be used but not the other (henceforth referred to as "categorical contexts"), and these need to be distinguished from those contexts in which – at least in principle – both constructions are potential variants (henceforth referred to as "choice contexts"); for an illustration of the difference between categorical and choice contexts, see figure 1 below.

As has been pointed out by Sankoff and Rousseau (1980: 12), in a quantitative analysis of grammatical variants first categorical contexts, or "knockout factors", need to be identified and excluded: "..., the traditional way of dealing with knockout parameters, namely setting them aside before proceeding to analyse the rest of the data, turns out to be mathematically justified."

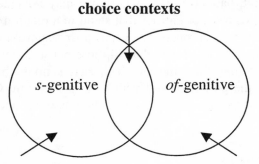

choice contexts

s-genitive   *of*-genitive

categorical contexts   **categorical contexts**

Figure 1.   Categorical versus choice contexts

In the following I will narrow down the range of possible grammatical variation between the two genitive constructions by identifying and consequently excluding categorical contexts for both the *s*-genitive and the *of*-genitive. It is in this way that I will show how the requirement of 'sameness' will be employed for the investigation of the two genitive constructions in the present study. Note that I am now turning to a semasiological approach: proceeding from two constructions, the *s*-genitive and the *of*-genitive, I will now determine which meanings and functions can be expressed by each construction, ultimately trying to isolate such contexts in which both constructions can be used (= choice contexts). What matters at this point is which sense relations can potentially be expressed by the two genitive constructions (in the sense of the linguistic repertoire or competence) and not how likely the occurrence of one or the other construction is, or what motivates the choice between them. It is only after we have figured out what are potential choice contexts that matters of motivation and likelihood will become important. Note, however, that the borderline between categorical and choice contexts is not clear-cut and can be rather blurred. In some cases there may remain a marginal choice, which is, however, so unlikely that we may regard it as a categorical context.

3.3.2.1.1   Genitive functions/meanings

As said, what the two genitive constructions have in common is that in both constructions a possessor is linked to a possessum on the nominal level, but the semantic nature of this relation can vary considerably. There is no one, clearly definable genitive relation, but rather there appears to be a whole range of relations that can be conveyed by the two constructions. To make things even more complicated, there is also no uniform classification or categorization of these multiple genitive relations (or "functions" as they are often called) in the literature; generally terms like "possessive", "subjective", "objective", or "partitive" are used in a very loose manner. The problems connected to the classification of genitive functions/ meanings will be further addressed in §4.3.1; here it will, for the time being, suffice to use the traditional labels (cf. table 10).

Table 10. Basic genitive functions/meanings

genitive relation	*s*-genitive	*of*-genitive
possessive	*John's arm*	*the arm of John*
(in a broad sense)	*my mother's car*	*the car of my mother*
	John's friend	*the friend of John*
	John's future	*the future of John*
	John's book (= that he wrote; that he owns, that he wants to buy,...)	*the book of John*
	John's strength	*the strength of John*
	**England's king*	*the king of England*
partitive	**my children's one*	*one of my children*
descriptive	* *an honor's king*	*a king of honor*
appositive	**London's city*	*the city of London*
idiomatic	*the king's grace*	* *the grace of the king*
expressions/	(as a title)	(as a title)
collocations	*for John's sake*	*for the sake of John*
	the water's edge	*the edge of the water*
subjective	*John's love* (= 'John loves')	*the love of John*
objective	*John's murder* (= 'someone murders John')	*the murder of John*

Partitive, descriptive and appositive relations[26] only occur with the *of*-genitive, as well as certain idiomatic expressions (e.g. *the king of England, the king's grace*) where there is also no choice between the two genitives. Only possessive meanings in a broad sense (I will come back to this notion in §4.3.1), subjective and objective genitives can be regarded as choice contexts.

3.3.2.1.2   Pronominal versus full NP possessors

In principle, pronominal possessors may occasionally appear with *of*-genitives if, as argued by Jucker (1993: 131) the pronoun is in focus, as e.g.

(31)   *He's nearly 60. This could be the death of him*
            (Sun, 17.10,1992, p.4, hn 98; example from Jucker 1993: 131)

Jucker's (1993) analysis does, however, also show that this is an extremely unlikely situation; in his corpus the vast majority of pronominal possessors (98.5%) are realized as possessive pronouns.[27] We can therefore regard pronominal possessors as a – although not absolute – categorical context for the occurrence of a special type of *s*-genitive, i.e. possessive pronouns (*my/your/her house* versus **the house of me/you/her*). Only possessors consisting of a full lexical NP, both proper nouns (*John's father* versus *the father of John*) and common nouns (*the man's house* versus *the house of the man*) represent potential choice contexts, although, as has been shown (cf. §4.1.2 below), depending on the specific noun class the *s*-genitive or the *of*-genitive will be more or less likely to occur.

3.3.2.1.3   Definiteness and reference tracking for whole possessive NP

Since the possessor in the *s*-genitive already occupies the determiner slot rendering the whole construction definite (cf. §2.3.1),[28] other reference tracking devices are not available for the *s*-genitive (cf. also Anschutz 1997). Therefore, all indefinite genitive constructions as in (32) must be excluded from the set of syntactic variants.

(32)   *a picture of a man ≠ a man's picture*

Also, all other reference tracking devices – even if they are definite –, such as demonstratives (33), possessive pronouns (34) or the definite article (35), cannot be used in the *s*-genitive. This is also due to the fact that the possessor in the *s*-genitive already occupies the central determiner slot:

(33)   *this head of the king* → **this the king's head*

(34)   *my picture of John* → **my John's picture*

(35)   *the head of the king* → **the the king's head*

Therefore, only such constructions may be compared in which the whole NP can be referred to by a definite article.

3.3.2.1.4   Grammatical function of the possessor

It has been shown in §2.3.1 that the possessor in the *s*-genitive and the *of*-genitive can express various grammatical functions. Modification of the type as in

(36)   *a king of honor*

(37)   *chains of gold*

constitutes a categorical context for the occurrence of the *of*-genitive and must therefore be excluded from the set of variants. Note that these modifier-constructions can also be ruled out for other reasons. Most typically, the whole possessive construction is indefinite (36) or a bare plural (37). Moreover, they correspond to descriptive genitives (cf. §3.3.2.1.1 above). Note also that the corresponding premodifying constructions for such *of*-genitives would be an adjective (i.e. *an honorable king, golden chains*), i.e. these constructions as such do not have an alternative pre*nominal* counterpart.

3.3.2.2 Comparable versus non-comparable contexts

Having identified the categorical contexts for the occurrence of the *s*-genitive or the *of*-genitive only, we have to turn now to the question whether all potential choice contexts may be legitimately compared in a quantitative analysis. In the following I will point out some further excluding criteria distinguishing, this time, between comparable and non-comparable contexts within the range of potential choice contexts.

3.3.2.2.1   Grammatical function of the possessor: specifying versus classifying genitives

Although classifying *s*-genitives, in which the possessor serves as a modifier (I) (*the [driver's seat]; a [bird's nest]*), can in principle be expressed by an *of*-genitive (*the seat of the driver; the nest of a bird*), in these cases – as shown in §2.3.1 – the possessor is [-referential] and serves not to identify the referent but restricts the denotational class of the head noun. Therefore, this constitutes a separate kind of genitive construction, which, as far as the *s*-genitive is concerned, has a strong affinity to compounding. These classifying genitives (or possessive compounds) may be subject to restrictions different from that for specifying genitives (see also §7.3 and §7.4.4.1 below). Also, as possessive compounds, such *s*-genitives very often are – or almost are – already idiomatized (*the driver's seat* probably is to a large extent) and may also allow for a third variant, namely an *s*-less, non-possessive compound (*the driver seat*). Note also, that other prepositional constructions than the *of*-genitive must often be considered the 'better' variants in such cases (*a seat for drivers; a nest for/with birds*). The (potential) availability of further variants for classifying genitives may obscure the quantitative analysis of the *s*-genitive and the *of*-genitive. For all these reasons, I exclude them from the variational study, focusing instead on *s*-genitives expressing a determination relation and *of*-genitives in a complement structure, i.e. 'specifying genitives', as defined in table 7, §2.3.1 above.

3.3.2.2.2 Structural equivalence

Two further genitive constructions need to be excluded from the set of variants since they are not structurally equivalent with the *s*-genitive or the *of*-genitive, i.e. double genitives and elliptic genitives. In double genitives (*a/that friend of John's*) the overall structure of the *of*-genitive is chosen, but, in addition to *of* as a relational marker also POSS '*s* marks the possessor. It seems that such a construction is especially favored in those contexts in which a *s*-genitive would be preferred but cannot be realized because the whole construction is either indefinite or headed by a demonstrative or pronoun.

In elliptic constructions the head (or possessum) is omitted. Two different types of elliptic genitive constructions can be distinguished. While in "absolute genitives" the head is implicitly interpreted as a place (38a), a church or parish (38b), in "independent' genitives" it is anaphorically given in the context with the possessor usually occurring predicatively (39).[29]

(38) a. *Let's meet at John's.* → **Let's meet at of John.* → *Let's meet at John's place/the place of John*
      b. *Let's go to St. Paul's.* → **Let's go to of St. Paul.* → *Let's go to St. Paul's church/the church of St. Paul.*

(39)   *These are not my shoes, these are John's/* of John.*

Although it has been argued that the choice between the *s*-genitive and the *of*-genitive in double genitives and in elliptic genitives seems to be subject to similar constraints as the choice between the *s*-genitive and the *of*-genitive in general (cf. e.g. Biber et al. 1999: §4.6.10-14), they will be excluded from the present analysis because they are, strictly speaking, not structurally equivalent to the 'simple' *s*-genitive and *of*-genitive.

3.3.2.2.3   Standard versus non-Standard forms

There are some other minor nominal genitive constructions which will not be considered here, such as the *his*-genitive (*John his book*), which can only be found in very colloquial or dialectal speech (cf. e.g. Seppänen 1997a, b; for its [possible] relevance in the diachronic development of POSS '*s* see however §7.5.2.3 below), some archaic northern English *s*-less genitives (*his father boots*) (cf. Seppänen 1997b; Klemola 1997) and the *to*-genitive (*secretary to the prime minister*). These nominal genitive constructions will be excluded for merely methodological reasons. First, they are extremely infrequent and therefore not very useful in a quantitative analysis. Second, and more importantly, the *his*-genitive and the *s*-less genitive are non-Standard forms, and although the distribution of genitive constructions within dialects is an intriguing question, it is beyond the aim and the scope of the present study to include it.[30] In particular, it would be extremely difficult to identify subjects for an experimental study who would have these forms in their linguistic repertoire. Therefore, the investigation of the genitive alternation in English will be restricted to the two major adnominal genitive constructions in Standard English, the *s*-genitive and the *of*-genitive.

3.3.2.2.4   Factors known to influence the choice between the *s*-genitive and the *of*-genitive

So far, we have been proceeding from a context-free notion of syntax for purely heuristic reasons, in order to identify comparable contexts allowing for a real choice between the *s*-genitive and the *of*-genitive. Yet, as argued in §3.2.1, from a strict functionalist point of view, even within comparable choice contexts there probably cannot be complete synonymy between two alternating constructions as – depending on the context – there will always be some kind of functional specialization determining which construction is more likely to be used. This means that we either investigate such contexts as factors or, otherwise, keep their effects controlled in our analysis. In the following I will present and discuss those factors already known to influence the distribution of the *s*-genitive and the *of*-genitive but not investigated and therefore to be controlled in the present analysis.

Phonological factor: final sibilant

When following a final sibilant POSS '*s* is often reduced orthographically to a simple apostrophe ('), as in *Jones' car* or *the boys' mother*. According to Quirk et al. (1985: §5.114) this reduced *s*-genitive or "zero genitive" is used "to avoid repetitive or awkward combinations of sounds." They notice that the zero genitive is generally used with Greek names of more than one syllable (*Socrates', Xerxes'*), in fixed expressions (*for goodness' sake*) and with regular plurals (*boys', cats'*); with sibilants ending in /z/ both POSS '*s* and the zero form are used (*Dickens', Dickens's*) and with sibilants not ending in /z/ POSS '*s* is generally realized (*niece's, George's*).

In Altenberg's (1982: 51) extensive corpus of the seventeenth century, the relative frequency of the *of*-genitive rises significantly with sibilant possessors, although he actually regards a final sibilant in the possessor rather as a contributory than a major factor, being subordinate to stylistic preferences (52-53).

Note, however, that POSS '*s* cannot be being avoided for purely articulatory reasons, because the – admittedly phonotactically difficult – succession of two sibilants can also be found when a regular plural-ending (*-s*) is attached to a base ending in a sibilant, as in *roses* or *races*.[31]

Morphological factor: plurality

According to Altenberg (1982: 58-9) possessors with a regular plural ending significantly more often take the *of*-genitive in the seventeenth century; with irregular plural possessors the frequency of the *s*-genitive is much higher. There are, however, several ways in which the different behavior of regular and irregular plural possessors can be interpreted. First, maybe it is the phonological property of the regular plural ending *-s*, i.e. a final sibilant, which is absent in irregular plurals (e.g. *children, men*) that triggers the use of the zero-genitive or the *of*-genitive to avoid awkward sibilant clusters, as discussed in the previous section. Plank (1985: 221), however, suggests that it is the morphological category of regular plural that conditions the absence or presence of POSS '*s* rather than the phonological properties of the preceding word.[32] This view seems to be supported by Jahr Sorheim (1980: 113), who finds in her corpus analysis of Modern English a distinctive difference in the frequency of the *s*-genitives with regular and irregular possessors. Yet, Jahr Sorheim's (1980) data also clearly show that irregular plural possessors behave differently than singular possessors in her corpus, in that they take much less *s*-genitives than singular possessors. This suggests that plurality as a concept may play a role. Some examples provided by Plank (1985: 222) do indeed point to this possibility (see examples [40] - [42] below). Although the realization of POSS '*s* seems to be governed by the morphological category of the directly preceding noun, it is the plurality of the internal head which determines the grammaticality of a group genitive, irrespective of the regularity or irregularity of its plural form or that of the final noun, as can be seen from the following examples given by Plank (1985: 222):

(40)   *the Queens' of England's common denominator*

(41)   *the queens of these countries' mutual dislike*

(42)   *the children of these women's/countries' education*

Syntactic factors: syntactic branching and weight

Within a genitive construction, both the possessor and the possessum can be further syntactically expanded. As will be shown below, it is both the branching direction (left- or right-branching) and the syntactic weight of this expansion that can influence the choice between the *s*-genitive and the *of*-genitive; the four logical possibilities of left- and rightbranching expansion of the possessor and the possessum are illustrated in table 11 by some examples.

Table 11. Branching direction of possessor and possessum – examples [emphasis mine]

	left-branching	right-branching
possessor	... *at the centre **of a guarded heart***. (Elizabeth George, *Missing Joseph*, 134) ...*his youngest **child's** life*. (Elizabeth George, *Playing for the Ashes*, 17)	*Suffering the agonies **of a woman who consistently disregards common sense in the selection of her footwear**,...* (Elizabeth George, *Playing for the Ashes*, 45)
	➔ preference for the *of*-genitive (depending on syntactic complexity of the possessor)	➔ strong preference for the *of*-genitive
possessum	*Lynley's **piously smoke-free domain*** (Elizabeth George, *Playing for the Ashes*, 61) ...*the **gabled roof** of the porch...* (Elizabeth George, *Playing for the Ashes*, 23)	*And then he had to smile at the unconscious mind's **ability to communicate through a medium he hadn't considered part of his world in years*** (Elizabeth George, *Playing for the Ashes*, 44) ... *a museum's **reproduction of a Victorian drawing room**.* (Elizabeth George, *Playing for the Ashes*, 74)
	➔ preference for the *s*-genitive	➔ strong preference for the *s*-genitive

Jucker (1993) tested syntactic factors focusing on the branching direction of the possessor and the possessum, not taking, however, their complexity into account. His data show that if the possessum is expanded to the right, i.e. postmodified, the likelihood for the occurrence of the *s*-genitive generally increases (cf. also Altenberg 1982: chapter 3; Quirk et al. 1985: §17.44). In contrast, the frequency of the *s*-genitive decreases with a further expanded possessor, particularly with a right-branching possessor (cf. also Altenberg 1982: chapter 3; Quirk et al. 1985: §17.44). [33] With left-branching possessors, it seems to be the syntactic complexity, i.e. the number of premodifiers that determines the frequency of the *s*-genitive. The frequency scores given in Biber et al. (1999: 304-305) show that *s*-genitives typically occur with simple possessors (proper noun, DET + noun, or premodifier+noun), consisting usually of one or two words only. If the possessor consists of three or more words, the *s*-genitive becomes increasingly infrequent.

What has not been empirically tested so far is, however, the *relative* weight within a possessive construction. [34] According to the *Gesetz der wachsenden Glieder* as formulated by Behaghel (1932) short elements should precede longer ones. As noted by Hawkins (1994), this general principle should apply for right-branching languages, such as English, which process language from left to right. We can therefore predict that, in general, the possessor and possessum should be arranged according to the principle "short > long", the *s*-genitive preferring the constellation "short possessor – long possessum", and the *of*-genitive favoring a short possessum and a long possessor. Note that complexity within Hawkins' (1994) approach is defined syntactically, in terms of number of words. [35] In §6.5 I will briefly discuss and test the "short-before-long" principle as defined phonologically, i.e. in terms of number of syllables. It is also arguable whether syntactic complexity is a genuine factor determining the choice of genitive construction or whether it results from more pragmatic principles; this question will be addressed below.

Moreover, the recursion of the possessor plays a role in the choice of the two genitive constructions. While there is in general no structural limitation as to the number of such recursions, Quirk et al. (1985: §17.118) argue that "there seems to be a practical limit of two [*s*-genitives] – anything more being stylistically objectionable, comic, and difficult to comprehend", which is also evident from the following examples (43a/b):

(43) a. *Annie's husband's trousers*   (Roddy Doyle, *A Star called Henry*, 156)
      b. ?? *Annie's husband's sister's trousers*

Jespersen (1961: 320) observes that the *of*-genitive is more easily repeated as the *s*-genitive, a view that is confirmed by Altenberg's (1982: §3.4) seventeenth-century data. For Altenberg this has stylistic reasons.[36] The most common pattern in his corpus is indeed a combination of the *s*-genitive and the *of*-genitive in such cases, as in (44) and (45) below; examples from Altenberg (1982: 114):

(44)   *give me so much of your time ... as to lay an amiable siege to the honesty of the honesty of this Fords wife*
        (Shakespeare, *The Merry Wives of Windsor*, 2.2.249, 1600?/ 1623)

(45)   *The safety of hir Majesties person is mutche procured*
        (*Diary of John Manningham*, 21, 1601-02)

Note that it has recently been argued by Rohdenburg (forthcoming) that there is a general processing principle which he calls "horror aequi" by which the repetition of the same form tends to be avoided.

Pragmatic factors: end-focus and end-weight

The effect of one particular pragmatic factor, i.e. givenness or topicality, will be addressed in this study in §4.2 and empirically tested in chapter 6 and chapter 7. In this section I will rather focus on the effect of the factors end-focus and end-weight on the choice of genitive construction. Moreover, I will briefly discuss whether the syntactic factors addressed in the previous section can possibly be reduced to such pragmatic principles, or whether syntactic and pragmatic factors must be regarded as independent principles affecting grammatical variation.

Quirk et al. (1985: §17.45, §18.3ff.) argue that the choice between the *s*-genitive and the *of*-genitive is, among other things, determined by the principles of end-focus and end-weight. According to these principles, the more complex and communicatively more important constituents tend to be placed towards the end of the NP.[37] Accordingly, the *s*-genitive should be preferred when the possessum is more important or focused on and more complex than the possessor, while the *of*-genitive should be favored if the possessor is the more communicatively important (and complex) element (cf. table 12 below).

Jucker (1993) argues that the preference for the *s*-genitive to occur with right-branching possessum nouns and the *of*-genitive to be preferred with complex possessors which he finds in his data, is only a syntactic reflex of the more fundamental and underlying pragmatic principles of end-focus and end-weight, without, however, providing any empirical evidence for this claim. That is, he does not directly test the effect of end-focus/weight against the effect of syntactic factors.

Table 12. End-focus and end-weight and the choice of genitive construction

	principles of end-focus and end-weight	
	communicatively less important and less complex	communicatively more important and more complex
s-genitive	possessor	possessum
of-genitive	possessum	possessor

It is, however, indeed striking that pragmatic principles seem to correlate to a large extent with syntactic factors. Whatever is given and accordingly less communicatively important within discourse,[38] is usually expressed by syntactically shorter constructions, while what is introduced as new information tends to get more formal marking, resulting in syntactically more complex constructions. Recently, Arnold et al. (2000) have empirically tested the question of whether grammatical complexity (i.e. heaviness) or discourse status (i.e. newness) can better account for grammatical variation, concluding that both factors influence word order and that the effect of one cannot be reduced to the effect of the other. While Arnold et al. (2000) have focused on heavy NP shift and dative shift as two constructions which allow for word order variation in English, a corresponding empirical study is still lacking for the English genitive variation; we may nonetheless hypothesize that their results hold true for word order variation in general, including the choice of genitive construction.

Socio-stylistic factors: text type, Standard variety and degree of formality

There is also striking evidence for a socio-stylistic conditioning of the two constructions. In particular, the distribution of the *s*-genitive and the *of*-genitive has been shown to vary considerably according to text type and the degree of formality (within and across text types). The *s*-genitive in Present-day English is generally reported to be most frequent and most progressive in journalistic language and in fiction while it is least productive in learned prose and scientific writings (cf. e.g. Dahl 1971; Jahr Sorheim 1980; Leech, Francis, and Xu 1994; Ljung 1997; Biber et al. 1999). As shown by Altenberg (1982), the stylistic conditioning of the *s*-genitive has firm roots already in early Modern English. In his seventeenth-century corpus, formal text types, in particular religious prose, strongly favor the *of*-genitive, while more informal texts show a higher proportion of *s*-genitives. According to Biber et al.'s (1999: 302) frequency scores, however, the *s*-genitive is particularly rare in conversation. In the light of the other empirical studies quoted above, this observation is somehow unexpected. If the *s*-genitive occurs more often in informal text-types, then we would certainly expect it to be much more frequent in the most informal mode, i.e. spoken language. Biber et al. (1999: 302) attribute the low frequency of *s*-genitives in conversation partly to the fact that the frequency of nouns in conversation is relatively low, and so, accordingly, should be nominal constructions. That is, the low frequency of the *s*-genitive in conversation may be an epiphenomenon, resulting from the overall low frequency of nominal constructions rather than from a genuine property of this register. The problems of using only the frequency of the *s*-genitive and not considering the potential possibility of the *s*-genitive to occur in contrast to the alternative *of*-genitive (= *relative* frequency) will be further discussed in chapter 4 below. Moreover, what is generally not considered in empirical studies investigating the impact of formality on the genitive variation is that it is maybe not so much the degree of formality that induces the choice of genitive construction but rather that the language user chooses the *s*-genitive or the *of*-genitive in order to achieve a certain effect. That is, the choice of genitive construction could create a certain formal context, and not vice versa, and "formality" may be less a genuine factor but rather an epiphenomenon. While such a perspective does probably not diminish the validity of the empirical findings, i.e. it does not affect the correlation between style/formality and the frequency of the *s*-genitive as such, it may nonetheless have implications for the way such findings are interpreted.[39]

The relatively high productivity of the *s*-genitive in journalistic language is usually attributed to the tight, short (and therefore space-saving) structure of the *s*-genitive (as compared to the *of*-genitive), which seems particularly apt for use in those genres in which information condensation is important (cf. e.g. Hundt 1998: 47). Likewise, the *s*-genitive is said to be particularly productive in the language of advertisement (cf. Leech 1966: 133). It has, however, also been shown that journalistic language as such is not a homogeneous genre as far as the distribution of the *s*-genitive is concerned. Jucker (1993) has shown that the frequency of the *s*-genitive varies considerably according to the degree of formality of British dailies in that its frequency is higher in more informal down-market papers than in the up-market papers. Jucker's (1993) data also indicate that the type of press section does play a role: in his newspaper corpus the *s*-genitive is more frequent in the sports section than in home news.

The frequency of the *s*-genitive also differs according to the different Standard varieties of English. Jahr Sorheim (1980) shows that American English is more advanced than British English in the use of the *s*-genitive with non-personal (i.e. inanimate) possessors (see also §4.1.2). Hundt (1998: 42-49) argues that the two Southern Hemisphere varieties, New Zealand and Australian English, are lagging behind in this development. However, "differences between national varieties of English are reflective of the time lag rather than constitute genuine regionalisms" (Hundt 1998: 48-49).[40] In the light of Jahr Sorheim's (1980) and Hundt's (1998) findings it is, however, somewhat surprising that Ljung (1997) in his corpus finds more *s*-genitives with non-personal nouns in the British newspaper (*The Independent*) than in the American newspaper (*The New York Times*) and magazine (*Time*). I will return to the question of which Standard variety is the more 'progressive' in the use of the *s*-genitive in chapter 6 below.

3.3.2.3 Implications for the empirical investigation

I have tried to establish a criterion of 'sameness' for the variation between the *s*-genitive and the *of*-genitive as the two major devices in Standard English to encode the relation between a possessor and a possessum. Apart from defining the set of variants, it is also necessary – and indeed crucial – for an empirical analysis of genitive variation to look only at those contexts in which the two genitive constructions can really compete and, ideally, only vary with respect to the factors under investigation. For this reason, the following potential choice contexts have been identified:[41]

Table 13. Choice contexts for genitive variation

choice contexts for the genitive variation (*s*-genitive and *of*-genitive)	
genitive function/meaning	• possessive
noun class	• possessor = full lexical NP
definiteness	• whole genitive NP = [+definite]
	• no reference tracking devices for whole NP

Moreover, having discussed all those factors hitherto known to bias the choice of genitive construction either towards the *s*-genitive or the *of*-genitive, these – potential – choice contexts can be further delimited to 'neutral', i.e. comparable contexts, as illustrated in table 14 below.

Having narrowed down the range of variation to real choice contexts in this way will serve as the main point of departure for the investigation of the three factors which the present study focuses on, i.e. animacy, topicality, and type of possessive relation. These factors will be introduced and discussed separately and in detail in chapter 4 and operationalized in §6.2 below.

Table 14. Comparable contexts within choice contexts

factor	comparable contexts within choice contexts
phonological	• possessor not ending in /s/, /z/, or /θ/
morphological	• singular possessor noun
syntactic	• non-complex, non-branching possessor and possessum
	• non-consecutive genitive constructions
socio-stylistic	• data must be either balanced or controlled for style

Note that only once the potential choice contexts have been identified can we go on and try to reveal which factors in these contexts influence the choice between the two genitive constructions. This procedure is, however, only possible if we already have sufficient information as to what constitutes in fact a categorical context and what does not. For the two genitive constructions this seems to be the case for the modern English situation, since, as shown in this chapter, the main contexts in which the two constructions are mutually exclusive can be inferred from the literature available. The strict distinction between categorical and choice contexts as outlined above may therefore apply to the investigation of Present-day English data. If, however, the potential choice context cannot be identified beforehand on independent grounds, then the logical procedure is that we need to take a more liberal view and include them in the study; in this case the analysis will identify those contexts in which there is no choice and it is only then that we may exclude these contexts from further analysis. Note that this was the procedure taken in the analysis of the historical data to be discussed in §7.4. From a diachronic perspective, another word of caution is in order: Even if there are, synchronically, categorical contexts, these may well change over time and become choice contexts. Therefore, from a long-term diachronic perspective, identifying categorical contexts is basically an empirical question. In the absence of diachronic native speaker intuitions about what is possible and what is not, only the empirical analysis will show us in which cases there was a potential context and in which there was not. Studying grammatical variation for previous stages of the English language, we therefore need to keep an open mind about categorical contexts and see whether they change. Again, the historical perspective pursued in this study will show that this is exactly what happened in the case of the *s*-genitive.

Chapter 4
Factors: Animacy, topicality, and possessive relation

Having discussed the various factors known to influence the choice of genitive construction (and therefore to be controlled for) in the previous chapter, I will now turn to the factors to be investigated in the present study, i.e. animacy, topicality, and possessive relation. It is well known from previous studies that the factors animacy, topicality, and possessive relation play some sort of role in the choice between the *s*-genitive and the *of*-genitive in English. In the following I will first introduce the factors and discuss the findings of previous research for the single factors. I will also go into the question of how these three factors interact in general, and with respect to the genitive constructions. In §6.2 I will then show how these factors can be related to the "choice"-based approach to be introduced in §5.3 below.

4.1   Animacy
4.1.1   The notion of animacy

"Animacy" is an inherent property of concepts and, as a first approximation, it refers to the distinction between living and non-living things or concepts. As a linguistic factor, shaping human language, however, animacy cannot be defined in a straightforward manner. The probably best-known linguistic treatment of animacy is Silverstein's (1976) "hierarchy of features of NPs", commonly referred to as "animacy hierarchy, in which he suggests a cline of decreasing animacy from left (1st person) to right (inanimate).

> 1st person > 2nd person >3rd person > pronoun > proper name > human
> >animate > inanimate   (based on Silverstein 1976: 122)

This hierarchy, however, mixes aspects of person, referentiality/topicality, and animacy. Rather than one single hierarchy, the Silverstein hierarchy comprises three logically independent though obviously highly interacting hierarchies (for a similar argumentation, see also Croft 1990: 112-113; Ortmann 1998: 78-79):

(1) person hierarchy: 1 > 2 > 3
(2) referentiality/topicality hierarchy: pronoun > proper name > common
     noun
(3) animacy: (a) animate > inanimate
                   (b) human > non-human

It is already obvious from Silverstein's animacy hierarchy that animacy as a linguistic factor cannot solely be defined on grounds of the living/non-living distinction; what matters are not so much the biological facts but rather what human beings conceive as being more or less animate or salient (see also §6.2.1.2 below). This explains why humans figure higher on the animacy scale than animals although the latter are no less animate.

It also varies from language to language how and to which extent animacy affects a language's grammar. There are some languages in which a conceived animate-inanimate distinction has been grammaticalized, for example in the organization of gender systems (cf. e.g. Ortmann 1998). Moreover, Corbett (2000: chapters 3 – 4) in his cross-linguistic study of number observes that the higher nouns are on the animacy hierarchy, the more likely they show number distinction (cf. also Croft 1990: 111-112). Dahl and Fraurud (1996) and Yamamoto (1999: chapter 2) give a good overview of the effects of animacy on grammar. Just to give a few examples: in some Australian languages animacy seems to determine if there is a separate accusative case (cf. also Comrie 1989: 189; Blake 1977: 13-15). In Spanish only referential and animate patients are marked with the preposition *a*, which is regarded as a kind of object marker. Most often, however, animacy seems to be manifested in terms of preferences rather than in grammaticalized distinctions. For example, animates are more likely to be selected as subjects than inanimates (see again Yamamoto 1999: 56-60 for a brief overview of the literature).

4.1.2   Previous studies

The dominant role of animacy in the choice between the *s*-genitive and the *of*-genitive has been stressed by almost every account on the English genitive alternation. The standard assumption expressed by grammars is that the *s*-genitive only occurs with human possessors, while with inanimate possessors the *of*-genitive is the rule (cf. e.g. Quirk et al. 1985: §5.117; Biber et al. 1999: 302-303). In addition, the use of the *s*-genitive seems to be sensitive to the lexical noun class of the possessor Quirk et al.

(1985: §5.1117) link the occurrence of the *s*-genitive to a "gender scale" (Quirk et al. 1985: §5.104), according to which, generally speaking, the *s*-genitive is favored for those noun classes which are highest on the gender scale. This predicts, strictly speaking, a decreasing frequency of the *s*-genitive according to the noun class of the possessor along the following scale:

personal	collective	higher	lower	inanimate
nouns >	nouns >	animals >	animals >	nouns
brother	*family*	*cow*	*ant*	*box*

As is, however, evident from Quirk et al. (1985: §5.118), the *s*-genitive may also occur with certain kinds of inanimate nouns, in particular geographical names (*Europe's future, Hollywood's studios, Harvard's Department of Linguistics*), locative nouns (*the earth's interior, the Gallery's rotunda*), temporal nouns (*the decade's events, a day's work*) and a dummy category called "other nouns of special relevance to human activity" (e.g. *the brain's total weight, my life's aim, the treaty's ratification*). It has long been observed by several scholars that the use of the *s*-genitive with such inanimate possessors seems to be on the increase in Modern English (e.g. Zachrisson 1920: 39-49; Jespersen 1961: 324-330; Thomas 1953; Barber 1964: 132-134; Potter [1969] 1975; Dahl 1971; Denison 1998: 119).[42] Most of the early empirical studies available focus mainly on a description of the noun classes (of the possessor), with which the *s*-genitive can occur and do not quantify their data at all (e.g. Zachrisson 1920; Svartengren 1949), or if they do, give the frequency of the *s*-genitive only (e.g. Thomas 1953; Dahl 1971). The latter is, however, not a reliable device to measure the productivity of the *s*-genitive since it may easily confound the frequency of nouns in general, or of noun classes which are more likely to take the *s*-genitive, as such with the frequency of the *s*-genitive as compared to its potential to occur at all, i.e. its relative distribution compared to its structural alternative, the *of*-genitive (= relative frequency). Genres or texts which tend towards a more nominal style will provide more potential contexts for the occurrence of nominal genitive constructions, which will in turn result in an overall higher number of *s*-genitives in these texts/genres than in texts/genres that use more predicative structures. Moreover, depending on what a text is about, some texts may exhibit more animate nouns while others contain more inanimate nouns; this again may bias the frequency rate of the *s*-genitive in absolute terms but may not tell us anything about its relative frequency.

Jahr Sorheim (1980) is the first to give the relative frequency of the *s*-genitive according to different genres and a fine-grained noun-class classification, considering only semantically equivalent, i.e. choice contexts. The main focus of her study is on the use of the *s*-genitive with inanimate possessors. Comparing the British *Lancaster-Oslo/Bergen corpus* (LOB corpus) with the corresponding American *Brown corpus*, her findings indicate that while the *s*-genitive is still most frequent with personal nouns (i.e. animate/human possessors), it can also occur with inanimate possessors; in this context it is most frequent with geographical nouns/names and temporal nouns (Jahr Sorheim 1980: 114-115). This increasing use of *s*-genitives with inanimate possessors according to Jahr Sorheim (1980), seems to have spread from American English to British English and is most prevalent in journalistic language and least likely in religious prose, i.e. the most formal genre. The extension Jahr Sorheim observes for the *s*-genitive is not an extension in its relative frequency but rather an extension of the possible contexts in which the *s*-genitive can occur:

> It is clear ... that the *s*-genitive is being used with types of nouns where it has been said not to occur, and that this expansion seems to develop faster i [sic!] present-day American English than in British English.
>
> (Jahr Sorheim 1980: 147)

Siemund (1993) is the first study to provide empirical evidence for a (short-term) diachronic extension in the frequency of the *s*-genitive (as quoted in Raab-Fischer 1995 and Hundt 1998: 44-45). His data indicate that the frequency of the *s*-genitive in the more recent *Freiburg-LOB Corpus of British English* (FLOB corpus) no longer runs along the lines of the gender scale in Quirk et al. (1985: §5.104), because less animate nouns (i.e. collective nouns) and inanimate nouns (i.e. geographical nouns) have become more frequent than the genuinely animate class of personal nouns.[43] In addition, his data show that in the more recent FLOB corpus the *s*-genitive has become more frequent in terms of absolute numbers. Raab-Fischer (1995) shows that this increase in the number of *s*-genitives from the LOB (1961) to the FLOB (1991) corpus in the said noun classes as observed by Siemund (1993) can be linked to a corresponding decrease of the *of*-genitive. So, while Siemund's (1993) findings are restricted to the frequency of the *s*-genitive only, the additional study by Raab-Fischer (1995) provides further evidence for a diachronic increase of – what now comes close to the – relative frequency of the *s*-genitive. Interestingly, Raab-Fischer (1995) comes up with a possible explanation of why the *s*-genitive is on the increase with personal names but not with personal nouns. She observes that the higher frequency of the *s*-genitive with personal names is, at least partly, due to the overall higher frequency of personal names in the more recent FLOB corpus than in the older LOB corpus, which, in turn, she attributes to a shift towards an increasing informality in the language of newspaper, to which her and Siemund's studies are restricted. This shows how problematic and indeed misleading it can be to look at the distribution of the *s*-genitive only and not taking into account how often it can be potentially realized within a certain context.

Hundt (1998: 45-46), comparing six newspaper corpora, in particular Siemund's (1993) figures from the LOB and FLOB corpus with the corresponding American corpora (Brown [1960s] and *Freiburg Brown Corpus of American English* [Frown corpus, 1990s]) as well as a New Zealand and Australian English corpus, not only confirms Jahr Sorheim's (1980) results showing that "AmE is leading the change towards a greater use of inflected genitives with nouns ranking low on the gender scale" (Hundt 1998: 46) but also "provides evidence that the younger colonial varieties [= New Zealand and Australian English] are closer to BrE in this respect than AmE" (Hundt 1998: 46). Hundt (1998) concludes, however, that the "diachronic change, on the whole, is likely to be more important than regional differences in the use of inflected genitives" (46), because the differences in the frequency of the *s*-genitive *within* the single varieties over time (LOB → FLOB; Brown → Frown) turned out to be more significant than the differences *between* the varieties, particularly with inanimate possessors. While Hundt's (1998) analysis is restricted to newspaper language only, Hundt (1997: 139) additionally shows that American influence on British English seems restricted to journalistic language; for other non-fictional writings the frequency of the *s*-genitive with inanimate possessors did not increase in the British corpora while it did so considerably in the corresponding American ones. Like Siemund (1993), however, also Hundt (1998) looks only at the frequency of the *s*-genitive without considering its distribution relative to the *of*-genitive. So, the fact that, for example, Hundt (1998) finds more *s*-genitives with inanimate nouns in the British and American corpora than in the corpora of the Southern Hemisphere varieties could be simply due to the fact that in the latter there are less inanimate possessors and that there is, for this very reason, a less likelihood of the *s*-genitive occurring with such nouns. As said above, only if the relative frequency of the *s*-genitive as opposed to the *of*-genitive is calculated for each noun class can this conflicting factor be ruled out: no matter how many overall inanimate possessors (or see also the other noun classes) there are, the relative frequency will not be affected by it.

Another empirical study which focuses on a newspaper corpus is Jucker (1993), who gives the relative frequency of the *s*-genitive as opposed to the *of*-genitive in British dailies according to the noun classes distinguished by Quirk et al. (1985: §5.118) as illustrated in figure 2 below (based on figures given in Jucker 1993: 127). Note that the order of noun classes corresponds to the decreasing scale of animacy as indicated in both the animacy hierarchy and Quirk et al.'s (1985: §5.104) gender scale.

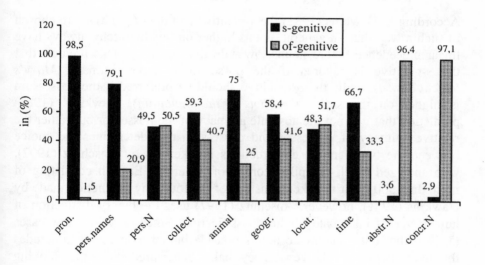

Figure 2. Relative frequency of the *s*-genitive versus the *of*-genitive in Jucker (1993)

Jucker's (1993) results correspond to a great extent to Siemund's (1993) in that the frequency of the *s*-genitive in newspapers in the 1990s does not decrease along the Quirkian gender scale; collective (59.3%), geographical (58.4%) and particularly nouns denoting time (66.7%) outnumber personal nouns (49.5%) in taking the *s*-genitive in Jucker's newspaper corpus.

Leech, Francis, and Xu's (1994) corpus data, drawn from the LOB corpus, basically confirm the findings of the other empirical studies reported so far. Although in their data human nouns (including proper names) are clearly most likely to take the *s*-genitive, place nouns/names and time nouns stand out among inanimate possessors by having a relatively high likelihood of taking the *s*-genitive, while abstract and concrete inanimate nouns are almost never realized by the *s*-genitive.

While all these studies have focused on the animacy, or rather lexical noun class, of the possessor, Hawkins (1981) argues that it is rather the *relative* animacy of possessor and possessum that determines the occurrence of the *s*-genitive versus the *of*-genitive, proposing the following hierarchy:

human >	human >	non-human, >	non-human,
	attribute	animate >	inanimate
Mary	*leg*	*cat*	*basket*

According to Hawkins (1981) the *s*-genitive and the *of*-genitive are chosen in such a way that, in general, nouns higher on this hierarchy always have linear precedence before nouns lower on the hierarchy. This predicts that the *s*-genitive is favored if the possessor is more animate (*Mary's leg/cat/basket*), while the *of*-genitive should be preferred if the possessum is higher on the scale (*the foot of the mountain*). Hawkins' (1981) prediction that it is not the absolute animacy of the possessor but rather the relative animacy of possessor and possessum that determines the choice between the two genitive constructions is taken up by Anschutz (1997), who analyzed a self-compiled corpus of American English consisting of more than 500 genitive tokens. Instead of the four-way distinction made by Hawkins (1981), however, Anschutz (1997) uses the binary distinction of human versus inanimate for her classification. Since only in a few cases (13% of her data) inanimate nouns precede human nouns, she concludes that the principle of relative animacy makes better predictions than looking at the animacy of the possessor only. Neither Anschutz (1997) nor Hawkins (1981), however, consider – beyond mere animacy – the lexical noun class, which, as already discussed, has been shown to strongly influence the frequency of the *s*-genitive. Moreover, the principle "animate > inanimate" also entails certain predictions as to which possessive relations should preferably take the *s*-genitive or the *of*-genitive, a question to which I will return in §4.4.2 and §6.2.2 below.

Interestingly, Dabrowska (1998) introduces a new argument into the empirical investigation of the factor animacy in the genitive alternation. Analyzing the relative frequency of the *s*-genitive versus the *of*-genitive in a corpus of computer manuals, she can show that the *s*-genitive occurs relatively frequently with a certain type of inanimate possessor not reported so far, i.e. computer nouns. Since computers tend to be often associated with human attributes and activities – they can be 'malicious', they have a 'memory', they 'give' instructions – they seem to be conceived of metaphorically as human and can therefore, as Dabrowska's (1998) argument goes, also linguistically be treated as human, thereby accounting for their ability to occur relatively easily with the *s*-genitive. Apart from the human metaphor, computers can also be thought of in a locational dimension: you can be 'within' a certain program or 'move' to another one. Note that locational/geographical nouns frequently take the *s*-genitive (see e.g. Siemund 1993; Jucker 1993 or Leech, Francis, and Xu 1994). This indicates again that it might not primarily be a question of what is and what is not animate (or "locational") that determines the use of the *s*-genitive but rather a matter of what we perceive and conceptualize to be animate-like or locational. As I will argue in §8.6.2.3 the capacity of certain inanimate nouns or noun classes to be conceptualized as animate may have given rise to analogical/metaphorical extension, thereby contributing to the systematic diachronic spread of the *s*-genitive.

4.2   Topicality

4.2.1   The notion of topicality

"Topicality" is a term widely used and defined within linguistics. What unites most notions of topicality is that in linear order topics tend to come first, at least in English. It is, however, less clear what constitutes a topic in the first place. Therefore, a brief overview of notions and concepts of topicality is in order.

First, we need to draw a general distinction between approaches which treat the notion of "topic" or "theme" as given or familiar information (see Prague School research, e.g. Firbas 1964; Halliday 1967; for an overview see Lambrecht 1994: chapter 4) and those in which the term "topic" refers to particularly salient, important – generally new – information (cf. the "principle of Actuality" by Jespersen 1961: 54, or topic as "important information", cf. e.g. Givón 1988, 1995: 51-54). In the following, I will be using the term "topic" to refer exclusively to given and familiar information. Usually, "givenness" refers to the speaker's assessment of what is given or familiar in the addressee's mind, and it links to notions such as identifiability and activation (cf. Chafe 1976, 1987; for a discussion, see e.g. Lambrecht 1994: chapter 3). A concept or referent is identifiable, if the speaker assumes it to be known by the addressee. In contrast to identifiability, which is knowledge-based and concerns the knowledge representations in long-term memory, the term activation refers to consciousness and what is currently focused on in the addressee's short-term memory. In particular, Chafe (1987) distinguishes between three activation states: "active" (= focus of consciousness), "semi-active" (= at periphery of consciousness, not directly focused on) and "inactive" (= knowledge not focused on).

Second, we need to keep the notion of "topic" as a purely conceptual entity in the sense of givenness as outlined above and its grammatical correlates logically apart. In this sense, the notion of topicality is closely interrelated with the grammatical category of definiteness. The concept of definiteness is strongly connected to the conceptual properties of familiarity (see e.g. Christophersen 1939; Hawkins 1978; Lyons, C. 1999: 2-7) and identifiability (cf. e.g. Lyons, C. 1999: 2-7, 12-13), and it is in this respect that definiteness overlaps to a great extent conceptually with topicality in the sense of givenness as outlined above. Formally, definiteness is expressed by the use of definite versus indefinite expressions. Proceeding from the formal expressions of definiteness, the general story is that the speaker, by using a definite expression, assumes that the hearer either knows the referent (= familiarity) or can identify it (= identifiability); cf. e.g. Lambrecht (1994: 79-87); Lyons, C. (1999: 6).[44]

Apart from the formal distinction between definite and indefinite expressions another semantic-conceptual distinction is important in accounts of definiteness, i.e. the distinction between referential and non-referential, or, in other terms, specific and non-specific expressions.[45] Referential expressions refer to an existing referent, while non-referential expressions are not referring and only describe, indicating class membership, typically represented by generic expressions (cf. e.g. Lyons, J. 1977: chapter 7; Givón 1984: §11.5; Lyons, C. 1999: §4.2). Table 15 below gives a broad overview of the relation between definiteness and referentiality, indicating how the respective categories are usually linguistically expressed.

Table 15. Definiteness and referentiality

definiteness		
referential definiteness		non-referential definiteness
definite NPs	indefinite NPs	generics
• personal pronouns: *I, you, he/she/it, we, you, they* • proper nouns: *Mary, Mr Brown*	• NPs formally marked by indefinite expressions: *a/one/some/a certain man*	• definite NPs: *The lion is a dangerous animal.* • indefinite NPs: *He has the shape of a woman.*
• NPs marked by definite article, demonstrative or possessive pronoun: *the/that/my book*		• plural: *Cats are lovely animals.*

Note that there is no absolute one-to-one relation between definiteness and referentiality on the one hand and the type of referring expression on the other. While referentially definite expressions are typically expressed by personal pronouns or proper nouns, both of which are inherently definite, or formally marked definites, the opposite does not necessarily hold true: both the definite and the indefinite article can be used to refer to a specific, referential referent and in a generic, non-referential sense. It is often particularly difficult to evaluate if an indefinite article is used referentially or generically, since referential indefinites and generics are conceptually very close. Sometimes the context forces a referential versus a non-referential reading; cf. the following examples:

(46)   *I bought a new book.*

(47)   *I'd like to have a book for my birthday, but I don't know yet which one.*

In (46) *a new book* must refer to a specific entity; the indefinite article is used because the speaker, although having a specific book in mind, does not expect the hearer to be able to identify it. In (47) he does not have a specific book in mind, therefore here *a book* is generic. The distinction between referential and non-referential expressions is crucial for the investigation of the English genitive constructions for two reasons. First, as argued in §2.3.1, it accounts for the inherent ambiguity of *s*-genitive containing an indefinite possessor which can very often be interpreted as both a specifying and a classifying genitive. Second, due to this ambiguity certain problems for the empirical investigation may arise. As argued in §3.3.2.2.1, only specifying genitives, i.e. genitives with a referential possessor, should be investigated as potential choice contexts. Yet when investigating topicality as defined in terms of definiteness, distinguishing between definite and indefinite possessors, the latter, even if referential, might often as well entail a non-referential reading, shading into a classifying genitive.

Gundel, Hedberg, and Zacharski (1993) explicitly link the shape of the NP to the cognitive status of these expressions, assuming that the type of referring (linguistic) expressing is indicative of the assumed cognitive status of the referent as formulated in the following "givenness hierarchy" (Gundel, Hedberg, and Zacharski 1993: 275):

in focus	> activated	> familiar	> uniquely identifiable	> referential	> type identifiable
it	*that, this* *this* N	*that* N	*the* N	*indefinite this* N	*a* N

In this framework definiteness is defined in that a definite noun phrase is taken to be definite if its referent is at least uniquely identifiable (Gundel, Hedberg, and Zacharski 1993: 277), which means that "the addressee can identify the speaker's intended referent on the basis of the nominal alone" (Gundel, Hedberg, and Zacharski 1993: 277). Since in the givenness hierarchy cognitive statuses are implicationally related to each other this implies that all cognitive statuses entailing "uniquely identifiable" are associated with definite NPs; i.e. 'uniquely identifiable' is both a necessary and a sufficient condition for definite reference (Gundel, Hedberg, and Zacharski 1993: 277).

Note, however, that there is no absolute one-to-one correspondence between formal definiteness and givenness. As, for example, Fraurud (1990) has shown in a corpus of Swedish prose, a definite NP does not necessarily encode anaphorically given information; the majority of definite NPs in her corpus (about 60%) are used as a first-mention.

Note also, that among the class of definite expressions, we may establish the following accessibility hierarchy: pronouns > proper nouns > definite NPs (common nouns). According to Gundel, Hedberg, and Zacharski (1993) pronouns are highest on the givenness hierarchy. Mulkern (1996) argues that proper names can be incorporated in Gundel, Hedberg, and Zacharski (1993) givenness hierarchy; in her account the use of single names (*John, Mary*) indicates familiarity while full names (*Glenn*

Robinson; University of Minnesota English professor Chester Anderson)
are regarded as uniquely identifiable, thereby ranging lower on the
hierarchy. In general, proper nouns are inherently given (cf. e.g.
Huddleston 1984: 230) and as individuals that can be named they can be
regarded to be the most individuated entities and therefore ontologically
more given than common nouns (cf. Fraurud 1996: 71).[46] Also, as shown in
§4.1.1, Silverstein's animacy hierarchy contains an implicit NP-type
hierarchy with pronouns ranking higher than proper nouns and common
nouns (see also Croft 1990: 113).

All this ties in to the general question of how a topic can be established
or is constituted. In an anaphoric and discourse-dynamic sense an entity can
become topical because it has been previously mentioned in discourse,
either explicitly or in the sense that it can be "inferred" from what has been
said before (cf. e.g. Prince 1981), in Chafe's terminology "active" or "semi-
active". A notorious problem for empirical studies is how to evaluate the
activation state of an entity from its occurrence in a text: is explicit mention
in previous discourse a sufficient criterion, and if so, how should "previous
discourse" be defined (cf. e.g. Givón 1983). And how should be dealt with
"inferrables" (Prince 1981), also called "associative anaphora" (e.g.
Hawkins 1978), i.e. expressions whose referent is implicitly associated with
a previously introduced discourse referent; as for example in

(48)   *John went into the house. The door was open.*

where, although *door* is a first-mention, it is given because of its
association with *house*.

Second, givenness in the sense of identifiability can be established on
the grounds of mutually shared knowledge between speaker and hearer, be
it that they currently share the same perceptual situation or are within the
same "frame", or that they are both members of a speech community
sharing certain kinds of cultural knowledge.

And third, as shown by Fraurud (1996) and Maes (1997) some entities
seem to be inherently more accessible and topical than others by their very
nature. Fraurud (1996) argues that besides the commonly accepted belief
that NP forms, such as e.g. pronouns, demonstratives, definite and
indefinite NPs are chosen on the basis of the speaker's assumptions about
the cognitive state of the referent in the addressee's mind irrespective of the
kind of entity in question, the ontological class of the entity correlates with
the type of NP chosen. In particular, Fraurud (1996) proposes a tripartite
referent   ontology,   distinguishing   along   the   two   dimensions   of
"relationality" and "individuation" between "individuals", "functionals"

and "instances". Individuals are entities conceived of in their own right and typically named; in fact, Fraurud (1996) considers them the most individuated entities in her cognitive ontology. Functionals are only identifiable via another entity (= anchor), as e.g. parts are in relation to their wholes (*windscreen* to *car*). Functionals are usually expressed by definite expressions, not by virtue of their givenness but by their identification through an anchor (for this, see also §4.3.1 and §4.4.3 below), and possessive constructions in which a possessor is linked to a possessum certainly fall under this category. Instances are instantiations of types (e.g. *a glass of wine*), usually expressed by an indefinite expression and typically answering the question 'what is it?' rather than 'which one?'.[47] Note that the distinction between functionals and instances as developed in Fraurud (1990) seems to be compatible with the distinction between specifying and classifying genitives drawn in §2.3.1 above. Specifying genitives, having a referential possessor functioning as a determiner, can be equated with functionals, while classifying genitives, which have a non-referential, modifying possessor, can be regarded as instances. Like Fraurud (1996), Maes (1997) maintains that the type of referring expressions depends on the inherent conceptual characteristics of the discourse referents rather than simply on the attentional state during discourse, providing evidence for an ontological distinction between common nouns and abstract nouns. Fraurud's (1996) referent ontology is innovative in that the choice of referring expressions is linked to the kind of entity referred to instead merely to the givenness status; it relates also to an account of definiteness proposed by Löbner (1985), which I will address in §4.3.1.

Finally, the term topic can be used in a relational and in a non-relational sense (cf. also Gundel 1988), that is, topic can be defined as given information (topic/theme) *in relation to* new information (comment/rheme) as explicated by the Prague School in the principle of "Functional Sentence Perspective" (e.g. Firbas 1964) and "Communicative Dynamism" (e.g. Firbas 1992) and in other theories of information structure (e.g. Gundel 1988). In this relational sense, it is generally assumed that a topic or theme precedes the comment or rheme in linear order. In a non-relational reading, topicality can be defined on the basis of the cognitive status of the intended referent, as e.g. in the framework by Gundel, Hedberg, and Zacharski (1993), the ontological type (cf. Fraurud 1996) or by the linguistic expression used (definite versus indefinite). Table 16 below sums up the various uses and definitions of topicality. This overview does not intend to give an exhaustive account of the various notions of topicality but rather serves as the point of departure for the discussion of topicality as applied in previous studies of the genitive alternation and as used in the present study.

Table 16. Notions and definitions of topicality

topicality			
conceptual basis	**linguistic expression**	**relational**	**non-relational**

• givenness:
   • identifiability
   • activation
 • referentiality
 • referent
   ontology
	• definiteness:
	 formally definite
	 versus indefinite
	 expressions
		• topic/theme >
		 comment/
		 rheme
			• cognitive
			 status
			 • referent
			 ontology
			 • definiteness

4.2.2   Previous studies

The studies by Jahr Sorheim (1980), Altenberg (1980, 1982) and Anschutz (1997) all use topicality in the relational sense, testing the principle that given information should precede new information (cf. e.g. Firbas 1964; Gundel 1988). If this principle, which has traditionally been applied to the clausal level only, can be transferred to the NP-level, then the following predictions should hold true for the two genitive constructions in the following four logically possible combinations of given/new possessors and possessum nouns:

(1)   given possessor- new possessum → *s*-genitive
(2)   given possessum – new possessor → *of*-genitive
(3)   given possessor – given possessum → *s*-genitive and *of*-genitive
                                      equally likely
(4)   new possessor – new possessum → *s*-genitive and *of*-genitive equally
                                        likely

Jahr Sorheim (1980: 129-133) classifies both previous mentions, i.e. anaphoric uses, and proper nouns as given, and her data indeed indicate that the *s*-genitive is preferred in the constellation "given possessor – new possessum"; never in her corpus does the *s*-genitive occur with a new possessor and a given possessum. However, as is apparent from her data (Jahr Sorheim 1980: 144), no matter which constellation is investigated, the preference for the *s*-genitive decreases if other principles, such as an inanimate or a plural possessor, which generally favour the *of*-genitive, come into play.

Jahr Sorheim's (1980) results are very much in line with the results for seventeenth-century English reported by Altenberg (1980, 1982). Defining givenness in terms of activation, i.e. as being previously mentioned in the immediate situation, Altenberg (1980: 152-153) explicitly excludes any knowledge-based notions of givenness from his analysis. His data indicate that a given possessor strongly favors the *s*-genitive when the possessum is new; in contrast to Jahr Sorheim's (1980) results, however, the *s*-genitive and the *of*-genitive do have roughly the same distribution for NPs with a given possessum and a new possessor. As in Jahr Sorheim's (1980) data, topicality alone does not seem to condition the frequency of the two genitive constructions. Rather, as Altenberg (1982: 287) puts it, "it is best described as a variable or potential force that comes into play under certain favorable conditions", i.e. topicality seems to interact strongly with other factors. Note, however, that both Jahr Sorheim (1980) and Altenberg (1980, 1982) seem to have proceeded from at times somewhat diverging definitions of topicality. While, for example, Jahr Sorheim (1980) classifies proper nouns always as given, Altenberg (1980, 1982) seems to regard them as new when first mentioned.[48]

Anschutz (1997) also defines "given" and "new" conceptually in terms of first mention (= new) versus second mention (= given/old). Her corpus data show that there are relatively few cases in which new information precedes old, and these are only realized by the *of*-genitive and never by the *s*-genitive; on top of that, Anschutz (1997: chapter 6) argues that most of these violators can be explained by having no semantically equivalent counterpart. For this reason Anschutz comes to conclude that topicality is a more important factor than animacy for the choice between the two genitive constructions. Note, however, that what turns out to be a knock-out context in Anschutz' (1997) data for the *s*-genitive, i.e. "new possessor – given possessum", is conceptually a very odd constellation: modifiers (possessors) are supposed to supply additional information that helps to narrow down the referent of the head (possessum); in this respect new modifiers/possessors as such are no good modifiers. And indeed, the data given by Anschutz (1997: 15) show that there are only 15 cases (out of more than 500 tokens) in which we find this constellation (new possessor-old possessum). The same can be observed for Altenberg's (1982) extensive seventeenth-century corpus; in his (sub)corpus (for "thematic structure") there are only 34 tokens (out of 801) for the context "new possessor/given possessum", of which 44% do occur with the *s*-genitive. That is, a new possessor and a given possessum as such is a very infrequent constellation and likewise also the *s*-genitive will be highly unlikely to occur in this context. And even if the relative frequency of the *s*-genitive as opposed to the *of*-genitive is taken into account (as it is in Anschutz 1997 and Altenberg 1980, 1982), the token frequency of genitive constructions will be too low to warrant any far-reaching conclusions.

The recent *Longman Grammar of Spoken and Written English* by Biber et al. (1999: 305-306) discusses the givenness of the possessor only and not the relative givenness of possessor and possessum. The frequency scores given confirm that the *s*-genitive is highly favored with given possessors, whereas the *of*-genitive is preferred with new possessors. While the *s*-genitive is certainly much less frequent than the *of*-genitive with new possessors, it nonetheless does occur in this context. Likewise, Anschutz' (1997: 14) data show that the *s*-genitive can occur with new possessors if the possessum is new as well, i.e. in 47 out of 241 obligatory contexts for "new possessor – new possessum" (= 19.5%).[49]

"Topicality" as used by Jahr Sorheim (1980), Altenberg (1980, 1982) and Anschutz (1997) is an essentially discourse-based notion, which proceeds from a definition of what is given in terms of previous mention in discourse, not taking into account other definitions of what can constitute a topic, as, for example mutually- or culturally shared knowledge or concepts or entities more prominent because of their ontological type. In neither Jahr Sorheim's (1980) nor Altenberg's (1980, 1982) study does a distinction seem to have been made between inherently definite – and topical – nouns, such as proper nouns, and anaphorical (second-mention) uses of nouns.[50] As we have seen in §4.1.2 above, however, proper nouns (= personal names) are much more likely to take the *s*-genitive than personal nouns are. That is, the frequency scores for topicality may have been confounded by the frequency of certain NP types (proper nouns versus personal nouns) in the respective corpora. Also, non-referential possessors seem to have been included in these studies, at least in Jahr Sorheim (1980)[51] and Altenberg (1980: 156-158, 1982).[52] As argued above (cf. §3.3.2.2.1), however, genitive constructions with non-referential possessors (= classifying genitives) form a rather different type of possessive construction and should therefore not be included in a quantitative analysis of the variation between the *s*-genitive and the *of*-genitive.

As was also apparent from Jahr Sorheim's (1980) data, topicality heavily interacts with animacy; topical inanimate possessors were much less likely to occur with the *s*-genitive than topical animate possessors. And also Altenberg (1982: 297-300) observes that topicality as a factor only seems to come into play if not other factors intervene. I will return to the question of how the factors interact in §4.4 below.

4.3   Possessive relation

4.3.1   Taxonomies and previous studies

The classification of the semantic relation that holds between the possessor and the possessum is a notoriously difficult enterprise (see e.g. discussions in Taylor 1996: 5-11 or Heine 1997: chapter 1). There are basically two different ways of approaching a taxonomy of the genitive meanings: (i) a form-based, semasiological approach, and (ii) a meaning-based, onomasiological approach.

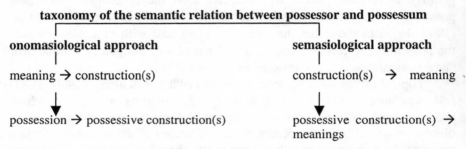

Figure 3.   Taxonomy of the semantic relation between possessor and possessum

In the semasiological procedure, we look first at the genitive constructions and determine which meanings can be expressed by them. In this case, the question arises which constructions are taken to be "possessive", i.e. from which constructions should we proceed? Only those constructions inflected for genitive case, or any constructions conveying possessive meanings? Note that such a form-based approach involves a classic chicken-and-egg problem and a certain circularity. Strictly speaking, only if we have a preconceived notion of what are possessive meanings can we identify the constructions from which we will proceed to identify, in turn – again – their meanings. In the second case, the onomasiological procedure, we need first to determine which are the genitive meanings and then look which constructions linguistically encode them. A precondition for an onomasiological procedure is, however, that there is indeed a clearly definable semantic-conceptual relation between possessor and possession. Yet note that a simple and innocent-looking expression, such as *John's book* can potentially convey – depending on the context – a wide variety of meanings: it can be (i) 'the book that belongs to John', (ii) 'the book that John is currently holding', (iii) 'the book that John wrote or is about to write', (iv) 'the book John is reading' or (v) 'John's most favorite book', and so on. It is also not clear what concepts such as kin terms, body parts, origin and location, typically associated with "possessive" should have in common. The only meaning-based definition of the genitive meanings that one could probably agree on is that there is *some* relation between a possessor and a possessum but that the nature of this relation is indeterminate and cannot be wholly captured. This is, in fact, a view expressed by Kempson (1977: 125; as cited in Taylor 1996: 9). Yet, this is far too general to serve as a useful point of departure for an onomasiological approach. Also, Taylor ([1989] 1995: 202) states that "possession is not a semantic primitive". For this reason, the semasiological procedure seems to be the only feasible one, and it indeed seems to be the procedure taken by most approaches trying to classify the semantic relation between possessor and possessum on the linguistic market. These approaches differ, however, in which linguistic expressions in which languages are taken as the point of departure for describing the genitive meanings. Basically, four main traditions can be distinguished: (i) the traditional taxonomies of genitive functions, (ii) the prototype approach, (iii) the typologically-oriented possession approach and (iv) accounts within the framework of definiteness. In the following I will briefly describe these individual approaches and their classifications and discuss the evidence available from previous studies.

   In the traditional taxonomy the set of genitive functions given is derived from the variety of sense relations that could be expressed either by the old Indo-European category of genitive case or by the Old English inflectional genitive, using terms shaped by Latin grammar such as possessive, subjective, objective, partitive, appositive or descriptive (see also §3.3.2.1.1 for such a taxonomy and examples), which still serve as the main reference point for most work on the English genitive alternation, diachronic (e.g. Mustanoja 1960: 79-87) and synchronic (e.g. Quirk et al. 1985: §5.116; Leech, Francis, and Xu 1994; Anschutz 1997). That this kind of taxomony is highly problematic has already been argued by Altenberg (1982: chapter 5) and Taylor (1996: 5-11). First, there are no clear criteria for defining these genitive functions. For example, the "possessive genitive" is usually regarded as one of the central genitive meanings. Yet, there seems to be no consensus as to what exactly should be covered by this term. It is also extremely difficult to delineate the borderline between possessive cases and subjective and objective genitives, i.e. genitive constructions in which the possessum is a noun derived from a verb, a problem which is discussed in Rosenbach and Vezzosi (2000: §3.1). While "possessive" is a semantic-conceptual category, "subjective" and "objective" are grammatical functions defined syntactically and it is often not clear on which grounds a genitive construction should be categorized as such. For example, should *Plinius' writings* be classified as subjective (since *writings* is a deverbal noun) or as possessive (since *writings* does not refer to the process of writing but rather to its result, i.e. books)?

Likewise, the category of "partitive genitives" is classified in various ways. Quirk et al. (1985: §5.116) include both body parts (*the baby's eyes*) and inanimate part-whole relations (*the earth's surface*) here, while these are both subsumed, for example, in Poutsma's (1914: 41) possessive category. Anschutz (1997: 9) in her corpus study has body parts in a category "inalienable" and "part-wholes" as a separate category. The latter category is reserved by Anschutz (1997) to a type of partitive in which the possessum represents a subpart of the possessor (e.g. *most of the fuel, the percentage of women in professional training*). It is, however, not clear from Anschutz' taxonomy where inanimate part-whole relations (*the earth's surface, the car's windscreen*) are subsumed.

It is beyond the scope and the aim of this section to give a detailed account of all taxonomies of genitive functions; what should have become clear, however, is that these taxonomies do their best to describe the various meanings that can be expressed by genitive expressions, yet, in absence of any clearly definable unique meaning and any theoretical backbone providing some unified description, they remain fairly arbitrary and *ad hoc* and do not provide a particularly valuable tool for the empirical researcher.[53] Actually, Quirk et al. (1985: §5.117) admit that their semantic classification "is in part arbitrary", discussing some examples which could be classified in various ways.

The only available empirical studies investigating the distribution of the *s*-genitive versus the *of*-genitive according to the semantic relation between possessor and possessum for Modern English make use of these traditional taxonomies. Anschutz (1997: 8-10) uses a tripartite system distinguishing between "genitive", in which she seems to have included what she labels as ownership (*Brower's inheritance, Varese's principles*), origin (*a native of Berkely, Joyce Kilmer's irritating ditty*), personal relation (*Mario's buddies*) and body parts (*his victim's throat*), "partitives" (*most of the fuel, the percentage of women in professional training*) and a dummy category "associative", which she does not specify further. Most *s*-genitives turn up in the genitive function in Anschutz' (1997) data and, not surprisingly, none in the partitive function, which she defines solely in terms of the type of partitive in which the possessum specifies the possessor and which has in §3.3.2.1.1 been identified as a clearly categorical context for the occurrence of the *of*-genitive.

Leech, Francis, and Xu (1994) seem to have adopted Quirk et al.'s (1985: §5.116) terminology; according to their data the relative frequency of the *s*-genitive decreases along the following cline: origin > subjective > possessive > attributive > partitive > objective. In contrast to Quirk et al. (1985: §5.116), where only a few examples and predicative paraphrases are given and no justification of the taxonomy, nor in Biber et al. (1999: §4.6.12.3), Leech, Francis, and Xu (1994: 63-64) do provide brief definitions of the categories used. Yet, the problems of classifying the data remain. While, for example, they include body parts in their "partitive" category, they give *the mind of a reader*, which might also be regarded as body part, as an example for "possessive".

Since Anschutz (1997) and Leech, Francis, and Xu (1994) use a different way of categorizing the genitive functions, their results cannot be compared. Second, and more importantly for empirical research, as an exclusively descriptive taxonomy the traditional way of classifying the genitive functions fails to provide us with any potential prediction as to which function is more likely to be expressed by the *s*-genitive or the *of*-genitive.

One attempt to motivate the diversity of semantic relations that can be expressed by the *s*-genitive is the prototype approach. Nikiforidou (1991), for example, shows how the different meanings are related to each other. In her account, "possession" is the basic meaning to which the other meanings, such as kin terms, body parts, subjective or objective are metaphorically related. One drawback of her analysis, according to Taylor (1996: 7-8), is, however, that she fails to characterize the basic meaning of possession. On the basis of the meanings that can be conveyed by the English *s*-genitive, Taylor (1995: 202-203) provides a set of defining criteria as to what constitutes prototypical possession:
The possessor is a specific human being.

(a) The possessed is a specific concrete thing.
(b) The relation is an exclusive one.
(c) The possessor has the right to make use of the possessed.
(d) The possessor's rights over the possessed are invested in him in virtue of a transaction.
(e) The possessor is responsible for the possessed.
(f) Possessor and possessed need to be in close spatial proximity.
(g) The relation of possession is a long-term one.

It is clear from this list that Taylor (1995) construes (permanent) legal ownership (*John's car*) as prototypical possession since in the ideal case it fulfils all criteria. In contrast, kin terms (*John's daughter*) or body parts (*John's head*) only partly match all requirements and are therefore less prototypical. What makes Taylor's defining criteria for prototypical possession valuable for empirical analysis is that he sees them as a tool measuring the productivity of the *s*-genitive rather than its grammaticality (cf. Taylor 1989: 669): *the poll's results* is not less grammatical than *John's car* (that he owns) but it is certainly less productive. It is, however, not at all clear how Taylor ranks his criteria for prototypicality; which of the criteria are more important than others? For example, should the animacy of the possessor be more important than close spatial proximity or a long-term relation, that is, should *John's exhaustion* be more productive than the *car's windscreen*? Also, Taylor (1989, 1995) seems to argue exclusively from the Modern English situation looking only at which relations tend rather to be expressed by the *s*-genitive but not by the *of*-genitive (??*the car of John*) but not regarding the historical development. Another problem, as Taylor (1999: 301) himself admits, lies in the fact that his prototype account fails "to capture the intuition that kinship relations and part-whole relations are probably no less basic, linguistically and conceptually, than possession narrowly construed".

The typological work on possession (cf. e.g. Seiler 1983; Nichols 1988, 1992; Heine 1997) provides a taxonomy of possession on the ground of ample cross-linguistic evidence. Seiler (1983) proposes a gradient from "inherent" (e.g. kin terms, body parts) to more "established" possession (e.g. social relationship, spatial orientation). Nichols (1988: 572) uses another terminology distinguishing between "alienable" and "inalienable" possession, proposing the following implicational hierarchy:

kin terms and/or body parts	>	part/whole and/or spatial relations	>	culturally basic possessed items

Heine (1997: §1.3) gives a thorough overview of the various taxonomies of possession in the literature and himself proposes a prototype taxonomy that is strongly influenced by Taylor's (1989, 1995) prototype approach, having (permanent) ownership ranking highest, followed by inalienable possession (e.g. kin terms, body parts) and other forms of ownership, and then by abstract possession (e.g. feelings, psychological states etc.) and inanimate possession.

But there are also problems with the typological work on possession: first, what is conceived of as alienable or inalienable differs considerably from culture to culture, and it is therefore not possible to establish a universal hierarchy of inalienability (cf. also Chapell and McGregor 1996: 8-9; Heine 1997: 11). It has also not been investigated which categories should be conceived of as inalienable in English. Second, this taxonomy has been solely applied to languages in which this distinction is grammaticalized and where there are clear morphological correlates to alienably versus inalienably possessed nouns. This is certainly not the case for English; here the distinction between alienable and inalienable possession could reflect certain preferences at best in the choice between the *s*-genitive and the *of*-genitive.

Another, completely different way of classifying the meaning of possessive constructions focuses on the semantics of the possessum rather than on the relation itself and comes from work on definiteness. Löbner (1985) classifies lexical nouns as follows:

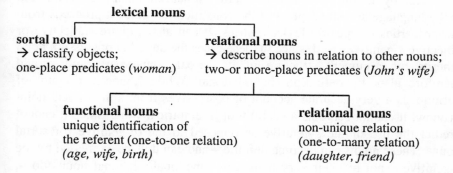

lexical nouns

sortal nouns
→ classify objects;
one-place predicates (*woman*)

relational nouns
→ describe nouns in relation to other nouns;
two- or more-place predicates (*John's wife*)

functional nouns
unique identification of
the referent (one-to-one relation)
(*age, wife, birth*)

relational nouns
non-unique relation
(one-to-many relation)
(*daughter, friend*)

Figure 4. Löbner's (1985) classification of lexical nouns

According to Löbner (1985) there is a basic distinction between sortal and relational nouns. While sortal nouns typically classify objects and are one-place predicates (*woman, table*), a relational noun can only be interpreted in relation to another noun, i.e. it is a two- or more-place predicate (*wife*). Relational nouns again can be further subdivided into nouns which have a unique referent (i.e. "functional nouns": e.g. *wife, birth*) and those where the relation is not unique but possibly one-to-many (i.e. "relational nouns": e.g. *daughter, friend*). Although Löbner's concern is primarily with an account of definite expressions, it can nonetheless be applied to grasp the semantics of possessives. Löbner's category of functional nouns is very similar to the category "functionals" in Fraurud's (1996) referent ontology, where this type of NP is also interpreted in relation to other nouns, a situation typical for possessive constructions (cf. §4.2.1). In Löbner's account of definites we can view the possessor as an "anchor" that helps to identify the referent of the possessum noun, thereby rendering the whole NP definite. In fact, the idea of possessors serving as anchors has, independently of Löbner's (1985) framework, been suggested for the English possessives, and I will come back to this issue in §4.4.3 below. Moreover, according to Löbner (1985), the taxonomy between sortal and relational nouns is not absolute but depends on the use of these nouns in the specific pragmatic context. While possession is typically the predicate-argument relation holding between possessor and possessum (– the latter ideally being a functional noun, or less ideally a relational noun –), a sortal noun (e.g. *table*) can also enter a possessive relation and become definite in and via context (e.g. *John's table*) as a "pragmatic definite". Löbner's taxonomy gives justice to both the semantic meanings and relations that are prototypically expressed by possessive constructions (kin terms and body parts, e.g., by definition always have a functional/relational possessum) and to the language-specific aspects of the constructions, since it proceeds from the properties of specific lexical entries. It can also capture subjective or objective *s*-genitives well, since in these cases the deverbal possessum noun inherits the argument structure of its verbal counterparts and should therefore also, by definition, be relational. While Löbner's account of definites is a very accurate account of possessives from a theoretical point of view, it cannot serve as a useful tool in empirical work, since it cannot predict the use of the *s*-genitive as opposed to the *of*-genitive for sortal nouns. These nouns can become definite – and can thus be expressed by the *s*-genitive – not by their very nature, as functional/relational nouns do –, but become definite, and therefore potentially possessive, in context only. We can therefore only acknowledge a possessive relation *posthoc* but never predict it. Note that this concerns all ownership relation, which typically has a sortal possessum.[54]

To conclude, classification of the possessive relations in English is extremely problematic. There are various proposals to describe the meaning of possessive constructions, but, due to the fuzzy nature of the concept of possession, there is so far no account at hand providing a convincing taxonomy of possessive relation for English. The only available empirical evidence are the studies by Anschutz (1997) and Leech, Francis, and Xu (1994), yet these studies are not comparable since they use different taxonomies. Most importantly, apart from Taylor's (1989, 1995) prototype account none of the taxonomies proposed for the English genitives entail any predictions as to the productivity of the *s*-genitive versus the *of*-genitive.

4.4 Interaction of factors

So far, the three factors animacy, topicality, and possessive relation have been discussed separately. In fact, however, these three factors very often go hand in hand as has already occasionally become apparent from the discussion of the factors above. In the following I will now look more closely at the interplay of the factors animacy, topicality, and possessive relation.

4.4.1 Animacy and topicality

In general, it is well-known that topics are usually animate, preferably human (cf. e.g. Yamamoto 1999: 60-67). For possessive constructions, there is cross-linguistic evidence pointing to an interplay of animacy and topicality. In Guerrero-Nahuatl, a Uto-Atztetic language, there are two patterns to link a possessive relation, and the choice of the construction depends on the relative animacy of possessor and possessum (cf. Stiebels 2000). Koptjevskaja-Tamm (2001, forthcoming) reports such possessor-splits also for some European languages, such as Faroese, Slavonic, Russian and even German. In all these cases it is, however, not only animacy that induces the split but also the degree of referentiality/topicality. For example, the prenominal genitive in German is basically restricted to highly topical proper nouns (*Peters Buch*), while common nouns, though not less animate, need to be expressed by the postnominal genitive (*das Buch des Lehrers*).

The correlation between animacy on the one side and topicality and definiteness on the other is also apparent in the many linguistic hierarchies that have been proposed (cf. e.g. Silverstein 1976; Givón 1984: 364; Allan 1987; Dahl and Fraurud 1996: 47-48); see the brief overview below. These hierarchies show that notions such as familiarity, topicality, definiteness, givenness, or animacy, although independent concepts, very often have the same effect. Generally speaking, in these hierarchies it is always the leftmost element which is more likely to undergo a certain grammatical operation than the elements to the right. In these hierarchies animates/humans cluster with given and familiar information, definites and referential expressions, i.e. they often have the same grammatical effect.

hierarchy of features	1st person > 2nd person >3rd person > pronoun
of NPs (animacy hierarchy):	> proper name > human > animate > inanimate
humanity/animacy:	human/animate > non-human/inanimate

familiarity hierarchies:	more familiar > less familiar topic > comment given > new
definiteness:	definite > indefinite
referentiality:	referential > non-referential

Moreover, as already noted above (§4.1.1), the animacy hierarchy fuses several logically independent hierarchies, a person hierarchy (1st > 2nd > 3rd), a NP-type hierarchy (pronoun > proper noun > common noun), an animacy hierarchy (animate > inanimate), and within the latter a humanness hierarchy (human > non-human), which also illustrates that these categories tend to go together. The same is true for the lexical noun classes as classified by Quirk et al. (1985), which have been empirically tested by a number of studies as discussed above (cf. §4.1.2). Their results basically confirm the sub-hierarchies entailed by the animacy hierarchy showing a preference for the *s*-genitive to occur with the following possessors:

(1)   proper names/nouns > common nouns
(2)   animate nouns > inanimate nouns
(3)   human nouns > non-human nouns

The correlation between animacy and topicality is so striking that some scholars have even contemplated suggesting only one single factor, i.e. "topicworthiness", subsuming both animacy and topicality. For example, Deane (1987) suggests that the effect of animacy in the choice between the *s*-genitive and the *of*-genitive can be reduced to an effect of topicality. Deane (1987) argues that the occurrence of the *s*-genitive depends on the position of the possessor on Silverstein's animacy hierarchy, i.e. the higher the possessor on this hierarchy, the more likely the *s*-genitive is to occur; the lower the possessor on this hierarchy, the more preferred the *of*-genitive becomes. This explains the almost obligatoriness of prenominal (possessive) pronouns (*my foot* versus **the foot of me*) and the decreasing acceptance of the *s*-genitive with inanimate (*?the room's edge* versus *the edge of the room*) and abstract nouns (*?the century's beginnings* versus *the beginnings of the century*). Viewing animates as intrinsically topical, Deane (1987) reduces the animacy hierarchy to a topic hierarchy, thereby subsuming animacy under what he regards to be the superior factor, topicality. In the same spirit, Deane (1992: 205-236) proposes that the Silverstein hierarchy should be regarded as an entrenchment hierarchy, being best interpreted in terms of a "natural topic and natural viewpoint hierarchy" (236). The same idea is taken up by Taylor (1996) in his account of the English *s*-genitive, to which I will return in §4.4.3 below.[55]

4.4.2   *Animacy and possession*

Work on possession generally proceeds from the assumption that the prototypical possessor is human (cf. e.g. Seiler 1983: 4; Taylor 1989: 679). Acknowledging an interplay between animacy and possession also entails interesting predictions for those accounts which have been suggested to reduce the choice between the *s*-genitive and the *of*-genitive to the *relative* animacy between possessor and possessum, always favouring the order "animate/more animate > inanimate/less animate" (cf. Hawkins 1981; Anschutz 1997), as briefly discussed in §4.1.2. If one adheres to this view, the following predictions should hold true:

more *s*-genitives   **either *s*-genitive or *of*-genitive**

───▶

animate > inanimate	animate > human attribute	animate > animate
permanent/legal ownership	body-parts	kin terms
the man's car	*the man's hand*	*the man's son*
abstract possession		social relation
the man's future		*the man's doctor*
the man's car (non-legal, associative sense)		

Figure 5.   Relative animacy of possessor and possessum: predictions

The *s*-genitive should be most likely in those possessive relations in which a human possessor possesses an inanimate possessum noun. Whether the relation is a prototypical one in the sense of Taylor (1989, 1995), i.e. whether there is a long-term and exclusive relation between possessor and possessum, or whether it is only peripherally possessive in the sense that it is only a temporary or associative relation, would not play a role. Hawkins' (1981) account would therefore predict the same likelihood for the *s*-genitive to occur with *the man's car* (= 'The car that the man owns') and *the man's car* (= 'The car the man always dreams of but has not bought yet'). A purely animacy-based account would also predict that there is the same likelihood of the *s*-genitive and the *of*-genitive occurring where the degree of animacy is the same for possessor and possessum, as for example in kin terms (*John's mother; the girl's brother*), where both the possessor and the possessum are animate. Also, the frequency of the *s*-genitive should not differ between kin terms (*the man's son*) and other social relations (*the man's doctor*). With body-parts the *s*-genitive should be somewhat more likely than with kin terms and social relations but less likely than with legal ownership or abstract possession. Yet, this is probably too simplistic a view. While this is certainly an empirical question, we already know intuitively that the *s*-genitive is quite common with kin terms and with body parts.

4.4.3   Topicality and possessive relation: possessors as anchors or reference points

It has recently been suggested that the possessor in a possessive construction has to be seen as an "anchor" or "reference point" that helps to identify the referent of the possessum noun (cf. e.g. Langacker 1995; Taylor 1996; Rosenbach and Vezzosi 2000; Haspelmath 1999a; Koptjevskaja-Tamm 2001, forthcoming). [56] Within the framework of Cognitive Grammar Langacker (1995) and Taylor (1996) both argue that possessive meanings can be captured best by the cognitive function of possessive constructions as reference point constructions. The general idea of reference points is that the world is conceived of as consisting of more and less salient objects. Non-salient entities are less accessible but can be identified *qua* their vicinity to more salient objects (cf. Langacker 1991: 170). It is in this respect that salient objects serve as reference points. In the following I shall focus on Taylor (1996), an elaboration of Langacker's (1995) account dealing exclusively with the English *s*-genitive as a reference-point construction, and which also captures the idea of the possessor as an anchor in the approaches mentioned above.

Taylor (1996: 16) analyzes the English *s*-genitive as a determiner, viewing it as "a rather special device for ensuring definite reference." By using the *s*-genitive the speaker instructs the hearer how to identify the referent of the possessum noun; the *s*-genitive is therefore seen as a reference-point construction with the possessor serving as the reference point, or anchor:

> The special character of the possessive construction lies in the fact that it invites the hearer to first evoke the possessor entity, and conveys that the referent of the possessee nominal is to be located in the neighbourhood of the possessor. The import of the possessor phrase is thus to *make explicit the mental path that the hearer must follow in order to identify the target* ...... in opting to use a possessive expression, the speaker is *instructing the hearer on how best to identify the referent that he, the speaker, intends*. The speaker, that is, invites the hearer to first conceptualize ('establish mental

contact with') the one entity (the possessor), with the guarantee that this will facilitate identification of the target entity (the possessee).
(Taylor 1996: 17)

To serve as a good reference-point the possessor itself should be highly accessible, and it is in this respect that there is a close interconnection between the function of the *s*-genitive as a reference point construction and the topicality of the possessor. The more topical the possessor is, the more effectively can it identify the referent of the possessum noun. Taylor (1996: chapter 8) distinguishes between two factors which determine the topicworthiness of the possessor: (i) "discourse-conditioned topicality", by which he means previously-mentioned possessors, and (ii) "inherent topicality", which refers to the inherent properties of the possessor and comprises factors such as animacy or egocentricity. Thus, Taylor's (1996) notion of topicworthiness, like Deane (1987), subsumes animacy as one aspect of topicality. Since various aspects contribute to the topicworthiness of an expression (e.g. animacy, previous mention, ontological status, person hierarchy), it is, however, not clear how the notion of topicworthiness should be operationally employed in empirical analysis.

4.4.4 The concept of individuation

So far we have seen that the factors animacy, topicality, and possessive relation not only do play individually an important role in the choice between the *s*-genitive and the *of*-genitive in English but that they also interact to a high degree. Now the question arises why these factors should go together at all in the first place – are they possibly subordinate to a superordinate, unifying principle? Timberlake (1977: 162) has proposed the concept of "individuation" under which factors such as topicality, definiteness, animacy, number and the count-mass distinction can be subsumed:[57]

individuated		**non-individuated**
proper		common
human	animate	inanimate
concrete		abstract
singular		plural
definite		indefinite

It is somehow striking that the *s*-genitive generally occurs with such possessors which show the properties of individuated entities. As has been shown in the discussion above, if the possessor is a proper human noun –

and as such definite, the *s*-genitive is very likely to occur. It is probably not a coincidence that Jahr Sorheim (1980) has also observed a certain inclination of the *s*-genitive to occur rather with singular possessors than with plural possessors (cf. §3.3.2.2.4 above). In other words, in the most optimal case the prototypical possessor in the *s*-genitive is a uniquely identifiable individual human being. Taking up the idea of the possessor functioning as an anchor in the *s*-genitive everything falls in its place. Only if the possessor is highly individuated can it serve as a good anchor in the *s*-genitive. It is, however, not at all clear how individuation as a *factor* can possibly be successfully employed in an empirical study, the major problem being the coding, quantification and evaluation of such items in which the properties of individuated referents do *not* go together and impinge on each other. Moreover, the question remains which factors contribute more to the individuation of an item than others.

4.4.5   Implications for empirical research

The discussion of the interaction of the factors animacy, topicality, and possessive relation in §4.4 has shown that these factors tend to have a clustering effect in the assignment of a possessive construction. This has major implications for the empirical analysis of the English genitive constructions when investigating these factors. How should the researcher know whether in a particular case, e.g. *John's mother*, it is (a) the high topicality of the proper-noun possessor, (b) the animacy of the possessor, or (c) the kin relation which determines the choice of the *s*-genitive? This means that we need to operationalize every single factor in such a way that only the effects of this one factor is tested but not simultaneously the effect of some other factor. Moreover, rather than looking at these factors in isolation or subsuming them under superordinate concepts such as "topicworthiness" or "individuation" we should investigate how these factors interact in the choice of the genitive construction and, in so doing, cast some light on the question of which of these factor(s) is/are more important when choosing between the *s*-genitive and the *of*-genitive.

4.5   Summary and discussion

I have discussed how the relevance of the factors animacy, topicality, and type of possessive relation on the choice of the genitive construction in English has been treated in the literature. The results of the empirical studies available for these three factors can be briefly summarized as follows:

(1)   *Animacy*: The *s*-genitive is most common with human possessors. It can, however, also occur with certain inanimate noun classes, particularly geographical nouns and temporal nouns; with these noun classes the *s*-genitive is more common in American English than in British English. Moreover, an increasing use of the *s*-genitive with such inanimate noun classes has been observed in twentieth-century English, particularly in journalistic language (cf. Jahr Sorheim 1980; Jucker 1993; Siemund 1993; Leech, Francis, and Xu 1994; Raab-Fischer 1995; Hundt 1998; Biber et al. 1999).

(2)   *Topicality*: There seems to be an ordering preference of given before new information within possessive constructions, resulting in a preference for the *s*-genitive to occur with given possessors and the *of*-genitive with new possessors (cf. Jahr Sorheim 1980; Altenberg 1982; Anschutz 1997; Biber et al. 1999).

(3)   *Possessive relation*: It is difficult to make any general statement here since the classifications of possessive relations (or "genitive functions") used in empirical studies are rather arbitrary and *ad hoc*. In a very general sense though we may say that the *s*-genitive is most common in possessive – although it is not clear how we should exactly define this category – and subjective functions (cf. Leech, Francis, and Xu 1994; Anschutz 1997).

All the studies discussed provide invaluable insights and empirical data for the question of what governs the choice between the *s*-genitive and the *of*-genitive in English. At the same time, however, they also point to a number of methodological problems:

(1)   In most of these studies it is not made explicit what has been included and excluded in the corpus; notable exceptions are the studies by Jahr Sorheim (1980) and Altenberg (1982), who make their inclusion/exclusion criteria very explicit.

(2)   Following from (1), for most of these studies it is somewhat difficult to evaluate whether indeed only comparable choice contexts in the

sense outlined in §4.2.1 have been considered, i.e. whether the factors analyzed were controlled for other intervening factors. In the optimal case, when analyzing a single factor all other factors should be kept neutral, otherwise facilitating and/or prohibiting factors (e.g. genre/style, variety, syntactic branching and weight, phonological and morphological factors) can intervene and bias the results.[58] This is, however, not only a difficult and time-consuming enterprise but also calls for an extremely large corpus which can be split up into several sub-corpora while still retaining enough tokens to justify quantification of the data.

(3)   Another general problem is that the ways of defining and classifying the data according to the factors seem to vary considerably from one study to another; these studies are therefore – if at all – not easily comparable. Particularly notorious is the classification of possessive relations/genitive functions.

(4)   As argued above, it is crucial to consider the frequency of the *s*-genitive as opposed to the *of*-genitive in clearly specified environments; the frequency of the *s*-genitive alone is certainly an indicator but not a particularly reliable one. However, only some of the studies discussed did take the relative frequency of the two genitive constructions into account (e.g. Jahr Sorheim 1980; Altenberg 1982; Jucker 1993; Leech, Francis, and Xu 1994; Anschutz 1997).

(5)   So far, the factors animacy, topicality, and possessive relation have been studied largely independently from each other. As, however, shown in §4.4 these factors interact to a high degree, which makes it difficult to evaluate the impact of each factor as operating independently from the others.

Given the multitude of factors involved in the choice between the *s*-genitive and the *of*-genitive in general and the interaction of the factors animacy, topicality, and possessive relation in particular, the question arises which factors need to be regarded as more important than others. There are only three studies which have attempted to approach such an evaluation, focusing, however, on different factors and using different ways of establishing a ranking between them. Altenberg (1982: 296) provides a hierarchy of some selected factors based on the relative frequency of the *s*-genitive. He argues that it is not the contexts favoring the *highest* frequency of the *s*-genitive which need to be regarded the most important factors but rather the most constraining factors. Therefore, Altenberg (1982: 300) argues that both an inanimate possessor and objective genitives are the most constraining factors for the choice of the *s*-genitive. A human possessor is only important in that it describes the range of contexts in which other factors, such as topicality, can play a role. Anschutz (1997) argues that topicality is a more important factor than animacy in her data, since the *s*-genitive does occur with inanimate possessors in her corpus (16%) but not with a new possessor. It must be stressed, however, that there were only 15 contexts for new possessors (and given possessum nouns) in her whole corpus, so that the overall chance for the *s*-genitive to occur was relatively small. Leech, Francis, and Xu (1994) also go into the intriguing and difficult question of ranking the relative strength of various factors, both within the factors and between the factors, using the statistical method of logistic modeling. Their results indicate that the noun class of the possessor is the most important factor for the choice of the *s*-genitive, followed by text type and then genitive function. Altenberg (1982: 300-301), however, seems to be skeptical about the application of logistic modeling in the genitive alternation since it "presupposes the existence of discrete variables whose effect can be calculated in a neutral context. ... , this requirement does not obtain for the GEN/OF variation" (301).

In general it must be noted that the empirical studies available have mainly focused on a description of *how* the *s*-genitive and the *of*-genitive are distributed in corpora but do not attempt any explanation of *why* the distribution could be the way it is. That is, these studies deal with the alternation between the *s*-genitive and the *of*-genitive in terms of "variation" rather than "choice" (see the following chapter for this distinction). A cognitive account of the *s*-genitive, which acknowledges the role of the individual language user is offered by the reference-point analysis in Taylor (1996), in which the *s*-genitive is analyzed as a reference-point construction, with the possessor serving as a reference point or anchor that models the mental route the hearer has to take when identifying the referent of the possessum (cf. §4.4.3). Taylor's (1996) reference point analysis, however, focuses solely on the *s*-genitive, not taking into account its structural alternative, the *of*-genitive. Thus, although it is an account based on the individual language user, in the strict sense it is not a "choice"-based approach, since only the *use* of the *s*-genitive but not the *choice* between the two genitives is accounted for. Moreover, it is essentially a theoretical account and non-empirical. It is also not clear (i) how the notion of topicworthiness, or the concept of individuation, which may even better describe the optimal properties of the possessor as an anchor, should be employed in empirical analysis, and (ii) how the – exclusively synchronic – reference-point analysis could possibly account for the diachronic development of the genitive variation as outlined in chapter 7 below. Note, however, that viewing the possessor in the *s*-genitive as a referential anchor provides a cognitive-functional motivation for the grammatical function of the *s*-genitive as a determiner (at least as far as specifying genitives are concerned).[59] In the discussion of the historical development of the *s*-genitive in §7.5.3 I will try to show how the need for a highly accessible possessor in the *s*-genitive correlates with the historical development and evidence and thereby link Taylor's (1996) reference-point approach with the historical development of the *s*-genitive and the genitive variation.

In sum, there is a notable and sorry gap between empirical studies providing valuable data on the genitive alternation but which lack a theoretical backbone and face a number of methodological problems on the one side, and a theoretical, cognitive account, which exclusively focuses on the *s*-genitive and lacks empirical application as well as a diachronic dimension.

Chapter 5
"Variation" versus "choice"

In this chapter I will now come to the question under which rationale grammatical variation (and change) is usually dealt with in linguistic approaches and, given this background, how the genitive variation will be investigated in the present study.

There is no such thing as *the* theory of grammatical variation. Rather, different linguistic frameworks seem to use the concept of grammatical variation as a tool, partly subservient to the respective theory, partly as a means to an end. Accordingly, there are various approaches to grammatical variation, which differ considerably from each other. In the following I will establish a systematic distinction between "variation"-based versus "choice"-based approaches and give an overview of how the prevailing linguistic approaches dealing with grammatical variation (and change) differ according to this distinction. I will then, finally, outline in §5.3 under which rationale the alternation between the *s*-genitive and the *of*-genitive is investigated in the present study.

Strictly speaking, variation implies choice. The basic difference between "variation" and "choice" is the locus of the choice context. In a broad sense, "variation" is used to capture the heterogeneous nature of a single language (cf. also Schulze 1998: 7), including, for example, such notions as dialects, registers or styles. Variation in a stricter sense and as introduced in this chapter operates on the single linguistic levels and concerns the investigation of concrete linguistic variables as "two ways of saying the same thing" (Labov 1972: 271). What is common to both the broad and the narrow use of variation is that even if the actual language use is the subject matter of investigation, it is not the individual language user. Variation, as defined here, accounts for the behavior of populations, either a whole language community or groups within a community, and not for the behavior of individuals. We may also distinguish between variation on the system-level and variation on the usage-level. On the level of the language system variation refers to the fact that the system provides variants; here variation operates on the repertoire level. On the usage-level variation deals with the question of how these variants are distributed, i.e. what is the statistical likelihood for the variants to occur within a speech community.

"Choice", however, seems to be an appropriate term to account for the various options an individual language user has when constructing a particular utterance in a concrete speech situation (cf. also Schulze 1998: 7). So here preferences as indicated by different frequency scores are not a reflection of group behavior but operate on the level of the individual. As far as the individual is concerned, choice is more of a psychological notion and is connected to theories of decision-making as developed in the framework of psychology (see van Hout 1984: 47-49; Coombs, Dawes, and Tversky 1970: chapter 5). The task of the investigator is to identify the conditions under which the decision is made. Choice may be, but does not necessarily have to be, situated within a real-time context. Such decision-making can be conscious but it does not need to be. Still lacking sufficient knowledge of what constitutes consciousness at all, it is also often very difficult to determine whether an action performed is conscious and intentional and to what degree. Whatever it is, it seems plausible to imagine a fine-grained continuum from highly conscious to completely unconscious on which we can then, accordingly, place the locus of choice.

maximally conscious   minimally conscious

$\longleftrightarrow$

While the term choice itself carries some active meaning, suggesting that the speaker consciously chooses among competing constructions, the present definition as such is neutral as to the question of intentionality and consciousness. In §5.3 below I will, however, narrow down the choice-based approach as proposed in the present study, to what may be regarded as largely unintentional, subconscious processes.

At first sight, the distinction between variation and choice seems to be an artificial one: one may argue that variation is indeed made up by individual choices. Looking at this more closely, however, this may turn out to be not entirely true. As, for example, argued by Greenbaum and Quirk (1970: 2) variation as defined above can be constituted by

(1)   the variant use of language options within individual speakers (i.e. intraspeaker variation), or
(2)   by the invariant use of one language option between individual speakers (i.e. interspeaker variation).

Only in the former case is the distribution of variants within a speech community a direct reflection of the choices made by individuals. In the latter case, variation occurs only as a cumulative effect within a speech community in that different individuals make different – though invariant – choices and the relation between the individual choice and variation on the level of the speech community is not one-to-one. A usage-based approach to variation can only capture the choice of individuals if the communities or social groups investigated are homogenous. See the following table 17 for a brief summary of the variation-versus-choice distinction:

Table 17. Grammatical variation: variation versus choice

	variation		choice
locus of variation	**language system**	**actual language use**	
mani-festation	as the structural availability of variables/variants	as preferences reflected in the distribution of variants in performance of social groups or the whole speech community	as preferences within individual speakers

In sum, the term "grammatical variation" is somewhat misleading and ambiguous, and it is more appropriate to differentiate between variation and choice. In the following an attempt is made to categorize the prevailing approaches to grammatical variation as to where they place the locus of change, i.e. whether they deal with variation and/or with choice, although this distinction is much clearer for some approaches than for others where the borderline between variation and choice can be fairly fuzzy. Since the conceptual distinction between variation and choice does not only affect synchronic approaches to grammatical variation, I will in the following also discuss how the various linguistic approaches model grammatical variation and change. Finally, I will give an outline of the choice-based approach taken in the present study.

5.1 Variation-based approaches
5.1.1 Formal approaches
5.1.1.1 Generative grammar

Although heuristically proceeding from the assumption that there is no variation among speakers of a speech community, generative grammar does account for grammatical variation in two ways (cf. also Radford et al. 1999: chapter 22). In a broad definition of variation as outlined above, grammatical variation within the Principles and Parameters approach is used in the sense of parametric variation to account for the typological diversity of languages. Although one of the core assumptions of generative grammar is the existence of a cross-linguistically invariant grammar core (Universal Grammar), variation among the languages of the world is accounted for by different parametric settings. In the narrow sense of grammatical variation, it accounts for word order options within a language by assigning different structures or transformations (or, in more recent versions, movements) to these options. It is this second sense which will concern us here.

Proceeding from a mentalist and nativist conception of language, generative approaches for heuristic and ontological reasons restrict themselves to the investigation of language competence (or "I-language"), i.e. the internalized mental grammar. Although this lays the emphasis on individual speakers, there are *a priori* no differences between speakers since the mental hardwiring is assumed to be the same for every individual speaker and language communities are taken to be homogenous. It is for this reason that interspeaker variation falls outside the scope of the generative framework; the only possible place to look for variation at all is within speakers' competence. As far as such intraspeaker variation is concerned, two further ways of coping with variation can be discerned. Categorical optionality in the sense that different linguistic contexts require categorically different syntactic constructions is quite unproblematic for formal approaches in general. What has, however, always been a notorious problem for rule-governed formal approaches is optionality of the more-or-less kind, i.e. when in a given context two (or more) variants are equally possible (though one may be preferred). As far as grammar-internal factors (as e.g. the application of optional transformations) can be held to be responsible, generative approaches can at least in principle cope with this type of variation, though even on the level of competence various generative approaches differ in coping more or less successfully with this; in the most recent Chomskyan framework, i.e. the "Minimalist Program" (Chomsky 1995), optionality is not permitted at all (cf. Lightfoot 1999: 92, and see particularly Müller 1999 for discussing the treatment of syntactic optionality in formal approaches). Inasmuch as extra-grammatical factors determine the occurrence of one or the other construction, and inasmuch as these variants are connected to certain probabilities, this type of optionality is attributed to performance (or "E-language"), accordingly lying outside the realm of formal analysis and usually referred to – and done away with – as randomly occurring "free variation" (cf. also Guy 1997b: 127). That is, generative approaches deal with grammatical variation, if at all, at the competence (i.e. the system) level only, in the sense of variation as outlined above. Note also that the generative notion of competence is a static concept, focusing on the representational aspects of language but not on how language is processed in real-time (for a different conception of "procedural competence" see §5.2.2 below); processing factors which thus count as extra-grammatical are considered to be performance factors too. Therefore, choice as outlined above is by definition not a subject matter of investigation in the generative model since it is completely in the realm of performance. Why a speaker prefers in a certain (non-syntactic) context one or the other variant is simply not an issue to be addressed. To sum up, the treatment of variation in generative grammar can now be sketched as follows:

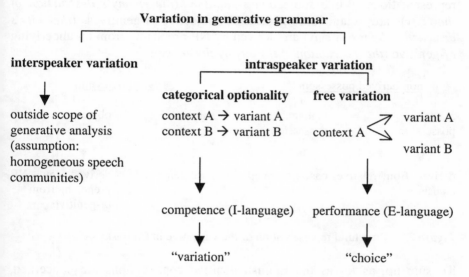

Figure 6.   Variation in generative grammar

In accordance with the theoretical orientation of generative grammar, the genitive alternation as outlined in chapter 3 above would mainly constitute a case of free variation; the alternation between the *s*-genitive and the *of*-genitive is only relevant inasmuch as these two constructions are representationally connected, i.e. derivationally related. Although the specific analyses have been constantly changed and modified, there is, I think, no change in the basic spirit of the argumentation.[60] Therefore, I will concentrate here – for the sake of illustration – on the treatment of the genitive alternation in a now classic work, i.e. Chomsky's (1970) "Remarks on Nominalizations". This article deals with an analysis of the structural representation of the *s*-genitive.[61] Chomsky (1970) proposes three different analyses for different types of *s*-genitives, which differ considerably in their structure and derivation. First of all, in this account a distinction between derived possessum nouns (*John's **murder***) and non-derived possessum nouns (*John's **car***) is crucial. Within non-derived possessum nouns, Chomsky (1970) draws on the semantic distinction between alienable and inalienable possession, suggesting that cases of alienable possession (*John's car*) are derived from a relative clause ('the car that John has'), while cases of inalienable possession (*John's head*) are base-generated, i.e. not derived. For derived possessum nouns, the distinction between subjective and objective *s*-genitives correlates with different structural representations. While subjective *s*-genitives (*the enemy's destruction of the city*) are again base-generated, objective *s*-genitives (*the city's destruction by the enemy*) are derived by NP-preposing from an underlying *of*-genitive (*the destruction of the city by the enemy*).

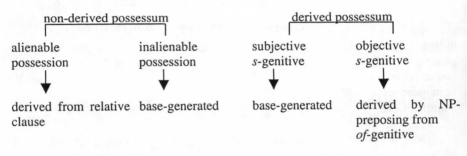

Figure 7.   Structural representation of the *s*-genitive in Chomsky (1970)

To sum up, as far as the English genitive constructions are concerned, generative grammar deals exclusively with the structural representation(s) of the constructions. Therefore, a relation between the *s*-genitive and the *of*-genitive is only seen as far as a derivational relation is concerned. In addition, such a relation is, according to Chomsky (1970), only given for a very specific type of *s*-genitive, i.e. the objective *s*-genitive, which is assumed to be derived from an underlying *of*-genitive. In all other types of *s*-genitives, there is no connection at all made to the *of*-genitive. Yet, note again, that even for the objective *s*-genitive the relation holding between *s*-genitive and *of*-genitive is of a representational type on the level of competence only.

Generative approaches to variation and change face the following problems. They inherit the rather limited capability of generative approaches to cope with grammatical variation at all, as discussed above. Moreover, they are faced with a methodological problem not trivial for the generative enterprise: the available data is restricted to textual evidence, i.e. performance data but the subject matter of investigation is competence (for good discussion on this see also Pintzuk, Tsoulas, and Warner 2000: §1.3). And while performance data necessarily reflect the underlying competence, competence is only *one* factor/component contributing to it and so performance is not a one-to-one image of the generative notion of competence. Variation therefore can have two reasons: it can be due to external, i.e. performance factors, or it can result from some genuine property of past speakers' competence. It is only the latter which generative approaches to variation and change want to address. That is, generative models need to postulate a model of variation as based in speakers' competence as well as a mechanism that allows this competence to change. With the locus of both variation and change necessarily lying in competence, there appears to be only one way for language to change in generative approaches, i.e. during language acquisition in the child.[62] Now of course the question arises why and how children's grammar should differ from that of their parents if their parents' competence, by definition, cannot change? Or, put differently by McMahon (2000: 123):

> The chicken and egg problem, put bluntly, is what comes first? Does a change in the grammar provoke surface changes in response? Or is there some sort of surface change, as a result of which the next population of speakers will inevitably develop a different grammar?

To my mind the most plausible solution to this problem has been put forward by Lightfoot (1999). He makes the methodological distinction between (a) what changes the triggering experience within adults' speech and (b) the reanalysis within the child's grammar during language acquisition. The key point in Lightfoot's argumentation is that while acknowledging that the triggering experience within adults' speech can and does change, he attributes those changes to external factors outside of the grammar. To him, the diachronic generative linguist's task is to account solely for the reanalysis of children's grammar on the basis of the triggering experience, but not for the change of the triggering experience itself. So while not ignoring change in adults' speech, he simply excludes it for heuristic reasons from generative approaches to change (see also the discussions in Harris and Campbell 1995: 36-45; McMahon 2000: 122-124, and Pintzuk, Tsoulas, and Warner 2000: 3-4).

So far we have seen that variation as manifested in performance, i.e. E-language, can have two possible sources: (a) performance factors, either as external factors influencing adults' speech and/or as free variation or (b) changes in the underlying competence of speakers caused during the process of language acquisition with generative approaches to variation and change restricting themselves to (b). Yet even when placing the locus of variation completely within competence, there are two principal possibilities by which, from a diachronic perspective, variation in performance can arise:

(1) *as interspeaker variation across individual speakers:* In such an account variation in a speech community is an artefact resulting from a situation where every speaker has one grammar each; variation arises because there are overlapping generations in a speech community with speakers from the older and the younger generation having different grammars (cf. e.g. Lightfoot 1999: § 4.7):[63]

(a) speaker A (= generation x) → grammar A → variant A
(b) speaker B (= generation x+1) → grammar B → variant B

In such a scenario individual speakers do not have any choice since their linguistic repertoire only consists of one option and the frequency of variants is only telling inasmuch as it reflects the distribution of speakers across generations, hence not interesting at all from such a generative linguist's point of view. The diffusion process by which linguistic variants spread through the speech community is simply a matter of one generation eventually replacing the other.

(2) *as intraspeaker variation within individual speakers*: In this conception of variation and change individual speakers are attributed co-existing grammars, a state that Lightfoot (1999: 92) calls "internalized diglossia". In such an account the individual speaker has more than one variant at his disposal;[64] this situation can be sketched as follows:

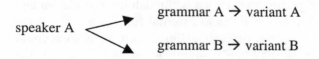

speaker A < grammar A → variant A
            grammar B → variant B

This is the approach taken by Kroch (1994) in his "Competing Grammar" model. Variation as represented in historical textual evidence over a longer period of time is attributed to the existence of two (or more) competing grammars within individual speakers. These variants are "doublets", i.e. two semantically and functionally equivalent but grammatically incompatible forms/constructions. That is, either a single grammar allows variant A or variant B but never both. In this respect, Kroch (1994) captures variation of the more-or-less sort by assuming categorical optionality but distributed over various grammars within an individual speaker. Two developments are possible in such a situation: (i) one variant eventually wins over the other in the course of time and becomes the sole form/construction, or (ii) the two variants will undergo functional specialization. It is the first possibility, called "winner-take-all competition" by Kroch (1994), which underlies the Competing Grammar approach. Under this perspective, variation is viewed as a transitory and unstable situation necessarily leading to the elimination of one variant (cf. also Kroch 1994: 180). It is not difficult to see that and why frequency of usage should matter in this approach: it can be viewed as a kind of diagnostics as to which variant will eventually take over and how far this diffusion – and replacement – process has proceeded, therefore reflecting speakers' underlying competence. One of the main findings of Kroch and his collaborators is the "Constant Rate Effect", i.e. the fact that such replacement processes seem to progress at the same rate across different contexts affected:[65]

> This is the Constant Rate Effect that is found repeatedly in empirical investigations. We take its general validity to indicate that what changes in frequency in the course of time during a syntactic change is language users' overall tendency to choose one abstract grammatical option over another in their language production. (Kroch 1994: 182)

The importance of frequency of usage has also led to the inclusion of quantitative statistical analysis within Kroch's Competition Grammar, otherwise only rarely found in generative research.

In figure 8 below the various possibilities for accounting for diachronic variation as occurring in performance are summarized as to where the locus of variation is assumed to be.

Although their data analysis (necessarily) proceeds from performance data, diachronic generative approaches account for variation in terms of speakers' competence, either as inter- or as intraspeaker variation. Performance factors – though acknowledged – lie outside the generative model. For this reason, the genitive variation lies outside the scope of generative analysis too; it can only constitute a topic within the generative framework inasmuch as the *s*-genitive and the *of*-genitive can be shown to be derivationally related on the competence level (which they barely ever are), but not when to use the one or the other since this depends to a large extent on factors external to grammar proper (cf. §3.3.2.2.4, and see chapter 4), i.e. performance. In the generative conception of grammatical variation most of the preferences for the choice-contexts discussed under §3.3.2.1-2 above – where both the *s*-genitive and the *of*-genitive could be used, would be regarded as cases of free variation and as such the genitive variation is simply not a research question a generative linguist would address in the first place.

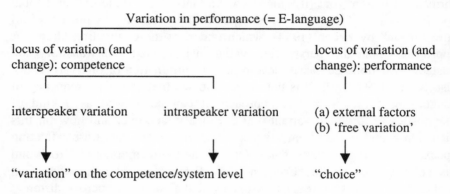

Figure 8.   Variation in performance (= E-language)

This has of course also serious implications for any diachronic account of the genitive variation. Since the *s*-genitive and the *of*-genitive are not two mutually exclusive grammatical variants, the Competing Grammar approach by Kroch (1994) is not applicable. Besides, Kroch's winner-takes-all approach cannot be applied either, since, as we will see in the discussion of the diachronic development in chapters 7 – 8, the *s*-genitive – although diachronically extending – does not, and probably is not going to – replace the *of*-genitive. Rather, what we can observe here is some kind of functional specialization which, however, again lies outside the generative model.

5.1.1.2 Optimality Theory[66]

A recent development within formal grammar is "Optimality Theory" (OT), as introduced in Prince and Smolensky (1993). The basic difference to the generative model is that (i) within OT there are no longer inviolable rules but violable and interacting constraints, and (ii) OT is output-oriented, i.e. OT analysis proceeds from the actual surface form/construction. According to Kager (1999: 8) the technical apparatus can be briefly sketched as follows:

> For a given input, the grammar generates and then evaluates an infinite set of output candidates, from which it selects the optimal candidate, which is

the actual output. Evaluation takes place by a set of hierarchically ranked constraints …, each of which may eliminate some candidate outputs, until a point is reached at which only one output candidate survives.

"Optimality" refers here to the fact that the 'winner' is that candidate which causes the least serious violations of constraints. That is, this notion of optimality as such is theory-internal as long as the constraints postulated do not have an underlying extralinguistic motivation (cf. §8.5 below for a different notion of "optimal" as underlying the present study). Some of OT's assumptions are not unproblematic though. For example, it is not clear where the input comes from, nor what delimits GEN, i.e. the generator that creates the candidate set (what precisely determines the language-specific candidates?), nor which constraints there are on constraints (particularly troublesome is the alleged all-embracing universality of constraints; for a particularly critical assessment of OT along such lines see McMahon [2000]).[67] Leaving such general conceptual-technical problems aside for a moment, what particularly concerns us here is how OT (a) considers extragrammatical factors, and (b) how it can handle variation. Just like generative approaches, classical OT accounts are concerned exclusively with an account of speakers' mental knowledge (i.e. competence) and not with performance. OT constraints are basically proposed on the grounds of markedness. There are various notions and concepts of markedness; the one applied in OT refers to cross-linguistic frequency of occurrence and hence remains language-internal (cf. Kager 1999: 2-3). Unless such markedness values are coupled with some independent extragrammatical, i.e. articulatory and/or cognitive foundations, the assumed universality of OT constraints remains a language- and theory-internal construct.[68]

As far as variation is concerned, it must be noted that, in general, whatever the account looks like in detail, the locus of variation in (classical) OT must lie within speakers' competence, for the very same reason as – and with the same implications as – the generative approaches discussed above. Now, at first sight it seems that doing away with inviolable rules in favor of violable constraints would open the door for variation. At a closer look, however, variation does not seem possible at all. For one input there is only one optimal output, i.e. one 'winner'.[69] However, grammatical variation, or, in formal terms "optionality", is a linguistic fact that cannot be completely ignored both within generative approaches and OT.[70] Within traditional OT we here envisage a situation where a single input produces two equally good candidates and there is no higher constraint which decides between the two. Variation arising from such an undecided state of grammar is, however, as noted by Anttila (1997: 46), "the poor man's way of dealing with variation" (cf. also McMahon 2000: 106). Moreover, it seems a rather unrealistic scenario. According to Green (1997: 31) in such cases neither candidate should be optimal. And even if we did allow two equally good candidates, there usually would be some lower ranked constraint eventually deciding between the two (cf. Green 1997: 31; see also Müller 1999: 4). Another problem concerning OT and free variation (= two outputs for a single input) is described by Kager (1999: 404) as follows:

> The fact that variation is 'free' does not imply that it is totally unpredictable, but only that no grammatical principles govern the distribution of variants. Nevertheless, a wide range of extragrammatical factors may affect the choice of one variant over the other, including sociolinguistic variables (such as gender, age, and class), and performance variables (such as speech style and tempo). Perhaps the most important diagnostic of extragrammatical variables is that they affect the choice of occurrence of one output in a stochastic way, rather than deterministically.

Here we can see that OT inherits the theoretical baggage of generative approaches. If there is variation of the more-or-less sort any formal approach runs into problems since this lies, as argued above (§5.1.1.1), by definition outside competence and hence outside the scope of formal analysis (see also Guy 1997b: 127).[71] Recently, however, some first and valiant attempts have been made within OT to account for free variation and assign probabilities to the output(s). What all these attempts to grasp variation in OT have in common is that they try to capture variation at the level of the constraint hierarchy. (In the same vein, cross-linguistic variation is accounted for in OT by assuming different rankings of the universal constraints.) In the following I will briefly discuss two different approaches to variation in OT, i.e. the partial-ranking approach introduced in Anttila (1997) and Stochastic OT as exemplified in Bresnan and Deo (2001).[72]

Underlying Anttila's (1997) OT approach to variation is the assumption that constraints need not be absolutely fixed but can be partially ranked. Predictions for the probabilities of various variants are then deduced by considering all logically possible rankings of constraints (t) and then looking, given these rankings, at how often a candidate wins (n), resulting in the probability n/t. The predicted probabilities for each variant are then compared to the actual frequencies as attested in corpora, and Anttila's (1997) analysis for Finnish genitive plurals shows surprisingly close matches between the two. One general methodological and/or conceptual problem I can see here, however, is that corpus data, i.e. E-language, may well be also determined by sociolinguistic and performance factors (cf. also Kager 1999: 404, as quoted above).[73] We therefore would not really expect a one-to-one match of the expected predictions derived from grammar and the actual observed frequencies from corpus data, because in the latter there are yet further, external factors at work influencing the frequency of variants not considered in the OT grammar-internal calculus (see also the discussion on the discrepancy between I-language and E-language as briefly discussed in §5.1.1.1 above.)

While the majority of OT analyses are still from the field of phonology (as is Anttila's analysis), some OT accounts from the area of morphosyntax have also emerged. Bresnan and Deo's (2001) analysis of variable subject-verb agreement with *Be* in non-Standard English varieties represents one recent OT approach to the modeling of morphosyntactic variation called Stochastic Optimality Theory.[74] Here the basic idea is that constraints are not ranked on a discrete ordinal scale but on a continuous scale. If the constraints selecting the output are located far enough from each other on that scale, there will be one winner; if, however, they are close to each other, two adjacent constraints can be ranked in such a way that the lower ranked constraint can dominate at some point and to some degree the higher ranked constraint, with a stochastic evaluation of the constraint interaction resulting in different frequencies for the possible outputs, i.e. the variants. Bresnan and Deo (2001) distinguish between inter- and intraspeaker variation in their analysis, concluding that both follow the same pattern, i.e. the same constraint ranking. Moreover, they seem at least to acknowledge that extragrammatical factors, in this case social meaning, can also affect the distribution of variants. It is, however, not precisely clear how to incorporate such social meaning into their approach. According to Bresnan and Deo (2001: 38), who in turn refer to Boersma (1997), such social meaning could partly be part of the grammatical system and partly constitute 'noise' outside grammar proper. Another advantage of their approach is that their Stochastic OT grammar only needs to assume one mechanism, i.e. one grammar for speakers to derive variation from grammar (unlike, for example, Kroch's Competing Grammar account discussed above, where it must be assumed that a speaker has access to more than one grammar).

The next question to ask now is how can OT account for variation and change? The standard way of modeling change within OT is to assume that constraints can get reranked in the course of time, thus resulting in a different output. Based on the conception of variation deriving from partial ranking of constraints, as briefly illustrated above, Anttila and Cho (1998) and Cho (1998) regard language change as both reranking and either fixing (> non-variation) or releasing of constraint ranking (> variation). In Bresnan and Deo's (2001) approach linguistic change can be accounted for by a change in the distance between two constraints: to the extent that the distance between two constraints on the continuous ranking scale increases, the probability for one construction (i.e. the 'winner') increases, that is, variation decreases. If, on the other hand, two constraints become more adjacent, variability increases.

What is, however, not clear is what should make constraints rerank, get fixed, get undone or move along scales in the first place. Do different surface forms force constraints to change, or does a change in the constraint ranking produce different surface forms? For this, see for example the following statement by Cho (1998: 50):

> The next stage in the development of the non-rhotic type can be characterized as undoing of the ranking between **Faithfulness** and **Coda**. Nonranking between these two constraints necessarily yields variation in the realization of coda *r*, as illustrated by (10). A weakening of the coda *r* most likely started with phonetic variation, which itself is reflected in the grammar by means of partial ranking of constraints. Variation occurs when the grammar underdetermines the output by partial ranking.

Here we can see how the argument runs: ranking between two constraints is undone, resulting in variation. Nothing is said, however, as to why the two constraints should get unranked at all. It rather looks as if the very fact of variation in the data leads the researcher to deduce a change in constraint-ranking (in the form of partial ranking in this case). This circularity in argument has been pointed out by McMahon (2000: 126-127) who refers to it as a "chicken-and-egg problem". According to McMahon (2000: 127) OT cannot really explain why a change takes place: "In OT, however, the motivation and the evidence for the constraint reranking are precisely the same, namely the change we are trying to explain in the first place". In her view, explanation within OT (as within most generative approaches) comes down to theory-internal description, and the explanation will be as good as the theory is. In addition, it has been argued by Hurch (1998: 135) that the simple fact of constraint reranking does not entail any predictions how constraints should be reranked, i.e. in which direction a change should proceed (whatever ultimately triggers it). These criticisms may turn out to be too strict, however. Rather, it seems to me that the whole issue of (possibly) explaining change within OT must be seen in the broader context of language acquisition, since this is – as in generative accounts of change in general – the locus of grammatical change. In a now somewhat outdated view on learnability, Anttila (1997) assumes that the initial state in language acquisition is a completely non-ranked grammar, with constraints becoming eventually ranked on the basis of positive evidence (for a critique on this account see e.g. McMahon 2000: 102-103). Recently, however, the process of language acquisition within OT is rather viewed as the demotion of markedness constraints (cf. Gnanadesikan forthcoming). [75] With language changing during language acquisition, accordingly, language change can be perceived of as changing towards an unmarked state of affairs (cf. also Vincent 2000: 44-45). Depending on the degree as to which markedness is grounded on general cognitive principles instead of mere cross-linguistic regularities (see also above), this could indeed entail some explanatory value to modeling change within OT. For a recent approach which tries to reconcile formal OT with the functional approach to grammaticalization (cf. also §5.2.1.2 below) see Vincent (2000), who provides an OT case study on Latin and Romance argument linking showing how the change proceeds along a markedness hierarchy and thereby building a diachronic vector in OT (as does, for example, Naturalness Theory, see §5.2.1.1.2 below). Vincent's (2000) study deals, however, with variation (between null and overt pronominal arguments) as a transient stage from Latin to Romance, but not with a situation of grammatical variation as a diachronically stable phenomenon due to functional specialization (if with possible diachronic shifts in the functional domains of the variants, as in the case of the genitive variation; see particularly chapter 7); moreover, Vincent (2000) does not address the question of probabilities (and how to incorporate these in his approach) either. In general, it must be noted that even OT analyses that do incorporate probabilities into grammar, such as Anttila's (1997) approach, cannot directly link these probabilities to specific contexts (particularly extralinguistic ones) in which one or the other variant should prevail. Rather, it appears that the probabilities given are overall frequencies derived *qua* differences in constraint ranking, which may (or not) account for the overall frequency of variants as attested in corpora, but this does not really explain why in a certain context one variant is more likely to occur than another one. [76] For this, see also Guy (1997b: 138): [77]

> ...it reduces variation to random selection, and derives specific quantities in the outputs as an epiphenomenon, arising haphazardly from the way the constraint hierarchy determines optimal forms. The result is a sophisticated version of the 'free variation' concept of the structuralists: outputs alternate randomly. As I have noted, this explanation failed when it was shown that

variation was not random; this OT version will likely fail for the same reason.

In general, it must be concluded that even not considering the general shortcomings of the theory (see particularly McMahon 2000) as well as the potential failure of OT to model variation (especially of the probabilistic kind) and change sufficiently (as e.g. argued by Guy 1997a and McMahon 2000: §3.4), the crucial point for the present argumentation is that classical OT, – and all this also applies to the generative approaches discussed above –, places the locus of variation and change into speakers' competence (and for the present argument it does not really matter whether one has to assume inter- or intraspeaker variation here) and deal with variation but not with choice as outlined above. Admittedly, however, in the Functional OT approach as recently programmatically laid out in Bresnan and Aissen (2002), in which constraints are supposed to be functionally motivated and which can also capture the probabilistic side of variation within a stochastic analysis, the gap between variation and choice does indeed seem bridgeable (see also note 68). This line of research is still in its infancy though, and it remains to be seen how many aspects of usage can be captured by it, and how well.

5.1.2   *Sociolinguistics and corpus linguistics*

In contrast to the structuralist and generative assumption that variation is random and as such outside the scope of linguistic analysis, the belief that variation is not random but structured (cf. the term "orderly heterogeneity" coined by Weinreich, Labov, and Herzog 1968) lies at the very heart of sociolinguistics (see also §3.1 above) and makes linguistic variation its primary object of investigation. The framework of sociolinguistics is primarily concerned with language in its social context. Accordingly, the locus of language (and hence variation) is assumed to be in society. The field itself today is extremely broad (for an overview see e.g. Romaine 1994); in the following I will be primarily concerned with the account of variation (and change) in the framework as introduced by the work of Labov. In this framework, statistical correlations are used to relate frequency scores on linguistic variables to linguistic as well as non-linguistic factors, i.e. social-demographic (e.g. class, age, ethnicity, gender) and stylistic-contextual (level of formality) factors. Although the focus is on the (empirical) investigation of language use, Labov does not want to break altogether with the structuralist tenet of *langue* being the primary object of linguistic inquiry.[78] It seems that for this reason, Labov (1969) has introduced the notion of "Variable Rule". These Variable Rules specify for a given context with which probability a certain variant is likely to occur according to linguistic as well as extralinguistic (i.e. social-demographic) factors. While Labov himself has been somewhat ambiguous as to where to place the locus of Variable Rules, in performance/*parole* or in competence/*langue* (cf. e.g. Romaine 1981: 95-96), the more common view seems to be that Variable Rules form part of speakers' competence (cf. e.g. Romaine 1981; Guy 1997b). This is not an unproblematic assumption. Given that Variable Rules are part of individual speakers' knowledge while at the same time variation (on which these Variable Rules are based) is supposed to manifest itself in groups (*qua* the underlying social conception of language), it is quite difficult to see how probabilities based on interspeaker variation should become part of individual speakers' linguistic knowledge (cf. also Botha 1992: §5.3, and Romaine 1981 for a good discussion of the conceptual problems involved).[79] Would this not imply that an individual speaker is (unconsciously?) aware of the distribution of variants in the group/speech community, constantly keeping mentally track of the probabilities attached to them (which in turn are derived from group behavior) (for this argument see also, e.g., Romaine 1981; Botha 1992: §5.3, and Lass 1997: 364-365)? Or, otherwise, when placing the locus of variation into the knowledge of individual speakers, this would imply that groups and/or speech communities are homogeneous (as far as the Variable Rules are concerned), which would lead the whole idea of sociolinguistics in a way *ad absurdum*.[80] In fact, Weinreich, Labov, and Herzog (1968: 188) explicitly talk about the "grammars of the speech community", which suggests that grammars exist or at least are defined above the individual in the group. In this respect, it is somehow difficult to decide whether sociolinguistics deals with variation or with choice as outlined above. On the basis of its general ontological claims, however, as well as other reasons to be dealt with below, I do discuss sociolinguistics under variation-based approaches here.

In sharp contrast to generative grammar, sociolinguists ideally proceed from a context-bound definition of 'sameness'. Within such a context-bound conception of syntax, however, it cannot be ruled out that the distribution of variants (also) results from an underlying difference in contextual and/or discourse-pragmatic meaning and therefore may not be attributed to social and stylistic factors only. As already said in §3.2.1, a definition of morphosyntactic variables and variants within such a strict context-bound approach does simply not seem practicable. This dilemma is manifest in Weiner and Labov (1983), who regard active and passive sentences as syntactic variants on the basis of truth-conditional equivalence for methodological reasons and were vigorously attacked for doing so for sociolinguistic-theoretical reasons (e.g. Lavandera 1978). Therefore, it seems that the investigation of (morpho)syntactic variation is incompatible with sociolinguistic objectives in the strict sense, unless contextual factors, which themselves are not the goal of the investigation, are controlled. It is probably for this very reason that there are not many studies of grammatical variation from a clear sociolinguistic angle. What seems to have happened instead is that a separate, independent field of grammatical variation has emerged, which, although it has strong historical and methodological affinities to sociolinguistic studies, is now generally concerned with the investigation of *any* factors that govern the choice between various structural alternatives, without necessarily committing themselves to the theoretical and ideological orientation of sociolinguistic studies. These theoretically more neutral approaches inherited the empirical, quantitative methodology, which was introduced into linguistics by the field of sociolinguistics. In this kind of empirical research the focus is not so much on what is possible and what is not, but rather on the probability with which a certain variant occurs (relative to an alternative one), it is the question 'how often' that matters. The main methodological tool of this newly developed field of grammatical variation is the analysis of corpora. The predominantly descriptive character of corpus linguistics has the advantage that the exclusion of (morpho)syntactic variation for theoretical-ideological reasons is not necessary, although the methodological problems involved in the investigation of grammatical variation certainly remain. Inductive generalizations are made over corpora using quantitative analyses (frequency scores and statistics). Such corpus studies do not – and probably need not for their purpose – distinguish between variation on the usage-level and choice on the level of the individual. Most often the result, i.e. the frequency distributions found within a corpus, is supposed to speak for itself,[81] and only rarely are the findings linked to factors operating on the level of the individual language user. This is not to say that all empirical approaches to grammatical variation using corpus analyses are descriptive and exclusively variation-oriented. A line of reasoning has also emerged among this field of linguistics which accounts for grammatical variation in English by way of cross-linguistic comparison; for this see, for example, the work by König and collaborators or the ongoing project on English dialect syntax at the University of Freiburg (cf. e.g. Kortmann 1999 for an introduction to this approach). Moreover, some scholars make reference to principles of language processing to explain why certain constructions occur more often than others (e.g. Bock 1982; Hawkins 1994; Rohdenburg 1996). The latter approaches certainly fall under choice-based approaches; and their general rationale will be introduced below (and see also §8.3).

In the Labovian sociolinguistic framework synchrony and diachrony are inextricably interwoven in that change presupposes variation, and variation is often indicative of ongoing change.[82] The study of variation has therefore an inbuilt diachronic perspective and as such is a useful tool for investigating the transmission of change(s).[83] In contrast to traditional historical linguistic approaches the present is, for methodological reasons, relatively important for the investigation of change in a twofold sense. First, since social mechanisms are easier to assess in the present than in the past, Labov (1972) transferred the "Uniformitarian Principle", a well-known principle from geology to the study of linguistic variation and change. According to this principle, "the same mechanisms that operated to produce the large-scale changes of the past may be observed operating in the current changes taking place around us" (Labov 1972: 161). This allows the investigator to deduce past processes from present ones (on the Uniformitarian Principle see also §5.3 and §8.5 below). Second, differences in the age of speakers are believed to reflect different diachronic stages of a language. In apparent-time studies, therefore, speakers from different age groups are investigated at a certain point in time in the present to deduce past changes (see also §6.4.3.2).

Since the locus of language and variation is assumed to be in society, i.e. the speech community, and social norms and prestige figure highly in determining the language of such speech communities, change in sociolinguistic thinking is necessarily located within performance and the speech of adults, in contrast to the generative conception of change as occurring within the process of language acquisition.[84] Moreover, it explicitly deals with the spread/transmission of variants through a speech community and not with their actuation, i.e. innovation.[85] To sum up, with the locus of variation – and accordingly change – being in the group or the speech community, in any case somewhere above the individual language user, sociolinguistic approaches to variation (and accordingly change) deal with variation on the usage/performance level. There are several empirical studies which investigate the factors governing the occurrence of the two genitive constructions within the broader framework of corpus studies on grammatical variation in general; these studies have already been discussed in §3.3.2.2.4 and chapter 4 above.

5.2   Choice-based approaches

We can broadly distinguish between two basic linguistic orientations dealing with choice in the sense outlined above, i.e. functional approaches and all cognitively-oriented models. In the following I will try to sketch in which respect these approaches capture variation and change, and finally, in §5.3, I will lay out the choice-based approach to variation and change as it underlies the present study.

5.2.1   Functionalism

Functionalism as such is not a uniform framework within linguistics but splits up into various single approaches.[86] What all these approaches have in common is that they proceed from a context-bound definition of grammar. In contrast to the generative tenet that syntax is autonomous (or context-free), functionalist approaches assume that (discourse-) context, communicative intentions and meaning determine the choice of a construction. In this respect, the notion of choice is almost inherently built into the notion of functionalism when taking an onomasiological procedure: given a certain meaning or intention (a) what is the set of options available and (b) which linguistic construction will be chosen to convey this meaning/intention? While question (a) refers to representational aspects of the language system, (b) addresses the question of language usage in concrete situations, and it is only in the latter that the individual language user and thus choice as defined above comes in. Both these aspects are combined in the following statement by Halliday (1970: 142):

> In speaking, we choose: ... The system of available options is the 'grammar' of the language, and the speaker, or writer, selects within this system: not in vacuo, but in the context of speech situations.

Within such a view, linguistic choices are never completely synonymous but taken to be functional, i.e. they are utilized to serve different cognitive and/or communicative needs (cf. also §3.3.2 above). In the following I will focus on those functional notions and approaches which seem particularly apt in dealing with grammatical variation in general and the genitive alternation in particular as a matter of choice.

5.2.1.1 Markedness, naturalness, and iconicity

Although there are very close links and interdependencies between naturalness, markedness, and iconicity, in that these concepts appear to form a triad, they are nonetheless logically distinct concepts arguing from different angles. In this section (as well as in §5.3) I will try to show how these three concepts are intermingled and how they can deal with grammatical variation in the sense of choice.

5.2.1.1.1 Markedness

As with functionalism, there is also no unique account of markedness, and it is certainly beyond the scope of the present study to provide an exhaustive overview of all the prevailing views on this concept. Instead, I will focus here on the concept of markedness as defined by Givón (1995: chapter 2),[87] which seems to me particularly apt to show how it links to naturalness and iconicity on the one side and to grammatical variation on the other. Givón (1995: 28) distinguishes conveniently between three criteria that constitute markedness:

(a) **Structural complexity**: The marked structure tends to be more complex (or larger) than the corresponding unmarked one.
(b) **Frequency distribution**: The marked category (figure) tends to be less frequent, thus cognitively more salient, than the corresponding unmarked category (ground).
(c) **Cognitive complexity**: The marked category tends to be cognitively more complex – in terms of mental effort, attention demands or processing time – than the unmarked one.

Ideally, these criteria for markedness should go together. According to this broad definition of markedness, a link to both variation and choice can be discerned. Variation in the sense of the availability of options in the system is already implicit since the notion of markedness as such presupposes the existence of a marked structure as opposed to an unmarked structure; in other words: there is by definition no marked form/structure without an unmarked counterpart. Concrete language usage and thus choice comes in with the other two criteria: while cognitive complexity operates on the level of the individual speaker during on-line processing, resulting in a preference for the unmarked form/construction, frequency can be seen as the surface manifestation in form of the accumulation of many such single preference choices (generally in favor of the unmarked member), as illustrated below.

language system		**language processing**		**language usage**
availability of a marked versus an unmarked form/construction	➔	preference for the unmarked form/construction	➔	frequency distribution of the marked versus the unmarked form/ construction

Markedness is a concept operating on all linguistic levels. It is, however, best explored for phonology and morphology; in syntax it is much more difficult to employ. Markedness relations usually hold between members of a paradigm. While it is relatively easy to identify the members of phonological and morphological paradigms, it is much less clear how to define a syntactic paradigm, i.e. what are interchangeable syntactic structures? Note that this is precisely the same problem the sociolinguists were facing when trying to extend the notion of the linguistic variable from phonology to syntax (see §5.1.2 above). Yet, apart from the problem of defining a paradigmatic syntactic set, markedness approaches on the level of syntax face the additional problem of having to assign a markedness value to the members of this set. Thus, in contrast to sociolinguistic studies, markedness as a concept is inherently evaluative on the structural level, having to decide which of the variants is the marked form/construction and which is the unmarked one. For morphosyntax, there are several ways in which this may be determined. (i) Using Givón's first criterion of "structural complexity" the more complex (or longer) form or construction can be taken as the more marked form/construction. For syntax in the sense of word order, the question as to what constitutes the basic word order in a language arises. Marked constructions are then, accordingly, those constructions that deviate from this basic word order. The problem, however, is on which grounds to decide what is indeed the 'basic' word order.[88] (ii) According to the criterion of "frequency distribution", a marked syntactic construction should be less frequent than its unmarked counterpart. And (iii), a marked construction should draw less on mental energy, i.e. it should be easier to process.

Now, according to these criteria, how can we assign markedness values to the two genitive constructions? As to Givón's first criterion of structural complexity, what does 'more complex' or 'longer' mean in this concrete case? In terms of structural substance, the two genitive constructions only differ in their respective relational marker (POSS '*s* versus *of*), and in this respect the *of*-genitive can be regarded as the marked member of the set, with *of* having more phonological substance and constituting a lexeme of its own. As to Givón's second criterion for markedness, i.e. frequency, the crucial question is: frequent relative to which contexts? If we take the overall frequency of the two genitive constructions within a corpus, then certainly the *of*-genitive is the overall more frequent variant (cf. e.g. Biber et al. 1999: 293). If, however, we take frequency relative to certain contexts and linguistic environments, then – as will be shown in the empirical part of this study (chapters 6 – 7) – the *s*-genitive can well be the more frequent variant. So, on which grounds should we establish markedness here? Likewise, Givón's third criterion, i.e. cognitive complexity, as the amount of mental effort, is not well enough defined. The crucial question is: more mental effort for whom – the speaker or the hearer? Gundel, Houlihan, and Sanders (1988) proceed from the assumption that the cognitive needs of the speaker and the hearer can well clash: what is easy for the speaker, may be difficult for the hearer, and vice versa (see also §8.2). In their view, unmarked constructions are by definition always easier for the hearer. Marked constructions, in contrast, arise through special needs of the speaker. While for the speaker short (but therefore not explicit) expressions are more optimal in the production process ("principle of least effort"), the hearer prefers more explicit (= longer) expressions in parsing the utterance, as illustrated in table 18.

Table 18. Markedness: speaker versus hearer (based on Gundel, Houlihan, and Sanders 1988)

marked structures	unmarked structures
• in certain contexts easier for the speaker	• in all contexts easier for the hearer
• short expressions, less explicit	• long(er) expressions, more explicit
➔ principle of least effort	➔ redundancy facilitates comprehension

So, according to Gundel, Houlihan, and Sanders's (1988) criteria the *of*-genitive as the more explicit and longer construction must be regarded the unmarked construction.

To sum up, it is not possible to decide on the basis of the markedness criteria given in Givón (1995) which of the two genitive variants is the marked and the unmarked one. It simply depends. Moreover, it is only with Givón's third criterion of cognitive complexity that the perspective of the individual using variants in concrete situations – and therefore choice – comes in.

5.2.1.1.2 Naturalness

The theory of naturalness, originally developed for phonology (Stampe 1972), has primarily been elaborated for morphology (cf. e.g. Dressler et al. 1987; Wurzel 1989). Although an explicit theory of syntactic naturalness is still lacking (cf. Mayerthaler and Fliedl 1993: 610), some basic tenets can be deduced and be shown to be fruitful for an approach to grammatical variation. As with functional theories in general, naturalness theory proceeds from the assumption that syntax is not autonomous and that variation is not only possible but also functional (cf. Mayerthaler and Fliedl 1993: 610-611). One major goal of naturalness theory is to find the extralinguistic bases of language, focusing on the following two domains (cf. Dressler et al. 1987: 11-12):

(a) neurobiological and psychological bases (e.g. working memory, processing)
(b) socio-communicational bases (communicative function of language)

Naturalness theory draws upon a large extent on the concept of markedness, with more and less natural being equivalent to less and more marked. Although the concept of markedness is used in a "pretheoretical" fashion (cf. Dressler et al. 1987:13-14), the following criteria are taken as diagnostics for a construction to be more marked/less natural, to name the most important ones given in Dressler et al. (1987: 13-14):

(1) What comes later in phylogenesis,
(2) what comes later in ontogenesis,
(3) what is more difficult to perceive,
(4) what is more likely/frequent subject to speech errors,
(5) what is usually lost first in aphasia,
(6) what is avoided by adults in 'motherese' speech,
(7) what is less frequent (type/token) cross-linguistically,
(8) what, diachronically, changes first, the direction of the change being: more marked > less marked,
(9) what is reduced first, or what emerges last, in pidgins and creoles,
(10) a category that is phonologically marked is likely to be morphophonologically marked as well,
(11) the less marked (morphological) form is zero.

It is in regard to this link to markedness theory in particular that grammatical variation needs to be seen in naturalness theory. Variants differ according to their markedness value, or, in other words, in their degree of naturalness. The parameters given for markedness above are, however, of a fairly heterogeneous type, going far beyond those proposed by Givón (1995) as discussed above. Some concern (synchronic) system-internal aspects (e.g. 10, 11), others language use (3, 4, 6), neurological aspects (5) or simply (cross-linguistic) frequency (7) but most of them are developmental (1, 2, 8, 9).[89] These developmental diagnostics are at the same time taken as predictive, the direction always proceeding from more marked/less natural to less marked/more natural. In this respect it is fairly dangerous to use the concept of markedness/naturalness as an explanatory notion. If the fact that a development runs from A to B is taken as evidence that B is less marked/more natural than A, and, if it is consequently argued that this change from A to B happened *because* A is more marked than B, then this is circular reasoning and a kind of *posthoc* explanation. Markedness values should therefore ideally be assigned by non-developmental, independent criteria (for a devastating critique of naturalness theory, see Lass 1980: chapter 2; for a more balanced criticism, see Keller 1994: §5.2).

5.2.1.1.3 Iconicity

The main assumption of the concept of iconicity is that the relation between a concept and its linguistic expression is not arbitrary – as was the basic tenet of structural linguistics as outlined by Saussure – but potentially motivated, in that properties of the concept may be reflected in those of the linguistic sign, either directly – as in the case of "iconic images", or more indirectly in "iconic diagrams", in the sense that the relation between different linguistic signs resembles the relation of their referents (cf. e.g. McMahon 1994: 84-86, or Fischer and Nänny 1999). It is usually the latter type of "diagrammatic iconicity" that is most relevant in linguistics, and various types of diagrammatic iconicity operating in various areas of grammar have been proposed (cf. e.g. Haiman 1985a, Haiman 1985b; Fischer and Nänny 1999), as for example:[90]

(1) *Isomorphism*: Two forms will never express exactly the same meaning; there will always be some additional semantic-pragmatic or functional distinction. There is no true synonymy.

(2) *Conceptual distance*: Concepts close to each other, should also linguistically occur in close proximity.

(3) *Constructional isomorphism*: More conceptual substance should be encoded by more linguistic substance.

(4) *Linear sequencing*: The order of how things happen in the world – or how we perceive them to happen – will be reflected in linear order.

The principle of isomorphism can be regarded as the fundamental principle underlying the whole concept of iconicity: whenever we have a choice between two forms/constructions, this choice will be motivated by some extra-linguistic property of the icon, and this is exactly where the notion of grammatical choice comes in.

Note that under a strict reading of iconicity, language should directly resemble properties of the real world, as, for example, exemplified in the sequential order in Caesar's famous *veni, vedi, vici*, where the order in which the events took place is reflected in linguistic serialization. In a more restricted and indirect sense, iconicity does not refer to properties of the world itself but rather to the way in which reality is perceived and conceptualized by human beings (cf. also Croft 1990: 171):

> The first question that comes to mind is, should the structure of language be compared to the structure of physical reality or the structure of human conceptualization of that reality? Since language is a human faculty, the general assumption on the part of the functional linguists has been that the structure of language should be compared to human conceptualisation of the world ... Thus, the iconically minded typologist should turn his or her attention to psychology.

But to which extent, if at all, is human conceptualization and language processing universal? This touches upon the old controversy brought up by the Sapir-Whorf hypothesis, whether – and in which respect – the way we speak influences the way we think, i.e. whether language can shape human thoughts. While modern linguistics generally seems to reject the view that language determines human thought in the way assumed by the Sapir-Whorf hypothesis (cf. e.g. Pinker 1994: chapter 3), a new line of psychologically and cognitively oriented research is currently emerging showing how language-specific grammatical structures can influence human conceptualization (cf. e.g. Gumperz and Levinson 1996; Bowerman and Levinson 2001), most prominently represented by Slobin's (1996) concept of "thinking for speaking".[91] The problem with all such approaches is, however, that not much is yet known about the structure of human conceptualization (cf. also Croft 1990: 172); human conceptualization is a kind of black box which is extremely difficult to investigate. And while it is certainly the case that the human processing system is subject to some language-specific requirements, it is not at all clear which of its aspects (e.g. processor, working memory) can be regarded to be universal or rather as language-specific? This brings us directly to the question of whether it is still legitimate to stretch the notion of iconicity as to cover matters of conceptualization and processing, if the cognitive system, including the language processor, is not the same across all languages, or would this run counter to the notion of iconicity as it was originally coined? With all these caveats in mind, I will make clear in §5.3 below how I will be using the notion of iconicity in the present study.

So far we have seen how the notion of choice is almost inherently built into the concepts of markedness, naturalness and iconicity. An implication directly following from this is that these concepts also entail certain predictions for the directionality of language change, to which I will return in §5.3 below. There I will also further elaborate on how considerations of iconicity and naturalness can be brought together when outlining the approach to grammatical variation and change as taken in the present study.

5.2.1.2 Grammaticalization

Grammaticalization, as e.g. elaborated in Hopper and Traugott (1993), has become one of the major functional approaches to language change. While I will further introduce and discuss grammaticalization in §8.6.3 below, the question to be addressed here is how approaches to grammaticalization can possibly model grammatical variation and change.

Variation in approaches to grammaticalization is primarily present as a transient situation between the different stages in the grammaticalization process in the sense that the non- or less grammaticalized construction may co-occur for some time with the newly developed one, a situation also known under the term "layering" (cf. Hopper 1991: 22; Hopper and Traugott 1993: 124-126). Variation studies within the framework of grammaticalization aim therefore at revealing significant transition stages in the development of a certain construction or grammatical concept.[92] It is not exactly clear, in which respect choice on the level of the individual speaker is incorporated in these approaches. This, of course, crucially depends on where the locus of change is supposed to be. While it is somewhat implicit in this essentially functionalist framework itself that the locus of language (and hence change) must be in the individual language user,[93] Janda (2001) has recently criticized grammaticalization research for taking notions such as clines too literally. That is, the concept of clines along which morphemes and language(s) move suggests that these lead a life of their own, in a way the metaphor, originally designed as a shorthand to describe language, eventually taken to be real (see particularly Janda 2001: 281-285).[94] While Janda (2001) advocates a sociolinguistic framework of grammaticalization he also makes a strong case for refocusing grammaticalization research again on the perspective of the single speaker as the main locus of language and change. This is not necessarily a contradiction, as one might assume from the discussion of the sociolinguist framework in §5.1.2 above. According to Janda (2001: 276, fn. 2) "grammars are properties of individual brains whereas a community has no (single) brain, there can be no such thing as a 'community grammar'." Janda's (2001) critique shows that grammaticalization research has somewhat moved away from its ontological claim of language residing first and foremost in individual speakers, rather treating structural concepts and language development as things standing outside the individual speaker.

5.2.2   Cognitive linguistics

The relatively recent field of cognitive linguistics is of a fairly heterogeneous nature. It can be divided into a more theoretical branch, which primarily focuses on the question of how language is represented in the human mind and into a more applied one (i.e. psycholinguistics), dealing with the question of how language is processed. Another dividing line can be drawn with respect to the assumptions made about the organization of the human mind. In modular approaches, the human mind is taken to be divided into several autonomous modules of which language is only one. But also language itself is supposed to have a modular architecture, with syntax regarded as autonomous from phonology or semantics. The investigation of the modular architecture of the human mind is the subject matter of theoretically-oriented work in modular cognitive approaches (e.g. Chomsky 1980; Fodor 1983) and can be more or less be equated with generative approaches as discussed in §5.1.1.1 above, while in the more applied-oriented field of psycholinguistics modular models are designed and tested, which take into account the process of on-line processing from conceptualization to articulation (in the case of speech production) or vice versa (in the case of speech perception). In §6.2.1.2 below, it will be shown how syntactic choices are explicated by the modular production model by Levelt (1989) and how – if at all – the choice between the two genitive constructions can be predicted from this model.

More holistic approaches assume that cognition is an inseparable whole, and that language, accordingly, follows the same cognitive principles as other cognitive abilities. The most prominent representative of this line of reasoning is what has become known as "Cognitive Grammar" (see e.g. the work by Langacker or Kemmer), where it is generally assumed that all syntactic structure follows from general cognitive strategies. (And for one particular account of the English *s*-genitive within Cognitive Grammar, see Taylor 1996). For different reasons, activation-spreading theories (e.g. Stemberger 1985; Dell 1986; MacKay 1987) based on connectionist theories (e.g. Rumelhart and McClelland 1982) model language processing in a non-modular, holistic way, assuming that linguistic elements are connected with each other in an associative neural network. These models have, however, not been explicated for syntactic choices so far, at least not to my knowledge. In table 19 a brief overview of the various approaches within cognitive linguistics is given.

Table 19. Cognitive linguistics – a brief overview

	cognitive linguistics	
approaches	**theory** (= representationally)	**psycholinguistics** (= procedurally)
modular	formal theoretical linguistics (e.g. Fodor 1983, Chomskyan linguistics)	modular models of speech production and perception (e.g. Levelt 1989)
holistic	Cognitive Grammar	connectionism (e.g. Rumelhart and McClelland 1986)

Note that except for the theoretical modular approach all other cognitively-oriented approaches are – more or less – easily compatible with the functional perspective on language. Holistic approaches can be regarded to be functionalist, since they proceed from a non-autonomous view of language and syntax, and, as argued by Bock (1982), even modular models of language processing are to some extent compatible with the functional perspective, because the inclusion of procedural aspects of language necessarily opens the interface between conceptualization and syntactic processing. In this respect it is also interesting to note that these approaches explicitly include language processing into competence by the very notion of "procedural competence":

> Dabei liegt der Kognitiven Linguistik ein erweiterter Kompetenzbegriff zugrunde: Mit Kompetenz wird nicht mehr nur das Kenntnissystem bezeichnet, sondern auch die Mechanismen, die dieses Kenntnissystem realisieren. Dabei wird die Sprachfähigkeit des Menschen sowohl strukturell (als mentales Kenntnissystem) als auch prozedural (als Verarbeitungsprozessor) definiert. ['Cognitive linguistics is based on an extended use of the notion of competence. Competence does not only refer to knowledge as a system but also to the mechanisms that realize this system. Accordingly, language capacity is defined both structurally (as mental knowledge system) and procedurally (as processor).']
> (Schwarz 1992: 39 [translation mine])

That is, according to this perspective, processing considerations do not belong to performance but to competence.

It is not difficult to see how cognitive linguistics links to the question of choice: the locus of language is placed inside the human mind, cognition becomes important, and – at least within the psycholinguistic approaches – aspects of on-line processing are taken into account. All this emphasizes the role of the individual language user. Given the availability of alternative syntactic constructions, these can be (a) due to general cognitive principles and/or (b) due to the make-up of the human processing system. Only rarely, however, are psycholinguistic arguments or even approaches applied to historical linguistics. One reason may be that psycholinguistics necessarily deals with present speakers and therefore is first and foremost a synchronic enterprise (apart from language acquisition studies, which are developmental, albeit along a relatively short time axis) and it is impossible to look into past speakers' minds. Notable exceptions are Tabor (1994) and Berg (1998), who both present a psycholinguistic (connectionist) approach to account for linguistic structure and change. While Tabor (1994) shows how syntactic categoriality emerges from probabilistic gradualness, Berg (1998) argues that psycholinguistic mechanisms as evident from speech errors can be held to be responsible for shaping linguistic structure and determine the course of linguistic change. Both Tabor (1994) and Berg (1998) do not, however, deal with grammatical variation in the sense of choice. Berg (1998) in fact explicitly excludes the impact of processing principles on language use from his investigation; that is, he does not address the question of what makes speakers use one variant rather than an alternative one in concrete speech situation. In the following section I will, however, come back to the central question raised by Berg (1998: 66-67): "What is the relevance of today's psycholinguistics to yesterday's language?" (For yet other functional-cognitive approaches of grammatical variation (and change) see also the discussion in §8.3 below.)

5.3 Towards a choice-based approach of the genitive variation: outline of approach to grammatical variation in the present study

The present study is a study of grammatical variation looking at why speakers use one genitive variant rather than the other in concrete speech situations. While not following one single of the approaches discussed above, there are various ways in which aspects of these frameworks will be utilized. First of all, the general theoretical orientation is certainly functional and not formal, for the very reason that formal approaches to variation and change deal with competence while the choice-based approach taken here is performance-based, or, alternatively, operates within the wider cognitive notion of procedural competence. Moreover, the functional stance of this study focuses on the cognitive-psychological aspects of choice (from the point of view of the speaker), and not on pragmatic-communicative speaker-hearer interactions. The cognitive-psychological factors investigated in the present study (and explicated in §6.2 below) are regarded as operating more towards the subconscious end of the consciousness scale in chapter 4 above.[95]

Most prominently, this study combines aspects of iconicity and naturalness theory in the following way. As said above, the concept of iconicity itself is closely linked to approaches to markedness and naturalness. In this study I will not deal with markedness, since markedness values in the sense of what is cognitively more optimal for the language user (cf. Givón's 1995: 28 criterion of 'cognitive complexity') can be assigned on the basis of iconicity and naturalness. That is, in this respect markedness is derivative of and follows from iconicity and naturalness and does not need to be evoked as a separate concept here. Likewise, another criterion for markedness, i.e. frequency distribution (cf. Givòn 1995: 28), can only determine *posthoc* what is marked as opposed to what is unmarked and cannot *predict* the distribution of variants in an empirical study.

The concept of naturalness provides the necessary bridge for an application of iconicity as a concept defined in terms of human conceptualization and processing. In particular, in the present argumentation the metatheoretical claim of naturalness theory to find the extralinguistic bases of language (cf. Dressler et al. 1987: 11) is important, and I will focus here on the neurobiological and psychological aspects of language. More and less natural, accordingly, is defined as "'more or less easy for the human brain'" (Dressler et al. 1987: 11). In this respect, naturalness theory can be seen as a preference theory building upon considerations of economy, and I will further elaborate on the notion of economy in general and as underlying the present study in chapter 8 below. In the present study, what is iconic will also be regarded to be easier to process (cf. also Givón 1985: 198 and Croft 1990: 254) and thus more economical,[96] and that genitive construction which is easier to process under certain conditions will be regarded as more likely to occur. It is in this very general sense that naturalness is exploited here. Note that in combining the genitive variation with such extralinguistically defined natural factors allows also for predictions (i) as to which genitive construction should be preferred in a certain context, and (ii) in which direction a change should proceed (if it occurs at all). Very generally, linguistic change should proceed from less natural to more natural. However, it is an empirical fact that languages as such do not become more natural (and, if this were so, how should *un*natural constructions arise in the first place?). It is well-known that there are conflicts of naturalness (cf. e.g. Wurzel 1997),[97] also called "competing motivations" (cf. e.g. DuBois 1985), which can be held to be responsible for dysfunctionality on both the variation, i.e. system level as well as on the level of choice, i.e. concrete usage, in the following way:

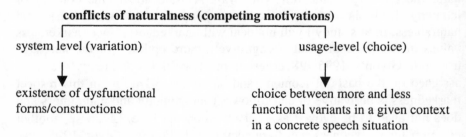

Figure 9.   Conflicts of naturalness (competing motivations)

The genitive variation is not a case of conflicts of naturalness or competing motivations on the system level – both the *s*-genitive and the *of*-genitive are fully functional, just that they are confined to and preferred in clearly specified contexts. It is only in these contexts that conflicts or competition can arise – in the sense of choosing that genitive variant which violates the least constraints, or, put positively, is the optimal one.

This does in fact very much 'sound' like OT-philosophy but it is not, since the competing motivations or constraints I will talk about, i.e. the factors animacy, topicality, and possessive relation, are supposed to operate on the conceptualization and processing (i.e. performance) level, which lies outside the classical OT approach as discussed in §5.1.1.2.[98] Although somewhat close in spirit, I will therefore not use the OT formal apparatus to model the genitive variation and change in the present study. Instead I will employ my own analysis to consider the fact of competing motivations in the choice of genitive construction in what I will call the "interaction of factors", and, based on the analysis in chapters 6 – 7, I will propose a preference structure built on the hierarchical ordering of the factors animacy, topicality, and possessive relation which captures, in my opinion, the competing forces in the genitive variation both synchronically and diachronically well.

Adopting such a choice-based approach to the genitive variation synchronically, will also throw light on the diachronic development of the *s*-genitive, as will be expounded in detail in chapters 7 – 9. The empirical analysis in chapter 6 will start off synchronically, arguing that the three factors investigated, i.e. animacy, topicality, and possessive relation, can be linked to extralinguistic, psycholinguistic principles, from which predictions can be derived, how these factors should affect the choice of genitive construction. These predictions will then be tested in the experimental study in chapter 6, first purely synchronically, and then, within an apparent-time approach, diachronically (over a very short period of time of about one generation). Then, in a second step, in chapter 7, the historical evidence for the genitive variation will be presented, with the empirical analysis focusing on the late Middle/early Modern English period. On the basis of both the synchronic and the diachronic evidence, in chapter 8 a diachronic scenario for the long-term diachronic development of the *s*-genitive from late Middle to Present-day English will be proposed.

Note, finally, that grammaticalization will be relevant to the present investigation of the English genitive variation in two ways. On the one hand I will discuss in §8.6.3 in which respect the diachronic development of the *s*-genitive is indicative of processes typically involved in grammaticalization. On the other hand, taking a choice-based stance to variation and change I will follow a speaker-based perspective on grammaticalization as, for example, underlying Hopper and Traugott's (1993: 63-67) approach, and recently reminded to us by Janda (2001), and study present-day variation (and across generations) in the ModE experimental part, although the speaker perspective underlying the present study is, in contrast to Janda's, not sociolinguistic but psycholinguistic/cognitive in nature.

Chapter 6
Modern English data: experimental study

The present study differs from previous empirical work on the genitive alternation in three important ways. First, in contrast to previous studies, which are all corpus analyses, in the present study a methodological tool is used, which has so far, at least to my knowledge, not been employed in the investigation of the English genitive alternation, i.e. a controlled experimental study. I will specify in §6.1 below why an experimental study is more promising than a corpus analysis for the purpose of the present study. Second, while previous empirical studies analyzing the grammatical variation between the *s*-genitive and the *of*-genitive have focused mainly on a description of the factors involved, the present study aims at providing a possible explanation of *why* the two variants are distributed the way they are by going beyond the mere descriptive/structural level and looking at how the make-up of human cognition and the processing system may influence the choice between the *s*-genitive and the *of*-genitive. Placing the locus of choice between these two constructions on the level of the individual speaker, in §6.2 I will derive predictions for the effects of the factors animacy, topicality, and possessive relation for this study. And third, the predictions for these three factors will not only be tested synchronically but also assessed diachronically, both along a very short time axis within the Modern English experimental study in this chapter (for this see the change-in-progress analysis in §6.4.3.2) as well as from a more long-term diachronic perspective, looking at how the choice of genitive construction was affected by the factors animacy, topicality, and possessive relation in past stages of English in the next chapter (chapter 7), with the empirical analysis focusing on late Middle/early Modern English. This will allow us to evaluate the role of the conceptual factors in the diachronic development of the genitive variation, i.e. in which way the choice of genitive construction in the past has been subject to the same cognitive pressures assumed to be at work – and tested in the experimental study – at present, and also help us understand why the development of the genitive variation may be the way it is in English, as argued in chapter 8.

6.1 Why using an experimental design?

Traditionally, studies on grammatical variation use corpus analysis as the major tool for analyzing the frequencies of the respective variants; it is mainly in psycholinguistic, model-oriented research that experimental methods are employed. There are advantages and drawbacks to both methodologies. In corpus analysis the researcher is restricted to what is available. There may be contexts which are as such infrequent and therefore underrepresented in a corpus; see for example the few occurrences of new possessors in corpora (e.g. Altenberg 1982; Anschutz 1997; cf. also §4.2.2). Also, in cases in which constructions are determined by many interacting factors – as in the choice between the two English genitive constructions – it may be difficult to find neutral contexts in which single factors can be analyzed and, ideally, no further factors intervene that possibly bias the results. And finally, there may be 'messy' data which do not properly fit into the categories deployed. For all these reasons, it may be necessary to compile very large corpora providing a sufficient number of neutral and clear-cut contexts for the factors investigated.

In contrast to corpus analyses, in experimental studies the items are not a matter of coincidence but are chosen by the researcher in such a way as to get typical representatives of the factors investigated and a balanced number of items for each condition. Intervening factors can be controlled to a large extent so that the researcher can focus solely on the factors he or she is interested in. However, concentrating on the clear cases and avoiding messy data may well prevent us from noticing phenomena that may eventually turn out to be crucial for our investigation. Also, in contrast to corpus data, experimental data are not set in natural speech situations; they are artificial and some linguists regard corpus data as the better and more natural performance data (cf. e.g. Leech, Francis, and Xu 1994: 58). In the present study, however, choosing an experimental study seemed most promising for the following reasons. First, many of the factors involved in the choice between the *s*-genitive and the *of*-genitive are already known from descriptions of English and previous studies. The primary goal of the present study is not to identify new factors hitherto unconsidered but rather to test the effect of some well-known factors in a controlled environment, using operational definitions and an experimental design which

(a) – given the multitude of factors involved – allows to investigate just the effects of animacy, topicality, and possessive relation, focusing on real choice-contexts only, excluding all non-comparable contexts and controlling to a large extent all other factors known to influence the choice between the two genitive constructions, and

(b) – given the interaction of the factors animacy, topicality, and possessive relation – makes it possible to study these three factors in isolation, independently of each other.

How these two goals will be achieved in the present study, will be further explicated in §6.4 below.

Using informants instead of text corpora has the further advantage of testing to which extent the *s*-genitive is potentially productive outside genre-specific environments. An experimental design is particularly apt to go beyond actual usage and explore the potential of the two genitive constructions by stretching them to the extreme cases (cf. also Greenbaum and Quirk 1970: 1-7). Furthermore, testing the same items with the same procedure makes it easier to compare the distribution of the *s*-genitive and the *of*-genitive in different groups, in the present study, the difference between American and British English, and within these two Standard varieties of English the difference between older and younger speakers; other things being equal, the difference in the results will then most likely reflect varietal and age differences rather than differences in the special composition of corpora or the peculiarities of particular tokens.

6.2   Deriving predictions in a choice-based approach: iconic and natural principles

In the following I will discuss in which respect the factors animacy, topicality, and possessive relation may be effective within the individual language user when choosing between the *s*-genitive and the *of*-genitive. I will first present the operational definitions for theses factors as used in the present study, considering (i) what is already known about the distributional preferences of the two genitive variants from previous studies as well as (ii) considering the interaction of factors as discussed in chapter 4. I will then derive the predictions for the distribution of the *s*-genitive versus the *of*-genitive on the basis of what is iconic/natural, i.e. the more optimal choice for the language user in the concrete speech situation in accordance to the choice-based approach as outlined in §5.3. Drawing on two morphosyntactic differences between the two English genitive constructions, I will address two different types of iconic/natural principles. To capture the complementary word order of the possessor and the possessum in the *s*-genitive and the *of*-genitive, I will introduce a linear sequencing principle, which will predict for the factors animacy and topicality under which conditions the possessor should occur first in linear order, thus resulting in the *s*-genitive. The principle of "conceptual distance", one of the classic iconic principles as proposed by Haiman (1985a), will predict the distribution of the *s*-genitive and the *of*-genitive according to the factor possessive relation, touching upon the degree of bondedness between the possessor and the possessum in the two genitive constructions, as reflected by the two different relational markers (POSS '*s* versus *of*) linking them.

6.2.1 Linear sequencing: the serial position of the possessor (factors: animacy and topicality)

6.2.1.1 Operational definitions

6.2.1.1.1 Animacy

Animacy as used in the present study refers to the animacy status of the possessor, [99] distinguishing between the central animate category, i.e. humans, and true inanimates, excluding collective nouns (*the government, the FBI*) and animals (*lion, cat, ant*) from the analysis. Moreover, as previous empirical studies have repeatedly shown (see §4.1.2 above), even within the [+human] and [-animate] categories the choice between the *s*-genitive and the *of*-genitive depends to a large extent on the noun class of the possessor. In particular, proper names are very likely to occur with the *s*-genitive (most likely due to their inherently high topicality), and, while the *s*-genitive has usually been reported to be rather uncommon with inanimate possessors, it has been shown to be quite frequent and even on the increase with certain inanimate noun classes, such as geographical and temporal nouns. To avoid any specific lexical effect and to test solely the difference in animacy and *only* animacy (rather than noun class and/or topicality), I will therefore focus on common nouns, comparing personal nouns (e.g. *girl, mother, boy, man*) and concrete nouns (e.g. *chair, bed, door, table*). [100] Within the respective categories of [+human] versus [-animate] possessors, personal nouns and concrete nouns are those noun classes which have been shown to be least likely to occur with the *s*-genitive. Note that in contrast to abstract nouns (*freedom, life, nature*), which relatively freely allow for personifications, concrete nouns (*chair, door, table*) cannot as easily be perceived of metaphorically as animates. Neither included in this study are inanimate possessors which are – or are associated with – computer nouns (cf. my discussion of Dabrowska 1998 in §4.1.2 above). Controlling the noun class of the possessor in this way, any differences in the distribution between the *s*-genitive and the *of*-genitive between [+animate] possessors (= personal nouns) and [-animate] possessors (= concrete nouns), must then be attributed to the difference in animacy and cannot be due to the membership in a certain noun class. Table 20 illustrates and summarizes how the factor animacy is operationally defined in the present study.

Table 20. Animacy of possessor: operational definition

animacy of possessor: operational definition	
[+animate] possessor	**[-animate] possessor**
• [+ human], [-animal], [-collective] • no proper nouns	• [-human], [-collective] • no proper nouns • no geographical and temporal nouns
↓	↓
personal nouns only (e.g. *girl, mother, boy, man, ...*)	concrete nouns only (e.g. *chair, bed, door, table,...*)

6.2.1.1.2   Topicality

In the present study I will use topicality in a non-relational sense referring both to the conceptual property of possessors as given versus new and to their formal marking as definite versus indefinite, while the topicality of the possessum noun is kept invariably new.

As argued in §3.3.2.2.1, in this study only referential possessors, i.e. specifying genitives, will be regarded while non-referential possessors, constituting classifying genitives, will not be taken into account here. Therefore, in this study a [+topical] possessor is always a specific referent or object which has been explicitly mentioned before in context and which is furthermore formally marked as definite, either by a definite article (*the girl, the chair*) or a possessive pronoun (*his father*). A [-topical] possessor is always a first-mention, indefinite expression (*a girl, one man, some composer*). Although indefinite expressions as such are highly ambiguous between a truly referential and a non-referential reading, the contexts in which they occur in the present study are designed in such a way that they at least potentially allow for referential interpretation; see the examples (49) – (51) from the questionnaire study:

(49)   *"Polly", he said urgently. He caressed her cheek. "I feel so much for you. I know you've seen it. Won't you please let me—". [**The headlamps of a car/A car's headlamps**] caught them like rabbits in its beam, not coming*

> *along the Clitheroe Road but bumping and jolting along the lane that led*
> *beyond the lodge up to Cotes Hall.*
>
> (Elizabeth George, Missing Joseph, 55)

(50) *The root of every trouble they'd experienced was with Kenny's departure*
      from Cardale Street. Trouble had started small, with the death of Jim's
      multicoloured mongrel, flip-flopped and crushed beneath [a lorry's
      wheels/ the wheels of a lorry]...

      (Elizabeth George, Playing for the Ashes, 521)

(51) *She would say, God damn it, Simon, don't tell me how to feel, you don't*
      know how I feel.... And she would weep the hardest with the greatest
      bitterness when she knew he was right. As he was now, when he was fifty-
      four miles away in Cambridge, studying a corpse and a set of X-rays,
      trying to decide with his usual dispassionate, clinical acuity what had
      been used to beat in [the face of a girl/ a girl's face]

      (Elizabeth George, Missing Joseph, 4-5)

Note, however, that it seems to be in the very nature of indefinite
expressions to be inherently ambiguous between a referential and a non-
referential reading, being always at the borderline to compounds (cf. §2.3.1
and §3.3.2.2.1); I will come back to this problem and the implications for
the present study in the discussion of the results in §6.5. Table 21 gives an
overview of how the factor topicality is operationalized in the present
study.

Table 21. Topicality of possessor: operational definition

topicality of possessor: operational definition	
[+topical] possessor	**[-topical] possessor**
• [+referential]	• [+referential]
• second mention	• first mention
• definite expression	• indefinite expression
↓	↓
e.g. *the girl, his father, the chair*	e.g. *a girl, one man, some composer*

6.2.1.2 Predictions

Having established the operational definitions for the factors animacy and
topicality, the questions arise (i) why the animacy and topicality of the
possessor should affect the choice between the *s*-genitive and the *of*-
genitive and (ii) why this can be regarded to reflect iconic/natural
principles?

As discussed in chapter 4, previous empirical studies have convincingly
shown that human possessors, and especially highly topical proper nouns,

tend to occur with the *s*-genitive in English. Moreover, there is cross-linguistic evidence that many languages which have more than one possessive construction make a distinction between constructions applying to animate/human and highly topical possessors versus less topical and inanimate possessors (cf. e.g. Koptjevskaja-Tamm 2001, forthcoming; Stiebels 2000). It is, however, not clear what should motivate such animacy/topicality (referentiality) splits and why in English it is the *s*-genitive that occurs with highly animate and topical possessors, and not the *of*-genitive.

The following discussion will draw on one morphosyntactic difference between the two genitive constructions as outlined in §2.1 and §3.3.1, i.e. the complementary word order of possessor and possessum. It will be argued that the animacy as well as the topicality of the possessor influence its position in serial order in a possessive construction. In what follows I will first discuss the general word order effect of animacy and topicality providing possible cognitive explanations, and then link the effects of these two factors to an iconic/natural principle, from which, finally, the predictions for the choice of the *s*-genitive will be derived.

That animacy has a pervasive influence in many areas of grammar has already been pointed out in §4.1.1 above. It is so pervasive, in fact, that some scholars, as e.g. Dahl and Fraurud (1996: 58), even view animacy as an "*ontological* category": "By this term we mean a category which is of a more fundamental kind than others; it would correspond to what is usually called 'type' in logic and computer science." Similarly, Sperber (1996: 69) refers to concepts of the living kind as "basic concepts", which stand out in several ways from other concepts (e.g. they are easy to learn and to grasp).

There is compelling cross-linguistic evidence for a preference to have animates preceding inanimates in linear order (cf. e.g. Siewierska 1988: 56-60; Ortmann 1998: 75-76; Yamamoto 1999: 52-56). According to Haspelmath (1999b: §6.5) this ordering preference is used in Optimality theory (OT) as a constraint (ANIM > INANIM). In his attempt to find a functional explanation for OT constraints, Haspelmath (1999b: 199) concludes that the constraint ANIM > INANIM "cannot really be called a constraint in the sense of a restriction put on speakers – it is what people naturally tend to do." This is certainly a true observation, albeit not a particularly helpful one, since he only postulates the effect of animacy on the ground of "frequency in performance" (199). So, *why* then should there be such a general tendency for animates to come first in serial position?

One possible account of the role of animacy on word order comes from those functionalist approaches, which argue that it is due to the anthropocentricity, or egocentricity, of human conceptualization (for a discussion see e.g. Yamamoto 1999: §1.1.1). No matter if we attribute the effect of animacy to "empathy", a notion explored by Kuno and Kaburaki (1977) or to "point of view" (cf. e.g. Dahl and Fraurud 1996: 59-62), as the argument goes, speakers tend to have a certain inclination to organize language around themselves. This is also evident in the so-called "Me-First" principle proposed by Cooper and Ross (1975), who argue that everything that comes close to the prototypical speaker tends to come first in frozen conjuncts, i.e. "freezes", with animacy being one such property for nouns to occur first in such freezes (e.g. *people and things, men and machines*). There is therefore some reason to assume that the effect of animacy is first and foremost connected to the perception of the speaker-ego; animacy in the strict sense comes in because speakers are by definition human. This would also account for the fact that humans, though not less animate than e.g. animals, are nonetheless linguistically treated in a special way. Based on Lakoff's (1987: chapter 6) prototype radial categorization, Yamamoto (1999: 22) proposes a "General Animacy Scale gradience", which shows the individual human in the centre and how the more peripheral categories, such as human organizations, supernatural beings or anthropomorphized animals (versus other animals) are organized around this prototype. It may vary from culture to culture – and language to language – whether and to what extent these entities are conceived of as being animate.

There is also evidence that the animate-inanimate distinction has neurophysiological correlates.[101] Several studies have shown that within the mental lexicon the semantic knowledge of either animate or inanimate objects can be selectively impaired in patients suffering from aphasia (e.g. Warrington and Shallice 1984; for an overview and review of these studies see also Garrett 1992: 150-156). Moreover, in brain-imaging studies it could be shown that the picture naming of animates causes activation in an area involved in visual processing, while the naming of inanimate objects led to an activation in another brain area typical for using objects and perceiving motion (cf. Martin et al. 1996). It is, however, still controversial whether the semantic categorization of the mental lexicon corresponds to the animate-inanimate distinction, or whether it is rather due to other, more general principles, i.e. a distinction between perceptual and functional attributes (see e.g. Farah et al. 1996) or even the product of a complex interplay of perceptual and functional properties within an associative/connectionist network as recently argued by Tyler et al. (2000). In this case the effect of animacy would only be indirect in that animates tend to be perceived due to their perceptual and visual properties while inanimate objects are perceived according to their functional properties. Whatever the ultimate reason for the animate-inanimate dissociation in the brain is, and however this may be integrated in a model of the mental lexicon, it undoubtedly remains a fact that it is in some way psychologically real and neurophysiologically grounded.

There is also compelling evidence from cognitively and psycholinguistically-oriented research that animates as highly salient and topics as familiar concepts tend to come first in utterances in English. In particular, Bock (1982) argues that the human processing system provides flexibility, i.e. linguistic word order choices, to accommodate information in the order in which it becomes available to the mind when producing utterances. In subsequent work, Bock and her co-workers have distinguished between two different types of accessibility, namely "Conceptual Accessibility" and "Lexical Accessibility" (cf. e.g. Bock and Warren 1985; Bock 1987a, 1987b; McDonald, Bock, and Kelly 1993). Conceptual Accessibility concerns the accessibility of lemmas from the mental lexicon and should affect the level of function assignment. The more conceptually accessible a concept is, the more easily can its lemma be retrieved from the lexicon and the more likely it is to be assigned the highest grammatical function,[102] with animacy and concreteness – but also topicality – as main determinants of Conceptual Accessibility.[103] That is, in their production framework an animate and/or topical concept will be conceptualized early, resulting in an early retrieval of its lemma from the lexicon; this lemma can then, in turn, be assigned the highest grammatical function, i.e. it will become the subject of the sentence. In contrast, Lexical Accessibility refers to the ease with which phonologically specified lexemes can be retrieved from the lexicon, and its main determinants are word length and frequency. The order of how lexemes are retrieved from the lexicon should influence their position in serial order: what is retrieved first will be serialized first. The hypotheses of Conceptual and Lexical Accessibility correspond to the speech production model proposed by Levelt (1989), where two successive levels of syntactic processing (functional and positional processing) and two successive levels of lexical retrieval (lemma and lexeme retrieval) are distinguished. The modular architecture of the Levelt model predicts that animacy and topicality should only affect word order via the assignment of grammatical functions but not directly in the serialization process on the positional level (cf. table 22 below).

Table 22. Levelt (1989) model: predictions for Conceptual and Lexical Accessibility

	Conceptual Accessibility	Lexical Accessibility
main determinants	animacy, concreteness, topicality	word length, frequency
affected lexical level	lemma retrieval	lexeme retrieval
word order effect	functional processing: via grammatical function assignment: subject > direct object > indirect object >...	positional processing: serial order (e.g. in binominal conjuncts)

What would this predict for the choice between the *s*-genitive and the *of*-genitive in English? The investigation of word order variation in English in general and in psycholinguistic research in particular is overwhelmingly based on studies on the active-passive alternation (e.g. Bock and Warren 1985; McDonald, Bock, and Kelly 1993; Ferreira 1994) and dative shift (e.g. Erteschik-Shir 1979; Bock and Warren 1985; Thompson 1990) and on word order in binominal conjuncts (see primarily work by Bock and co-workers, and work on freezes, e.g. Cooper and Ross 1975). The speech production model by Levelt (1989) has, however, not been explicated for adnominal possessives, and it is altogether unclear on which syntactic level the choice between the *s*-genitive and the *of*-genitive should be made in the first place. Is it a matter of function assignment, comparable to the assignment of subjects via the semantic roles of agents, or is it simply a matter of serialization of possessor and possessum taking place on the positional level? While it would make sense intuitively to assume that processes of function assignment are involved in the production of possessive constructions involving relational or functional nouns (e.g. *wife, father*), which are two-place predicates (cf. e.g. Löbner 1985, see also §4.3.1 above), this may be less well motivated for the ordering of possessives containing a sortal possessum noun (e.g. *John's car*). Also, while it is in principle possible for concepts to be realized alternatively by subjects or objects in active and passive sentences, it is not at all clear how the accessibility of a concept should influence whether this concept ends up as the possessor or the possessum (leaving aside for a moment the further problem of which of these should be regarded as the hierarchically 'higher', comparable to the subject of a sentence)? In the possessives *John's car* versus *the car of John* it is invariably *John* who is the possessor and *car* which is the possessum. The only thinkable exception are kin terms. If we wish to express the relation between John and Mary, we can (a) think of John as *Mary's father*, or (b) think of Mary as *John's daughter*.

If the choice between the *s*-genitive and the *of*-genitive were a matter of strict serialization, then, according to Levelt (1989) and the hypotheses of Conceptual and Lexical Accessibility, it should not be influenced by animacy. Note, however, that there is also evidence from several experimental studies showing that animacy can affect word order in binominal conjuncts, i.e. on the positional level (cf. e.g. McDonald, Bock, and Kelly 1993), and this is also evident from analyses of frozen conjuncts (freezes); see e.g. Cooper and Ross (1975) and Allan (1987). Also, Dietrich and van Nice (forthcoming) provide experimental evidence for a unique firstness effect of animacy, independent of grammatical role assignment. That is, the effect of animacy, though most widely attested for grammatical function assignment, can also be observed for serialization on the positional level.

It is not the aim of the present study to test the predictions made by the Levelt (1989) model. Lacking any appropriate account of possessives both theoretically and in models of language processing, asking the question of whether the complementary word order of possessor and possessum as reflected in the *s*-genitive and the *of*-genitive is due to function assignment or serialization remains an idle pursuit. What is important for the present study is, however, that, very generally, animacy and topicality have indeed been shown to influence word order in a number of experimental studies and that models of language production account for this effect by assuming that the perceived animacy of concepts can determine the order in which they are processed and then linearized, taking into account the requirements of real-time processing in that what first comes to the mind should be processed and linearized first.

Additional psychological evidence for the effect of topicality comes from the work by Fenk-Oczlon (1983, 1989). Based on arguments from information theory she tries to give a cognitive explanation for the question of why given information should precede new information in linear sequence. At the beginning of an utterance the hearer has least information about what is going to be said. Since our cognitive resources are informationally restricted, her argument goes, it is therefore cognitively more economical to place first what is informationally poorer, i.e. given information, in an utterance thereby saving processing costs. Note that this is now a hearer-based account. Also Taylor's (1996) reference-point analysis as briefly discussed in §4.4.3 seems to argue from the cognitive point of view of the hearer: the topicworthiness of the possessor (subsuming animacy and topicality as defined in the present study) facilitates its accessibility for the hearer thereby allowing for a better and quicker identification of the possessum noun. All this shows that both perspectives, that of the speaker and that of the hearer are not necessarily incompatible in this respect. While the speaker undoubtedly has the advantage of already knowing what he is going to say, it is certainly also advantageous for him to place already given and activated information first, since this will give him time to plan the rest of his utterance. It is a common experience that we as speakers often start sentences without having them fully planned ahead.[104]

Going one step further, we might now ask in which respect such a processing principle should be regarded as non-arbitrary, i.e. iconic coding and as reflecting natural principles? I will take it to be iconic in that linguistic serialization reflects the order of processing which in turn reflects the order of conceptualization and perception. Since this reflects a procedure which is easier for the human processing system, this can also be regarded as a natural serialization principle.

order of
conceptualization & ➔   order of
language processing ➔   linguistic serialization
perception

Similarly, in his reference point analysis Taylor (1996: 18) – although not using language processing as an intermediate step – argues that the serialization of the possessor in the *s*-genitive reflects the conceptualization (for the hearer) and can therefore be regarded as iconic:

> Consider, for example, a seemingly trivial aspect of the English construction – the fact that the possessor is named before the possessee. Constituent order *iconically diagrams* the mental route that the conceptualizer needs to follow in order to identify the possessee.

On similar grounds, Cooper and Klouda (1995) treat the Me-First principle in freezes as a case of syntactic iconicity, since what is psychologically easier to process tends to be placed early in utterances.[105] Finally, Dotter (1990: §4.4.2) explicitly allows for an extension of constructional iconicity as to encompass not only a direct resemblance of conceptual structure and linguistic structure but also the way the language user perceives, processes and utilizes concepts as to achieve the most efficient information flow.

Note, finally, that while there is good reason to assume that the preference for animates to precede inanimates in linear order is a cognitive universal, found in most languages of the world – provided they allow for such flexibility – and having neurological correlates in the brain, the "given > new" ordering is most likely not a cognitive primitive. As shown by Hawkins (1994: §4.4), the relative order of given and new information is sensitive to the typological branching direction of a language; while "given > new" ordering seems to be true for right-branching languages such as English, the order "new > given" is more frequent in left-branching languages, such as Japanese. Yet, for the present study, which investigates a word order choice in English, it is sufficient to notice that "given > new" is a processing principle operating in the English language.

So far we have seen that there is multiple evidence that animate and topical elements tend to come first in linear order, at least in English, and that this serialization principle is cognitively motivated in the sense that (i) what first comes to the mind tends to be processed and then linearized first (from the point of view of the speaker) or (ii) the more retrievable the first element is (for the hearer), the more easily can he identify what follows. Given the complementary word order of possessor and possessum in the *s*-genitive and the *of*-genitive this serialization principle now makes the following predictions for the choice of the *s*-genitive:

[+animate]	highly	early	early	
[+ topical] ➜	accessible ➜	processing ➜	linearization ➜	*s*-genitive
possessor				

Due to the high conceptual accessibility of an animate possessor and a topical possessor, such possessors should be processed early and accordingly occur first in linear order. Yet, only in the *s*-genitive does a [+animate] and/or [+topical] possessor have the chance to be realized first, in the *of*-genitive the possessor follows the possessum. We can therefore predict that the *s*-genitive is more likely to occur with animate possessors and/or with topical possessors.

6.2.2   *The principle of conceptual distance (factor: possessive relation)*
6.2.2.1   Operational definition

The discussion in §4.3.1 above has shown that an operational definition of possessive relations for empirical analysis is far from being straightforward and easy. It is beyond the aim and scope of the present study to introduce a new and improved taxonomy of possessive relations. Rather, I will try to provide a working definition which combines the – to my mind – most useful aspects of the prototype and the typologically-oriented possession accounts, both from a semantic and a heuristic point of view.

Although possession as such is certainly rather a gradient – and not categorical – concept, for the sake of empirical analysis a binary categorization is adopted in this study in which the most prototypical instances of possession are contrasted with less prototypical cases of possession. I will distinguish between [+prototypical] possessive relations versus [-prototypical] possessive relations as illustrated in table 23:

Table 23. Type of possessive relation: operational definition

type of possessive relation: operational definition			
[+animate] [+human]		**[-animate]**	
[+prototypical]	**[-prototypical]**	**[+prototypical]**	**[-prototypical]**
body parts: *hand, eyes*,...	states: *exhaustion, pride, joy*,...	part/whole: *frame/chair; bonnet/car; door/building*	non-part/whole: *contents/bag; condition/car*
kin terms: *father, brother*,...	abstract possession: *future, career*,...		
permanent/legal ownership: *car, house*,...			

Kin terms and body parts are the most uncontroversial representatives of inalienable possession cross-linguistically; they range on top of most possession scales (e.g. Seiler 1983: 13; Nichols 1986: 77; Nichols 1988: 572-573; cf. also Chappell and McGregor 1996 for discussion). There are, however, other accounts of possession which regard (permanent/legal) ownership as the most prototypical instance of possession (cf. Taylor 1989, 1995; or Heine 1997), and, as shown by Taylor (1989, 1995), this is certainly one central meaning of the English *s*-genitive. I will therefore consider kin terms (*father, brother*), body parts (*hand, eyes*) and (permanent/legal) ownership (*house, car*) as prototypical instances of human possession; these relations have also recently been identified as the most prototypical cases of possessive NPs in the typological work on possession by Koptjevskaja-Tamm (2001, 2002, forthcoming).

Unlike inalienable possession, alienability is an open-ended category (cf. e.g. Heine 1997: 172; Nichols 1988: 562); therefore, [-prototypical] possessive relations are best captured in terms of what is not prototypical, examples are abstract ownership (*future*) or states (*exhaustion, pride*) for animate possessors. For inanimate possessors the situation is considerably complicated by the fact that the prototypical possessor is *by definition* human (cf. e.g. Seiler 1983: 4; Taylor 1989: 679). In this study, I will regard (permanent) part/whole relations as [+prototypical] instances of inanimate possession because parts are inherently inseparable from their wholes (as e.g. *frame* from *chair* or *bonnet* from *car*), while non-part/whole relations, such as *condition/car* or *contents/bag* are treated as the respective [-prototypical] counterpart.[106]

Although the distinction between alienable and inalienable possession so far has not been applied to account for the distribution of nominal possessives in English, it seems to be relevant in other areas of English grammar as well. Doyle and Szymanek (1997: 1379-1384), for example, have shown that inalienability plays a role in English word formation. Possessional adjectives (*-ed* adjectives) only allow an inalienably possessed head noun as a base (*red-haired, three-legged, blue-eyed;* but: **two-carred [family], *big-Alsatianed [woman]*, cf. also Katamba 1993: 78); privative adjectives (*fingerless, headless*), and privative verbs (*core [an apple], bark [a tree]*) also seem to be sensitive to the notion of inalienability. This may independently motivate the classification of part/whole versus non-part/whole relations for the distinction between [+prototypical] and [-prototypical] inanimate possession: note that there may be a *four-wheeled car* but not a **bad-conditioned car.*

I will not deal with deverbal possessum nominals in this study (i.e. subjective [*John's translation*] and objective genitives [*John's murder*]), since they seem to be subject to yet further restrictions. In English as a Subject-Verb-Object language *s*-genitives are much more likely to occur in subjective than in objective relations, since the former reflect Subject-Verb word order on the nominal level, while the latter, resembling Object-Verb, goes against the typologically preferred linearization pattern (see also Fischer 1992: 226-227; Rosenbach, Stein, and Vezzosi 2000: 192). It is also not clear how such valency relations should be treated and integrated in frameworks of possession.[107]

Note finally, that legal ownership and abstract possession imply most difference in the relative animacy of possessor and possessum, always involving a human possessor and an inanimate possessum, resulting in an "animate > inanimate" ordering in the *s*-genitive. Comparing animate/human possession with inanimate possession, as outlined in table 23, may therefore confound the factor possessive relation and animacy. Ownership per definition contains an animate/inanimate difference. Therefore, in the present study predominantly kin terms and body parts are used in the [+prototypical] animate/human category.[108] In kin terms the effect of the relative animacy is completely neutralized (= animate/animate, e.g. *the boy's father*), and in body parts it is weakened (e.g. *the boy's eyes*), since body parts are generally viewed as intermediate between animate and inanimate (cf. e.g. Hawkins 1981; see also §4.1.2 above); for inanimate possessors there is generally no difference in the relative animacy of possessor and possessum (i.e. inanimate/inanimate, e.g. *the building's door, the car's condition*). It is therefore only in the [-prototypical] animate/human category (e.g. *the mother's future*) that a difference in the relative animacy of possessor and possessum remains and cannot be neutralized.

6.2.2.2 Predictions

In the typological work on possession it has been observed that languages often show an opposition between alienable and inalienable possession in that two different grammatical constructions are used to express these two types of possession, a phenomenon also found under the name "alienability splits" (cf. Koptjevskaja-Tamm 2001). Where these alienability splits occur, they fairly systematically have the following structural properties:

(1) Alienable possession receives more grammatical marking than inalienable possession (cf. e.g. Heine 1997: 172).
(2) Inalienably possessed nouns are structurally more bonded with their possessor than alienably possessed nouns (cf. Nichols 1992: 117; Heine 1997: 172)

A functional explanation of these systematic structural correlates of the semantic alienable-inalienable distinction has been proposed by Haiman (1985a) on the basis of the iconic principle of conceptual distance. This principle predicts that "the greater the formal distance beween X and Y, the greater the conceptual distance between the notions they represent" (Haiman 1985a: 106). Applied to possessive constructions this principle predicts that inalienable possessive relations, in which possessor and possessum form a very tight, if not inseparable, relation should be encoded by more implicit linguistic means:

> It seems intuitively clear that conceptual distance is greater when possession is *alienable* than when it is not: possessor and possessum are not indissolubly bound together where possession is alienable, either in fact or in the perception of speakers. ... The motivation hypothesis now predicts that where the distinction between alienable and inalienable possession is grammaticalized, inalienable possession will be indicated by the structure in which the linguistic distance between possessor and possessum is *less*; alienable possession will be indicated by the structure in which the linguistic distance between possessor and possessum is *more*.
>
> (Haiman 1985a: 130)

Although English is not a language in which the distinction between alienable and inalienable possession has been grammaticalized, the principle of conceptual distance may nonetheless well reflect preferences in the choice of the *s*-genitive and the *of*-genitive, i.e. may predict distributional frequency patterns. The distinction between [+prototypical] and [-prototypical] possessive relations established in the previous section reflects the conceptual distance between possessor and possessum: [+prototypical] possessive relations are close relations between possessor and possessum. In contrast, [-prototypical] possessive relations rather express loose possession. Structurally, the *s*-genitive shows (a) less formal substance in its relational marker than the *of*-genitive ('*s* versus *of*), and, (b) as a clitic it is structurally more bonded with the possessor than the preposition *of*. The degree of structural bonding is also apparent when applying some structural tests. In the *of*-genitive the relational marker can be stranded but not in the *s*-genitive, see example (52) as quoted from Plank (1992a: 34):

(52)   *They stole* (a) *the portrait of Dr Johnson* / (b) *Dr Johnson's portrait.*
        Dr Johnson was the only lexicographer they stole (a) *the portrait of _* /
        (b) **_ 's portrait.*

Moreover, only in the *s*-genitive can the possessum be omitted, while such elliptic constructions are ungrammatical with the *of*-genitive, indicating that the relation is more implicit in the *s*-genitive than it is in the *of*-genitive (53):[109]

(53) a.   *The girl's bicycle was green, while the boy's _ was blue.*
     b.   *The bicycle of the girl was green, while *_ of the boy was blue.*

Having established the *s*-genitive as the more implicit genitive construction which has more structural substance and is more bonded than the *of*-genitive we can now derive the following predictions for the choice between the *s*-genitive and the *of*-genitive (cf. figure 10 below).

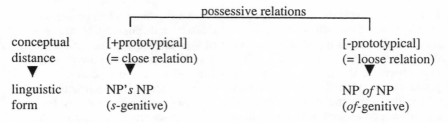

Figure 10.   Possessive relations: predictions for choice of genitive construction

The *s*-genitive should be more likely to occur with [+prototypical] possessive relations while the *of*-genitive should occur more often in [-prototypical] possessive relations. Note that in the category of [+prototypical] possessive relations for human possessors only kin terms and body parts map to the inalienable category in the strict sense, while legal ownership is generally not considered inalienable. As pointed out above, however, in the present study most [+prototypical] possessive relations for human possessors are kin terms or body parts; for the only two remaining items expressing ownership in the questionnaire study it may be argued that legal ownership is more permanent and inherent than temporary and/or associative ownership; e.g. *John's car* (= 'the car belongs to John') is more closely connected to John than *John's car* (= 'the car John always speaks of and wants to buy').

Having established the predictions arising from the principle of conceptual distance for the distinction between [+prototypical] and [-prototypical] possessive relations we can turn now to two further structural correlates with the alienability splits, which have been reported from the typological work on possession apart from the criteria of formal marking and structural bondedness:

(1)   Inalienable constructions are typically head-marked, i.e. the head is structurally marked for possession, while alienable constructions correlate with dependent-marking, i.e. the marking of the possessor (cf. Nichols 1992: 117; Heine 1997: 172-173; Koptjevskaja-Tamm 2001: chapter 4).[110]

Having predicted the *s*-genitive to encode [+prototypical] possessive relations, it should follow that the *s*-genitive is also a head-marking construction. This typological prediction is, however, difficult to evaluate for the English possessive constructions, since it crucially hinges on the question of what is the head in a possessive construction. While the *of*-genitive is quite uncontroversially a case of dependent-marking (the relational marker *of* belongs to the possessor), the *s*-genitive could be both interpreted as dependent-marking (with POSS *'s* belonging to the possessor which in turn functions as a determiner to the possessum as the head) in traditional analyses; on the basis of some recent formal DP-analyses, which view POSS *'s* as the head of the DP (see also §2.3.2 above), the *s*-genitive could equally well be regarded as a head-marking construction.[111]

(2)   The markers of inalienable possession are more archaic, i.e. they are "etymologically older" than those used for alienable possession (cf.

Heine 1997: 172; see also Nichols 1988: 562; Koptjevskaja-Tamm 2001: chapter 4).

Again, this typological prediction cannot easily be transferred to the English genitive constructions. The *s*-genitive is certainly the more archaic, older construction if we see it as a continuation of the Old English inflectional genitive case ending. As will be shown in §7.5, however, POSS '*s* has undergone a considerable change from a case-marker into a clitic and a determiner in the course of late Middle and early Modern English. If we only consider the phonological form of POSS '*s*, then the *s*-genitive may be regarded as the older construction, because the *-(e)s* suffix was already a genitive-ending in the Old English genitive paradigm, albeit not the exclusive one. *Of* as a possessive relational marker, however, did not emerge until the end of the Old English period and only became productive during the Middle English period (see also §7.1 and §7.2). If, however, the grammatical status of POSS '*s* is taken into account, the *s*-genitive as a clitic must be seen as an early Modern English innovation and the more recent construction; it therefore depends on the perspective and approach taken, whether it is viewed as a genuine innovation or rather as a reanalysis of older forms. Since it is beyond the aim and scope of the present study to settle theoretical controversies about the headedness and the diachronic reasons for the change from an inflection to a clitic, I will restrict the predictions for the type of possessive relation to the predictions made by the principle of conceptual distance as outlined above.

6.2.3 Summary

I have argued that the factors animacy, topicality, and possessive relation can be linked to certain iconic/natural principles. In particular, I have shown that there is ample cognitive, cross-linguistic and psycholinguistic evidence for animate and topical concepts to occur first in linear order in English. Accordingly, we may also predict that animate and topical possessors will occur first in linear order when choosing between the two English genitives, resulting in the *s*-genitive rather than the *of*-genitive. Moreover, I have argued that the choice between the *s*-genitive and the *of*-genitive may be determined by the degree of prototypicality of the possessive relation in that the closer, i.e. [+prototypical] relations get encoded by the structurally more bonded and less implicit construction, i.e. the *s*-genitive. The following table 24 summarizes and illustrates the predictions for the choice of genitive construction according to the factors animacy, topicality, and possessive relation:

Table 24. Predictions for the choice of genitive construction according to the factors animacy, topicality, and possessive relation

morpho-syntax	factor(s)	iconic principle	predictions	
			s-genitive	*of*-genitive
word order	animacy & topicality of possessor	linear sequencing: order of conceptualization → order of processing → linguistic serialization	[+animate] possessor [+topical] possessor	[-animate] possessor [-topical] possessor
relational marker	possessive relation	conceptual distance	[+prototypical] possessive relation	[-prototypical] possessive relation

6.3 Research questions for the present study

Having established the predictions for the factors animacy, topicality, and possessive relation, let me now outline the research questions, which I will address in the empirical part of this study.

(1) What is the impact of the factors animacy, topicality, and possessive relation – studied in controlled choice contexts and in isolation – on the relative frequency of the *s*-genitive and the *of*-genitive? Will the predictions made by iconic principles in §6.2 be confirmed or not, i.e. will the *s*-genitive occur more often with a [+animate] possessor, a [+topical] possessor, and in a [+ prototypical] possessive relation?

(2) I will also try to establish what is the relative importance of these factors when choosing between the two genitive constructions. Which factors will turn out to be more important than others?

(3) How, if at all, do the results for (1) and (2) differ according to
 (a) (short-term) diachrony; i.e. is there any evidence for change-in-progress?
 (b) Standard variety, i.e. in which respect does British English differ from American English?

In particular, special attention will be paid to the question whether an increasing use of the *s*-genitive with inanimate possessors, reported by previous studies (cf. e.g. Jahr Sorheim 1980; Raab-Fischer 1995) can be confirmed or not. Note that in contrast to these previous studies, the present study

- focuses solely on concrete nouns, which have been shown to be the most unproductive – and *not*-increasing – inanimate noun class,
- investigates the productivity of the *s*-genitive in individual language users and not in the genre with which the increasing use of the *s*-genitive with inanimate possessors is generally associated, i.e. journalistic language.
- allows for a direct comparison between American English and British English in that the same procedure and the same items are used for all subjects, thereby making it possible to test whether American English is more progressive in the use of the English *s*-genitive as claimed by Jahr Sorheim (1980) and Hundt (1997, 1998).

6.4   Experimental study
6.4.1   Experimental design
6.4.1.1 Subjects

My subjects are 56 native speakers of British English and 48 native speakers of American English, aged between 18 and 81, both female and male, who were all willing to participate as volunteers in the present study. Only subjects with a relatively advanced education have been selected; in fact, most of the subjects come from a university background; otherwise for the British subjects the minimum requirement was grammar school, for the American subjects a high-school degree at least. Controlling the educational background of the subjects also helped to minimize the influence of possible dialectal and/or regional influences. Higher education, at least in England, often goes hand in hand with an approximation of what might be called "Standard English". Furthermore, it was made sure that all subjects are monolingual native speakers,[112] since it is not at all clear how the influence of a second first language might affect the use of possessive constructions in English. Excluded from the study are also those subjects who left out or changed too many items when filling in the questionnaire.[113] Altogether, 122 subjects originally participated in the study; because of the criteria mentioned above 18 subjects had to be excluded, resulting in 104 subjects entering the analysis. The subjects are not controlled for sex; both female and male subjects are included. An overview of the subjects participating in the present study, specified for the respective Standard variety, sex and average age, is given in table 25 below.

Table 25. Subjects: Standard variety, sex, and age.

sex	British subjects			American subjects		
	n	age	∅ age	n	age	∅ age
male	18	18-81	34.7	27	20-74	40.3
female	38	18-66	33.4	21	24-71	39.9
total	56	18-81	33.8	48	20-74	40.1

6.4.1.2 Procedure: questionnaire elicitation

Experimental studies investigating actual language use differ in referring either to language comprehension (= parsing) or to language production. In parsing experiments language serves as the point of departure in the experimental design; it is language that is – and easily can be – manipulated according to the variable to be tested (= independent variable), and what is measured is the subjects' response to it, which is, in most cases, the time the subject needs to read, parse or make a decision (= dependent variable). Production experiments are a completely different matter. Here it is language itself that is measured (= dependent variable), and the independent variable which needs to be tested is the conceptual structure. Conceptual structure is, however, not well understood at present (see also §5.2.1.1.3 above) and not at all 'visible' and can therefore also not easily be manipulated. This makes production experiments an extremely difficult enterprise. It is probably for this methodological reason that production experiments are considerably underrepresented in experimental studies (cf. Butterworth 1980: 2; Schwarz 1992: 166; Pechmann 1994: 10-11; Bock 1996).

The present study primarily intends to model language production and faces this problem in a twofold sense: Even given that we can design and fix conceptual settings that exactly test the three conceptual factors under investigation, i.e. animacy, topicality, and possessive relation, and only these, the subjects still have various possibilities to express this linguistically. Apart from the nominal possessive constructions investigated in the present study, there is a whole range of predicative structures that can all express possessive relations (cf. also §3.3.2). In a picture elicitation task, for example, a picture depicting a woman holding a book would very likely lead to responses such as *The woman has a book*, *The woman is holding a book*, *The book belongs to the woman* or *There is a woman and she is holding a book*. A nominal possessive could be enforced by asking *whose book* it is, but this might well bias the answer to the *s*-genitive. As the study by Weiner and Labov (1983) has shown the syntactic frame of the question does influence that of the answer. To avoid these methodological pitfalls I therefore decided to use a questionnaire for the elicitation of nominal possessive constructions, having the advantage that the subjects are forced to use the *s*-genitive or the *of*-genitive but no other possessive construction. A questionnaire is also an excellent tool for providing a short, well-controlled context for each item, which is particularly important for varying the factor topicality in terms of first- and second mention of the possessor. And although a questionnaire elicitation is not a genuine production task where the subjects can freely choose to use a construction it is generally assumed in the psycholinguistic literature to model production rather than comprehension.[114]

The questionnaire used contains little text passages providing contexts for nominal genitive constructions. To use language material as authentic as possible, most text passages are taken from novels, sometimes slightly adapted to match the control requirements.[115] The choice of the novels – and their authors – was deliberate. Particularly Elizabeth George from whose novels most of the text passages are taken, proves to be an unusually innovative and 'playful' author when using the *s*-genitive. Her novels are therefore an ideal base for the compilation of the questionnaire, since her use of the *s*-genitive comes probably very close to what can be considered the ultimate potential of the construction. The following examples (54) – (58) from the questionnaire illustrate what the task and the contexts looked like (and see also examples [49] – [51] for [-topical] possessors in §6.2.1.1.2 above).

(54)   *My mother was fully confident of how her meeting with Jean Cooper would play itself out. She had had many such meetings with unwed mothers-to-be before, and her track record of orchestrating those encounters to a successful conclusion was a stellar one. Most of the girls who had fallen within [the purview of my mother/ my mother's purview] had seen reason in the end. My mother was expert in the art of gentle persuasion, her focus always fixed on [the mother's future/the future of the mother].*   (based on: Elizabeth George, *Playing for the Ashes*, 137)

(55)   *He passed through the entrance where a sign identified the park as Island Gardens. At its far west end, a circular brick building stood, domed in glass and mounted by a white and green lantern cupola. A movement of white shimmered against the red bricks, and Lynley saw Jimmy Cooper trying [the door of the building/ the building's door].*
        (Elizabeth George, *Playing for the Ashes*, 585)

(56)   *The boy must have known his father intended to push forward with the divorce. And he spoke to his father that same afternoon. He may have known where Fleming was headed. The way I see it, Fleming had hurt* **[the mother of the boy/ the boy's mother]**, *he'd hurt the boy himself, he'd hurt* **[the boy's brother/the brother of the boy]**, *he'd made promises he wasn't willing to keep-.'*
(based on: Elizabeth George, *Playing for the Ashes*, 381)

(57)   *Lynley felt his lips twitch in a smile that he did the best to control. The masseur was more efficient than a polygraph. Abruptly, Gabriella shook* **[the masseur's hands/the hands of the masseur]** *from her body. ...'I think I've had enough for today'.*
(based on: Elizabeth George, *Playing for the Ashes*, 364)

(58)   *A helicopter waited on the nearby grass like a sleeping insect, its pilot standing outside with Marino. Whit, a perfect specimen of male fitness in a black flight suit, opened* **[the helicopter's doors/the doors of the helicopter]** *to help us board.*
(based on: Patricia Cornwell, *The Body Farm*, 52)

The subjects had to choose the *s*-genitive or the *of*-genitive as spontaneously as possible in the given contexts (= "forced-choice selection" according to Greenbaum and Quirk's [1970: 3] classification of experimental tests). The subjects were explicitly asked to mark that option which sounded better to them and not to take into account what grammar books would tell them. To avoid the subjects would be to be tempted into giving stereotype responses, the order in which the items were presented was randomized so that the same conditions were not tested repeatedly in a row. Moreover, the order of presentation of the two genitive constructions between which a choice had to be made, was randomized, so that the same genitive construction did not always occur as the first choice in brackets. Although it was obvious that the use of the *s*-genitive versus the *of*-genitive was being investigated, the subjects generally commented that they did not have a clue which factors exactly were tested. Therefore, the subjects' responses can be taken to approximate their unconscious knowledge of the language and habitual usage.

6.4.1.3 Conditions and items

The factors animacy, topicality, and possessive relation have already been introduced, discussed and operationalized as used in the present questionnaire study in §6.2. Note that apart from focusing on potential choice contexts as outlined in table 13 (see §3.3.2.3 above), the items used in the questionnaire were further controlled for the following factors, which have been discussed in §3.3.2.2 as non-comparable contexts, in the following way:

(1)   The possessor noun never ends in /s/, /z/ or /θ/ as it is well-known that POSS *'s* is often avoided in this phonetic environment, either resulting in the alternative *of*-genitive or in the zero-genitive (*Jones' house*) (cf. e.g. Altenberg 1982: §2.5; Quirk et al. 1985: §5.114).

(2)   The possessor is always a singular noun, never a plural noun (neither regular nor irregular plural). As discussed in §3.3.2.2.4, it is possible that the concept of plurality as such – or as a property contributing to the individuation of a possessor (cf. §4.4.4) – rather than, or additionally to, its phonological realization (ending in *-s*) constrains the use of the *s*-genitive.

(3)   Contexts for consecutive *of*-genitives have been excluded from the questionnaire. Such constructions, where one *of*-genitive is embedded in another one, are generally avoided for stylistic reasons (cf. e.g. Zachrisson 1920: 46) and would probably favor the *s*-genitive (see also §3.3.2.2.4). There is also ample evidence for an effect of syntactic repetition from experimental research in that subjects tend to use the same syntactic frame currently open for a following construction (cf. e.g. Weiner and Labov 1983; Bock 1986; Bock and Loebell 1990). For non-embedded genitive constructions, however, this factor could not be controlled, since it is the very nature of this questionnaire to provide consecutively genitive constructions. It may have helped though that the presentation of the genitive choice was randomized, so that the *s*-genitive and the *of*-genitive are equally affected by this.

(4)   As Altenberg (1982: §3.1) and Jucker (1993) have shown, right-branching expansions of the possessor or the possessum may affect the choice of genitive construction considerably. Therefore, no items have been included in which the possessor or the possessum is further postmodified.

(5)   Left-branching modification of the possessum and possessor (i.e. premodification) correlates with the factor of syntactic weight, which is controlled inasmuch as only one further syntactic modifier to the possessor or the possessum is admitted, which is no longer than one word. As shown by Biber et al. (1999: 304-305) there is still considerable variation between the *s*-genitive and the *of*-genitive with a two-word possessor (cf. also §3.3.2.2.4).

(6)   Finally, the factor style has been controlled by keeping it constant throughout the questionnaire. The text passages used all come from

novels, sharing the same stylistic level. No matter whether subjects might have been responding to the style of the text passages in which they had to choose the genitive construction, or whether they deliberately imposed a genitive construction to keep to the style given by the text passages (cf. discussion in §3.3.2.2.4), the style was always the same. Therefore, different frequencies of the *s*-genitive for single items or conditions cannot be attributed to different styles in which these items/conditions are embedded.

Controlling the items in this way, the present study attempts to investigate the choice between the *s*-genitive and the *of*-genitive in what can approximate real choice contexts where the influence of other factors is kept to a minimum. In the following I will now demonstrate how the factors animacy, topicality, and possessive relation, which have been shown to be highly interdependent in §4.4, are kept apart from each other in the present study (– apart from considering this interaction in the operational definitions of the factors given in §6.2 –) and how this allows for a ranking of these factors with respect to their relative impact on the choice between the *s*-genitive and the *of*-genitive.

The combination of the three nominal variables investigated, animacy, topicality, and the type of possessive relation leads to eight conditions with at least 10 items per condition, altogether the questionnaire contains 93 items.

Table 26. Experimental study: conditions and items (examples), *[± p] = [±prototypical] possessive relation

[+animate]				[-animate]			
[+topical]		[-topical]		[+topical]		[-topical]	
[+p]*	[-p]	[+p]	[-p]	[+p]	[-p]	[+p]	[-p]
the boy's eyes/ the eyes of the boy	*the mother's future/ the future of the mother*	*a girl's face/ the face of a girl*	*a woman's shadow/ the shadow of a woman*	*the chair's frame/ the frame of the chair*	*the bag's contents/ the contents of the bag*	*a lorry's wheels/ the wheels of a lorry*	*a car's fumes/ the fumes of a car*

Table 26 illustrates the single conditions, giving an example for each condition (for a list of all items used according to these eight conditions, see Appendix, §10.1). In the following, the predictions and the data analysis will always refer to these eight conditions (either singlely or subsumed under the three factors [±animate], [±topical], [±prototypical]) and the presentation will, accordingly, be rather technical in tone. For the sake of illustration the items in table 26 will be referred to as representative for the single conditions although of course always all items for each condition were tested in each analysis.

In a pilot study with two British and two American native speakers it was tested that the task would be well understood and that the items chosen are always a possible option in the given contexts, although – due to the different conditions – certainly with varying degrees of likelihood. The test subjects were asked to indicate those options in the questionnaire which would be virtually impossible for them. There was only one option in this pilot questionnaire which was regarded by one test subject as an absolute non-option and taken out for this reason from the set of test items. Also excluded from the main study were those items which sounded odd or caused difficulties for the test subjects.[116]

There were more items tested in this pilot study than those eventually included in the final questionnaire. Only three items were added to the questionnaire after the pilot study had been conducted; these three items did, however, not cause any problems to the subjects in the main study and proved to be potential choice-contexts. Also, some of the items tested were slightly modified as to better match the (control) conditions set for the study.

6.4.2   Refined predictions

In §6.2 above, the predictions for the factors animacy, topicality, and possessive relation were presented, according to which the *s*-genitive should occur more often with a [+animate] possessor, a [+topical] possessor, or in a [+prototypical] possessive relation. This general prediction needs now to be further specified. There are in principle two ways in which these factors can affect the relative frequency of the *s*-genitive. The first concerns the distribution of the *s*-genitive versus the *of*-genitive within the single contexts. According to prediction (I) the *s*-genitive should be more frequent than the *of*-genitive with a [+animate] possessor, a [+topical] possessor, or in a [+prototypical] possessive relation (cf. table 27 below).

Table 27. Prediction (I): distribution of *s*-genitive and *of*-genitive within the single contexts

prediction (I)	*s*-genitive versus *of*-genitive	
[+animate]	*s*-genitive	> *of*-genitive
[+topical]	*s*-genitive	> *of*-genitive
[+prototypical] possessive relation	*s*-genitive	> *of*-genitive

A somewhat weaker implication of the general prediction in §6.2 concerns the relative distribution of the *s*-genitive between the positive and negative values of the single factors:

Table 28. Prediction (II): distribution of the *s*-genitive between positive and negative contexts within one factor

prediction (II): relative distribution of *s*-genitive	
more *s*-genitives	**less *s*-genitives**
[+animate]	[-animate]
[+ topical]	[-topical]
[+prototypical] possessive relation	[-prototypical] possessive relation

According to prediction (II) the *s*-genitive should be more frequent with [+animate] than with [-animate] possessors, with [+topical] than with [-topical] possessors and with [+prototypical] rather than with [-prototypical] possessive relations.

Note that in both types of prediction it is always the frequency of the *s*-genitive as opposed to that of the *of*-genitive that is taken into account, i.e. its relative frequency, and never the frequency of the *s*-genitive alone. Even for prediction (II), which is explicated here for the relative distribution of the *s*-genitive solely, the corresponding predictions necessarily follow for the *of*-genitive in a kind of mirror image. Taking the relative frequency of the *s*-genitive into account, to the same extent that the *s*-genitive is getting less frequent the *of*-genitive will become more frequent.

Testing all eight logically possible combinations of the three factors as indicated in table 26 makes it furthermore possible to keep their effects apart in the empirical analysis and to look more closely at how these factors interact. Particularly important are those contexts in which the factors do not go together. That is, there are cases in which there are [+animate] but [-topical] possessors (*a girl's face*); [+animate] possessors in a

[-prototypical] relation (*the mother's future*) or [-animate] [+prototypical] cases (*the chair's frame*), just to give a few examples.

In this way we can then also make predictions as to the relative importance of these three factors. If, for example, animacy is a more important factor than topicality for the choice of the *s*-genitive, then a [+animate] [-topical] possessor (*a girl's face*) should take more *s*-genitives than a [-animate] [+topical] possessor (*the chair's frame*), when balanced for [+prototypical] possessive relation. Likewise, if topicality is more important than possessive relation in the selection of the *s*-genitive, then we would expect to find more *s*-genitives with [+topical] possessors in a [-prototypical] possessive relations (e.g. *the mother's future*) than with [-topical] possessors in a [+prototypical] possessive relation (e.g. *a girl's face*). What is crucial in this argumentation is that testing all possible combinations of [±animate], [±topical] and [±prototypical] possessive relation enables us to separate the effects of the single factors, look at them in isolation and, subsequently, evaluate their relative strength in the assignment of the *s*-genitive as opposed to the *of*-genitive. Note that the right- and leftmost conditions in table 26 are, strictly speaking, irrelevant for evaluating the relative importance of the three factors; no matter what the ranking is, a [+animate] [+topical] possessor in a [+prototypical] possessive relation should present the optimal context for the occurrence of the *s*-genitive, while a [-animate] [-topical] possessor in a [-prototypical] possessive relation should be the least likely context for the realization of the *s*-genitive. It is only those contexts, where the factors do not map one-to-one on each other which are crucial for ranking the three factors.[117]

Moreover, the predictions pertaining to the interaction and the relative importance of the three factors as entailed in the eight conditions in table 26 can be further subdivided into two sub-predictions in the same way as the predictions for the single factors above. First, the *s*-genitive can be predicted to be more frequent than the *of*-genitive in the single conditions (= prediction I); this type of calculus indicates under which conditions (i.e. in which combinations of the three factors) the *s*-genitive is (still) favorable and in which it is not. In this case it is, however, not exactly clear from which condition onwards the *of*-genitive should become more frequent, i.e. how many negative values are needed for the *s*-genitive to become disfavored. Second, depending on the relative importance of the factors animacy, topicality, and possessive relation, the *s*-genitive should become less frequent in the single conditions (= prediction II); it should be most frequent with a [+animate] [+topical] possessor in a [+prototypical] possessive relation and least frequent with an [-animate]

[-topical] possessor in a [-prototypical] possessive relation. It remains to be seen, however, how the *s*-genitive is distributed over those conditions in which the positive or negative values of the factors do not cluster (cf. table 30). The various predictions are summarized in tables 29 and 30.

Table 29. Predictions for single factors (not considering their interaction), ([+proto] = [+prototypical])

	animacy		topicality		possessive relation	
	[+animate]	**[-animate]**	**[+topical]**	**[-topical]**	**[+proto]**	**[-proto]**
(I)	*s*-genitive > *of*-genitive	*of*-genitive > *s*-genitive	*s*-genitive > *of*-genitive	*of*-genitive > *s*-genitive	*s*-genitive > *of*-genitive	*of*-genitive > *s*-genitive
(II)	more *s*-genitives	less *s*-genitives	more *s*-genitives	less *s*-genitives	more *s*-genitives	less *s*-genitives

Table 30. Predictions for the interaction of factors

[+animate]				[-animate]			
[+topical]		**[-topical]**		**[+topical]**		**[-topical]**	
[+p]*	**[-p]**	**[+p]**	**[-p]**	**[+p]**	**[-p]**	**[+p]**	**[-p]**
the boy's eyes/ the eyes of the boy	*the mother's future/ the future of the mother*	*a girl's face/ the face of a girl*	*a woman's shadow/ the shadow of a woman*	*the chair's frame/ the frame of the chair*	*the bag's contents / the contents of the bag*	*a lorry's wheels/ the wheels of a lorry*	*a car's fumes/ the fumes of a car*

prediction I (frequency of *'s* versus *of*):

 ????

s-genitive > *of*-genitive ⟶ *of*-genitive > *s*-genitive

prediction II (relative distribution of *s*-genitive):

 ????

more *s*-genitives ⟶ less *s*-genitives

6.4.3 Analysis and results
6.4.3.1 Synchronic state of affairs

For each subject it was recorded in a database whether the *s*-genitive or the *of*-genitive was chosen for each single item. Since each item pertained to one of the eight conditions given in table 26, for each item the choice between the *s*-genitive and the *of*-genitive was recorded, specified for each of these eight conditions. After that, the frequencies of the *s*-genitive and the *of*-genitive for the single conditions were summarized for each subject, resulting in another database which contained the frequency of the *s*-genitive and the *of*-genitive for each subject according to each of the eight conditions. Based on this data, in the following the predictions in §6.4.2 will be tested separately for the British and the American subjects. First I will look at how the two genitive constructions are distributed over the single factors, distinguishing between [±animate], [±topical] and [±prototypical] possession, i.e. not yet considering their interaction. This analysis will show whether the general predictions for the three factors hold true, i.e. whether the *s*-genitive is indeed more frequent with a [+animate] possessor, a [+topical] possessor, and in a [+prototypical] possessive relation. In a second step, the interaction – and ranking – of the factors will be investigated, presenting the relative frequencies of the *s*-genitive versus the *of*-genitive for each of the eight conditions.

6.4.3.1.1 Animacy, topicality, and possessive relation
British English

Figure 11 below shows the relative frequency of the *s*-genitive and the *of*-genitive according to the three factors animacy [±animate], topicality [±topical] and possessive relation [±prototypical] for the British subjects. Figure 11 shows that the *s*-genitive is more frequent than the *of*-genitive in the [+animate] and [+ topical] and in [+prototypical] possessive relations, while the *of*-genitive is more frequent than the *s*-genitive in the [-animate], [-topical] and [-prototypical] possessive relations. A *goodness-of-fit* test was conducted on the data to test whether the difference found in the frequency of the *s*-genitive versus the *of*-genitive in each context is random or significantly non-random.[118] Table 31 below shows that the difference in the frequency of the *s*-genitive versus the *of*-genitive is always highly statistically significant, except for the [+prototypical] conditions, where the distribution seems to be random. Note that in the following I will present the statistical analyses to illustrate and make explicit the general procedure, i.e. what precisely was compared in which way. Once each type of analysis has been introduced, the statistical results will only be referred to but not further explicated in detail here.

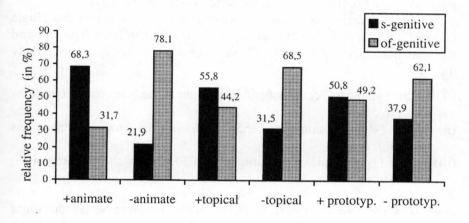

Figure 11. British subjects (n=56): relative frequency of the *s*-genitive versus the *of*-genitive for the factors animacy [± animate], topicality [± topical], and possessive relation [± prototypical], cf. also table 1, Appendix §10.1.

Table 31. British subjects: prediction (I) – statistical analysis (*Yates corrected, *df* 1)

predictions (I): frequency of '*s* versus *of*	goodness of fit test*	result
[+animate]	chi-square = 341.494, *p*<0.001	*s*-genitive (68.3%) > *of*-genitive (31.7%)
[+topical]	chi-square = 38.086, *p*<0.001	*s*-genitive (55.8%) > *of*-genitive (44.2%)
[+prototypical] possessive relation	chi-square=0.728, not significant	*s*-genitive (50.8%) ≈ *of*-genitive (49.2%)
[-animate]	chi-square = 823.786, *p*<0.001	*of*-genitive (78%) > *s*-genitive (21.9%)
[-topical]	chi-square = 318.357, *p*<0.001	*of*-genitive (68.5%) > *s*-genitive (31.5%)
[-prototypical] possessive relation	chi-square = 139.551, *p*<0.001	*of*-genitive (62.1%) > *s*-genitive (37.9%)

As predicted, the *s*-genitive is significantly more frequent than the *of*-genitive in the positive values of the three factors (not significantly though for [+prototypical] possessive relation), while the *of*-genitive is always significantly more frequent when the factor values are negative.

When considering how the *s*-genitive is distributed *within* the single factors,[119] the following picture emerges. As is apparent from figure 11 and the statistical analysis in table 32, the *s*-genitive is always significantly more frequent

(i)   in the [+animate] conditions (68.3%) than in the [-animate] conditions (21.9%),

(ii) in the [+topical] conditions (55.8%) than in the [-topical] conditions (31.5%), and

(iii) in the [+prototypical] conditions (50.8%) than in the [-prototypical] conditions (37.9%).

Table 32. Predictions II: relative frequency of the *s*-genitive within the single factors, statistical analysis (* Yates corrected, *df* 1)

prediction (II): relative distribution of *s*-genitive	chi-square*	*p*-level
[+animate] (68.3%) > [-animate] (21.9%)	1121.983	$p<0.001$
[+topical] (55.8%) > [-topical] (31.5%)	304.660	$p<0.001$
[+prototyp.] possessive relations (50.8%) > [-prototyp.] possessive relations (37.9%)	86.259	$p<0.001$

Moreover, figure 11 indicates that the *s*-genitive varies in frequency according to the three factors. The frequency of the *s*-genitive decreases along the following cline:

[+animate] > [+topical] > [+prototyp.] > [-prototyp.] > [-topical] > [-animate]
(68.3%)   (55.8%)   (50.8%)   (37.9%)   (31.5%)   (21.9%)

The differences are all highly statistically significant (chi-square, $p<0.001$).[120] Note that the positive and negative values of the three factors appear as a kind of mirror image. Animacy exerts the strongest influence on the choice of the *s*-genitive, since most *s*-genitives occur in the [+animate] condition, while least *s*-genitives can be found in the [-animate] condition. Likewise, the factor possessive relation has least impact on the choice between the two genitive constructions; [+prototypical] possessive relations are less likely to take the *s*-genitive than [+animate] or [+topical] possessors, while, on the other hand, [-prototypical] possessive relations also exert the least constraining force on the *s*-genitive. This suggests that animacy is the most important factor, followed by topicality, followed by possessive relations. The final evaluation of the relative importance of the three factors will, however, depend on the analysis of their interaction in §6.4.3.1.2; it remains to be seen whether this ordering holds true.

American English

The results for the American subjects, as illustrated in figure 12, are comparable to those obtained for the British subjects.

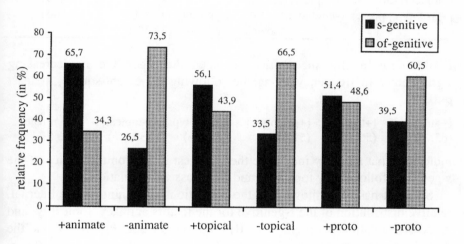

Figure 12.   American subjects (n = 48): relative frequency of the *s*-genitive versus the *of*-genitive for the factors animacy [± animate], topicality [± topical] and possessive relation [± prototypical], cf. also table 2, Appendix §10.1.

First, in the [+animate], [+topical] conditions, the *s*-genitive is significantly more frequent than the *of*-genitive, while the *of*-genitive is always more frequent than the *s*-genitive in the [-animate], [-topical] and [-prototypical] conditions (chi-square, $p<0.001$). Again it is only in the [+prototypical] conditions that the difference in the distribution of the *s*-genitive and the *of*-genitive does not reach any statistical significance.

Moreover, looking at the internal distribution of the *s*-genitive within the single factors, table 33 shows that the *s*-genitive is, as predicted (prediction II), always (highly) significantly more frequent in the [+animate], [+topical] and [+prototypical] conditions than in the corresponding [-animate], [-topical] and [-prototypical] conditions.

Table 33. Predictions II: relative frequency of the *s*-genitive within the single factors, statistical analysis

prediction (II): relative distribution of *s*-genitive within factors	chi-square, *p*-level
[+animate] (65.7%) > [-animate] (26.5%)	$p<0.001$
[+topical] (56.1%) > [-topical] (33.5%)	$p<0.001$
[+prototyp.] possessive relations (51.4%) >[-prototyp.] possessive relations (39.5%)	$p<0.001$

Furthermore, as for the British subjects, the *s*-genitive is decreasing significantly in frequency along the following cline (chi-square, at least $p<0.01$),

[+animate] >	[+topical] >	[+prototyp.] >	[-prototyp.] >	[-topical] >	[-animate]
(65.7%)	(56.1%)	(51.4%)	(39.5%)	(33.5%)	(26.5%)

indicating that animacy may have the strongest impact on the choice of the *s*-genitive, followed by topicality and then possessive relations.

So far it has been shown that the predictions pertaining to the internal, relative distribution of the *s*-genitive for the factors animacy, topicality, and possessive relations (= predictions II) hold true for both the British and the American subjects; the predictions concerning the distribution of the *s*-genitive versus the *of*-genitive (= predictions I) can be confirmed for the factors animacy and topicality but only partly for the factor possessive relations, i.e. for the [-prototypical] possessive relations; while in both British and American English the *s*-genitive is slightly more frequent with [+prototypical] possession, this difference is not statistically significant.

6.4.3.1.2   Interaction of factors

Let us now go a step further and look at how the *s*-genitive and the *of*-genitive are distributed in all possible combinations of the factors animacy, topicality, and possessive relation, thereby taking into account how these factors interact. This will, in turn, cast more light on the relative importance of the three factors and enable us to evaluate whether or not the relative importance of these factors as suggested by the results obtained for the single factors – for both the British and American subjects –, i.e. animacy > topicality > possessive relation, does indeed hold true.

British English

Figure 13 below gives the relative frequency of the *s*-genitive and the *of*-genitive according to the eight conditions as specified in table 26 for the British subjects, with the four [+animate] conditions preceding the four [-animate] conditions in linear arrangement.

Let us first consider in which of these eight conditions the *s*-genitive or the *of*-genitive is the more frequent option (= prediction I). First of all, a goodness-of-fit test conducted on the data shows that in any of the eight conditions the two genitive constructions are not randomly distributed but that the difference in the relative frequency of the *s*-genitive and the *of*-genitive is always statistically significant at the 0.001 level.

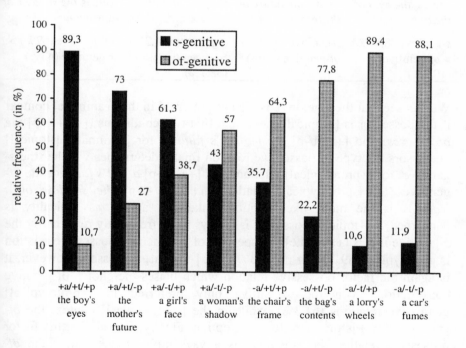

Figure 13. British subjects (n=56) – interaction of factors: relative frequency of the *s*-genitive versus the *of*-genitive according to the eight conditions (±a = [±animate]; ±t = [±topical]; ±p = [±prototypical] possessive relation); cf. also table 3, Appendix §10.1.

Moreover, it appears that a [-animate] possessor never favors the *s*-genitive; the analysis of the interaction of the factors topicality and possessive relation can therefore be restricted to the context of [+animate] possessors as illustrated in table 34.

Table 34. British subjects – interaction of factors: relative frequency of the *s*-genitive versus the *of*-genitive (prediction I) for the [+animate] conditions (cf. also table 3, Appendix §10.1)

[+animate]			
[+topical]		[-topical]	
[+prototypical]	[-prototypical]	[+prototypical]	[-prototypical]
the boy's eyes versus *the eyes of the boy*	*the mother's future* versus *the future of the mother*	*a girl's face* versus *the face of a girl*	*a woman's shadow* versus *the shadow of a woman*
s-genitive (89.3%) > *of*-genitive (10.7%)	*s*-genitive (73%) > *of*-genitive (27%)	*s*-genitive (61.3%) > *of*-genitive (38.7%)	*of*-genitive (57%) > *s*-genitive (43%)

We can see that the s-genitive is always preferred in the [+animate] context if the possessor is [+topical], i.e. in the first two conditions ([+a/+t/+p] *the boy's eyes*) and ([+a/+t/-p] *the mother's future*); for [+animate] [-topical] possessors the type of possessive relation finally determines whether the *s*-genitive (for [+prototypical] relations, i.e. [+a/-t/+p] *a girl's face*) or the *of*-genitive (for [-prototypical] relations, i.e. [+a/-t/-p] *the shadow of a woman*) is the more likely option. Likewise, as far as topicality is concerned, a [+topical] possessor is always more frequently realized by the *s*-genitive if it is [+animate], irrespective of whether the possessive relation is prototypical (89.3%) or not (73%). For [-topical] possessors, however, it is again the factor possessive relation which biases the choice of genitive construction, with the *s*-genitive only preferred in [+prototypical] possessive relations (61.3%), while in the [-prototypical] context the *of*-genitive (57%) is the more frequent option. Finally, considering the factor possessive relation the *s*-genitive is always more frequent than the *of*-genitive with [+prototypical] possessive relations in the [+animate] context, irrespective of the topicality of the possessor. That is, both items of the type *the boy's eyes* (89.3%) as well of the type *a girl's face* (61.3%) are more frequent than the corresponding *the eyes of the boy* (10.7%) and *the face of a girl* (38.7%). And if the possessor is [+animate] *and* [+topical], even [-prototypical] possessive relations (the type *the mother's future*) are more frequently realized by the *s*-genitive (73%). The differences in the frequency between the two genitive constructions are in every condition highly significant (chi-square, $p<0.001$).

To sum up, looking at the interaction of the factors animacy, topicality, and possessive relationship makes it possible to pinpoint more precisely those contexts in which the *s*-genitive is still favorable and those in which the *of*-genitive is preferred. In so doing we can see the delicate interplay of the three factors. In particular, it could be shown that not just *any* [+animate] or [+topical] possessor occurs more often with the *s*-genitive but that it depends on the special constellation of factors. Likewise, the negative values of the factors do not necessarily result in a preference for the *of*-genitive to occur. It is only for the [-animate] contexts that the *of*-genitive is always the more preferred option; for the [-topical] and the [-prototypical] contexts the *s*-genitive can be more frequently realized than the *of*-genitive if the possessor is [+animate]. Moreover, while looking at the factor possessive relation in isolation yielded a random distribution of the two genitive constructions for the context [+prototypical] in §6.4.3.1.1, in this section it could be shown that [+prototypical] possessive relations do become more frequently realized by the *s*-genitive under certain conditions, i.e. if the possessor is [+animate].

So far, we have only looked at the relative frequency of the *s*-genitive versus the *of*-genitive *within* each of the eight conditions (= prediction I). Considering the relative frequency of the *s*-genitive *between* the eight conditions (= predictions II), we are now able to further determine the relative importance of the factors animacy, topicality, and possessive relation. The analysis of the single factors in §5.4.3.1 suggested the hierarchical order "animacy > topicality > possessive relation". Table 35 below illustrates under which conditions the *s*-genitive should be more frequent if this ordering holds true, already indicating the relative frequency of the *s*-genitive for the critical conditions.

First, if animacy is more important than topicality, then the *s*-genitive should be more frequent in the [+animate] [-topical] conditions than in the [-animate] [+topical] conditions. As we can see in table 35, this is indeed the case. When balanced for prototypical possessive relations, items such as *a girl's face* ([+a/-t/+p], 61.3%) are significantly more frequently realized by the *s*-genitive than items such as *the chair's frame* ([-a/+t/+p], 35.7%), with chi-square, $p<0.001$. Accordingly, for [-prototypical] possessive relations, items such as *a woman's shadow* ([+a/-t/-p], 43%) take significantly more *s*-genitives than items such as *the bag's contents* ([-a/+t/-p], 22.2%), (chi-square, $p<0.001$).

Table 35. British subjects – interaction of factors: comparing the relative frequency of the *s*-genitive between the single conditions (= prediction II)

---

prediction II: relative frequency of the *s*-genitive *between* the single conditions

animacy > topicality	animacy > possessive relation	topicality > possessive relation
[+a/-t] > [-a/+t], for [+p]	[+a/-p] > [-a/+p], for [+t]	[+t/-p] > [-t/+p], for [+a]
a girl's > the chair's	*the > the chair's*	*the > a girl's*
face frame	*mother's frame*	*mother's face*
(61.3%) > (35.7%)	*future*	*future*
	(73%) > (35.7%)	(73%) > (61.3%)
[+a/-t] > [-a/+t], for [-p]	[+a/-p] > [-a/+p], for [-t]	[+t/-p] > [-t/+p], for [-a]
a woman's > the bag's	*a woman's > a lorry's*	*the bag's > a lorry's*
shadow contents	*shadow wheels*	*contents wheels*
(43%) > (22.2%)	(43%) > (10.6%)	(22.2%) > (10.6%)

Second, we can observe in table 35 that animacy is more important than the type of possessive relation, since in the context of a [+animate] possessor in a [-prototypical] possessive relation the *s*-genitive occurs significantly more often (=73%) than in the context of a [-animate] possessor in a [+prototypical] possessive relation (=35.7%) (chi-square, $p<0.001$); i.e. the type *the mother's future* ([+a/+t/-p], 73%) is a better context for the occurrence of the *s*-genitive than *the chair's frame* ([-a/+t/+p], 35.7%) when balanced for topical contexts, and items such as *a woman's shadow* ([+a/-t/-p]), 43%) outnumber the type *a lorry's wheels* ([-a/-t/+p], 10.6%) significantly in [-topical] contexts (chi-square, $p<0.01$).

And third, topicality turns out to be more important than the type of possessive relation. As is apparent from table 35, a topical possessor in a [-prototypical] possessive relation is more frequently realized by the *s*-genitive than a [-topical] possessor in a [+prototypical] possessive relation for both [+animate] and [-animate] possessors (chi-square, $p<0.001$). That is, the type *the mother's future* ([+a/+t/-p], 73%) is preferred by the *s*-genitive over the type *a girl's face* ([+a/-t/+p], 61.3%) in the [+animate] conditions; likewise items such as *the bag's contents* ([-a/+t/-p], 22.2%) more frequently take the *s*-genitive than items such as *a lorry's wheels* ([-a/-t/+p], 10.6%) in the [-animate] conditions.

The results for the predictions pertaining to the relative importance of the factors animacy, topicality, and possessive relation are summarized in table 36 below.

Table 36. British subjects: relative importance of animacy, topicality, and possessive relations (hypotheses, predictions, and results), * '+' = predictions confirmed.

hypo-thesis	predictions for the relative frequency of the *s*-genitive	results *
animacy > topicality	• [+animate] [-topical] possessor (*a girl's face*) > [-animate] [+topical] possessor (*the chair's frame*) (in control condition: [+prototypical] possessive relation)	+
	• [+animate] [-topical] possessor (*a woman's shadow*) > [-animate] [+topical] possessor (*the bag's contents*) (in control condition: [-prototypical] possessive relation	+
topicality > possessive relation	• [+topical] possessor in [-prototypical] possessive relation (*the mother's future*) > [-topical] possessor in [+prototypical] possessive relation (*a girl's face*) (in control condition: [+animate] possessor	+
	• [+topical] possessor in [-prototypical] possessive relation (*the bag's contents*) > [-topical] possessor in [+prototypical] possessive relation (*a lorry's wheels*) (in control condition: [-animate] possessor	+
animacy > possessive relation	• [+animate] possessor in [-prototypical] possessive relation (*the mother's future*) > [-animate] possessor in [+prototypical] possessive relation (*the chair's frame*) (in control condition: [+topical] possessor)	+
	• [+animate] possessor in [-prototypical] possessive relation (*a woman's shadow*) > [-animate] possessor in [+prototypical] possessive relation (*a lorry's wheels*) (in control condition: [-topical] possessor)	+

The results for the interaction of factors therefore confirm the hierarchy already indicated after the analysis of the single factors, i.e. animacy > topicality > possessive relation. On the basis of this hierarchy, we can now propose a preference structure for the English *s*-genitive, as illustrated in figure 14 below.

This preference structure is based on two findings:

(1)   As has been shown in §6.3.1.1 the positive values of the factors ([+animate], [+topical], [+prototypical]) generally favor the *s*-genitive while the negative values ([-animate], [-topical], [-prototypical]) are more frequently realized by the *of*-genitive.

(2)   As has been shown in this section, animacy is a more important factor
      than topicality, and topicality, in turn, exerts a stronger influence on
      the choice of the *s*-genitive than the factor possessive relation.

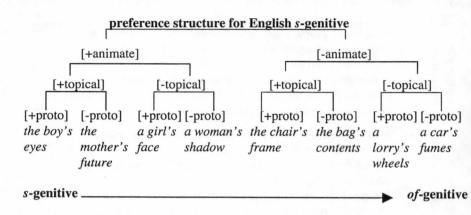

Figure 14.   Preference stucture for the English *s*-genitive

Taken together, both findings point to a preference structure for the choice
of the genitive construction in English as outlined above. This preference
structure now also predicts that the relative frequency of the *s*-genitive
should decrease from the optimal context on the left ([+animate] [+topical]
[+prototypical]) to the least optimal context for the occurrence of the *s*-
genitive on the right ([-animate] [-topical] [-prototypical]). Figure 13 above
shows the relative frequency of the *s*-genitive and the *of*-genitive according
to the eight conditions in the order given in the preference structure, and is
repeated below for convenience (as figure 15).

As can be seen from figure 15, the relative frequency of the *s*-genitive
does indeed decrease steadily from left to right as predicted by the
preference structure, and it is only the difference in the relative frequency
of the *s*-genitive between the two rightmost conditions ([-a/-t/+p], 10.6%,
versus [-a/-t/-p], 11.9%) that goes against this general tendency and which
is not significant. For all other conditions, the differences in the relative
frequency of the *s*-genitive as opposed to the *of*-genitive are always
statistically significant between the single conditions (see also table 38
below).

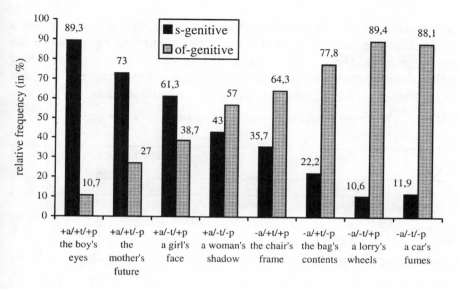

Figure 15. British subjects (n=56) – interaction of factors: relative frequency of the *s*-genitive versus the *of*-genitive according to the eight conditions (±a = [±animate]; ±t = [±topical]; ±p = [±prototypical] possessive relation), see also table 3, Appendix §10.1)

In addition to the chi-square test a matched *t*-test (for repeated measures) was conducted on the data. While the chi-square test compares the absolute number of occurrences of the *s*-genitive versus the *of*-genitive between the single conditions summarized for all subjects, the matched *t*-test (for repeated measures) compares the relative frequencies (percentages) of the *s*-genitive between the single conditions for each single subject. The difference in methodology and calculation between the chi-square test and the matched *t*-test are briefly illustrated in table 37 below.[121]

For the sake of exposition the two statistical procedures are illustrated somewhat grossly simplified in table 37. Note, for example, that although the input data for the chi-square test are raw frequencies and not percentages, it takes into account, as does the *t*-test, the relative frequency of the *s*-genitive versus the *of*-genitive in its calculation. Also, both the chi-square test and the *t*-test essentially test the same question, i.e. whether the difference in the frequency of the *s*-genitive between one condition and another one is to be considered random or statistically significant. Yet, it is the general difference in the procedure of these two statistical tests that matters here. Conducting the chi-square test over the frequencies summarized for all subjects presupposes, in a way, that the subjects are a homogeneous group with respect to the distribution of the *s*-genitive versus the *of*-genitive. Having more *s*-genitives in one condition may indeed reflect the uniform behavior of all subjects, it may, however, very well also be an artefact ignoring possible variation between the subjects.

Table 37. Chi-square test versus *t*-test (subj. = subject; '*s* = *s*-genitive, *of* = *of*-genitive

	chi square test				matched *t*-test (for repeated measures)	
	[+a/+t/+p]		[+a/+t/-p]		[+a/+t/+p]	[+a/+t/-p]
	'*s* (n)	*of* (n)	'*s* (n)	*of* (n)	'*s* (relative frequency, in %)	'*s* (relative frequency, in %)
subj. 1	13	1	10	1	92.86 ⟷	90.91
subj. 2	11	0	9	1	100 ⟷	90
subj. 3	14	0	11	0	100 ⟷	100
......						
total	696	83	448	166		

In the present study, an additional *t*-test provides therefore a valuable methodological tool to take such potential intersubject variation into account. The chi-square values and *t* values for the differences between all the single conditions are both provided in table 38 below. As is evident from table 38, both the chi-square test and the *t*-test yield the same results.[122]

Table 38. British subjects – interaction of factors (predictions II): results for matched *t*-test (for repeated measures) and chi-square test.

matched condition pair	*t* value	*df*	*p*-level (2-tailed)	chi-square	*df*	*p*-level
[+a/+t/+p] – [+a/+t/-p]	10.171	55	0.000	61.654	1	*p*<0.001
[+a/+t/-p] – [+a/-t/+p]	5.606	55	0.000	17.456	1	*p*<0.001
[+a/-t/+p] – [+a/-t/-p]	6.788	55	0.000	38.258	1	*p*<0.001
[+a/-t/-p] – [-a/+t/+p]	2.306	55	0.025	7.957	1	*p*<0.01
[-a/+t/+p] – [-a/+t/-p]	6.060	55	0.000	28.727	1	*p*<0.001
[-a/+t/-p] – [-a/-t/+p]	5.006	55	0,000	26.508	1	*p*<0.001
[-a/-t/+p] – [-a/-t/-p]	-0.828	55	0.411 (n.s.)	0.381	1	n.s.

Note, finally, that establishing that the relative frequency of the *s*-genitive significantly decreases along the preference structure proposed above, constitutes the most exhaustive indication for the validity of this preference structure, and will therefore, in the following, be taken as a sufficient criterion for it.

American English

We may now go on and look at whether the same preference structure can also account for the American subjects when choosing between the two genitives. In figure 16 the relative frequency of the *s*-genitive and the *of*-genitive according to the eight conditions in the order as indicated in the preference structure proposed for the British subjects in figure 14 above is presented for the American subjects.

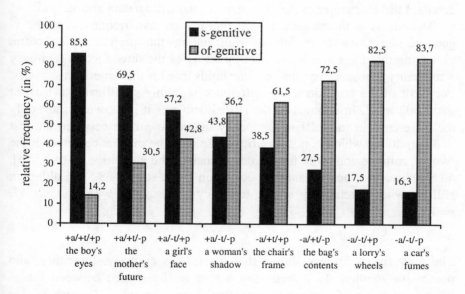

Figure 16.   American subjects (n=48) – interaction of factors: relative frequency of the *s*-genitive versus the *of*-genitive according to the eight conditions (±a = [±animate]; ±t =[±topical]; ±p = [±prototypical] possessive relation); cf. also table 4, Appendix §10.1)

Again, the results correspond to a great extent to those obtained for the British subjects. First, the *s*-genitive is a more frequent option than the *of*-

genitive for the first three [+animate] conditions. For [+animate] and [-topical] possessors in a [-prototypical] possessive relation ([+a/-t/-p]) as well as for all inanimate conditions the *of*-genitive is more frequently realized. The difference in the relative frequency of the *s*-genitive versus the *of*-genitive in each condition is significant at least at the 0.01 level, indicating that the two genitive constructions are not distributed randomly within the eight conditions.

And again, the results obtained for the single factors in §6.4.3.1.1 need to be modified in the light of the data on the interaction of factors. A [+animate] possessor, a [+topical] possessor and a [+prototypical] possessive relation do not in themselves favor the *s*-genitive; it is only a certain interplay of these factors which determines whether the *s*-genitive or the *of*-genitive is more likely to be used. In this respect, the results for the American subjects do not differ from those for the British subjects; for details, I therefore refer to the discussion of the British data above.

Second, as with the British subjects, the relative frequency of the *s*-genitive decreases from left to right along the preference structure, indicating that the same hierarchical ordering of the three factors (animacy > topicality > possessive relation) also holds true for the American subjects. For most of the conditions this difference is highly significant, at least at the 0.002 level. In contrast to the British subjects it is, however, not only the difference in the relative frequency of the *s*-genitive between the last two conditions which is not significant but also the difference between the 'worst' animate condition for the occurrence of the *s*-genitive (= [+a/-t/-p], 43.8%) and the 'best' inanimate condition (=[-a/+t/+p], 38.5%), although still showing a relatively strong tendency (chi-square, $p<0.10$; t, df 47, $p=0.133$).

6.4.3.1.3 Summary

The analysis so far has shown that the factors animacy, topicality, and possessive relation do indeed play a role in the choice between the *s*-genitive and the *of*-genitive in both British and American English in that the *s*-genitive is, in general, more likely with a [+animate] possessor, a [+topical] possessor, and in [+prototypical] possessive relations. Looking at this more closely and considering how these three factors interact with each other rather than looking at them separately revealed for both the British and the American subjects that the factors animacy, topicality, and possessive relation are highly sensitive with respect to how they co-occur.

Moreover, considering the interaction of factors also enables us to pinpoint the relative importance of these factors, which turned out to be the same for both the British and the American subjects, i.e.: animacy > topicality > possessive relation. This hierarchical order of the three factors, which represents the relative strength in their assignment of the *s*-genitive, has been translated into the (modified) preference structure given in figure 17 below.

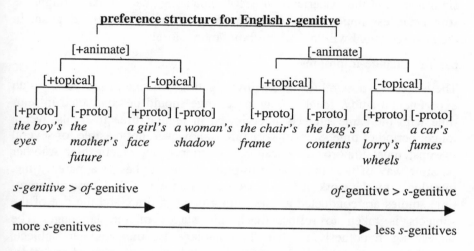

Figure 17. Preference structure for English s-genitive (modified)

This preference structure, to be read as a kind of decision tree, specifies the general likelihood with which the *s*-genitive can occur, with a decreasing likelihood for the *s*-genitive to occur from left to right, thereby capturing the results for predictions (I) and (II) as outlined in §6.4.2 in the following way:

(1) It indicates those contexts in which the *s*-genitive is more frequent than the *of*-genitive, clearly delineating the point from which onwards the *of*-genitive becomes more frequent, i.e. from the [+a/-t/-p] condition (*a woman's shadow*) onwards (= prediction I).

(2) It illustrates the relative frequency of the *s*-genitive as opposed to the *of*-genitive in relation to the eight conditions (= prediction II), with the *s*-genitive decreasing significantly in frequency from the leftmost, i.e. optimal context for the occurrence of the *s*-genitive, to the rightmost, i.e. least optimal context along this preference structure, as the data for the British and American subjects as discussed in §6.4.3.1.2 have shown.

It is only towards the rightmost end of the scale, that the otherwise very neat picture is disturbed in that the relative frequency of the *s*-genitive is not significantly different between the last two conditions. Note also, that in contrast to the British speakers the difference between the two conditions marking the borderline between the animate and inanimate conditions is not significant for the American subjects, indicating that animacy might be somewhat less important in American English than in British English. In the next sections I will look at this point more closely.

6.4.3.2 Change-in-progress

There are two possibilities when investigating "change-in-progress" in an experimental study. Ideally, ongoing change should be conducted in real-time with the same subjects interviewed in regular time intervals over a longer period of time. Such a procedure is, however, not feasible for several reasons; most importantly because it is simply not practicable. Another possible way of tracking change-in-progress are studies in apparent time, introduced by the work of Labov, as e.g. in Labov (1972). These apparent-time studies are conducted at one certain point in time, and the age of the subjects is taken to reflect diachronic stages of the language. The underlying hypothesis is that the language of the younger subjects represents more recent language usage, while the language of the older subjects reflects an older language state. If differences are found in the language of the younger and the older subjects, these differences should then, accordingly, reflect ongoing change. Of course, apparent-time studies crucially hinge on the assumption that differences in age genuinely reflect ongoing change and not differences in language usage which are simply characteristic of certain age groups. That is, we can never completely rule out the possibility that younger people just speak differently because they are young people and not because they grow up at a different time and are surrounded by a changing language.[123]

With these caveats in mind, the present study is a study in apparent-time. To test whether there is evidence for ongoing change in the choice between the *s*-genitive and the *of*-genitive, I divided the British and American subjects into two age groups, older and younger ones, drawing the line at the age of 40. An overview of the number and average ages of the British and American subjects, specified for age group and sex is given in table 39 below.

Table 39. British and American subject groups for apparent-time approach (m= male; f= female; # = toal)

sex	British subjects						American subjects					
	younger subjects (age < 40)			older subjects (age ≥ 40)			younger subjects (age < 40)			older subjects (age ≥ 40)		
	n	age	∅ age	n	age	∅ age	n	age	∅ age	n	age	∅ age
m	11	18-32	22.3	7	45-81	54.3	15	20-39	29.6	12	40-74	53.7
f	25	18-38	23.2	13	42-66	53.2	11	24-33	28.5	10	44-77	52.5
#	36	18-38	22.9	20	42-81	53.6	26	20-39	29.1	22	40-77	53.1

In what follows I will proceed from the assumption that differences in the usage of the younger subjects in contrast to that of the older subjects can be taken to reflect ongoing change in the respective Standard varieties. A first indication for ongoing change comes from a comparison of the overall relative frequency of the *s*-genitive according to the two age groups in the two Standard varieties. As is apparent from figure 18, the younger subjects use more *s*-genitives than the older subjects in both varieties, and this difference is more striking in British English (chi-square, $p<0.001$) than in American English (chi-square, $p<0.05$).

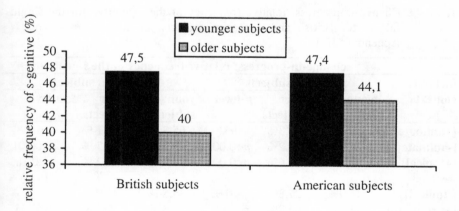

Figure 18. British and American subjects: younger versus older subjects – overall frequency of the *s*-genitive (cf. also table 5, Appendix §10.1)

In the following I will analyze the data from the questionnaire elicitation according to these two age groups in the same way as for the synchronic state of affairs in §6.4.3.1. That is, I will first look at whether there are differences in the distribution of the *s*-genitive and the *of*-genitive between these two age groups according to the three factors. After that, I will analyze in which respect there are differences between the younger and the older subjects when looking at the interaction of factors. In particular, I will examine whether the general increase in the relative frequency of the *s*-genitive, as observed above in British and American English, is evenly distributed across all three factors or whether some factors contribute more to this development than others. Moreover, I will investigate whether the relative importance of the three factors as indicated in the preference structure above has been changing or not. The results for the two Standard varieties, both synchronically and diachronically will then in a second step be compared in §6.4.3.3.

6.4.3.2.1   Animacy, topicality, and possessive relation

Table 40 gives the relative frequency of the *s*-genitive for the positive and negative values of the three factors animacy, topicality, and possessive relation for the younger and the older British and American subjects. Additionally, it is indicated whether and at which significance level the difference in the relative frequency between the two age groups is statistically significant for the single contexts.

Table 40. Change-in-progress: relative frequency of the *s*-genitive for the single factors for British and American subjects (cf. also tables 6 and 7, Appendix §10.1)

factors/ contexts	change-in-progress: relative frequency of the *s*-genitive					
	British subjects			**American subjects**		
	younger subjects	older subjects	*p*-level	younger subjects	older subjects	*p*-level
[+animate]	69.4%	66.3%	n.s.	65.3 %	66.1 %	n.s.
[-animate]	26.2%	14.2%	*p*<0.001	29.7 %	22.7 %	*p*<0.001
[+topical]	58.7%	50.6%	*p*<0.001	57.7 %	54.2 %	*p*<0.10 (n.s.)
[-topical]	33.9%	27.3%	*p*<0.01	34.8 %	31.9 %	n.s.
[+prototyp.]	53.6%	45.8%	*p*<0.001	53.3 %	49 %	*p*<0.05
[-prototyp.]	40.5%	33.3%	*p*<0.001	40.4 %	38.4 %	n.s.

For the British subjects it can be observed that the younger subjects use more *s*-genitives than the older subjects in every context. This difference in the relative frequency between the two age groups is always significant, except for [+animate], which indicates that this context is not participating in the ongoing change towards a higher frequency of the *s*-genitive in British English.

In the American English subject group, the older subjects show a slightly (and not significantly) higher proportion of *s*-genitives than the younger subjects in the [+animate] context. In all other contexts, the younger subjects use more *s*-genitives than the older subjects. In contrast to the British subjects, however, the increasing use of *s*-genitives as indicated by the higher frequency of *s*-genitives by the younger subjects, is only significant for the contexts of [-animate] and [+prototypical], suggesting that it is particularly in these contexts that the *s*-genitive is spreading in American English.

To sum up, having divided the British and American subjects into two age groups (younger and older subjects) to trace possible change-in-progress, a general tendency towards an increasing use of the *s*-genitive in both British and American English could be discerned. The two Standard varieties differ, however, in the extent to which the *s*-genitive is increasing and the contexts participating in this overall increase. For the British subjects this shift towards a higher frequency of the *s*-genitive is stronger and can be observed for all conditions, except for [+animate] possessors, while for the American subjects it is only constituted for the [-animate] and [+prototypical] conditions.

6.4.3.2.2   Interaction of factors

Proceeding from the indications for ongoing change in the previous section let us now, in a second step, look more closely at how this change-in-progress is distributed over all eight possible combinations of the factors, thereby taking into account their interaction. This will allow us to isolate even more precisely those contexts, in which the *s*-genitive is becoming more frequent in Present-day English, and, additionally, enable us to evaluate whether the relative importance of the factors has been changing or remained the same in British and American English when comparing the two age groups.

British English

Let us first try to evaluate whether the relative importance of the three factors is the same for the younger and the older subjects in British English. If the preference structure suggested for all subjects independent of age in §6.4.3.1.2/3 (animacy > topicality > possessive relations) is diachronically stable, then for both age groups the frequency of the *s*-genitive should be decreasing along the eight possible combinations of the three factors as indicated in this preference structure from left to right. In figure 19 the relative frequency of the *s*-genitive for the eight conditions is given in the order of the preference structure.

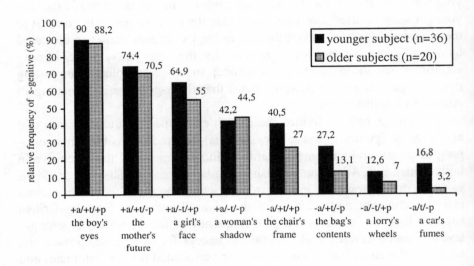

Figure 19.   British subjects – interaction of factors: relative frequency of the *s*-genitive for the younger and the older subjects (±a = [±animate]; ±t = [±topical]; ±p = [±prototypical] possessive relation) (cf. also tables 8 and 9, Appendix §10.1)

As we can see, for both age groups the *s*-genitive decreases along the preference structure from left to right; the difference in the relative frequency of the *s*-genitive between the single conditions is always statistically significant, except for the following contexts. First, the difference in the relative frequency between the last two conditions ([-a/-t/+p] versus [-a/-t/-p]) is – when specified for the two age groups – again not as predicted. The younger subjects use more *s*-genitives in the rightmost [-a/-t/-p] condition (16.8%) which should constitute the 'worst' context for the occurrence of the *s*-genitive, than in the preceding [-a/-t/+p] condition (12.6%); this difference is, however, not statistically significant for the younger subjects, nor is it for the older subjects, who use least *s*-genitives in the rightmost [-a/-t/-p] condition. Another notable difference between the two age groups is to be observed at the borderline between the [+animate] and the [-animate] conditions. While for the older subjects the difference in the relative frequency of the *s*-genitive between the [+a/-t/-p] (=44.5%) and the [-a/+t/+p] condition (=27%) is highly significant (*t*, *df* 19, *p*=0.000), it is not significant for the younger subjects (42.2% in [+a/-t/-p] versus 40.5% in [-a/+t/+p]). That is, while for the older British subjects *the chair's frame* is still significantly worse than *a woman's shadow*, for the younger British subjects this is no longer the case, indicating that animacy is becoming somewhat less important in British English in the choice of genitive construction.

In general, we can conclude so far, that both age groups use the *s*-genitive according to the same preference structure as outlined in §6.4.3.1.2/3, which suggests that the relative importance of the three factors (animacy > topicality > possessive relation) has remained the same in British English from a short-term diachronic perspective.

To identify more closely in which contexts the younger subjects use more *s*-genitives than the older subjects, we need now to compare the relative frequency of the *s*-genitive between the two age groups for each single condition. As we can note from figure 19, the younger subjects use more *s*-genitives than the older subjects in all conditions, except in the [+a/-t/-p] condition, and in this condition the difference in frequency between the two age groups is not significant. Most difference in the relative frequency of the *s*-genitive between the older and the younger British subjects can be observed in the [-animate] conditions, and it is particularly in the four [-animate] conditions that this difference reaches statistical significance (at least *t*, *p*=0.027). This shows that the increasing use of the *s*-genitive turns out to be first and foremost a development restricted to the [-animate] conditions. The effects for topicality and possessive relations, as observed in the analysis of the single factors in table 40 above turn out to be secondary to the effect of [-animate].

American English

In figure 20 below the relative frequency of the *s*-genitive for the younger versus the older American subjects is now presented for the eight conditions, again arranged in the order given in the preference structure.

Apparently, both age groups follow the same preference structure; the relative frequency of the *s*-genitive decreases for both the younger and the older subjects along this preference structure from left to right. Again, the last two [-animate] conditions do not conform to the otherwise clear picture, for both age groups the difference in the relative frequency of the *s*-

genitive between these two conditions does not yield any statistical significance.

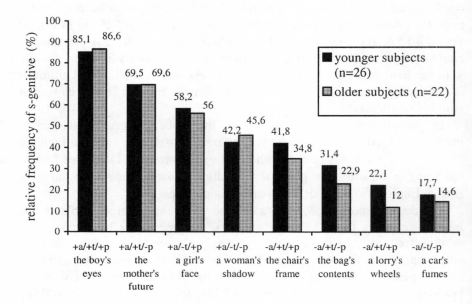

Figure 20. American subjects – interaction of factors: relative frequency of the *s*-genitive for the younger and the older subjects (±a = [±animate]; ±t = [±topical]; ±p = [±prototypical] possessive relation) (cf. also tables 10 and 11, Appendix §10.1)

And, as for the British subjects, it is the borderline between the [+animate] and the [-animate] conditions ([+a/-t/-p) versus [-a/+t/+p] conditions) where the greatest difference between the two age groups can be observed. While for the older subjects the difference between these two conditions (*a woman's shadow* versus *the chair's frame*) is statistically significant (*t*, *df* 21, *p*=0.051), the younger subjects use the *s*-genitive almost equally frequently in these two conditions, indicating – as for the British subjects – that the impact of the factor animacy is on the decrease in Present-day American English.

Comparing the relative frequency of the *s*-genitive of the two age groups for each single condition, it is, again, striking that it is almost exclusively in the [-animate] conditions that a higher use of the *s*-genitive in the younger American subject group can be observed. It is, however, only in the [-a/-t/+p] condition that this difference reaches any statistical significance (*t*, *p*=0.016). The increasing frequency of the *s*-genitive for [+prototypical] possessive relation as observed for the younger subjects in §6.4.3.2.1 above seems therefore to be predominantly restricted to [-animate] contexts in American English.

6.4.3.2.3   Summary

It has been shown that the *s*-genitive is on the increase in both British and – albeit to a somewhat lesser extent – in American English, as reflected in the higher frequency of the *s*-genitive in the younger subject group as compared to the older subjects in these two Standard varieties of English. In particular, this ongoing change towards a higher use of the *s*-genitive could be identified to be predominantly restricted to the context of [-animate] possessors. Again, as in the analysis of the synchronic state of affairs in §6.4.3.1, it has been demonstrated that looking at the interaction of factors yields the more precise results, since it helps us to better identify the contexts in which this change takes place. This was particularly striking for the British data, for which it could be shown that although the factors topicality and possessive relation are indeed participating in the overall increase of the *s*-genitive, they only play a secondary role in this development, since restricted to the context of [-animate] possessors.

6.4.3.3 Comparing British and American English

Having established the effects of the factors animacy, topicality, and possessive relation from both a synchronic and a diachronic point of view separately for the British and American subjects, I will now address the question in which respect there are any differences in the choice between the two genitive constructions between the two Standard varieties. For this purpose, I will first compare the two varieties from a synchronic point of view, i.e. irrespective of age, and then discuss the interplay of Standard variety and change-in-progress in the increasing use of the *s*-genitive in Present-day English.

6.4.3.3.1   Synchronic state of affairs
Animacy, topicality, and possessive relations

In general, the analysis of the single factors for the British and American subjects in §6.4.3.1.1 above has yielded essentially the same results as to the impact of the factors animacy, topicality, and possessive relation on the choice of genitive construction. Therefore, the two Standard varieties can only differ with respect to the relative frequency of the *s*-genitive in these six contexts, which is illustrated in figure 21.

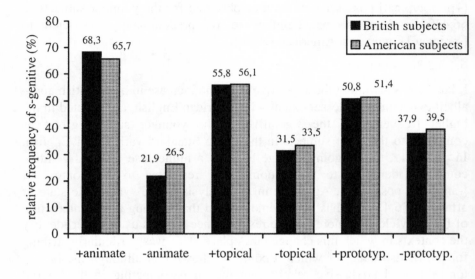

Figure 21.   British versus American subjects: relative frequency of the *s*-genitive according to the single factors (cf. also tables 1 and 2, Appendix §10.1)

Figure 21 compares the relative frequency of the *s*-genitive when looking at the single factors for the British and the American subjects. And, again, it is the [-animate] context that is most conspicuous in that in this context the American subjects use more *s*-genitives (26.5%) than the British subjects (21.9%) and this difference is highly significant below the 0.001 level. On the other hand, the British subjects choose the *s*-genitive more frequently with [+animate] possessors (68.3%) than the American subjects (65.7%), this difference is, however, not significant. This indicates that animacy as such, i.e. the distinction between a [+animate] and a [-animate] possessor, is more important in British English than it is in American English for the choice of the *s*-genitive. For the factors topicality and possessive relation the main tendency is that the American subjects always use more *s*-genitives than the British subjects in both the positive and the negative contexts, the differences in the relative frequency of the *s*-genitive in these contexts are, however, only slight and not significant.

Interaction of factors

Comparing the interaction of the three factors in the two Standard varieties can, again, not reveal any qualitative differences in the use of the s-genitive but, as with the analysis of the single factors, only point to differences in the relative frequency of the *s*-genitive, since the analyses in §6.4.3.1.2 for the synchronic state of affairs for the interaction of factors yielded the same preference structure for both the British and American subjects.

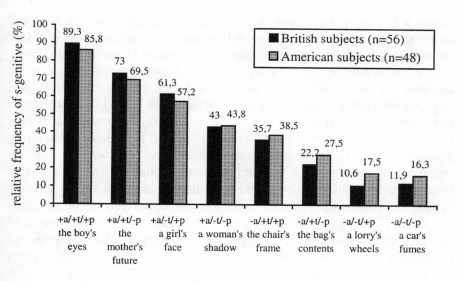

Figure 22. British versus American subjects – interaction of factors: relative frequency of the *s*-genitive (±a = [±animate]; ±t = [±topical]; ±p = [±prototypical] possessive relation) (cf. also tables 3 and 4, Appendix §10.1)

First of all, it is noticeable from figure 22, that the British subjects use more *s*-genitives than the American subjects in the first three [+animate] conditions, although none of these differences reach any statistical significance. In contrast, the American subjects show a higher proportion of *s*-genitives for *all* [-animate] conditions. Yet notice, that only for one inanimate condition (= [-a/-t/+p]) does this difference turn out to be significant (*t, df* 76.809, *p*=0.009); for the [-a/-t/-p] condition still a strong tendency can be observed (*t, df* 91.973, *p*=0.085). That is, the difference between the British and American subjects is most pronounced at the extreme ends of the preference structure: while the British subjects tend to use more *s*-genitives in the contexts more optimal for its occurrence (i.e. with [+animate] possessors) – albeit not significantly so –, the use of the *s*-genitive with the less optimal [-animate] conditions is much more productive for the American subjects. In the 'middle-field' the differences between the two varieties are not very pronounced.

6.4.3.3.2   Change-in-progress

So far it has been shown that it is the factor animacy which shows most differences in the use of the *s*-genitive when comparing the two Standard varieties and when investigating change-in-progress in that a significantly higher frequency of the *s*-genitive with [-animate] possessors can be observed for (i) the younger subjects, and (ii) the American subjects. Yet how can we evaluate which of the two factors is the more important one in this increasing use of the *s*-genitive with [-animate] possessors? Is it age, i.e. the diachronic change-in-progress factor, or is it rather the factor Standard variety? For this reason, I will now compare the relative frequency of the *s*-genitive for the [-animate] conditions according to age (younger versus older subjects) and according to Standard variety (British versus American subjects). As a first approximation, figure 23 below gives the relative frequency of the *s*-genitive summarized for all [-animate] contexts, specified for the two age groups in the two Standard varieties. As is apparent from figure 23, the diachronic change-in-progress factor seems to be the more important factor in the higher use of the *s*-genitive with [-animate] possessors.

Overall, irrespective of the Standard variety, the younger subjects use more *s*-genitives with [-animate] possessors than the older subjects. Standard variety comes into play only as a secondary factor in that the American subjects show a higher frequency of the *s*-genitive than the British subjects in the respective age groups.

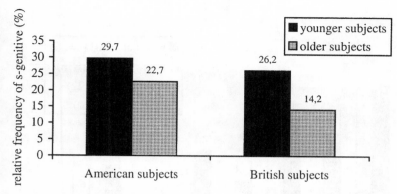

Figure 23. Change-in-progress (younger versus older subjects) and Standard variety (British versus American subjects) for [-animate]: relative frequency of the *s*-genitive (cf. also tables 6 and 7, Appendix §10.1)

The interplay of change-in-progress (age) and Standard variety in the use of the *s*-genitive with [-animate] possessors can be briefly illustrated as follows:

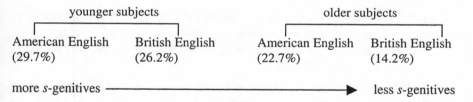

Figure 24. Interplay: change-in-progress versus Standard variety

The differences in the relative frequency of the *s*-genitive between the four groups (younger American subjects [29.7%] > younger British subjects [26.2%], younger British subjects [26.2%] > older American subjects [22.7%], older American subjects [22.7%] > older British subjects [14.2%]) are all statistically significant at least at the 0.05 level.

If we look at this more closely, however, and consider how the frequency of the *s*-genitive is distributed over the *single* [-animate] conditions for the four subjects groups, the general picture needs to be slightly modified. In figure 25 below the relative frequency of the *s*-genitive for the four [-animate] conditions is given in (a) the order of the preference structure, and (b) according to the hierarchical order "age (younger > older subjects) > Standard variety (American English > British English)" as observed above.

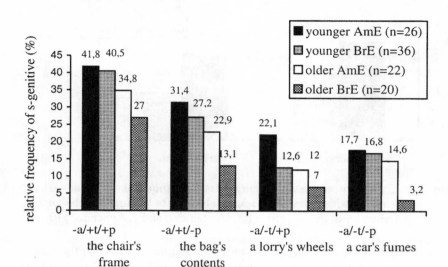

Figure 25.   Change-in-progress versus Standard variety – interaction of factors in [-animate]: relative frequency of the *s*-genitive (-a = [-animate]; ±t = [±topical]; ±p = [±prototypical] possessive relation) (cf. also tables 8-11, Appendix §10.1)

First, while the younger American subjects use more *s*-genitives than the younger British subjects in every single [-animate] condition, the difference in the relative frequency of the *s*-genitive between these two groups is only slight in the optimal [-animate] condition for the occurrence of the *s*-genitive (= [-a/+t/+p]) and in the least optimal context (= [-a/-t/-p]); it is most pronounced in the (-a/-t/+p) condition, which is also the only condition in which the difference in the relative frequency of the *s*-genitive between the younger American and British subjects is statistically significant (*t, df* 36.445, *p*=0.018).

Second, it also appears from figure 25 that the difference in the relative frequency of the *s*-genitive between the two Standard varieties is much more pronounced for the older subject groups. Except for the least optimal context for the occurrence of the *s*-genitive, the [-a/-t/-p] condition, the older American subjects show a much higher proportion of *s*-genitives in the single [-animate] conditions than the older British subjects. In the [-a/+t/-p] and the [-a/-t/-p] condition this difference is significant ([-a/+t/-p]: *t, df* 37.947, *p*=0.045; [-a/-t/-p]: *t, df* 29.421, p=0.000), and in the

[-a/-t/+p] the *t* value (*df* 39.679) at least points to a strong tendency at the 0.076 level.

Therefore, it appears, that in the increasing use of the *s*-genitive with [-animate] possessors, Standard variety as a factor seems to have been more important in the past than it is in the present, indicating that the increasing use of the *s*-genitive is a development which may have originated in American English and has been spreading from there to British English. While American English is still leading this trend, today the difference between the two varieties seems to be leveling out. What needs to be further explained, however, is why for one particular [-animate] condition, i.e. [-a/-t/+p], the picture is completely different. While in this condition no significant difference in the frequency of the *s*-genitive can be found for American and British English usage in the past, as represented by the older subjects, there is, however, a significant difference between American and British English in the present (as represented by the younger subjects). This suggests that the increasing use of the *s*-genitive in this particular [-animate] condition is a recent development originating in American English and having not yet spread to British English. Note that it is again a [-animate] [-topical] condition which stands out throughout almost all analyses and which will be discussed in more detail in the following section.[124]

6.5 Summary and general discussion

The results from the questionnaire study can now be summarized and discussed as follows.

Table 41. Predictions and results

factor	choice of *s*-genitive	
	+ iconic/natural contexts	**- iconic/natural contexts**
animacy	[+animate] possessor	[-animate] possessor
topicality	[+ topical] possessor	[- topical] possessor
possessive relation	[+ prototypical] possessive relation (*only partially)	[- prototypical] possessive relation
prediction (I)	*s*-genitive > *of*-genitive	*of*-genitive > *s*-genitive
prediction (II)	more *s*-genitives	less *s*-genitives

First, the *s*-genitive is generally more frequent with a [+animate] possessor, a [+topical] possessor and with [+prototypical] possessive relations than with a [-animate], a [-topical] possessor and [-prototypical] possessive relations, both with respect to its distribution as opposed to the *of*-genitive within each context (= prediction I) and to its internal distribution within the single factors (= prediction II), thereby confirming the predictions following from iconic/natural principles as outlined in §6.2, as illustrated in table 41 above.

Second, the relative importance of the three factors turned out to be: animacy > topicality > possessive relations, and can be illustrated by a preference structure, in which the three factors are hierarchically ordered with respect to their decreasing impact on the choice of the *s*-genitive; this preference structure was introduced in §5.4.3.1.2/3 and is repeated here for convenience as figure 26.

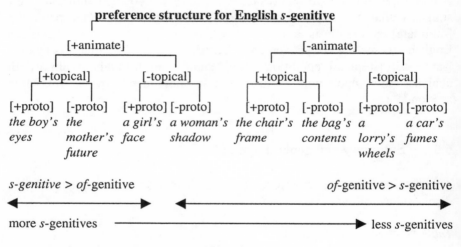

Figure 26. Preference structure for English s-genitive

This preference specifies the decreasing likelihood for the occurrence of the *s*-genitive in two ways. (i) It indicates in which contexts the *s*-genitive is the more preferred option as opposed to the *of*-genitive (= prediction I), and (ii), it specifies the contexts along which the *s*-genitive decreases in frequency (= prediction II). This preference structure has proved to be stable, unaffected by the factors change-in-progress and Standard variety. It therefore appears that the language user makes his or her choice for the *s*-genitive or the *of*-genitive following this general preference structure. What may vary, however, is how much advanced a subject group or the individuals within these groups may be along this scale, i.e. whether all the possible contexts on this preference structure are fully explored by using the *s*-genitive and how frequently the *s*-genitive is used in the single contexts. This is particularly striking for the lower end of the scale, i.e. for [-animate] [-topical] possessors. There are, for example, subjects who never use the *s*-genitive with these two conditions, not surprisingly these are primarily older British subjects, i.e. part of that subject group which shows a very low proportion of *s*-genitives in these contexts anyway. Note also that there was one item included in the pilot study which was regarded by one test subject as an absolute non-option, and for this reason excluded from the main study, namely (59):

(59)   *She moved closer to the chair. She examined the point of [the fire's origin/the origin of the fire], an uneven carbon wound from which bled wiry lengths of kindling stuffing.*
(Elizabeth George, Playing for the Ashes, 31)[125]

According to this test subject *the fire's origin* is impossible in English. Interestingly, however, the other three test subjects participating in the pilot study not only did not rule out *the fire's origin* as a possible choice, they even considered it the preferred option; so did the author (Elizabeth George) in the original text from which this passage is taken. Again, it may not be a coincidence that this test subject was an older British person, who has been very hesitant to use the *s*-genitive with [-animate] possessors throughout the test questionnaire.

Third, adopting the concept of change in apparent time, there is also evidence for ongoing change in that the younger subjects use more *s*-genitives than the older subjects, particularly with [-animate] possessors. The fact that the frequency of the *s*-genitive for [+animate] possessors is only minimally affected by ongoing change, may indicate that in this context the potential of the *s*-genitive is already – more or less – fully explored and that there is no much room left for change, so to speak.

Fourth, the results for the British and American subjects conform with respect to the findings in (1) – (3). Yet although both varieties essentially follow the same preference structure, animacy seems to have a lower impact on the choice of the *s*-genitive in American English than it has in British English. Moreover, it has been shown that the increasing use of the *s*-genitive with [-animate] possessors seems to be a development that has spread from American English to British English but that today the difference in the use of the *s*-genitive with [-animate] possessors is gradually fading. The results of the present study therefore essentially confirm the findings by Dahl (1971) and Jahr Sorheim (1980), who reported an increasing use with [-animate] possessors, and particularly those by Hundt (1998: 46) who already speculated that the diachronic factor within one variety has a stronger impact on this development than the difference between regional varieties. Note, however, that in contrast to those previous studies the present study shows that the increasing use of the *s*-genitive with [-animate] possessors is much more productive than has hitherto been assumed. In particular, in this study this diachronic change has been constituted for a noun class, which has been reported to be the most unproductive inanimate noun class and not participating in this change, i.e. concrete nouns. Moreover, while previous studies so far have observed this increasing use of the *s*-genitive in one particular genre only, i.e. journalistic language, which is particularly apt to use the *s*-genitive as the shorter – and as Hundt (1998: 47) terms it the "'more snappy'" – construction, the present analysis has investigated the choices of individual language users outside this particular genre. Of course, the findings of the present study crucially hinge on the assumption that (i) an experimental study can reflect the potential of language usage, and (ii) that the apparent-time approach is indeed valid. It can also not completely be ruled out that the higher frequency of the *s*-genitive with [-animate] possessors in the younger subject group is in fact due to other changes, e.g. a change in the educational schedule over time in such a way that older subjects may have been taught in school not to use the *s*-genitive with [-animate] possessors while the younger subjects might not have been instructed likewise. That is, the increasing use of the *s*-genitive with [-animate] possessors may not be genuine diachronic language-internal development but may be secondary to a change in what is conceived of as 'correct' or 'incorrect' within a language community. Yet, would this not still be a change, albeit that factors external to language come into play? Also, this factor would be the same for experimental studies and those studies which compare two corpora from two language periods.

In general, the analysis of the three factors animacy, topicality, and possessive relation within an experimental setting proved to be advantageous from a methodological point of view in a number of ways. It was possible to investigate the impact of these conceptual factors in what may approximate real choice contexts in a neutral setting, i.e. controlled for other factors. Also, even for such contexts a sufficient number of items were able to be tested which in naturally occurring speech are only infrequently attested; this was particularly relevant for the context of [-topical] possessors. And finally, the effects of the single factors could be kept apart from each other by (a) operationalizing them in such a way as to test only the effect of one factor and not, simultaneously, the effect of the other factors too, and (b) by testing all eight logically possible combinations of the three factors. It was also in this way that the interaction of factors could be assessed. The present study has shown that an analysis of the interaction of the factors animacy, topicality, and possessive relation yields even more precise results than when investigating them independently. Testing all logically possible combinations of factors allows us to pinpoint in which contexts the *s*-genitive is still favorable and in which it is not. In particular, it could be shown that the *s*-genitive is highly probable when the possessor is [+animate], [+topical] *and* in a [+prototypical] possessive relation with its possessum noun, i.e. when all three factors go together. If not, the likelihood for the occurrence of the *s*-genitive decreases orderly along the preference structure suggested. Analyzing the three factors in such a way therefore reveals that not *any* [+animate] or [+topical] possessor or a [+prototypical] possessive relation will trigger the *s*-genitive but that it is the way these factors co-occur along the hierarchy animacy > topicality > possessive relation that determines the likelihood for the *s*-genitive to be chosen. Moreover, only by considering how the three factors interact could their relative importance be safely established, as reflected in the preference structure above. And third, it is only by looking at the interaction of factors that the (short-term) diachronic increase in the frequency of the *s*-genitive could be shown to be primarily a development essentially restricted to [-animate] possessors.

What still needs to be explained, though, is why particularly the [-animate] [-topical] conditions show a somewhat deviating behavior throughout the analysis. This might be due to the fact that these two conditions ([-a/-t/+p] and [-a/-t/-p]) represent the 'worst' contexts for the occurrence of the *s*-genitive and that, at the lower end of the scale, subjects are more insecure in their choice. Another explanation may be that [-topical] possessors, although chosen to convey a referential interpretation, are, as discussed in §2.3.1 and §4.2.1, inherently ambiguous and close to receiving a non-referential compound reading. In the pilot study, where the test subjects were explicitly asked to comment on the items chosen, it was exactly such [-animate] [-topical] contexts, which caused most problems. In the following two examples, which were subsequently taken out of the questionnaire, non-possessive compounds were suggested by two of the test subjects as the more natural option (*torchlight* or *flashlight* in (60) and *bridge railing* in (61)).

(60)   *It was painstaking work, a wordless scrutiny of every centimetre by [the*
          light of a torch/by a torch's light]
                      (based on: Elizabeth George, Playing for the Ashes, 32)

(61)   *They dawdled at [the railing of a bridge/a bridge's railing]* .....
                      (based on: Elizabeth George, Playing for the Ashes, 219)

This shows how easily such [-animate] [-topical] contexts can be
interpreted as compounds, and although the conspicuous items have been
taken out for this reason it is still possible that this context in general is –
though not necessarily for every subject and for every item – open for a
compound interpretation, which may have biased the results. As Altenberg
(1982: §4.9) has shown for his seventeenth-century data, possessive
compounds do much more easily allow for a [-animate] possessor (see also
§7.3 and §7.4.4.1 below).

It is also possible that the choice of the possessor *car* in some of the
items may have played a role. Note that although *car* is a genuine concrete
inanimate noun, it might belong to those noun classes which have certain
affinities to animates. Some people care a lot about their cars, even give
them names so that maybe this noun is open for being treated by some
subjects as metaphorically animate, very much in the sense that Dabrowska
(1998) has shown computer terms to be treated as metaphorically extended
animates, resulting in a greater preference for the *s*-genitive (cf. §4.1.2).

Table 42. Items with *car* as possessor

condition	items with *car* as possessor	relative frequency of *s*-genitive for younger British subjects	relative frequency of genitive for older British subjects
[-a/+t/+p]	*the car's security system*	88.9%	85%
	the car's bonnet	63.9%	50%
	her car's wings	37.1%	30%
[-a/+t/-p]	*the car's condition*	38,9%	40%
[-a/-t/+p]	*a car's headlamps*	61.1%	45%
[-a/-t/-p]	*a car's silhouette*	27.8%	0%
	a car's fumes	44.4%	0%
	a car's driver	2.8%	5%

When looking at the single choices in the questionnaires it is somehow
striking that indeed those items containing *car* as a possessor show a
relatively high frequency of the *s*-genitive in contrast to the other items, cf.
the table 42 above for an overview of the relative frequency of the *s*-

genitive with *car*-items, exemplified for the British subjects. So, maybe the fact that what should be the 'worst' inanimate condition ([-a/-t/-p] contains more *car* items than its prototypical counterpart ([-a/-t/+p]) may then account for the uneven distribution of the *s*-genitive in these two conditions.[126] Moreover, when comparing the two age groups, it is rather striking that especially the younger subjects use the *s*-genitive much more freely with such *car* items in the 'worst' [-animate] [-topical] conditions, while the older subjects almost never use the *s*-genitive in this context. This may indicate that concrete nouns such as *car* because of their ability to be metaphorically interpreted as animates form a kind of bridging context for the use of other [-animate] [-topical] nouns in general.[127] I will return to the question of bridging contexts in the process of analogical/metaphorical extension again in §8.6.2.3 below.

There is, however, another aspect in which *car* is outstanding: it is an extremely short word. It has already been discussed in §3.3.2.2.4 that syntactic 'shortness' in terms of syntactic complexity plays a role in the choice of the *s*-genitive. What has so far, however, not been considered as a factor for the choice between the two genitive constructions is length as defined as word length, which also conforms to Behaghel's "Gesetz der wachsenden Glieder". And indeed, it has been shown in psycholinguistic research that shorter words tend to precede longer words in linear order in English (cf. e.g. Pinker and Birdsong 1979; McDonald; Bock, and Kelly 1993).[128] Evidence for a word order effect of word length comes also from the analysis of frozen binominal conjuncts (freezes) in Cooper and Ross (1975). Word length in these studies is defined in terms of number of syllables. To test whether word length may have played a role in the choice between the two genitives in the present questionnaire elicitation, I will, in the following, classify the items used according to the relative length of possessor and possessum determined by the number of syllables, broadly dividing each of the eight conditions in table 26 into three sub-conditions: (i) a controlled condition, where the difference in word length is kept to a mininum (maximally 1 syllable difference, e.g. *the girl's cheeks, her husband's hair*),[129] (ii) a "short > long" condition, where the possessor is short and the possessum is long, with a minimum of 2 syllables difference (e.g. *the boy's exhaustion, the car's security system*), and (iii) a "long > short" condition where the possessor is minimally 2 syllables longer than the possessum (e.g. *his sister-in-law's shoulder, a sixteen-year-old boy's future*). If there is indeed a length effect in the data, then the following predictions should hold true: Relative to the control/neutral condition, the *s*-genitive should be more frequent in the "short>long" condition, while the *of*-genitive should be more frequent in the "long > short" condition. Figures 27 (for the British subjects) and 28 (for the American subjects) show the relative frequency of the *s*-genitive according to these three word length conditions. Note that only those contexts have been quantified for which there were at least 2 items.[130]

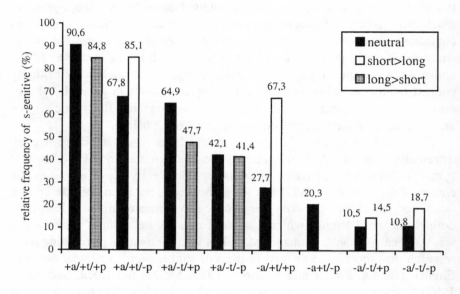

Figure 27. British subjects (n=56) – word length: relative frequency of the *s*-genitive (±a = [±animate]; ±t = [±topical]; ±p = [±prototypical] possessive relation) (cf. also tables 12 and 13, Appendix §10.1)

Figure 27 and figure 28 show that for both the American and British subjects word length does indeed affect the choice between the two genitive constructions in that the *s*-genitive is used more frequently with a short possessor and a long possessum ("short>long" condition) and less frequently with a long possessor and a short possessum ("long<short" condition), always relative to the control condition in which word length has been largely neutralized. Yet note, that the impact of word length seems to depend on the particular context. It is most pronounced in the following conditions: [+a/+t/-p], [+a/-t/+p] and [-a/+t/+p]. This indicates that word length mainly exerts an influence on the choice of the *s*-genitive in particularly sensitive contexts, which are neither the most optimal nor the worst for the occurrence of the *s*-genitive. The [+a/+t/+p] condition already

so strongly favors the *s*-genitive that a short possessor/long possessum would probably have resulted in a floor effect showing hardly any further improvement; this context can only be slightly weakened by a long possessor/short possessum. Likewise, if the condition is already 'bad', as with the [-animate] [-topical] conditions at the lower end of the preference scale, a "long>short" ordering does not make it much less likely for the *s*-genitive to occur.

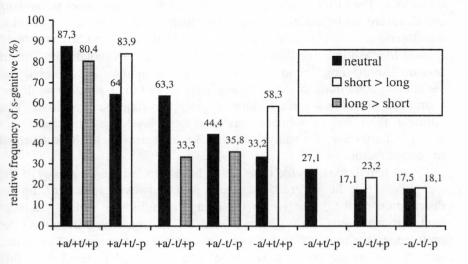

Figure 28. American subjects (n=48) – word length: relative frequency of the s-genitive (±a = [±animate]; ±t = [±topical]; ±p = [±prototypical] possessive relation) (cf. also tables 14 and 15, Appendix §10.1)

Also, a "short>long" ordering does not considerably improve the frequency of the *s*-genitive at the lower end of the [-animate] scale. Particularly striking is the strong influence of word length on the frequency in the most optimal [-animate] condition at the borderline to the [+animate] condition (= [-a/+t/+p]). Here "short>long" dramatically improves chances of choosing the *s*-genitive suggesting that this context is very sensitive to word length in that it needs only a 'little push' to be more apt to take the *s*-genitive. It may therefore turn out that word length is a decisive factor, tipping the scales toward the *s*-genitive or the *of*-genitive where the choice would have been otherwise undecided. Having observed an impact of word length on the frequency of the *s*-genitive, the question arises whether this may have biased the overall results for the distribution of the two genitive constructions? It may have, but only a little, for the following reasons. First, it must be noted that most items used in the questionnaire appear to be neutral to word length. Moreover, when comparing the single subject groups (British versus American subjects; younger versus older subjects), the word length effect is leveled out, since all subjects had to choose the *s*-genitive or the *of*-genitive for the same set of items, i.e. under the same conditions. The observed differences, particularly for [-animate] possessors, can therefore not be attributed to a word length effect but must be a genuine development. Note also that in general most [+animate] conditions contain more "long>short" conditions, while the [-animate] conditions rather contain "short>long" conditions, i.e. word length may have biased the [+animate] conditions towards a lower frequency of the *s*-genitive while the [-animate] conditions contain items slightly favoring the *s*-genitive. Yet, although the effect of animacy may have been leveled by this somewhat skewed distribution, the analysis in §6.4.3 nonetheless yields it as the most important factor.

Word length may, on the other hand, have affected the *frequency* of the *s*-genitive along the preference structure. As is, however, apparent from the distribution of the *s*-genitive in the control condition – which is almost neutral to word length – in figures 27 and 28, the *s*-genitive still follows the preference structure outlined above. One notable difference is, however, that the difference between [+a/+t/-p] and [+a/-t/+p] is leveled in this control condition and no longer significant for both the American and the British subjects. Yet, the difference in the corresponding [-animate] conditions ([-a/+t/-p] versus [-a/-t/+p]) remains significant (chi-square, $p<0.001$), confirming topicality as a more important factor than possessive relation.

Although the data indicate that word length does indeed affect the choice between the *s*-genitive and the *of*-genitive, they are nonetheless too sketchy and can only give a first impression of the impact of word length; more research on this factor, and particularly on its interaction with factors as – and other than – the ones investigated in the present study, is certainly in order.

To put the results of the ModE experimental study into a more long-term diachronic perspective, I will discuss in chapter 7 the diachronic development of the genitive alternation from Old English to early Modern English.

Chapter 7
Historical development of the genitive variation

The discussion of the historical development of the genitive variation in this chapter will be organized in the following way. First, I will give an outline of what is already known from handbooks and previous research concerning the genitive variation from Old English (OE) to early Modern English (EModE), with special emphasis paid to the role of animacy, topicality, and possessive relation in this development. I will then present and discuss evidence from a corpus analysis showing the *s*-genitive to have become more frequent – at the expense of the *of*-genitive – in the period from 1400 to 1630. These corpus data will be analyzed according to the factors animacy, topicality, and possessive relation considering their interaction, on the basis of which a preference structure modeling the preference for the *s*-genitive for the period investigated will be introduced in the same way as for the ModE data in chapter 6. Finally, the observed increase of the *s*-genitive along that preference structure will be linked in detail to the structural development of POSS '*s* from an inflectional ending to a clitic and determiner.

7.1   Old English: prenominal versus postnominal genitive

In Old English the *of*-genitive is only a marginal construction (cf. e.g. Faiß 1989: 124); according to Thomas (1931) the *of*-genitive constitutes only 1% of all adnominal genitive constructions (i.e. as opposed to the inflectional genitive) in the late tenth century (see also figure 29 in §7.2). It is mainly used to indicate source (*hē...hēt ʒetrimbian cyrican of treowe* 'he had a church of wood built') or partitive relations (*sume of þām sundor-hālʒan*, 'some of the saints'),[131] and it seems to have arisen from the original local meaning 'out of' of the preposition *of* (cf. Mustanoja 1960: 74). Stahl (1927: 14-15) points out that the *of*-genitive may have resulted from a reanalysis of a predicative construction; the phrase *se cyning of Englum cōm* may have had the original meaning 'the king of (= from) England came' and from which the adnominal meaning 'the king of England came' developed.

Although the *of*-genitive has not yet been established as the major grammatical variant as opposed to the inflected genitive, there is already in Old English a word order option with respect to the variable realization of the possessor (before or after the possessum). Within the inflected genitive the possessor can be realized prenominally (62) or postnominally (63):

(62)   *þæs   cyninges   þegnas*
       the-GEN   king-GEN   thanes
       'the king's thanes'
                                                    (Chron A 755)

(63)   *heafod   ealra   haligra   manna*
       head   all-GEN   holy-GEN   men-GEN
       'the head (leader) of all saints'   (ÆCHom ii. 14.23)

Therefore, as far as grammatical (word order) variation is concerned, the variants to be compared are – not yet – the inflected genitive versus the *of*-genitive, but the alternative word order of the inflected genitive, i.e. the prenominal versus the postnominal genitive.

In the course of Old English the postnominal genitive (NG) becomes increasingly substituted by the prenominal genitive (GN), and in this process animacy already was a decisive factor. While proper-name possessors had a strong preference to occur prenominally already throughout the Old English period (see Thomas 1931: 104; Timmer 1939; Mustanoja 1960: 76-77), the increasing shift from postnominal genitives (NG) towards prenominal genitives (GN), as shown by Timmer (1939), begins with common nouns denoting persons (e.g. *mann, cyning*) (i.e. [+human]) and gradually also comes to include common nouns denoting things (i.e. [-human]), a development that seems to run along the animacy hierarchy (cf. §4.1.1). The preference of proper names, which are inherently more topical than common nouns (cf. §4.2.1), to occur prenominally points also to topicality as a factor at work already in Old English. Moreover, Brown (1970: 40-41; as cited in Harris and Campbell 1995: 208) in his investigation of the *Pastoral Care* shows that the postnominal genitive seems to be preferred if the possessor is modified by an adjective and if there is a partitive relation. Thomas (1931: 105-106) has argued that primarily structural factors, i.e. both the loss of the article/determiner and strong adjective inflection as well as the shift towards fixed word order to indicate grammatical relations contributed to the restriction of the inflected genitive to prenominal position only.

7.2   Middle English: the gradual decline of the *s*-genitive

In the Middle English period three major developments can be observed for adnominal genitive constructions. First, at the beginning of Middle English the inflected genitive is restricted to the prenominal genitive; the alternative word order (possessum-possessor) is now displayed by the *of*-genitive (cf. Mustanoja 1960: 77). Second, the various inflectional genitive endings are generalized to the *-(e/i/y)s* ending; this process seems to be completed by the fourteenth century at the latest (cf. Mustanoja 1960: 71; see also §7.5.2.1 below). And third, in the course of Middle English the *s*-genitive becomes increasingly replaced by the periphrastic *of*-genitive. The corpus analysis by Thomas (1931) on the distribution of the *s*-genitive versus the *of*-genitive from late Old English to the fourteenth century is to this day the most exhaustive study on the quantitative distribution of these two genitive constructions, the results of which are illustrated in figure 29 below.

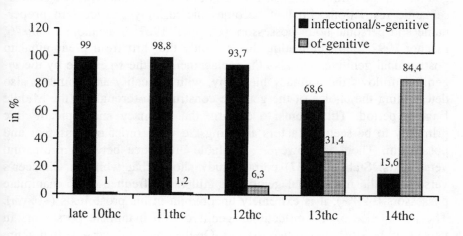

Figure 29.   Distribution of the inflectional genitive versus the *of*-genitive from the late tenth to the fourteenth centuries (Thomas 1931)

Figure 29 shows that while the *of*-genitive was at best marginal at the end of the Old English period (1%), from the twelfth century onwards the *of*-genitive increasingly replaces the *s*-genitive until in the fourteenth century it is by far the more frequent variant (84.4%). Some scholars assume that the similarity to French *de* may have accelerated the spread of the *of* genitive (cf. Mustanoja 1960: 74). In contrast, Thomas (1931: 120) attributes the increasing use of the *of*-genitive not only to the principle of analogy but also to more structural reasons, finding in his data a "direct relationship between loss of inflection in the definite article and strong adjective and the increased use of the periphrastic genitive." As it appears from Thomas' (1931) account, both the fixation of the inflectional genitive to prenominal position and its replacement by the *of*-genitive seem to be due to the same underlying structural pressures.

The process of replacing the *s*-genitive by the *of*-genitive is most notable with plural possessors and in prose (see e.g. Mustanoja 1960: 76 Brunner 1962: 28; Fischer 1992: 226). Whether there are any dialectal differences in this development is difficult to establish because of the uneven distribution of prose versus verse texts in the various dialects of English throughout the Middle English period (cf. Mustanoja 1960: 76 Fischer 1992: 226). It is interesting to note that the sharp decline of the *s* genitive in the Middle English period goes hand in hand with two lexical semantic restrictions. First, it becomes increasingly restricted to proper name and personal-noun possessors (cf. Stahl 1927; Mustanoja 1960: 76 Fischer 1992: 226), indicating that not only the shift from prenominal to postnominal genitives but also the replacement of the *s*-genitive by the *of* genitive follows the animacy hierarchy, with topicality and animacy also determining the choice of the genitive construction throughout the Middle English period. This seems to confirm that animacy and topicality are primarily to be seen as factors affecting the word order of possessor and possessum. There is, however, a notable difference between prose and verse texts: Stahl's (1927) corpus study shows that while in Chaucer's verse texts the inflectional genitive is still fairly frequent with inanimate possessors (~20%), it is extremely uncommon in his prose texts (~0.4%). The persistence of the inflectional genitive with inanimate possessors in verse may be attributed to two reasons. On the one hand, verse is that genre in which the inflectional genitive lingered on longest in general; according to Fischer (1992: 226) "poetic language often shows archaic features, and besides, it gave the poet the opportunity to vary rhythm and stress patterns." On the other hand, it is particularly in poetic language that personifications are used, i.e. inanimate nouns conceived of as animate (see also §7.3; and on personification particularly §8.6.2.3).

Moreover, it has been noted that the *s*-genitive becomes more and more restricted to certain genitive functions, i.e. the possessive and the subjective function (cf. Fischer 1992: 226-227), although there is, as for Modern

English, no unifying definition of what should exactly be included in these categories. The *of*-genitive, on the other hand, seems to have gained ground first in partitive functions, and it is somehow striking that in the course of Middle English it is in this function – apart from the descriptive function – that the *of*-genitive eventually becomes the sole genitive construction (cf. e.g. Stahl 1927: 14-15; Brunner 1962: 28-29).[132]

7.3   Early Modern English: no further change?

Since, as we have seen, the 'dramatic' period in the history of the genitive variation is undoubtedly the Middle English period, the few empirical investigations (Stahl 1927; Thomas 1931) that compare the distribution of the *s*-genitive versus the *of*-genitive from a long-term diachronic perspective concentrate on this very period. Thomas (1931), however, only gives the overall distribution of the two constructions, not further specifying his data according to specific environments. Also, Thomas' study ends with the fourteenth century. Stahl (1927), in contrast, does distinguish between animate and inanimate possessors, but his corpus relies on single texts or authors for whole centuries. Although Stahl includes EModE data in his study, this data come exclusively from works by Shakespeare, which cannot be taken to be representative for the whole period (cf. also Altenberg 1982: 19). Den Breejen (1937) provides very detailed observations on the distribution of the *s*-genitive versus the *of*-genitive in EModE prose texts, but his study is restricted to the first half of the sixteenth century, and he does not quantify his data at all. The only extensive quantitative study of the genitive alternation for early Modern English comes from Altenberg's (1982) corpus study, in which he analyses the frequency of the *s*-genitive and the *of*-genitive for a wide variety of factors in several controlled sub-corpora. Apart from phonological, syntactic and stylistic factors, which have already been briefly discussed under §3.3.2.2.4, his data show that animacy, topicality, and the relation between possessor and possessum affect the choice between the two genitive constructions. In particular, animacy seems to have the strongest impact on the choice of the *s*-genitive, since in his corpus this construction very rarely occurs with an inanimate possessor. If the *s*-genitive occurs at all with [-animate] possessors in Altenberg's corpus, then – as in Stahl's (1927) corpus (see above) – preferably in verse rather than in prose, in possessive compounds and mainly with abstract nouns, either as expressions of time (*thy last nights work, yesterday foolery*) or as personifications (*natures hands, fates ministers*), see Altenberg (1982: 132ff.). With concrete nouns, the *s*-genitive occurs – if at all – only in verse, and here mainly with geographical nouns and names (*the Seas entrance, all earths pleasures, Jordan's Sand, Egypts Queene*). According to Altenberg (1982: 297-300) it is only within the context of a [+animate] possessor that other factors, as e.g. topicality may further influence the variation between the two genitive constructions. Topicality is important in that the *s*-genitive is more likely if the possessor is given and the possessum new (cf. §4.2.2). The semantic relation between the possessor and the possessum is also important in the seventeenth century. Altenberg (1982), however, works with a very delicate classification based on Fillmorean case roles and his results for this factor resist a closer comparison with other studies and the present one. In general, Altenberg (1982: 297-298) stresses the restricting force of an objective relation, which, in contrast to subjective genitives, almost categorically calls for the *of*-genitive (cf. also §4.3.1 above). The fact that animacy is the major factor for the choice of the *s*-genitive is confirmed by Raumolin-Brunberg (1991) in her study on the noun phrase in the early sixteenth century, which focuses on the language of one particular author, i.e. Thomas More.

For the early Modern English period it is difficult – if not even impossible – to compare the results of the various empirical studies available. Different scholars use different types of corpora, applying different inclusion and exclusion criteria and classify their data in their own way, very much in the sense as it was already apparent for the empirical studies dealing with Modern English in chapter 4 above. As argued in §3.3.2.1 and shown in chapter 6, the choice and frequency of the *s*-genitive does, however, crucially depend on the specific linguistic or extralinguistic environment. There is not a single study investigating the distribution of the *s*-genitive versus the *of*-genitive in any systematic and comparable way covering the period between the fifteenth century and the sixteenth century. And although recently the diachronic investigation of the English genitive has gained much attention in the literature, these studies either focus on the discussion about the grammatical status of the *s*-genitive as an inflection or a clitic (see §7.5 below) or on the role of the *s*-less genitive in the development of the category of genitive case (see §7.5.1.1 below), but none of them aims at providing any empirical data concerning the relative frequency of the *s*-genitive as opposed to its morphosyntactic variant, the *of*-genitive. Appropriate data on the distribution of the two genitive constructions for the time span between the fifteenth and the sixteenth centuries are therefore lacking, which seems to have given rise to the somewhat silent impression we get from the handbooks that there was no further change in the distribution of the two genitive constructions from the fourteenth century onwards. What certainly also contributed to this impression is the fact that the figures presented by Thomas (1931) (cf. figure 29 above) have served as the main – and often only – reference point for the distribution of the two genitive construction in the handbooks on the history of English (cf. e.g. Mustanoja 1960; Brunner 1962; Fischer 1992). And these figures very clearly show the replacement of the *s*-genitive by the *of*-genitive as a typical *S*-curve process. From the late tenth to the twelfth centuries the process advances very slowly, between the twelfth and the fourteenth centuries the replacement of the *s*-genitive by the *of*-genitive rapidly accelerates and gains momentum with the *s*-genitive figuring only about 15% in the fourteenth century, lingering on in the English language in very restricted contexts to the present day. Such a development is fully in accordance with theories of language change and corresponds to the typological development of English (see also §7.4.3 below). So why should anyone doubt that anything unexpected in the distribution of the *s*-genitive and the *of*-genitive may have happened after the fourteenth century? And why conduct further empirical case studies on this issue? Altenberg (1982: 302) seems to be silently assuming that the *s*-genitive must have been further reduced throughout the fifteenth and the sixteenth centuries, concluding his study of the genitive alternation in seventeenth-century English with the remark that the process of replacing the *s*-genitive by the *of*-genitive seems to have "reached its peak in the 17th century" and that "a functional and stylistic balance between the two variants had established itself". As I will show in the next section, the former statement may well have to be rethought, while the latter certainly contains a grain of truth. Likewise – and probably based on Altenberg's (1982) observation – Rissanen (1999: 201) states that "[i]n the sixteenth and seventeenth centuries, the distribution of the *s*-genitive and the *of*-genitive developed roughly to what it is today." It is one of the main findings of this study that this observation cannot be maintained.

It is only in recent research, which I conducted in co-operation with Letizia Vezzosi and Dieter Stein, that new empirical evidence for the development of the genitive alternation in general, and for the impact of the factors animacy, topicality, and possessive relation in particular has been brought forward for the period between the fifteenth and the early seventeenth centuries, which altogether calls for a re-evaluation of the history of the *s*-genitive and its alternation with the *of*-genitive.

7.4   Against all odds? The revival of the *s*-genitive in early Modern English

The late Middle/early Modern English data (henceforth referred to as "EModE data") as used in this section stems mainly from the analyses in Rosenbach and Vezzosi (2000) and Rosenbach, Stein, and Vezzosi (2000) and will be referred to accordingly. I will focus here on those aspects of these studies which are crucial for the argumentation of the present study, and will conduct some additional analyses and interpretations on the data in such a way that makes the EModE data more easily comparable with the results from the experimental study in chapter 6.

Contrary to what has traditionally been assumed, we were able to show in this research project that the *s*-genitive was increasing again in its relative frequency from the fifteenth to the early seventeenth centuries. In this section I will first give a brief description of the corpus and the general methodology. I will then present the evidence for the revival of the *s*-genitive and discuss how it can be evaluated. Finally, the impact of the factors animacy, topicality, and possessive relation in this development will be addressed.

7.4.1   Corpus analysis (1400 – 1630): methodological preliminaries

In Rosenbach and Vezzosi (2000) we analyzed a corpus consisting of prose texts covering the period from 1400 to 1630. The corpus mainly contained a selection of text excerpts taken from the *Helsinki Corpus* as well as some other selected texts (for a list of the texts used, see Rosenbach, Stein, and Vezzosi 2000), having the advantage that the corpus is fairly heterogeneous, including various authors and ranging from informal to formal texts thereby avoiding the results being biased towards the stylistic preferences of single authors or certain text types. The fact that we were mainly dealing with short excerpts of larger texts should not have influenced our results, since obligatory contexts for genitive constructions are in general very common. So we should not expect to find serious imbalances within single texts. That is, the distribution found within say five pages can be regarded to be representative of the distribution in the whole text.

The corpus was subdivided into four time intervals, which were taken to represent synchronic stages: 1400 – 1449 (I), 1450 – 1499 (II), 1500 – 1559 (III) and 1560 – 1630 (IV). Although the comparison of several synchronic stages is the essence of the structural approach to historical linguistics, which somewhat ignores the gradualness of the process, it remains nonetheless the only feasible methodological procedure. In order to spot changes at the level of the language system we need to generalize over a longer period of time and over several speakers, although in fact the changes most likely operate in a much more subtle way and more slowly on the level of the individual. In the choice-based approach to grammatical variation of the present study, the underlying assumption is that if the factors animacy, topicality, and possessive relation can be shown to have been operative in the EModE data, this implies that the natural/iconic principles introduced in §6.2 can be evoked in the same way as for the ModE experimental data.

7.4.2   Analysis and results: the revival of the s-genitive (1400 – 1630)

For a first approximation in Rosenbach and Vezzosi (2000) all occurrences of the *s*-genitive and the *of*-genitive were recorded irrespective of whether these were choice- or categorical contexts. As said in §3.3.2.3 above, for heuristic reasons this may be a useful procedure: we first proceed from all possible occurrences, then identify the categorical versus the choice contexts and only subsequently narrowing the investigation down to an approximation of real choice contexts. The whole corpus consisted of more than 10,000 tokens, and initially all nominal constructions that could possibly express a genitive relation were counted; the relative frequency of these constructions are listed in table 43 below (for the classification and the figures, see also Rosenbach and Vezzosi 2000: 290).

Table 43 reveals two things: (i) The *s*-genitive and the *of*-genitive are indeed the major competing nominal genitive constructions in the period investigated; all the other constructions are – in quantitative terms – marginal and on this ground ignored in the further analysis.[133] (ii) The frequency of the *s*-genitive increases from 8% in the first interval (1400 – 1449) to 19.1% in the last interval (1560 – 1630) at the expense of the *of*-genitive (decreasing from 90.7% in interval I to 77.5% in interval IV). The analysis in Rosenbach and Vezzosi (2000) also showed that in the first interval the *s*-genitive is not only very infrequent but it also occurs preferably with certain lexical possessors (e.g. *God, king, queen, man*), which moreover often combine to almost idiomatic uses (e.g. *in Goddes lufe, Goddes name, owr Lordys mercy, Godes grace, ye kyngis pece*).

Table 43. Distribution of genitive constructions in corpus (1400 – 1630) (*column "s-genitive" comprises both the old orthographical -*(e/i/y)s* form and the ModE apostrophe '*s* spelling)[134]

genitive variant	possessor-possessum								possessum-possessor			
	s-genitive*		zero-genitive		*s*-less genitive		*his*-genitive		*of*-genitive		*to*-genitive	
example	the constable's son		certin howers tasks		the butcher wyff		Monsieur Boissy his army		the father of Simon		servant to Polonius	
time interval	n	%	n	%	n	%	n	%	n	%	n	%
(I)	119	8	6	0.4	9	0.6	1	0.1	1341	90.7	3	0.2
(II)	371	14.9	8	0.3	14	0.6	39	1.6	2059	82.6	1	-
(III)	320	11.8	10	0.4	84	3.1	11	0.4	2257	82.8	41	1.5
(IV)	449	19.1	12	0.5	31	1.3	10	0.4	1826	77.5	29	1.2

The low frequency of the *s*-genitive together with its restricted lexical applicability may indicate that the *s*-genitive was further on the decrease in the first half of the fifteenth century.[135] If we contrast the relative frequency of the *s*-genitive and the *of*-genitive in our corpus with that of the preceding centuries provided by Thomas (1931), then the following picture emerges.[136]

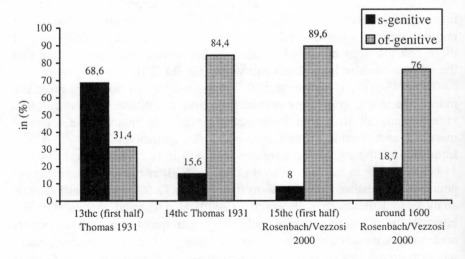

Figure 30. Relative frequency of the inflected/*s*-genitive versus the *of*-genitive from the thirteenth to the early seventeenth centuries

Figure 30 suggests a somewhat U-shaped trajectory of the *s*-genitive. It may, however, be difficult to directly compare the distributions found by Thomas (1931) with our corpus data, since the corpora and the way the constructions were classified and counted may well not be comparable. No matter, however, whether there is indeed a further decline of the *s*-genitive from the late fourteenth to the early fifteenth centuries or not, it can be safely noted that within our corpus the increase in the relative frequency of the *s*-genitive from the first interval (1400 – 1449) to the last interval (1560 – 1630) is well constituted and in itself remarkable.

In Rosenbach and Vezzosi (1999) we investigated in which respect the dialectal stratification of our corpus may have played a role in this resurgence of the *s*-genitive. Note that it is possible that the observed increase of the *s*-genitive is a development restricted to a certain dialect but not a genuine development of *the* English language. It turned out, however, that most of our corpus data before 1500 belonged to the East Midlands dialect and that it was also in this dialect that the increase of the *s*-genitive was most apparent. Since the East Midlands dialect is generally considered to be the forerunner of the emerging English Standard, and since our corpus data from 1500 onwards is supposed to reflect Standard English,[137] we concluded that the new productivity of the *s*-genitive is a feature of the emerging English Standard language (Rosenbach and Vezzosi 1999: 6).

7.4.3 *Interpretation: Why the revival of the* s-*genitive is surprising – or is it?*

The revival of the *s*-genitive as shown above is a development that seems to run counter to what would have been predicted from both a typological point of view and from theories of language change.

The term "drift" as coined by Sapir (1921) describes the typical morphosyntactic pathway of languages from synthetic characters, in which sentence relations are marked by a rich case system, to analytic characters, in which the same sentence relations become expressed by invariable words and, configurationally, by fixed word order; this term fits the typological development of the English language well. From Old English to Middle English most case distinctions were lost; this development was compensated by more and more periphrastic constructions and an increasingly more rigid (Subject–Verb–Object) word order. Therefore, the *s*-genitive as a synthetic device, should – if anything – have further decreased in favor of the analytic *of*-genitive but not have been revived.

Moreover, apart from some case residues in the pronominal paradigm, genitive case was the only case left intact in late Middle English. This fact is in itself remarkable. Genitive case is generally considered one of the most marked cases in the nominal paradigm, certainly more marked than, for example, accusative case (cf. e.g. Greenberg 1966: 38; Silverstein 1976: 162). Note also, that in the NP accessibility hierarchy as formulated by Keenan and Comrie (1977) it is the genitive which figures lowest on the scale; it is that syntactic function which is least easily to be relativized in a relative clause. Taken together, why should genitive case-marking be maintained longest and even be reinforced? Typologically, such a constellation looks extremely odd (cf. e.g. Janda 1980: 245, Plank 1985: 229-230, Taylor 1996: 118 for such an argumentation).[138]

Also, in terms of word order languages tend to be typologically consistent, and if not, they should at least strive to become so. Work on syntactic typology (e.g. Greenberg 1963, Vennemann 1974, Hawkins 1983) correlates the general word-order type of a language (Verb-Object [VO] versus Object-Verb [OV]) with the relative placement of the head and its modifiers. VO-languages, such as English, are typically head-first, so likewise modifiers should follow their heads, which predicts "head – modifier" as the typologically consistent order for possessum and possessor in English.

VO ⊃ head-modifier/NG (possessum-possessor) → *of*-genitive
OV ⊃ modifier-head /GN (possessor-possessum) → *s*-genitive

The revival of the *s*-genitive, having the order "modifier – head" (possessor – possessum), is a development back to a typologically inconsistent word order and therefore contradicts the predictions of syntactic typology. If anything, the development should have been towards total loss but not towards an increasing frequency of the *s*-genitive.

Taking all these arguments together, the comeback of the *s*-genitive looks like an altogether odd and unexpected development in the light of the general laws of typology and language change. But then, maybe, it is not as surprising as it looks at first glance.

While it is generally assumed that it is typologically awkward to have the genitive as the only remaining case in a language, this may be too sweeping a statement which fails to separate genitive as a case operating on the sentence level, assigned by verbs, and genitive as a purely adnominal case. While genitive case assigned by verbs is undoubtedly a marked case as opposed to the accusative, it does not have any *inflectional* competitors on the nominal level. There are, to the best of my knowledge, no cross-linguistic studies, which in fact show that the genitive as an *adnominal* case is a marked case.[139] Moreover, it is striking that English has various head-final constructions on the NP level (in the traditional sense of "head", see below): adjectival modifiers typically *precede* their heads (word order: AN), and also in compounds we find head-final (OV) structures (cf. *truck-driver*), while VO-structures such as *pick-pocket* are very rare (cf. also Harris and Campbell 1995: 201).[140] So, the view implicit in syntactic typology that word order on the sentential/VP level should ideally correlate with word order on the NP level may have some cross-linguistic validity,[141] yet English does not seem to care too much about its inconsistency in this respect, allowing adjectives, compounds and the *s*-genitive to go against the preferred clausal word ordering.[142]

In addition, syntactic typology proceeds from a – from today's point of view – monolithic conception of headedness. While Nichols (1986: 57) still maintains that within linguistics it is generally agreed on what the head of a given construction is, classifying the possessum as the "head" and the possessor as the "dependent" (i.e. modifier), in more recent linguistic (formal) theory the emergence of functional categories and heads turns this classic concept of headedness completely upside down. As shown in §2.3.2 above, within DP-analysis POSS *'s* can function as the head of the functional category DP. In such a conception, the *s*-genitive would be head-first and hence typologically consistent.[143]

Last, but certainly not least, as will be shown in §7.5 there is a striking chronological correlation between the structural change of POSS *'s* from a fully-fledged inflection to a more clitic-like determiner and the observed revival of the *s*-genitive, which is, most likely, not accidental. As will be argued, it may have been this change in the grammar which has given rise to a higher productivity of the *s*-genitive. Moreover, given this structural change, it must be stressed that the increasing use of the *s*-genitive does not necessarily contradict the general drift towards more analyticity: the *s*-genitive becomes more productive as a clitic/determiner, not as an inflection.

Adding all this together, at second glance the revival of the *s*-genitive may look somewhat less odd. Largely based on the analyses in Rosenbach and Vezzosi (2000) and Rosenbach, Stein, and Vezzosi (2000), I will now, in the following section take a closer look at the impact of the factors animacy, topicality, and possessive relation in this development.

7.4.4   The role of the factors animacy, topicality, and possessive relation in the revival of the s-genitive
7.4.4.1 Animacy

The distribution of the *s*-genitive as opposed to the *of*-genitive according to a [-animate] possessor in the corpus is as follows (cf. also Rosenbach and Vezzosi 2000: 297-299):

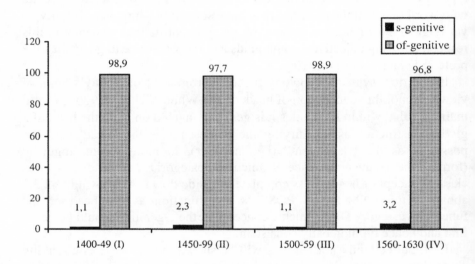

Figure 31.   Distribution of the *s*-genitive and *of*-genitive according to [-animate] possessor (in %)

As can be seen from figure 31, the *s*-genitive is extremely rare with a [-animate] possessor. Moreover, looking at the few cases recorded shows that they are generally almost idiomatic, compound-like expressions (e.g. *new yere's eve, his death's-bed, a new year's gift, a hair's breadth, an hour's talk, a longe summers day*) or instances of personification, where the [-animate] possessor seems to be conceptualized like an animate one (e.g. *my mind's eye, for furtune's finger, offence's gilded hand, sin's true nature, fortune's cap, in love's fire*). Note that these contexts for *s*-genitives with [-animate] possessors correspond to those observed by Altenberg (1982) in his seventeenth-century corpus (cf. §7.3 above). In our corpus, there are only a *very* limited number of tokens which seem to be productive cases of what could come close to a truly inanimate possessor (e.g. *on the houses top, the world's diameter).* This extremely low frequency of the *s*-genitive with [-animate] possessors and its restriction to mainly idiomatic uses and personifications rules it out as a real choice-context for the period investigated.

As a [-animate] possessor turned out to be a (quasi)knock-out criterion for the occurrence of the *s*-genitive, a [+animate] possessor marks the range of choice-context, in which both genitive constructions have a chance to be realized. Among the sub-corpus of [+animate] [+human] possessors, the following further contexts could be identified as categorical contexts for either the use of the *s*-genitive or the *of*-genitive and were therefore excluded from the further analysis:

(1) Partitive constructions (e.g. *some of the footmen, one of his servants*) have been shown to exclusively take the *of*-genitive in the corpus under investigation (cf. Rosenbach and Vezzosi 2000: §3.2).

(2) Expressions such as *the king/queen's grace/highness/majesty* or *the king of England* are fixed formula – or idiosyncratic chunks – that never allow for the occurrence of the alternative construction. Other formula-like expressions, such as *in god's name*, though no longer semantically transparent, still show variation between the two genitive constructions in the corpus (*in god's name* versus *in the name of god*) and were therefore treated as choice contexts.

(3) *Of*-genitives in modifier-relations, such as *a daughter of noble fame, chains of gold*) are never expressed by a corresponding *s*-genitive (**noble fame's daughter*; * *gold' chains*) throughout the corpus. Finally, further excluded from this [+animate] sub-corpus were [-referential], i.e. generic, possessors (e.g. *a butcher's knife, a Christians soul, the shape of a woman, the office of a tutor*) for reasons already discussed under §2.3.1 and §3.3.2.2.1. Altenberg (1982: §1.6.2) also discusses the problematic status of compound-like expressions and concludes that such compounds (= *s*-genitives in modification relation) are "structurally invariable" forms, which "are never completely analogous" with a corresponding *of*-genitive (Altenberg 1982: 25).

The relative frequency of the *s*-genitive versus the *of*-genitive within this restricted [+animate] context, focusing on possessive relations only, is shown in figure 32 below.[144] In this restricted [+animate] context the diachronic increase of the *s*-genitive is even more apparent: while in the first interval (1400 – 1449) the *of*-genitive (72.2%) is still the far more frequent option, in the last interval the *s*-genitive (64%) has become clearly more frequent than the *of*-genitive (36%). The increase in the relative frequency of the *s*-genitive between the single time intervals is always statistically significant (cf. table 44 below).

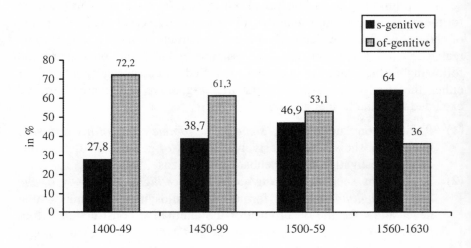

Figure 32.   Distribution of the *s*-genitive and *of*-genitive within a restricted [+animate] context (cf. table 16, Appendix §10.2)

Table 44.   Relative frequency of the *s*-genitive with [+animate] possessors (1400→ 1630)

relative frequency of the *s*-genitive within [+animate] (1400 – 1630)			
time intervals	chi square value	*df*	*p*-level
1400-1449 (I) →1450-1499 (II)	7.107	1	*p*<0.01
1450-1499 (II) → 1500-1559 (III)	6.108	1	*p*<0.025
1500-1559 (III) → 1560-1630 (IV)	20.410	1	*p*<0.001

Note that a statistical analysis should be restricted to potential choice contexts and that therefore the revival of the *s*-genitive – as noted in §7.4.2 – not only is more apparent in the contexts given in figure 32 and table 44, but it can also only be safely be concluded in such a restricted [+animate] sub-corpus.

The analysis of the interaction of the other two other conceptual factors, topicality and possessive relationship in §§7.4.4.2-3 is accordingly confined to this [+animate] sub-corpus.

7.4.4.2 Topicality

The factor topicality as analyzed in Rosenbach, Stein, and Vezzosi (2000) refers to the distinction between referentially given and new possessors. Within the given category we further distinguished between more given and less given possessors. Proper nouns, divine entities (e.g. *god, Christ, angels*) and persons of high-rank (e.g. *the king*) as extra-contextually- or culturally known referents were regarded as more readily accessible and given than otherwise definite, more context-bound referents (*my/the father*). [145] Referentially indefinite expressions were coded as new possessors. Note that in Rosenbach, Stein, and Vezzosi (2000) we have shown that, in general, truly referentially indefinite possessors figured very low in the corpus in contrast to definite possessors and for this reason they were excluded from the further analysis.[146] For the present purpose these indefinite (= [-topical]) possessors are included for the following reason. Although the results for this context certainly need to be taken cautiously in the light of the overall low rate of occurrence and therefore will not enter any statistical analysis here, nonetheless some tendencies in the behavior of the *s*-genitive in this context can be discerned, which can be linked to the patterns observed in the experimental study in chapter 6. For a brief overview of the classification of topicality in the EModE corpus and the respective predictions see figure 33.

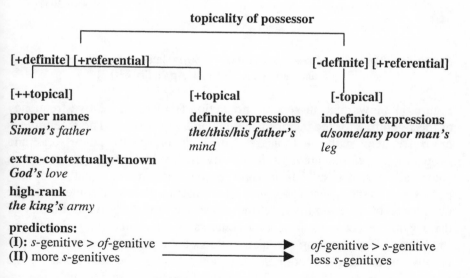

Figure 33. Topicality: operational definition and predictions

According to prediction (I) in §6.4.2 the *s*-genitive should be more frequent than the *of*-genitive with topical possessors than with non-topical possessors. In addition, within the category of topical possessors more *s*-genitives are to be expected with highly topical possessors (= [++topical]) possessors than with less highly topical possessors (= [+topical]), while least *s*-genitives should occur with [-topical] possessors.[147]

Figure 34 shows the relative frequency of the *s*-genitive according to the [++topical], [+topical] and [-topical] contexts for each time interval.[148]

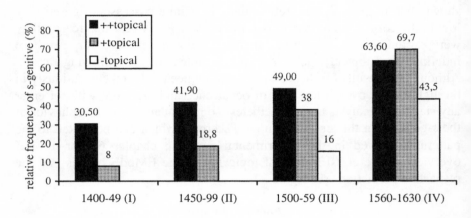

Figure 34. Topicality of possessor (1400 – 1630): relative frequency of the *s*-genitive (cf. also tables 17a and 17b, Appendix §10.2)

Figure 34 shows that, in general, prediction (II) for the relative frequency of the *s*-genitive for the factor topicality can be confirmed. The *s*-genitive is more frequent with [++topical] than with [+topical] possessors, and [-topical] possessors are less frequently realized by the *s*-genitive than [+topical] possessors.[149] It is only in the last interval that [+topical] possessors slightly oust [++topical] ones as the preferred context for the occurrence of the *s*-genitive, yet the difference in the relative frequency of the *s*-genitive between these two contexts is not statistically significant. Prediction (I) concerning the distribution of the *s*-genitive versus the *of*-genitive in the single conditions, can, however, only be confirmed for the last time interval (1560 – 1630). In the first two time intervals the *of*-genitive is always the significantly more frequent option than the *s*-

genitive, irrespective of the degree of topicality (chi-square, *df* 1, *p*<0.001).[150] The third time interval (1500 – 1559) marks a turning point: the two genitive constructions are now equally distributed within the [++topical] context, and in the last interval (1560 – 1630) the *s*-genitive has become the significantly more frequent option than the *of*-genitive in both the [++ topical] and the [+ topical] context (chi-square, *df* 1, *p*<0.001).

7.4.4.3 Possessive relations

In contrast to the analysis in Rosenbach, Stein, and Vezzosi (2000) I have not included subjective and objective genitives in the present sub-corpus but will focus here solely on possessive relations, as in the experimental study in §6.4. The type of possessive relation has been classified as defined under §6.2.3.1, distinguishing between [+prototypical] and [-prototypical] possessive relations, [151] resulting in the same predictions as for the experimental study, namely:

(I) The *s*-genitive should be more frequent than the *of*-genitive with [+prototypical] possessive relations.

(II) The *s*-genitive should be more frequent in [+prototypical] than in [-prototypical] possessive relations.

Figure 35 below illustrates the relative frequency of the *s*-genitive as specified for the type of possessive relation for the four time intervals.

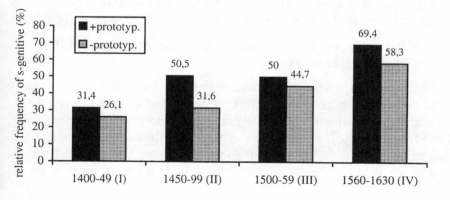

Figure 35. Possessive relation (1400 – 1630): relative frequency of the *s*-genitive (cf. tables 18a and 18b, Appendix §10.2)

As is apparent from figure 35 the *s*-genitive is, as predicted, always more frequent in [+prototypical] than in [-prototypical] possessive relations (= prediction II). Note, however, that this difference is only statistically significant for time intervals II (chi-square, *df* 1, *p*<0.001) and IV (chi-square, *df* 1, p<0.025).

Contrary to what has been predicted, however, the *of*-genitive is the (significantly) more frequent option than the *s*-genitive even with [+prototypical] possessive relations in the first time interval (1400 –1449) (chi-square, *df* 1, *p*<0.01). It is again from the second interval (1450 – 1499) onwards that the *s*-genitive gains ground, becoming as frequent as the *of*-genitive in the [+prototypical] contexts, and in the last interval (IV) the *s*-genitive has become significantly more frequent than the *of*-genitive with [+prototypical] possessive relations (chi-square, *df* 1, *p*<0.001).

So far we have seen that the factors topicality and possessive relation determine the choice between the *s*-genitive and the *of*-genitive within the categorical domain of [+animate possessors] for the late Middle and early Modern English period investigated. The frequency of the *s*-genitive correlates with the degree of topicality and the prototypicality of the possessive relation. Moreover, these two factors, as is the case with animacy (cf. §7.4.1), seem to play a significant role in the overall increase of the *s*-genitive. While throughout the fifteenth century the *of*-genitive is, as a rule, the more frequent option in *every* [+animate] context, in the last interval (1560 – 1630) the *s*-genitive has become significantly more frequent with topical possessors and in prototypical possessive relations. In a next step, I will now try to evaluate the relative importance of topicality and possessive relation in each time interval within the [+animate] context.

7.4.4.4 Interaction of factors: topicality and possessive relation within [+animate] contexts

As argued in chapter 6, it is important to study the factors independently from each other to keep their effects separate and evaluate their relative impact on the choice between the two alternating genitive constructions. The three types of topicality as defined in figure 33 and the basic distinction between [+prototypical] and [-prototypical] possessive relations lead to six possible combinations of these two factors in the [+animate] context, as exemplified in table 45.[152]

Table 45. Interaction of topicality and possessive relation (1400 – 1630): contexts (+ proto = + prototypical possessive relation)

[+animate]					
[++topical]		[+topical]		[-topical]	
[+proto]	[-proto]	[+proto]	[-proto]	[+proto]	[-proto]
Simon's father	*the authority of the true Pope*	*my father's book*	*the violence of my said ancestors*	*a poor man's leg*	*the image of a naked man*

Figure 36 below shows the relative frequency of the *s*-genitive (as opposed to that of the *of*-genitive) according to these six conditions for each of the four time intervals. Note that in contrast to the experimental study in chapter 6 where the items and conditions to be tested could be deliberately chosen in advance, yielding a representative number of tokens for each condition, in the EModE corpus the number of genitive occurrences in the single conditions are not equally distributed over all conditions and all time intervals.

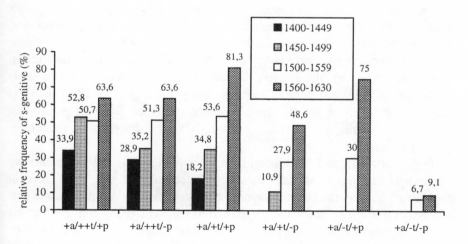

Figure 36. Relative frequency of the *s*-genitive according to the interaction of the factors topicality and possessive relation in [+animate] sub-corpus (±a = [±animate]; ++t = [++topical], ±t = [±topical], ±p = [± prototypical] possessive relation) (cf. tables 17a and 17b, Appendix §10.2)

Figure 36 shows that in the first two intervals (1400 – 1449 and 1450 – 1499)

(1)   the *s*-genitive is mainly restricted to highly topical [++topical] possessors,
(2)   if the *s*-genitive occurs at all with less topical [+topical] possessors, this is first (interval 1400 – 1449) in [+prototypical] possessive relations only, only in the second interval (1450 – 1499) does it also extend to [-prototypical] contexts, although in this context the *s*-genitive is less frequent than with [+prototypical] possessive relations.

Therefore, we concluded in Rosenbach, Stein, and Vezzosi (2000: 194-196) that the degree of topicality turns out to be a stronger factor than possessive relation throughout the fifteenth century.

In the third (1500 – 1559) and last interval (1560 – 1630) the type of possessive relation does not influence the frequency of the *s*-genitive with [++topical] possessors. It does, however, affect the frequency of the *s*-genitive with less topical [+topical] possessors, and – although the overall number of tokens is very low for [-topical] possessors, it is nonetheless evident that the *s*-genitive occurs more often in this context if the possessive relation is prototypical. In the last interval (1560 – 1630) two columns 'disturb' the otherwise orderly picture: (i) [+topical] possessors have now become the more preferred context than [++topical] possessors, yet note, that the difference in the relative frequency of the *s*-genitive versus the *of*-genitive between these two conditions is not statistically significant. And (ii), the relative frequency of *s*-genitives with [-topical] possessors is unusually high. The latter, however, may be attributed to the very low number of tokens (nine *s*-genitives versus three *of*-genitives), which, as mentioned earlier, prohibits our drawing far-reaching generalizations in this context.[153]

In the following the two topical categories [++topical] and [+topical] are subsumed under one single category [+topical] to see how topical possessors in general interact with the prototypicality of the possessive relation. Figure 37 shows the relative frequency of the *s*-genitive for all topical possessors and non-topical possessors according to the type of possessive relation within the domain of [+animate] possessors for the four time intervals. As can be seen from figure 37 the prototypicality of the possessive relation affects the frequency of the *s*-genitive with topical possessors. In every time interval the *s*-genitive occurs more often with [+topical] possessors in [+prototypical] possessive relations than in a [-prototypical] one, although this difference is only statistically significant in interval II (1450 – 1499) (chi-square, *df* 1, *p*<0.001). Likewise, the type of possessive relation determines the frequency of the *s*-genitive with [-topical] possessors: the *s*-genitive is less frequent in [-topical] [-prototypical] contexts than in [-topical] [+prototypical] ones.

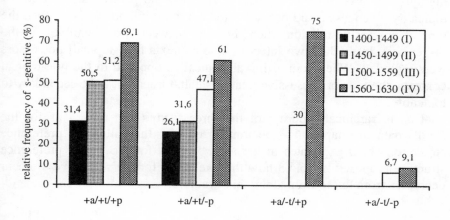

Figure 37. Relative frequency of the *s*-genitive according to the interaction of the factors topicality and possessive relation in the [+animate] sub-corpus (±a = [±animate]; +t = [+topical]*, ±p = [±prototypical] possessive relation), *including [++topical] and [+topical] categories from figure 36 above (for [+topical] see also tables 19c and 19d, for [-topical], see tables 20a and 20b, Appendix §10.2)

We can also observe that as a main tendency the preferred context for the occurrence of the *s*-genitive decreases from left to right, although the differences in the relative frequency of the *s*-genitive – except in the context mentioned above – never reach any statistical significance.

7.4.5   *Preference structure for the* s-genitive *(1400 – 1630)*

The results for the corpus data (1400 – 1630) point therefore to the following relative importance of the three conceptual factors: animacy > topicality > possessive relation. Animacy can be regarded the most important factor because an [-animate] possessor proved to be a knock-out factor for the occurrence of the s-genitive. It is only within the [+animate] context that topicality and possessive relation can exert any further influence on the relative frequency of the s-genitive. In the first two intervals the investigation of topicality had to be restricted for heuristic reasons to referentially given possessors. Distinguishing between more highly and less highly topical possessors, however, the degree of topicality/givenness could be shown to be a more important factor than the type of possessive relation when choosing between the s-genitive and the of-genitive. In the last two intervals also contexts for [-topical] possessors were included. When contrasting all topical as opposed to the non-topical contexts, the type of possessive relation again turned out to be secondary to topicality.

This hierarchical ordering of the three factors can now – as for the ModE data in chapter 6 – be transferred into the following preference structure, which explicates in the same way as for the ModE preference structure proposed in §6.4.3 how the likelihood for the *s*-genitive to occur decreases from left to right along this structure:

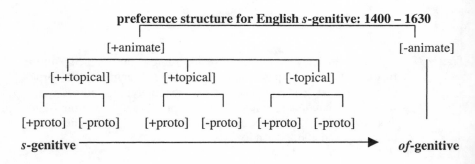

Figure 38.   Preference structure for English *s*-genitive: 1400 – 1630

For the period under investigation (1400 – 1630) two kinds of diachronic extension can be observed for the *s*-genitive along this preference structure: (i) an extension of the possible contexts, in which the *s*-genitive can occur, and (ii) an increase in the relative frequency of the *s*-genitive within these contexts. Note that all these extensions occur within the [+animate] domain only. This finding is in accordance with Raumolin-Brunberg (1991), who stresses the important role of animacy in the choice of the *s*-genitive for the early sixteenth century. For the seventeenth century, the importance of animacy is confirmed by Altenberg's (1982) corpus analysis:

..the great variation in GEN/OF selection gives an indication of the power and flexibility of the lexical factor. Its impact is most uncompromising at the inanimate end of the scale, where OF is practically obligatory with many noun classes and seldom replaced by GEN even in rhetorical or poetic contexts. (Altenberg 1982: 148)

Altenberg's (1982) findings thereby also suggest the validity of the preference structure – at least with respect to the relative order of the factors animacy and topicality for the seventeenth century. Throughout the early Modern English period an [-animate] possessor is and remains the knock-out criterion for the occurrence of the *s*-genitive; only within the [+animate] domain do other factors, such as topicality and the kind of possessive relationship further determine the occurrence and frequency of the *s*-genitive.

7.5 The revival of the *s*-genitive and the structural change of POSS *'s* from inflection to clitic and determiner

Having investigated the impact of the factors animacy, topicality, and possessive relation in the revival of the *s*-genitive from 1400 to 1630, the question remains *why* the *s*-genitive should be increasing along the preference structure in figure 38 at all, and why at that particular time and not earlier, or later? While I will discuss the former question in chapter 8 below, I will here offer a possible explanation of why the *s*-genitive started to become productive again around the sixteenth century and continues to be so throughout the period investigated, i.e. until the early seventeenth century. In particular, I will argue that (i) the change of POSS *'s* from a fully-fledged inflection in Old English to a clitic in Modern English is the structural precondition for the *s*-genitive to become more productive again, and (ii) that the increase in the relative frequency of the *s*-genitive along the proposed preference structure corresponds well to the new function of the clitic *s*-genitive as a determiner.

In the following I will first describe the structural change of POSS *'s* from an inflection to a clitic, discuss the various accounts of it and point out further developments possibly been involved in this development, hitherto not considered in the literature. I will then sketch the development of the *s*-genitive from an inflection to a determiner and discuss in which respect the empirical evidence corresponds to the newly acquired determiner status of the *s*-genitive.

7.5.1   From inflection to clitic: what happened ...

In Old English, there was still a genitive paradigm with various genitive endings according to gender, number and noun class (see table 46), and POSS '*s* used to be a fully-fledged inflection.

Table 46. Old English genitive paradigm

genitive suffixes	strong declension				weak declension	
	masc. sg.	**fem. sg.**	**neut.sg.**	**pl.**	**sg.**	**pl.**
noun	-(e)s	- e	-(e)s	-a /-ra	-an	-(e)na
adjective	-(e)s	-re	-(e)	-ra	-e(n)	-a/-e

Note also, that in Old English genitive case could not only be assigned by nominal elements but also by adjectives (64) and verbs (65):

(64)   *ðu   art   deaðes*   *sceldi(h)*
       you are   death-GEN   guilty
       'You are guilty of death'   (Vices and Virtues [1] [Stw], p. 51:23-4)154

(65)   *þæt folc   ne   cuðe   þæra   goda*
       that people   not   know   the-GENpl   gods-GENpl
       'that people do not know the gods'   (AECHom I.12)

There was also still obligatory agreement in case, gender and number among the single elements within the Old English NP, i.e. between determiners, adjectives and nouns (for this see example (65) and also examples (62) and (63) in §7.1 above). And, as already said in §7.1 above, in Old English the inflected genitive could still occur both prenominally (*Godes lufe*) and postnominally (*lufe Godes*).

Only in the course of the Middle English period was POSS '*s* generalized to all noun classes – first to all singular nouns and later also to plural nouns –, thereby becoming the sole genitive ending, it lost the gender and number distinctions, could eventually only be assigned by nouns and became restricted to prenominal position only. In this process POSS '*s* also began to lose typical characteristics of an inflection and increasingly began to behave as a clitic. Note that this is not an abrupt but a gradual development: between the late fifteenth century and at least the seventeenth century POSS '*s* can be interpreted as both an inflection and a clitic. Anticipating some of the discussion of §7.5.2 below, the following criteria can be taken as indicative for this process:

(1)   Until at least the fourteenth century irregular genitive forms still persist, which indicates that during that time it could still be

interpreted as an inflection (cf. Carstairs 1987; Allen 1997a: 115; see also §7.5.2.1 below).

(2)　The *s*-suffix stops triggering voice alternation in early Modern English, which is indicative that it does not behave as an inflection any longer; again there is a period of transition in this development, roughly from the sixteenth to the eighteenth centuries (see Plank 1985, Lass 1999: 144-145; see also §2.2 above).

(3)　As an inflection, POSS '*s* used to be attached to the head of the possessive construction. First evidence for a clitic-like behavior of POSS '*s* is reported for the late fourteenth century in Chaucer (*[the grete god of Love]*NP*s name*) (see Allen 1997a). There are, however, up to the early seventeenth century, still instances of "split constructions", in which POSS '*s* attaches to the head of the possessive construction (cf. e.g. Rissanen 1999: 202-203). Altenberg (1982: §2.8) still reports a few examples of split constructions for the seventeenth century, although he notes that "[i]n the present material, the modern group genitive shows almost complete domination (32/37)".[155] This indicates that in the seventeenth century the development towards POSS '*s* as a clitic was already very advanced, though it is difficult to evaluate when precisely the Modern English situation was fully established. To my knowledge, no systematic empirical investigation of the *s*-genitive exists covering the period from the eighteenth to the twentieth centuries. Jespersen (1960: 304) gives a nice example from Thackeray (*Ballads*: 64), which shows that in the nineteenth century POSS '*s* cannot have been felt as an inflection but as something separate from the head noun (if in poetic language):

(66)　　*He lay his cloak upon a branch,*
　　　　To guarantee his Lady Blanche
　　　　's delicate complexion.

It is certainly striking that the observed increase in the relative frequency of the s-genitive in §7.4 above covers precisely the alleged transition period for POSS '*s* changing from an inflection to a clitic. In Rosenbach and Vezzosi (1999) we therefore analyzed this corpus according to the criteria given in table 47 below (cf. Rosenbach and Vezzosi 1999: 38).[156] Our analysis showed that in the first interval (1400 – 1449), in which the relative frequency of the *s*-genitive is lowest, there is only evidence for inflectional *s*-genitives within our corpus. Although the generalization process towards *-(e)s* is already advanced in this period, there is still variation among the inflectional genitive endings.

Table 47. POSS *'s* – inflection versus clitic: criteria

POSS *'s* as inflection	POSS *'s* as clitic
• other inflectional endings than *-(e)s* still present	• *-(e)s* as the exclusive genitive ending
• still agreement within NP	
• POSS *'s* only attaches to head of NP:	• POSS *'s* attaches to whole NP:

• split constructions:
    the kings of England daughter
	• 'group genitive':
	    the parson of Sparrammys
	    dowter

• split conjoined NPs:
    þe kynges peas and þe quensyse
	• conjoined NPs:
	    women and mens flesche

Most importantly, only split constructions (67b) and split conjoined NPs (67a) are attested in this period but no evidence for a phrasal attachment of POSS *'s* can be found. From the second interval (1450 – 1499) onwards the *s*-genitive in the corpus shows both characteristics of an inflection (cf. [68a – 68b] and [69a – 69b]) and of a clitic (cf. [68c – 68d] and [69c – d]). Even in the last interval (1560 – 1630), though, we still find one split construction (70d), reflecting some residual inflectional features of the *s*-genitive besides the now prevailing group genitives (as in [70a-c]), indicative of the newly emerging clitic status of POSS *'s*.[157]

(67) 1400 – 1449 (interval I)
    a. *in goddess peas and the kynges*   (Chancery: 28)
    b. *Goddes Sone of heuen*   (Gaytridge: 4)

(68) 1450 – 1499 (interval II)
    a. *the dukis brothir of Bretayn*   (Capgrave: 246)
    b. *the dukys sone of Burgay*   (Gregory: 114)
    c. *my Lady off Norffolkys disposicion*   (Paston Letters: 449)
    d. *a man or a wommanys eye*   (Methan: 125)
    e. *the Counte of Charlys sone*   (Gregory: 114)

(69) 1500 – 1559 (interval III)
    a. *the kyngs daughter of Ethiopia*   (Elyot: 151)
    b. *the kyngs Dowghter of that yle called Costus* (Torkington: 56)
    c. *in Theodore th'archbisshop of Cantwarbyri's tyme* (Leland: PI, 143)
    d. *my lord of Wynchesteres lyvere*   (Mowntayne: 201)

(70) 1560 – 1630 (interval IV)
    a. *the king of Portingales ship*   (Richard Madox: 133)
    b. *the Duke of Millaynes daughter*   (John Stow: 567)

c. *ane Yrish man of my Lord of Bedfords*   (Madox: 139)
d. *too of Godfries sonnes of the Swane*   (Simon Forman: 8)

It is, however, noticeable that all occurrences of group genitives in our EModE corpus are of the pattern [TITLE *of* PLACE] *'s* X, as in *the king of Portingales ship*, which constitutes a close unit that can be perceived as one name. There are also no occurrences of the more 'progressed' group-genitive type, such as POSS *'s* attaching to non-nominal elements or even to relative clauses.[158] Altenberg (1982: §2.8), however, reports cases of phrasal POSS *'s* from his seventeenth-century corpus which clearly appear to be more productive than the ones attested in our corpus. First, there are group genitives which are not restricted to the [TITLE *of* PLACE]*'s* X-type, as in (71) and (72), both cited from Altenberg (1982: 61):

(71)   *the Ruler of the Synagogues house*   (Mark 5.35)

(72)   *a Woman of Quality's Porter*   (WW 1.341)

Second, there are cases in which POSS *'s* attaches to a non-nominal element, as in (73).

(73) *a year or two's Intrigue*   (EW 132, cited from Altenberg 1982: 62)

As Altenberg (1982: 62) notes, however, it is only in idiomatic combinations such as (73) that the group genitive seems possible; in the parallel – though less idiomatic – construction in (74) a split construction is still preferred:

(74) *two hours work, or three*   (Her 48, cited from Altenberg 1982: 62)

All this indicates that the extension of POSS *'s* to phrasal groups proceeded piecemeal, from idiomatic phrasal units to less idiomatic phrasal, and from smaller units to bigger units (cf. also Allen 1997a: 121-122; Norde 2001: 253). I will come back to this observation in §7.5.2.4 below.

7.5.1.1 Excursion: the *s*-less genitive and elliptic genitives

It is interesting to observe that besides the *s*-genitive another variant with the word order possessor-possessum is attested in our corpus data, i.e. the *s*-less genitive. While in many cases the *s*-less genitive is a continuation of the Old English genitive for words ending in *-r* (e.g. *father, brother*), it also comes to be used with noun classes originally not taking the *s*-less genitive (for a good discussion and data see particularly Wyld 1936: 316-318), which shows that at some time the *s*-less genitive was a possible alternative to generalized *-(e)s*. In general, *s*-less genitives have always been more productive in northern English where they have have been in wide use up until the twentieth century (cf. Klemola 1997; and see Allen 1997b, 1998 on the *s*-less genitive in northern Middle English). According to Wyld (1936: 316) *s*-less genitives become frequent in Middle English and persist into the early Modern English period also in non-northern dialects. The following examples are from our corpus:

(75)   *Croft wife*   (Plumpton Correspondence: 184)

(76)   *the bucher wyff*   (Machyn: 8)

(77)   *the man name*   (Machyn: 21)

While in our corpus they only occur relatively rarely as opposed to the *s*-genitive, Altenberg (1982: 13, §2.4) regards the *s*-less genitive as an extremely common construction in late Middle and early Modern English, a serious competitor to the *s*-genitive in certain contexts and dialects. In fact, one may view the *s*-less genitive as the natural endpoint in the development of the inflectional genitive; in accordance to the general collapse of the nominal inflectional paradigm and the loss of inflectional endings in English, zero would simply have been the ultimate stage in this process, resulting in juxtaposition of possessor and possessum.[159]

Sometimes one author uses the *s*-genitive and the *s*-less genitive in precisely the same context, which shows how variable the use was at that time as evident in examples (78a/b) and (79a/b) below.

(78)   a.   *Barnard Castle*   (Leland: PI, 77)
       b.   *Barnardes Castle*   (Leland: PI, 76)

(79)   a.   *Gascoyne-tower*   (Leland: PI, 140)
       b.   *Gascoyne's-tower*   (Leland: PI, 140)

These examples also indicate how difficult it often is to decide whether an *s*-less genitive is a specifying or a classifying *s*-less genitive (cf. also §2.3.1 and §7.5.2.4). Apart from a determiner reading, in both (78) and (79) the proper-noun possessors can also be understood as modifiers, i.e. compounds, also indicated orthographically by the hyphens in (79a) and (79b) (see also §2.3.1 above for a discussion of proper nouns functioning as modifiers).

Finally, we can also observe *s*-less 'group genitives', see examples (80) – (82):

(80)   *Rafe of Raby tyme*   (Leland: 76)

(81)   *the duke of Somerset dowther*   (Machyn: 253, cited from Wyld 1936: 317)

(82)   *bishop of London palles*   (Machyn: 204, cited from Wyld 1936: 317)[160]

It therefore appears that the *s*-less genitive, in which the possessive relation is only marked by mere juxtaposition of possessor and possessum, has been an alternative to the *s*-genitive and we may ask why the *s*-less genitive did not eventually make it? Why retaining POSS *'s* after all but not the *s*-less genitive? In this respect, it is interesting to observe that genitive marking, i.e. the *s*-genitive, was often obligatory – even in northern dialects – in elliptic constructions where the possessum noun was omitted (cf. also Seppänen 1997b: 196; Allen 1998).[161] This is nicely illustrated in the following two examples from Middle Scots where the *s*-genitive is consistently used in the ellipted part but omitted in the the the non-ellipted one (cf. Rosenbach and Vezzosi 1999: 46):

(83)   *my uncle guid will, nor yit the guid breithring's*   (Melvill: 83)

(84)   *the man was neir blo on the father syde to the Erl of Glencarn and on the mother's to the Lord Boid*   (Melvill: 71)

Naturally, the indication of possessive relation by mere juxtaposition with the strict order possessor – possessum is only possible if both the possessor and the possessum are overtly realized. If the possessum is omitted, juxtaposition cannot work by definition and an *s*-less genitive cannot discriminate meaning differences, at least not with "independent genitives" (*That one is John* versus *That one is John's*; cf. Seppänen 1997b: 197). This might be one reason why POSS *'s* is more likely to occur than be omitted in such constructions. Interestingly, the two types of ellipted genitive construction, the independent (*this book is John's*) and the absolute genitive (*at Mary's*), do not make their appearance into the English language until 1300 (cf. van der Gaaf 1932: 50; Brunner 1962: 38); one of the earliest occurrences given by van der Gaaf (1932: 50) is example (85):[162]

(85)   c. 1280 South Eng. Leg., 109.91, *he was at seint poules.*

These elliptic absolute genitives, appearing as late as in the late thirteenth century in the English language, with a strong preference for the *s*-genitive (rather than the *s*-less genitive, even in northern dialects), may be one possible reason for why the *s*-genitive stayed in English and was not superseded by the *s*-less genitive. Allen (1998) also mentions the influence of the emerging Standard in early Modern English as one external reason why the *s*-less genitive was eventually banned from the Standard language (if persisting in northern dialects). Another internal reason for why POSS *'s* was not dropped completely will be given in §7.5.3 below, i.e. its new function as a determiner. Whether there is any relation between the newly emerging independent genitives, obligatorily occurring with the *s*-genitive and the structural change of POSS '*s* is not clear to me; the correspondence in timing may be accidental as well as meaningful.

7.5.2   *How the structural change of POSS 's from inflection to clitic is accounted for....*

Table 48 sums up the most important steps in the structural development of the *s*-genitive from Old English to Middle English.

Table 48. Structural development of the *s*-genitive from Old English to Modern English: overview

	genitive paradigm	grammatical status of relational marker	agree-ment within NP	word order
Old English	different inflectional endings according to gender, number and noun class	inflection	agreement within entire NP	possessor can be in prenominal and postnominal position
Middle English	gradual generalization of masculine and neuter genitive singular -*(e/i/y)s* (*s*-less genitives)	late 14th century: first evidence for clitic-like behavior appearance of absolute genitives	fading agreement within NP	possessor becomes restricted to prenominal position only
early Modern English	-*(e/i/y)s* as the sole inflectional ending (*s*-less genitives)	transition period: inflection → clitic	no agreement within NP	prenominal possessor only
Modern English	apostrophe '*s*	clitic (hybrid status)		

To my knowledge there are currently three major accounts for the development of POSS '*s* from an inflection to a clitic, which will be introduced and discussed in the following sections. Note that one recurring question often dominating the discussions around the possible reasons for this development is the question of whether this should be regarded as a genuine case of degrammaticalization, i.e. a counter-example to the alleged unidirectionality of grammaticalization processes, usually proceeding from clitic to affix but not the other way round. In the following sections I will be primarily concerned with the accounts themselves; as to the question of degrammaticalization – or not – see §8.6.3.2 below.

7.5.2.1 Collapse of the genitive paradigm

According to Carstairs (1987) POSS 's as an inflectional affix can turn into a clitic only after it has become the one and only marker in the genitive paradigm (see also §2.2 above). Carstairs (1987) observes that the chronology of the change seems to be such that first the s-suffix had been generalized by about the late fourteenth century, and that this made its reanalysis as a clitic possible. This kind of reasoning can be found as early as in Jespersen (1960: 298-299), who was not – like Carstairs – concerned with the theoretical distinction between affixes and clitics, but who had already observed the striking chronological correlation between the decreasing diversity of the genitive endings and the first appearance of group genitives (see also Plank 1992b: 58). Jespersen (1960: 298-299) also observed that "we find no trace of the group genitive with any of the O.E. genitive endings -a, -ra, -an, -e, -re, etc. ... but only with -(e)s."

Along a very similar line Allen (1997a) argues that when the s-suffix became the only genitive ending and the genitive paradigm collapsed, it could be reanalyzed as a clitic. The general rationale behind Allen's argumentation is that when there are no formal distinctions left within a paradigm, a paradigm stops being a paradigm. What seems crucial in her argumentation is the fact that -(e)s has become a *possible* variant for any genitive rather than the one and only genitive suffix. Allen (1997a: 115) observes that irregular genitive forms persist into the fifteenth century. In general, Allen (1997a: 120) acknowledges the gradient character of the process of reanalyzing inflectional POSS 's as a clitic by regarding the newly emerged clitic variant as an option that became available for a language learner rather than an abrupt reanalysis from inflection to clitic between two successive generations of speakers. In contrast to Carstairs' and Allen's account, Norde (1998, 2001) has recently suggested on the basis of Swedish, which, very similar to English, also had an inflectional s-genitive in Old Swedish which subsequently turned into a clitic, that the reanalysis of the *s*-genitive from an inflection to clitic occurred much earlier, i.e. *before* the *s*-suffix was generalized as the only genitive ending; in her view, the extension of the *s*-suffix is a consequence of the reanalysis, and not its cause. Although she admits that the empirical evidence for English does indeed point to the interpretation given by Carstairs (1987) and Allen (1997a), she suspects that "this particular chronology may be purely accidental" (Norde 2001: 254). While negative evidence, however, is certainly of a more shaky type than positive one, Norde's (1998, 2001) chronology for English itself solely rests on cross-linguistic comparison with Swedish. Which of these two types of evidence is stronger remains ultimately in the eye of the beholder. In §7.5.4 below I will come back to the methodological question of what kind of evidence can be evoked for evaluating the different accounts for the development of POSS '*s*.

In fact, Norde (1998, 2001) proposes yet another account for the structural change of POSS '*s* in English that will be discussed in the next section.

7.5.2.2 Looking at the NP as a whole (I): deflexion and loss of NP-internal agreement

While NP-internal agreement was still obligatory in Old English, in the course of Middle English it began to fade and eventually became completely lost. The development can be sketched as follows:

Old English:	[Det-INFL------Adj.-INFL----Noun-INFL]
end of Middle English:	[Det---Adj-----Noun-GEN]

Apart from the genitive all other nominal case-markings and, accordingly, subject-verb agreement, were lost in the course of Middle English, and on the sentence level the grammatical relations came to be expressed by fixing word order to SVO. Likewise, the fixation of the inflected genitive to prenominal position in Middle English is probably due to the loss of the inflection of the article/demonstrative and strong adjective and NP-internal agreement (see e.g. Thomas 1931: 105-106). However, as argued by Seppänen (1997b: 200-201) – almost in passing, as it were – the loss of agreement within the NP could also have had an effect on the interpretation of POSS '*s* as an inflection or a clitic.

Old English: [Det-GEN------Adj.-GEN ----Noun-GEN]   Noun
                          possessor   possessum

end of Middle English: (i) [Det----Adj.-----Noun-GEN-*es*]   Noun
                            possessor   possessum
                        (ii) [Det----Adj.-----Noun] GEN -*es*   Noun
                            possessor   possessum

Figure 39.   Loss of NP-internal agreement affecting a clitic interpretation of
POSS '*s* (based on Seppänen 1997b: 200)

In Old English the genitive suffix attached undoubtedly to the head of the
possessor. When agreement within the NP had been lost at the end of
Middle English, however, the genitive could be analyzed in two ways: It
could still be interpreted as an inflection to the head noun (i), and it was
now also possible to interpret it as a phrase-final suffix to the whole NP
(ii). Therefore, the loss of internal NP-agreement led to ambiguity in the
bracketing of POSS '*s*, thus now allowing the analysis of POSS '*s* as a
phrase-marker. Seen like this, it can be argued that even in 'simple' *s*-
genitives where the possessor is not further postmodified, such as *the old
man's daughter* or even *the king's son* the possessor is an NP and hence
POSS '*s* a phrase-marker (cf. Seppänen 1997b: 201). One might even go a
step further and argue that with a proper-name possessor, as in *John's book*,
POSS '*s* can be a phrase-marker too since proper names can fill an NP
position too. Note that Seppänen (1997b: 210) comes to the conclusion that
the genitive as an inflectional category remained in English, only having
changed into a category of NPs rather than N (see also §2.2 above for the
various ways of theoretically dealing with the status of POSS '*s*).[163] While
Seppänen's (1997b) account points to fading NP-internal agreement as a
possible reason for why POSS '*s* became a phrase-marker it remains rather
sketchy, to be understood rather as a possible and tentative (but to my mind
very reasonable) suggestion than a wholesale analysis.

Similarly, Norde (1998, 2001) discusses the development of POSS '*s* in
the context of deflexion, i.e. the loss of concordial case. While proceeding
from Swedish, the angle of her studies is cross-linguistic, comparing what
appears to be a very parallel development of prenominal genitives in
various Germanic languages (such as Scandinavian languages, English,
German, Dutch, Afrikaans). One consequence of this process of deflexion
is that agreement is fading and case becomes marked only once within the
NP. While in Swedish (as in German) case-marking is predominantly on
the article/adjective but not on the noun, genitive -*s* is the odd exception
being always attached to the last element of the NP (which does not

necessarily have to be a noun in Swedish). Combined with Seppänen's (1997b) proposal, this account would also make sense for English, although in English case loss has been much more advanced than in the other Germanic languages, leaving no NP-internal agreement at all. The crucial point, however, is that NP-final genitive-marking makes a reanalysis of POSS 's as a phrase-marker possible.[164]

Note that while the account proposed by Carstairs (1987) and Allen (1997a) has centered – more or less – locally on the grammatical behavior of the *s*-genitive, Seppänen (1997b) and Norde (1998, 2001) show that it is beneficial to take a broader perspective and have a look at what happened diachronically to the English NP as a whole. Here it might be useful to go even a step further and include more phenomena within the NP than just NP-internal agreement. As recently demonstrated by Demske (2001) for the history of the German NP, individual changes within the NP can be accounted for if single constructions within the NP are not seen in isolation but studied in relation to other constructions within the same structural domain. In particular, Demske (2001) relates the development of the strong/weak adjective inflection, the use of the definite article, the reanalysis of possessive constructions and an increasing productivity of nominal compounding to each other; in her account all these developments can be captured by a single change, i.e. a change in the relation between article and noun, which she models within the framework of "Head-Driven Phrase Structure Grammar" (HPSG). Since the *s*-genitive not only turned into a clitic but has also acquired a determiner function in Modern English (see §7.5.3 below), a closer look at the relation between the evolution of the definite article and the development of the *s*-genitive looks most promising, particularly if considering the developments within the German NP, where, as shown by Demske (2001), the development of the definite article also has been shown to be the crucial trigger for the other developments within the NP. In §7.5.2.4 below I will address yet another development in the broader context of the English NP at the interface between the word and the phrasal level. i.e. the development towards phrasal compounding in English as possibly being related to the development of POSS 's towards a phrase-marker or clitic.

7.5.2.3   The *his*-genitive: causal, contributory or no role at all in the development of POSS 's towards a clitic?

Parallels between the *s*-genitive and the so-called *his*-genitive, i.e. a periphrastic construction in which the relational marker is a possessive pronoun (*John his book*) have been pointed out already by EModE grammarians (see e.g. discussion in Graband 1965: 112-119) and in modern linguistics as early as in Jespersen (1960: 304-312) and Wyld (1936: 314-316). What is indeed striking is that from about the thirteenth century onwards the weak, unstressed form of *his* (= *is, ys*) could be homophonous with the syllabically pronounced *-(i/y)s*, which made it possible to confuse *the kyngys sonne* (= *s*-genitive) with *the kyng hys sonne* (= *his*-genitive) (cf. Wyld 1936: 314-315; see also Jespersen 1960: 309). Particularly ambiguous constructions in this respect are those in which *ys* is orthographically separated from the possessor noun so that, in written language, it is difficult indeed to tell whether *Harlesdon ys name* (Margret Paston, as cited in Wyld 1936: 315) should be interpreted as an *s*-genitive ('Harlesdon's name') or a *his*-genitive ('Harlesdon his name'). Now, the question is how should the two constructions, the *s*-genitive and the *his*-genitive be related, if at all? And how should this bear on the interpretation of the development of POSS *'s* from an inflection to a clitc? Various interpretations on the role of the *his*-genitive exist, and to this day there is no consensus whatsoever on this issue. Wyld (1936: 314-316) suggests that the OE inflectional genitive ending *-(y)s* got reinterpreted as *his* because of the confusion resulting from the homophony between the two as described above. Essentially the same argument is used by Janda (1980) who links this alleged reanalysis to the new clitic status of POSS *'s*. In Janda's view, the Middle English *-s*-suffix *-(e)s* was reanalyzed as the possessive pronoun *his*, eventually becoming enclitic to the possessor noun. This scenario would go along the following lines:

(86)   *John(y)s* [inflectional] *book* → *John his book* → *John's* [clitic] *book*

Since derived from the reanalyzed *his*-genitive, ModE POSS *'s* can now also attach to phrases. Note that a linking possessive pronoun is not bound to heads but can easily be attached to whole NPs; in fact, such examples are attested as in (87):

(87)   *the busshop of Rome his power*
                    (Archbp. Cranmer, 1536, as cited in Wyld 1935: 315)

While Janda's scenario crucially hinges on the assumption that the *his*-genitive originates in Middle English (cf. Janda 1980: 247), other scholars trace the *his*-genitive clearly back to Old English times (cf. Jespersen 1960: 306; Mustanoja 1960: 159-161; Brunner 1962: 31; Fischer 1992: 230; Seppänen 1997b: 202).[165] On the other hand, the *his*-genitive only starts becoming particularly popular in the fifteenth century and remains so up to the seventeenth century (cf. Wyld 1936: 315; Mustanoja 1960: 161;

Brunner 1962: 31; Altenberg 1982: 43-45; Lass 1999: 146), which is indeed the crucial period for the transition of the *s*-genitive from an inflection to a clitic. Although never very frequent the popularity of the *his*-genitive can be witnessed in its use by writers such as Shakespeare (*Neuer did the Cyclop hammers fall On Mars his armours*, Hamlet, ii, 2, 512 – quoted in Jespersen 1960: 310) and by its occurrence even in the book title of a play by Ben Jonson (*Seianus His Fall*).[166] While it is generally believed that the *his*-genitive has become obsolescent by the late seventeenth century (cf. e.g. Lass 1999: 146), Jespersen (1960: 310) mentions that the *his*-genitive can still be found in "the vulgar speech or burlesque style of our days". In any case, today the *his*-genitive – if it does occur at all – is restricted to very colloquial and/or dialectal speech (cf. also Seppänen 1997a: 160) and is clearly banned from the standard language. For the question of whether ModE POSS *'s* goes back to the *his*-genitive, the presence of the *his*-genitive in Modern English is, however, not that important; far more important is the question as to whether the *his*-genitive is attested already in Old English or whether its occurrence coincides with the transition period for POSS *'s* to change towards a clitic, as discussed above.

Janda's (1980) account is quite controversial. In particular Allen (1997a) argues against Janda's proposal on various grounds (and see, e.g., also Fischer 1992: 230-231 for criticism). Probably most importantly, Allen (1997a) argues that there are considerable problems with the timing. If the ModE clitic *'s* derives from the *his*-genitive, then we should also find the first group genitives with the *his*-genitive; however, first evidence for such phrasal attachment of *his* like (88) is attested not earlier than the late fifteenth century (cf. Allen 1997a: 116):[167]

(88)   *my Lord of Canterbury ys cortte*
         'my Lord of Canterbury's (his) court'   (Cely 153.24, 1482)

Also, as argued by Allen (1997a: 116), if *ys* were a true possessive pronoun, one would expect the *his*-genitive construction to spread to feminine (89) and plural possessors (90) as well. Such a spread occurred, but it is not attested before the late sixteenth century (cf. Allen 1997a: 116).[168]

(89)   *Juno hir bedde*   (Lyly, *Eupheus*, 86; cited from Wyld 1936: 316)

(90)   *Canterbury and Chillingworth their books*
         (Verney Memoirs II.222.11, letter of c.1645, cited from Allen 1997a: 116)

All in all, Allen (1997a: 119) observes that the *his*-genitive had precisely the same distribution as the inflectional *s*-genitive (at least before the sixteenth century), concluding that "this *his* of ME was just an orthographical variant of the inflection" (118). Maybe it is this homography as well as the homophony between the old inflectional -(*e/i/y*)*s* ending and the *his* that has given rise to some popular meta-interpretation of *'s* as the shortened form of *his*, as was commonly expressed by grammarians throughout the early Modern English period up to the nineteenth century; on this see particularly Jespersen (1960: 310-311) and Graband (1965: 112-119).

Janda (2001: 301-303) has recently come up with a slightly modified version of his (1980) account, proposing that in late Middle and early Modern English there were in fact two different types of *his*: "a gender-neutral clitic vs a masculine-only free form" (303). It seems as if in his new account it is only the gender-neutral clitic *his* that Janda (2001) considers to be resulting from a reanalysis of the inflectional -(*y*)*s* suffix. According to Janda (2001: 302) this invariant *his* was "homophonous but not identical with the masc[uline] s[in]g[ular] possessive *his*". Thereby he tries to account for the fact that it was not until the late sixteenth century that the *his*-genitive became sensitive to gender distinctions as in (89) above. In general, it is interesting to note how the very same type of evidence can get interpreted in two exactly opposite ways. While Allen (1997a: 118) considers examples in which *his* is used with non-masculine possessor nouns as in (91) as evidence that *his* must be regarded as an orthographical variant, Janda (1980: 248-249; 2001: 302-303) interprets the same type of examples as proof for a gender-neutral clitic.

(91)   *...to be enfformyd that Margere ys dowghter ys past to Godd*
                    (Cely 188.3, 1482; cited from Allen 1997a: 118)

What does, according to Tabor and Traugott (1998) and Norde (1998), speak against Janda's account for the change of POSS *'s* from an inflection to a clitic is the fact that in the Scandinavian languages there has been a development parallel to that in English in that the Danish, Norwegian and Swedish *s*-genitive has been changing from an inflection to a clitic, too. In contrast to English, however, there has not been a functionally equivalent construction with a linking possessive pronoun; therefore – at least for these languages – this cannot be the ultimate reason for this development as argued by Tabor and Traugott (1998) for Danish and Norwegian, and also by Norde (1998: 220) for Swedish. Yet, again, upon closer scrutiny these statements might not hold entirely true. Jespersen (1960: 305), for example, observes that possessive dative constructions are "extremely common in Danish, Norwegian and Swedish dialects". Likewise, Koptjevskaja-Tamm (forthcoming) shows that Modern Norwegian does have a construction comparable to the English *his*-genitive, i.e. a reflexive pronoun bound to the possessor, as in:

(92)   *Jan og   Maria   si-ne   barn*
        Jan and   Maria   refl.poss-pl children
        'Jan and Maria's children'

Maybe the fact that these constructions do occur in dialects or spoken language has so far been overlooked, and therefore their presence and influence on the process of turning a genitive inflection into a clitic in the Scandinavian languages has not been acknowledged yet and may well need to be rethought (cf. also Janda 2001: 303).[169]

So far we have seen two extreme viewpoints on the role of the *his*-genitive in the change of POSS '*s* from an inflection to a clitic: (i) a causal role of the *his*-genitive, as put forward by Janda (1980), and (ii) no role at all, as argued by Allen (1997a). A somewhat more cautious view may be to regard the *his*-genitive in early Modern English as a contributory – but not necessarily a causal – factor in the development of POSS '*s* towards a phrase-marker (cf. e.g. Jespersen 1960: 311-312; Plank 1992a: 57, 1995: fn. 17; Seppänen 1997b: 202-203). So maybe a much 'messier' but somewhat more realistic scenario may be that both the old inflectional *-(e/i/y)s* ending and the *his*-genitive have been sitting around in the English language; for one reason or the other the old inflectional genitive ending, which was almost on its way out of the language, became 'reactivated' for other functional needs (see also §7.5.3 below), and in this process the apparent structural as well as functional overlaps with another possessive construction, i.e. the *his*-genitive, which has also been available in the English language, may have facilitated or even accelerated – but in any case certainly not impeded – this process.

Moreover, Seppänen (1997b: 202) points out an interesting parallel development with the English relative pronouns, i.e. the emergence in non-Standard Present-day English of new genitive relativizers such as *that's*, *what's*, etc., resulting from a reanalysis of the *his*-genitive along the following lines, which shows that such a *his*-reanalysis into an enclitic possessive '*s* is a somewhat familiar mechanism in English: [170]

(93)   *a man that his father was killed* → *a man that's father was killed.*

It must be noted that methodologically it is extremely difficult to ascertain evidence for or against a particular theory. Given the general infrequency of the *his*-genitive as well as its clearly more colloquial and/or dialectal status, any quantitative, or even statistical methods are not applicable. So the only possible empirical approach is in terms of when the *his*-genitive is attested first, or not. However, the non-occurrence of the *his*-genitive does not represent the strongest type of evidence, because the fact that a certain form/construction is not attested (i.e. negative evidence) could be meaningful as well as a pure artefact of the textual evidence, particularly in the case of infrequent and colloquial forms/constructions such as the *his*-genitive). And even if the linguistic facts as such are clear, it is a completely different matter how to interpret them, as the discussion above has shown. So, for example, in order to assess the role of the *his*-genitive in the development of POSS '*s* a lot hinges on the question of whether it is an 'old' English construction, already available in Old English, or whether it only came into being in Middle or even early Modern English. The few relevant examples attested, however, can get interpreted in various ways so that this question may remain unsettled for the time being (cf. note 165). Or see the discussion of the use of *his* with non-masculine possessors above, where Allen (1997a) and Janda (2001) come to very different, in fact opposing conclusions. In the end it might be a matter of argumentation, i.e. of how convincingly the pieces given by the relatively poor empirical evidence are put together, which may tip the scales towards one rather than the other account. For future research, it certainly looks very promising to look at linking possessive pronouns in other Germanic languages. It may not be a coincidence that such constructions are attested, albeit in colloquial and/or dialectal language, in German, Dutch, Afrikaans and the Scandinavian languages (for examples, see Norde 1998: 214-216) whose prenominal genitives underwent a parallel development to the English *s*-genitive (see also §7.5.3.3 below). For the time being, we must conclude, however, that the role of the *his*-genitive remains obscure.

7.5.2.4 Looking at the NP as a whole (II): of words and phrases
7.5.2.4.1   The development towards phrasal compounding

While in §7.5.2.2 above deflexion and the loss of NP-internal agreement have been argued to be relevant for the changing grammatical status of POSS '*s* (cf. Seppänen 1997b; Norde 1998, 2001), I will address in this section another development within the English NP possibly having contributed to POSS '*s* turning into a phrase-marker, i.e. the change towards phrasal compounding in English. This is yet another case in which a grammatical process is no longer confined to the lexical level but begins to operate on the phrasal level as well, thereby very much resembling the change of POSS '*s*, although to my knowledge so far the two have not been connected in the literature. As said in §2.2, in English today we find both lexical compounding (*playground,   summer   school*) and phrasal compounding (*the Charles and Di syndrome; an off-the-rack dress*). Diachronically, two observations are of interest here. First, it is only in the Middle English period that lexical units can be derived from syntactic phrases, such as *mother-in-law, milk-and-water* or *what-d'ye-call-'em* (cf. e.g. Koziol 1972: 70-71). Examples such as *Bere-no-false-witnesse* or *Bileef-so-or-thow-beest-noght-saved* (*Piers Ploughman*, 14thc; quoted from Koziol 1972: 67), where imperatives function as the name for (allegorical) persons may also be subsumed here. This type of lexicalization becomes considerably more productive in early Modern English (cf. Wolff 1975: 51-63), as for example witnessed in loan translations for plant names such as *forget-me-not* (16thc; Old French *ne m'oubliez mie*) or *touch-me-not* (16thc; Latin *noli-me-tangere*); cf. Koziol (1972: 68). Second, as noted by Mutt (1967: 403), such compound nouns could serve again as premodifiers for compounds (e.g. *film-star divorce, part-of-speech approach*) only from the latter half of the fourteenth century onwards in English. It may not be a mere coincidence that this development should have started about the same time as the change of POSS '*s* towards a clitic. We could therefore hypothesize that, very generally, the development of POSS '*s* may be viewed in the light of the context of the general development in English of morphological processes extending to the phrasal level. The whole process may have started as a word-internal development (with syntactic lexical units, such as *mother-in-law*) and from there expanded to the phrasal, i.e. the NP level (i.e. *s*-genitives), with syntactically complex premodifiers and/or phrasal compounding (*part-of-speech approach, the Charles and Di syndrome*) at the borderline between words and phrases; a possible scenario for this development will be suggested in the next section.[171] Note, in passing, that this may also be diachronic evidence for the fact that the borderline between derivation and inflection is not as tight as usually has been assumed.

7.5.2.4.2   Gradience in the *s*-genitive: from determiners to compounds?

The analysis of the two genitive constructions in §2.3.1 has demonstrated that their structure is closely connected with their semantics. In particular, the role of definiteness plays an important role when discussing the different relations expressed by the *s*-genitive. As has been shown, some constructions are inherently ambiguous in that the determiner and the modifier/possessive compound function of the *s*-genitive cannot always be clearly distinguished. In this section I will suggest that this ambiguity is due to the gradient character of the determiner/modifier distinction, both synchronically and diachronically. The following scenario follows and draws upon Taylor (1996: 311), who proposes a continuum of conventionalization from what he calls "prenominal possessives" (*[the driver's] license*) to – in his terminology – "non-possessive compounds" (*a [driver license]*):

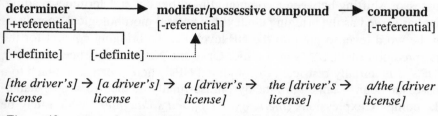

Figure 40. conventionalization pathway: from determiner to compound

What I would like to suggest here, is that an indefinite possessor provides the crucial link from a determiner reading to a modifier/compound reading in that it is inherently ambiguous. It can potentially have a truly referentially indefinite reading (= an individual driver) as well as a non-referential, generic reading (drivers in general).

It is interesting to note that Taylor (1996: chapter 11) points out that referentiality motivates the presence or absence of POSS *'s* in a compound. According to Taylor (1996: 309), a possessive compound is favored over a non-possessive compound if the possessor can potentially – though not necessarily – invoke the conception of a specific instance rather than a type, i.e. if the possessor (also) allows for a referential interpretation. If this is true, possessive compounds seem to be the ideal bridging context between (non-possessive) compounding and indefinite determiner *s*-genitives.

We need, however, to distinguish between the development of single expressions and the development of grammatical constructions. The scenario suggested above in the spirit of Taylor (1996) refers to the conventionalization of single expressions (from *[the driver]'s license* to *a/the [driver license]*), which may be called an instance of lexicalization. As far as the development of a grammatical construction is concerned, however, the picture may be very different, if not exactly the opposite. I suggested in the previous section that the development of POSS *'s* may have started as a word-internal process in that first phrasal words and phrasal compounding became possible. The possibility for a morphological process to operate over phrases to be subsequently expanded to the NP-level may have enabled POSS '*s* to be attached to phrases. This extension may have been made possible by a close link, i.e. the gradience, between compounding and the *s*-genitive as it is evident in possessive compounds, such as *the driver's seat*. Once the constraint on word-formation, namely that only single-word lexical units may enter compounding, was relaxed, bigger units, i.e. the NP, could also be affected by this process. In particular, it may have been the inherent ambiguity of a [-referential] possessor, shifting between a compound/modifier and a determiner reading, that has served as the bridging context for phrasal morphological operations on the word level to jump to the NP level, i.e. the bridging context for the interpretation of POSS '*s* as a clitic. Once the NP-level has been reached, POSS '*s* is initially restricted to conjoined NPs where it can still attach to a possessor noun – although already phrase-finally –, then to proper-name-like complex expressions (*the king of England's daughter*), which may be conceived of as a name-unit,[172] and where POSS '*s* attaches to a non-possessor noun (= *England*), and finally, POSS '*s* can also attach to non-nominal elements (*people who hurry's ideas*). To sum up, as one possible way for POSS '*s* to develop from an inflection to a clitic I propose the following scenario as illustrated in figure 41:

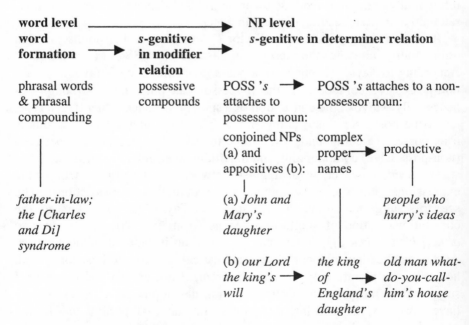

Figure 41.   POSS '*s*: from word-level to NP-level ? – A possible scenario

This is, admittedly, a very general and highly hypothetical scenario, which still needs to be looked at in more detail, tracing the possible occurrences of the respective constructions.[173]

First evidence for the steps within the development of the *s*-genitive as sketched above is given in Allen (1997a: 121):

> There is some evidence that that the transition from an inflection to a clitic which attached to the end of NP was not made in a single step, but went through a stage in which the new clitic attached only to constituents smaller than NPs or to NPs which ended in a possessor noun.

In particular, Allen (1997a: 121-123) argues that in her corpus the new clitic POSS *'s* certainly occurs first with appositive constructions and conjoined NPs (though, according to Allen, the empirical evidence in the latter case is too scarce to warrant a definite chronology) before the group genitive is attested. As far as the transition stage from (phrasal) compounding to the genitive constructions is concerned, it is, however, arguable whether this 'jump' occurred in concrete phrases or whether we rather need to understand it as operating very generally, resulting from the general affinities of phrasal compounding to the *s*-genitive due to the potential ability of possessors to shift from a referential to a non-referential interpretation. That it is already in Old English often very difficult to distinguish in examples such as *winter's day* or *sunnandæg* ('sun's day' → 'Sunday') between compounds and genitive constructions (as syntactic phrases) has repeatedly been pointed out in the literature (cf. e.g. Koziol 1972: 48-49; Kastovsky 1992: 362-363; Lass 1994: 194). For single expressions the reason for the difficulty in classification is most likely diachronic, since such compounds most often originate in (syntactic) genitive constructions, i.e. represent fossilized genitive phrases (cf. e.g. Lass 1994: 194), in accordance with the conventionalization pathway proposed by Taylor (1996) and sketched above. According to Koziol (1972: 60-61), however, there are also cases in which the genitive *-s* is a later addition (cf. OE *winterdæg* > ModE *winter's day*). Also, variation between a possessive and a non-possessive compound (as in *craftsman* versus *craftman*, or *the driver's seat* versus *the driver seat*) can already be found in Old English (e.g. *heofonrice* versus *heofonarice*, 'kingdom of heaven', or *stēorman* versus *stēoresman*, 'steersman'); cf. Koziol (1972: 60). And even if the causal chain may not turn out to be as outlined above, the chronological correlation between morphological processes on the word-internal level (possibility of phrasal compounding) and the level of the NP (attachment of POSS *'s* to phrases), both having started in the late fourteenth century, still is a striking coincidence.

What may, however, speak for such a scenario is the fact that for other NP-internal elements a similar pathway has been proposed. Plank (1992b) has argued on the basis of possessives after demonstratives in German (*dieses unser Land* 'this our country')[174] that the distinction between determiners and modifiers is not a tight one, but that "determinerhood is gradient,..., shading off into modifierhood" (466). Note that the same construction (*this our friend*) used to be possible in English until the seventeenth century (cf. Rissanen 1999: 206); today it needs to be expressed by a double genitive (*this friend of ours*); see also §7.5.3 below. Plank (1992b: 462) states:

> Diachronically, in view of the earlier suggestion.... that German, like English, has been moving away from strict AG status in so far as possessives have ceased to co-occur with definite articles, *the directionality to be assumed here would be one of possessives exchanging modifier for determiner properties rather than the other way round* [emphasis mine]

That is, Plank (1992b) proposes for German possessive pronouns a development from modifier to determiner status, and the same may be hypothesized for English.

Moreover, Adamson's (2000) case study on the development of *lovely* from a descriptive adjective to an intensifier also points to an NP-internal pathway which is compatible with the view that POSS '*s* may have developed from the compounding/modifier level to a determiner. Adamson (2000: 56) uses the following configurational model for English pre-modifiers, where different functions are associated with different elements within the NP:

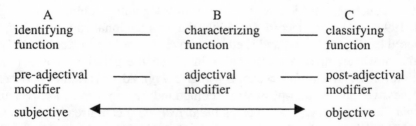

A		B		C
identifying function	———	characterizing function	———	classifying function
pre-adjectival modifier	———	adjectival modifier	———	post-adjectival modifier
subjective	◄———————————————►			objective

Figure 42.   A configurational model for English premodifiers within the NP (cf. Adamson 2000: 56)

Synchronically, the different meanings of *lovely* correspond to a different word order within the NP. Used in a descriptive sense, *lovely* has a characterizing function and can be regarded as an adjectival modifier (e.g. *a* *kind **lovely** woman*). In its subjective meaning it becomes a pre-adjectival modifier (e.g. *a **lovely** kind woman*). Diachronically, *lovely* has been expanding from a descriptive adjective to a subjective adjective, and this difference – and change – in meaning corresponds to a shift in word order within the NP, with *lovely* used subjectively moving to the left of the NP and eventually becoming reanalyzed as an intensifier (e.g. ***lovely** warm room*).[175]

If we expand Adamson's scheme to the whole NP we get the following order of elements within the NP (see also Quirk et al. 1985: §17.113-114), which may, given both the diachronic development for descriptive adjectives proposed by Adamson and the one proposed above for the development of POSS *'s*, translate to the following general pathway within the NP as such, which corresponds to the general semantic subjectification cline (from less subjective/objective to more subjective) as proposed by Traugott (1995).

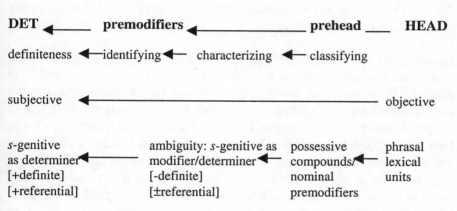

Figure 43. The *s*-genitive: from lexical units to determiner

While Adamson's analysis captures the relatively small step from characterizers (descriptive adjective) to identifiers (intensifier) for single adjectives, an analysis of the development of POSS *'s* along the above-sketched line would go within the NP all the way from the head (phrasal lexical units: *mother-in-law*) to compounding (*the Charles and Di syndrome*) to (referential) determiner *s*-genitives (*John's book*) via the intermediate step of possessive constructions which are inherently ambiguous between a determiner (= referential) and a modifier (= non-referential) reading, as e.g. in *a driver's license* (*[a driver's] license* versus *a [driver's license]*; see above). In §8.6.3.2 I will also briefly address the question whether the link between leftward position and subjectivity, which is stressed by Adamson (2000) in her analysis, may also be true for the *s*-genitive in its specifying determiner function.

Note finally, that specifying genitives do not only have an affinity to (possessive) compounds due to the ambiguity in referentiality of the possessor, but also to nominal premodifiers as shown in §2.3.1 above. In this respect it is interesting to note that Raumolin-Brunberg (1991: 275) observes a diachronic expansion of more complex NPs as manifested in nominal premodification to have taken place between early Modern and Modern English (on this see also §8.6.4.2 below). Here we once again witness a chronological correlation between (i) the structural change of POSS 's towards a clitic, (ii) the shift towards phrasal compounding and (iii) an increasing productivity of nominal premodification.

7.5.3   From inflection to determiner: the new grammatical function of the s-genitive as a determiner

Research on the history of POSS 's has so far primarily focused on the change of this relational marker from an inflection to a clitic, and it is particularly for the functionally-oriented theory of grammaticalization that this development is of special interest since it poses a serious challenge to the presumed unidirectionality of linguistic change which predicts clitics to turn into affixes but not vice versa (see also §8.6.3 below). What has, however, been somewhat neglected in these discussions is that POSS 's not only becomes a clitic but also acquires determiner status (but see brief notes in Norde 2001: 253, and Janda 2001: 302).[176] As argued in §7.5.1, in Old English POSS 's is undoubtedly an inflection; as described in §2.3.1, in Modern English it is quite uncontroversially to be analyzed as a determiner, be it in grammars of English (e.g. Huddleston 1984; Quirk et al. 1985), in Cognitive Grammar (Taylor 1996), or in formal DP-analysis (e.g. Radford 1990; de Wit 1997). At some point in the history of English this change must have taken place, although not much is yet known about the chronology of this process. I would assume that it was in the same period observed for the transition of POSS 's towards a clitic and the re-rise in the relative frequency of the *s*-genitive. It is clear from the examples below that in Old English the inflectional genitive was neutral as to the question of definiteness (as would be expected for an inflection).

(94) *sume   wæstmas   godra   weorca*
      some   fruits   good-GENpl   works-GENpl
      'some fruits of good works'
                            (ÆlfHom 3.1829; cited from Traugott 1992: 175)

(95) *on   Godes   þa   gehalgodan   cyricean*
      in   God-GEN   that   hallowed   church
      'in that hallowed church of God'
                      (BlHom X.111.8-9; cited from Traugott 1992: 173)

In (94) the possessum *wæstmas* is marked with the indefinite *sume*, which shows that the inflected genitive (*godra weorca*) itself does not necessarily render the whole possessive NP definite as in Modern English (cf. §2.3.1). In (95) the possessum occurs with the demonstrative *þa*, so there is not yet any restriction which prohibits the co-occurrence of genitive marking and some other determiner. That is, either the possessor was not a determiner yet but an adjective or Old English was typologically like Italian which allows two determiners to co-occur (as in *il mio libro* '(the) my book'). Given that the genitives in Old English were clearly inflectional I prefer the former interpretation. While definiteness in Old English was primarily signaled by the weak/strong adjective inflection (weak adjective → [+definite] NP; strong adjective → [-definite] NP) (cf. Fischer 1992: 217), the Middle English period sees the emergence of the invariant (uninflected) definite article *the*, which had become the norm by the late fourteenth century (cf. Fischer 1992: 217-218). Likewise, the indefinite article *an*, originating in the OE numeral *an* ('one'), developed its modern functions during the Middle English period (cf. Fischer 1992: 218). It may therefore be assumed that the evolution of the definite article in English made a structural determiner position available in English in the course of Middle English. Structurally, so to speak, there was now a place for POSS *'s* to fit in as a determiner. In early Modern English we still find constructions in which a demonstrative co-occurs with a possessive pronouns, as in the following examples (96) and (97), cited in Rissanen (1999: 206):

(96) **This his goodness** *stood not still in one or two*   ([HC] Ascham, 280)

(97) *your Highness will be as good a Lord to* **that your Monastery,** *as your noble Progenitors have been*   ([HC] Wolsey 19)

Again, we must either assume that the possessive pronoun was not yet a definite determiner, or, alternatively, this co-occurrence of two definite determiners points to the fact that the ModE situation has not yet been reached.[177] As noted by Rissanen (1999: 206) it is only by the end of the seventeenth century that these constructions get superseded by the double genitive ('this X of mine [yours, etc.]').[178]

7.5.3.1 The *s*-genitive as a semantic-pragmatic anchoring device

If we now tie the emerging (syntactic) determiner function and position to its semantic-pragmatic function, i.e. that of a referential anchor (cf. also Haspelmath 1999a and the discussion in §4.4.3 above), then the observed re-rise of the *s*-genitive along the preference structure in §7.4.5 fits in very well. As argued by Taylor (1996), as a referential anchor, the possessor in the *s*-genitive must be highly accessible and high accessibility should correlate with animacy and topicality (in Taylor's account both subsumed under topicworthiness). Moreover, according to Haspelmath (1999a: 235-236) inalienable possession provides for particularly effective pragmatic anchoring since in this case the relation is inherently given and does not need to be inferred by the hearer. The analysis of the EModE data in §7.4 has shown that the preferred contexts for the *s*-genitive indeed correlate with the animacy and the topicality of the possessor as well as with prototypical possessive relations. That is, the effects of the factors animacy, topicality, and possessive relation in the revival of the *s*-genitive can be neatly linked to its new anchoring function (cf. also Rosenbach and Vezzosi 2000: 301).

7.5.3.1.1   Descriptive and partitive genitives

If the *s*-genitive has turned into a determiner, it is also not surprising to find the *s*-genitive dropping out completely in those functions which are altogether incompatible with that determiner status and the possessor as a referential anchor. In Old English the inflectional genitive could still be used with a descriptive (98) as well as a partitive function (99):

(98)   *haliges   lifes   mann*
      holy-GEN life-GEN   man
      'a man of holy life'   (ÆCHom ii.298.17; cited from Mitchell 1985: 543)

(99)   *sumne   dæl þæs   felles*
      some   part that-GEN   skin-GEN
      'some part of that skin' (ÆChom i.92. 34; cited from Mitchell 1985: 545)

While partitives of the type as in (99) are said to have been completely replaced by the *of*-genitive in the course of Middle English (cf. §7.2), it is not clear from the handbooks when descriptive genitives should have stopped occurring with the *s*-genitive. Mustanoja (1960: 80-81) still gives some examples with descriptive *s*-genitives for early Middle English; in Present-day English such descriptive genitives are obligatorily realized by the *of*-genitive (**a holy life's man*). Now, in which respect should such descriptive and partitive genitives be incompatible with the anchoring function of the possessor? In partitives as in (99) it is the possessum ('some part') that functions as an anchor to specify the possessor ('that skin'), that is, the anchoring relation is precisely the other way round.[179] Therefore, in such partitive constructions POSS 's is not a referential anchor. Neither is it in descriptive genitives. Here the possessor does not identify the referent of the possessum noun but simply qualifies it, i.e. this is a case of modification and not determination; in fact, descriptive genitives correspond to the second type of modifying possessors introduced in §2.3.1 (*a king of honour*) where the prenominal modifying counterpart would be an adjective today (*an honorable king*) but never a *s*-genitive (**an honour's king*). This is also reflected by the fact that the possessor noun in such descriptive genitives is never referential itself; moreover, such descriptive genitives are usually indefinite, which rules out the *s*-genitive as a definite determiner on structural grounds too.

7.5.3.2 The Topic Schema and the *his*-genitive revisited

Further evidence which points to a connection between the preference of the *s*-genitive to occur with animate and topical possessors and its newly acquired determiner status comes from Heine's (1997) work on possession. Heine (1997) identifies eight basic conceptual "event schemas" for the grammaticalization of possessive constructions in the languages of the world, one of which is the "Topic Schema". This Topic Schema (*As for X, X's Y*) predicts that the possessor is a topic which precedes the possessum, and it is interesting to note that Heine (1997: 158-163) suggests that whenever the Topic Schema is involved it will result in "possessor specification" (see also §8.6.3.2 for further discussion of the Topic Schema). By "specification" Heine seems to refer to a (definite) determiner function, since he characterizes the specifier, among other things, as "narrowing down the range of possible referents that may qualify as the specified" (Heine 1997: 157), i.e. it has precisely the same function as a referential anchor. As pointed out by Koptjevskaja-Tamm (forthcoming: chapter 5) the Topic Schema typically underlies constructions with linking pronouns, such as the English *his*-genitive. In this respect, it is also interesting to note that in creoles the Topic Schema commonly involves linking constructions with a possessive pronoun, as shown in Heine and Kuteva (2001: §§5.1-5.2). The following example is from Seychellois, a French-based creole (cf. Corne 1986: 167, as cited from Heine and Kuteva 2001: §5.2).

(100) a. *Sesil,   son   lisyen   ti   malad*
           Cécile,   her   dog   PAST   ill
           'Cécile, her dog was ill'
       b. **i   ti   war   Sesil   son   lisyen*
           he   PAST   see   Cécile   her   dog
           (*'He saw Cécile's dog')

According to Heine and Kuteva (2001) this example exemplifies an early stage in the evolution of adnominal possession along the Topic Schema with a linking possessive pronoun. At this stage, the possessive construction still exhibits obligatory agreement of the linker with the possessor and is only possible when the (human) possessor is in subject position (100a) but not when it is in object position (100b); only at a later stage will it also extend to non-human possessors and object positions, with the linking pronoun losing agreement and becoming an invariant marker. Note that the initial restriction to subject position is precisely what is to be expected if the possessor is a topic – topics naturally are more likely to occur in subject than in object position. Considering that the example above comes from a French-based creole is particularly remarkable, because French usually does not have the order possessor-possessum in possessive constructions, only the periphrastic *de*-construction (possessum-*de*-possessor). This may indicate that the Topic Schema is indeed a natural pathway for the evolution of adnominal possessive constructions. Given that the English *his*-genitive occurs typically with a human and topical possessor and given the cross-linguistic evidence discussed above, maybe a re-evaluation of the role of the *his*-genitive in the history of the English *s*-genitive will be necessary. What, however, still remains a problem for assigning any causal role to the *his*-genitive in the development of the ModE POSS *'s* is the relatively late occurrence of feminine and plural possessive pronouns indicating agreement between the possessive pronoun and the possessor (as in *Juno her bed*, see also §7.5.2.3 above).

7.5.3.3 The development of adnominal possessive constructions in other West-Germanic languages

It is also worthwhile having a brief look at the development of possessive constructions in other West-Germanic languages closely related to English, which, as already mentioned, seem to show a number of parallels to the development in English. Very similar to English, in both Dutch and German there has been a large-scale process of replacing the inflectional genitive by (i) a prepositional *van*/*von*-construction, and (ii) additionally, the prenominal genitive by an invariant *s*-construction to be analyzed as a determiner. While according to Weerman and de Wit (1999) genitive case has been completely lost in Dutch, in German it is still retained in the postnominal genitive. According to Demske (2001: chapter 4) in German the prenominal possessive construction in (101) is to be interpreted as a determiner, while the postnominal possessive construction in (102) is still an instantiation of genitive case.[180]

(101)   *Annas*   *Buch*
            Anna-GEN   book
            'Anne's book'

(102)   *das Buch*   *des*   *Lehrers*
            the book   the-GEN   teacher-GEN
            'the teacher's book'

What speaks in Demske's (2001) account, among other things, for a determiner analysis of the prenominal possessive in German is that (i) it does not co-occur with other articles, (ii) it renders the whole NP definite, (iii) the suffix is invariably -*s,* even with feminine nouns which do not have -*s* in the genitive paradigm (*Großmutters Buch,* 'grandmother's book'), and (iv) it only occurs with a semantically very restricted class, i.e. proper nouns. [181] That is, both in German and in Dutch there has been, diachronically, a shift from the inflectional prenominal genitive to a determiner. And just as in English, this transition is accompanied in German by the same semantic restrictions, i.e. a restriction to animate and topical possessors and to possessive relations, while inanimate possessors and those genitive functions incompatible with a determiner function as argued above, i.e. partitive and descriptive genitives, get realized postnominally, either by the inflectional genitive or the periphrastic *von*-construction, as illustrated (and somewhat simplified) in table 49 below for German (cf. Demske 2001).

There are, however, two notable differences between German and English:

(1)   The prenominal determiner *s*-construction is semantically more restricted, i.e. to highly topical possessors only, in Modern German, i.e. proper names, while in Modern English it can also occur with less topical and inanimate possessors as shown in chapter 6.

(2)   The German possessive prenominal -*s* (as the Dutch *s*-construction, cf. Weerman and de Wit 1999) attaches to heads only, unlike in English and Swedish, where POSS '*s* is a clitic, i.e. a phrasal marker.

Table 49. Historical development of genitive constructions in German: overview

	Old High German	(in the course of) Early New High German	Modern German
syntactically	predominantly prenominal inflectional genitives	**reanalysis**: prenominal GEN → determiner postnominal GEN → remains inflectional	
semantically	no semantic restrictions	GN → possessor: [+animate] [+definite]; possessive relations	GN → proper names & [+definite]
		NG → possessor: [-animate]; partitive & descriptive genitives	NG *von-* construction ⎤ [±animate] ⎦ [±definite]

7.5.4   Summary

In this section it has first been demonstrated *that* POSS *'s* has been changing gradually from a genuine inflection into a more clitic-like element in the late Middle/early Modern English period, and some suggestions as to the *why* of this process have been discussed. In addition to the three prevailing accounts for this development, i.e. (i) the collapse of the genitive paradigm (cf. Jespersen 1960; Carstairs 1987; Allen 1997a), (ii) deflexion and loss of NP-internal agreement (Seppänen 1997b; Norde 1998, 2001) and (iii) the reanalysis *qua* the *his*-genitive (cf. Janda 1980, 2001), another possible pathway for this change has been sketched here, arguing that the development of the *s*-genitive should not be looked at in isolation but seen in the broader context of developments within the whole NP. In particular, the shift towards phrasal compounding, blurring the distinctions between words and phrases in the domain of word-formation as well as the close interconnections between specifying genitives on the one hand and classifying genitives/compounds and nominal premodification on the other seem to be correlated to the development of POSS *'s* towards a phrasal marker. Further research along such a more 'holistic' NP-based approach is certainly in order to pinpoint more closely how these processes are interrelated.

What makes an assessment of conflicting theories particularly difficult in this case is the extreme scarcity of relevant data. Constructions in which POSS *'s* attaches to elements larger than the head (e.g. group genitives, conjoined NPs) are extremely rare and also most likely to occur in colloquial/informal language barely attested in Middle English textual evidence (cf. also Kroch 1997: 134-135). For this reason, any kind of evidence brought forward concerning the timing of the process, in terms of 'first occurrence' or 'not-attested-yet' must be taken very cautiously, and the precise chronological as well as causal chain in the development towards a phrasal POSS 's are extremely difficult to assess. The same methodological caveats discussed in the section on the *his*-genitive (§7.5.2.3) also hold for the empirical evidence for or against the status of POSS 's as a phrasal marker in general. For the time being, the question as to the ultimate origin of ModE POSS 's must remain unsettled.

Besides the shift towards a clitic, attention has been drawn to the development of the *s*-genitive from an inflection to a definite determiner, which (although the evidence is admittedly still weak) is also assumed to have taken place in the late Middle/early Modern English period, made possible by the availability of a structural determiner position due to the evolution of the definite article in the course of Middle English. Looking at the semantic-pragmatic correlate of a definite determiner, i.e. a referential anchor, it can be explained why (i) the *s*-genitive is initially restricted to and preferred with animate and topical possessors, and in prototypical possessive relations, and (ii) why the *s*-genitive drops out completely of those functions which are incompatible with such an anchoring function, i.e. descriptive and partitive genitives. The determiner/anchoring function of the *s*-genitive was also shown to be well compatible with Heine's (1997) Topic Schema. Invoking the Topic Schema as a possible source for the ModE *s*-genitive also brings the *his*-genitive back into the discussion as a contributory, if not a causal factor, given cross-linguistic evidence and evidence from the evolution of possessive construction in creoles.

What is certainly striking is that other Germanic languages, such as German, Dutch and Swedish, underwent a very similar development with prenominal inflectional genitives becoming reanalysed as determiners. Given these parallels it is interesting to observe that it is only in English and Swedish that this determiner-possessive has also acquired clitic-status, i.e. has become a phrasal marker. This cross-linguistic dissociation between the development of prenominal possessive constructions from inflections to (i) clitics (in English and Swedish) and (ii) determiners (in English, Swedish, German and Dutch) suggests that these two processes are logically distinct and need not necessarily go together (even though they are in practice interacting). [182] In general, given the methodological problems in the investigation of the development of POSS 's towards a clitic and determiner mentioned above, a systematic cross-linguistic comparison, particularly among the Germanic languages, seems most promising.

What is crucial for the present study, however, is not to offer a new and ultimate explanation for the development of POSS '*s* towards a clitic and determiner. Rather, it is sufficient to note *that* this change has taken place. And, given this structural change of POSS '*s* from late Middle throughout early Modern English, this can then, in turn, explain *why* the *s*-genitive has become more frequent from the fifteenth century onwards as observed above – the *s*-genitive becomes more productive in a new function, a determiner with a clitic POSS '*s*, not as an inflectional genitive.

7.6   General summary

This chapter has been dealing with both the historical development of the genitive variation as well as of POSS '*s*. As far as the genitive variation is concerned, the impact of the factors animacy, topicality, and possessive relations in the choice of genitive construction from Old English to early Modern English can be briefly summarized as illustrated in table 50 below.

There are two kinds of replacement processes to be observed in the domain of adnominal genitive constructions from Old English to early Modern English, both concerning the quantitative distribution of the two adnominal genitive variants.

(1)   Beginning in the Old English period the postnominal inflected genitive is becoming replaced by the prenominal genitive, and it eventually drops out of the language.

(2)   In Middle English, the *of*-genitive is gaining ground, taking over the functions of the postnominal genitives and increasingly replacing the inflectional genitive as the preferred adnominal genitive construction.

It is striking that in both replacement processes, animacy and topicality already have played a decisive role in that constructions with the possessor first (prenominal inflected genitive/ *s*-genitive) obviously favor an animate and highly topical possessor and eventually become restricted to this context. It may also be no coincidence that the two constructions exhibiting the alternative word order of possessum-possessor, i.e. the postnominal genitive and the *of*-genitive, take over the function of partitives when substituting their adnominal counterparts, and as in the case of the *of*-genitive, becomes the almost exclusive genitive construction with [-

animate] possessors and preferred with less topical or non-topical possessors.

Table 50. Genitive variation from Old English to early Modern English – impact of the factors animacy, topicality, and possessive relation: an overview

	adnominal genitive variants	
	possessor-possessum	**possessum-possessor**
Old English	**prenominal (inflected) genitive (GN)** increasingly restricted to: • [+human] possessor • [+topical] possessor (proper names) ↓	**postnominal (inflected) genitive (NG), marginally:** *of-*genitive(~ 1%) • [-animate] possessor • partitive meanings ↓
Middle English	**s-genitive** becomes less frequent; increasingly restricted to: • [+human] possessor • [+topical] possessor (proper names) • possessive and subjective meanings	**of-genitive** becomes increasingly more frequent, particularly with: • [-animate] possessor • partitive meanings
Early Modern English	restricted to: • [+animate][+human] possessors preferably with: • (highly) topical possessors • [+prototyp.] possessive relations new developments: • structural change of POSS *'s* from inflection to clitic & determiner • revival of the *s*-genitive	• almost exclusive construction for [-animate] possessors preferably with: • less topical or non-topical possessors • [-prototyp.] possessive relations

Moreover, it has been shown in the studies by Rosenbach and Vezzosi (2000) and Rosenbach, Stein, and Vezzosi (2000) that, somehow unexpectedly – after a long period of continuous replacement by the *of-*genitive –, the *s*-genitive again increases in frequency in the period between 1400 and 1630. Most importantly, this revival takes place within the context of [+animate] possessors; within this context the *s*-genitive becomes more frequent along a preference structure, based on a hierarchical ordering of the three factors as it was proposed for the Modern English data in chapter 6 as well, i.e. animacy > topicality > possessive relation.

Besides an increasing frequency of the *s*-genitive in the period from 1400 to 1630 there is also evidence for the changing status of POSS *'s* from an inflection to a clitic and a determiner. That is, within the corpus investigated (1400 – 1630) we can not only observe the *s*-genitive significantly increasing in its relative frequency but also gradually changing from an inflection into a more clitic-like element. Therefore, I assume that the change of POSS *'s* from inflection to clitic was the structural precondition for the *s*-genitive becoming more productive again, i.e. it made it possible for the factors animacy, topicality, and possessive relation to exert an increasing influence on the choice of the *s*-genitive. That fact that it gained a new function (as a definite determiner) and was becoming more syntactic in nature (a clitic) and in this way did not go against the general typological make-up of the English language, may indeed have paved the way towards a more frequent use of the *s*-genitive.

While the structural setting may explain the timing of the change, i.e. why the *s*-genitive starts becoming more frequent in that particular period, i.e. in early Modern English, I will, in the next chapter (chapter 8), offer a possible scenario of how the conceptual factors investigated in the present study, i.e. animacy, topicality, and possessive relation can be regarded as driving forces in the observed extension of the *s*-genitive, thereby trying to come to grips with the particular direction of the change along a unified preference structure to be proposed in which both the results of the EModE corpus analysis and the ModE experimental study are drawn together.

Chapter 8
A diachronic scenario: the extension of the *s*-genitive from late Middle to Modern English – economically-driven language change?

The empirical evidence presented in this study has confirmed the predictions based on iconic/natural principles in §6.2 in that the *s*-genitive has been shown to be more likely to occur with a [+animate], [+topical] possessor, and in a [+prototypical] possessive relation. Moreover, the effect of the factors animacy, topicality, and possessive relation on the choice of genitive construction – already present in Old English – has been observed to become stronger from early Modern English onwards. Within early Modern English the *s*-genitive has been shown to be increasing along the hierarchical order of animacy > topicality > possessive relation as illustrated in the preference structure in §7.4.5. For Modern English the same relative importance of the three conceptual factors could be observed with the same preference structure extended to – and still extending within – the inanimate domain.

In the following I will first bring the ModE and EModE data together, proposing one unified preference structure to model the observed change(s). To account for the long-term diachronic extension of the *s*-genitive I will refer to principles of economy, finally proposing a possible diachronic scenario of how different types of economy may have interacted leading to a greater preference for the *s*-genitive. First, however, I will discuss which notions of "economy" prevail in the linguistic literature and under which premises the term economy will be used in the present study.

8.1   Notions of economy in linguistics

The notion of economy is used in various ways in linguistics. On the one hand, it is a criterion in linguistic theorizing requiring that theories should proceed from the least possible set of assumptions, a principle also known under the name "Occam's razor", aiming at a maximally elegant theory. Here, for example, we can subsume the notion of economy as implicit in Optimality Theory as discussed in §5.1.1.2 in that what is optimal is defined in terms of the least serious violations of constraints.[183] On the other hand, it can be transferred beyond the realm of linguistic theory to human cognition, assuming that the way language is acquired and processed should be as economical as possible. Let us call this type of economy "cognitive economy". In this case, economy is no longer a theoretical construct but assumed to have an underlying psychological reality (for a discussion of these two basic types of economy see e.g. Wilder and Gärtner 1997). Note that this is not an uncontroversial step; some scholars in fact see no reason at all to believe that biological systems in general should be subject to considerations of economy (e.g. Johnson and Lappin 1997). In the present study, however, I will follow the assumption implicit in many orientations of cognitive linguistics that principles of economy do indeed play a role within human cognition and language processing.[184] The probably best-known and most widely applied economy principle within linguistics is Zipf's "principle of least effort". This principle is particularly bound to frequency as a precondition for formal reduction. Frequent, hence predictable, forms or constructions are more likely to be formally reduced than infrequent, less predictable items.[185] The same idea is also underlying Haiman's (1983) concept of "economic motivation": "Reduction of form is an ECONOMICALLY motivated index of familiarity" (Haiman 1983: 802). For Haiman (1983: 802), familiarity is identical to frequency of occurrence, and it will turn semantically transparent forms or constructions into semantically opaque ones. (I will briefly return to frequency as a factor in §8.6.2.2 below). Considerations of "least effort" also play a role in Relevance Theory (Sperber and Wilson 1986), which predicts utterances to be structured in such a way that they can be processed with a minimum amount of effort (cf. also Nicolle 1998: 2).

Another assumption of cognitive economy implicit in production frameworks such as Bock (1982) and Levelt (1989) is the distinction between two modes of processing, i.e. automatic and controlled processing (cf. Schneider and Shiffrin 1977). Controlled processes are intentional, strategic devices involving speakers' consciousness and therefore demanding more working memory than automatic processes, which are employed unintentionally, operate outside awareness, run very fast and thus do not need any capacity, i.e. are extremely economical. In language production these two processing modes have their typical domains: while automatic processing is primarily applied for routine matters, controlled processing is required whenever evaluation and attention on the side of the speaker comes into play. Put into a diachronic perspective, we can observe for frequently occurring constructions or patterns a shift from the controlled processing mode to the automatic mode (on this process see further §8.6.2.2 below). Note that Deacon (2000) is currently investigating into the question of the neurological correlates and the evolutionary process of automatization, which should give us further insights into how, diachronically, certain controlled processes become automatic routines from a neurobiological perspective. According to Deacon (2000), the evidence so far suggests that automatic processes take place in the basal ganglia, which are brain structures assumed to be also involved in other motoric routines, such as car driving.

In the present study I will use "economy" exclusively in the sense of "cognitive economy", under which I will subsume any states and or/processes which are (i) easier to conceptualize or process for the human mind (= synchronically user-optimal constructions) and/or (ii) run in the automatic processing mode.

8.2   Speaker versus hearer economy

Having established a notion of cognitive economy the question arises: economical for whom – the speaker or the hearer? Very often the different communicative and processing needs of the speaker and the hearer are ignored by assuming that the speaker, when constructing an utterance, always has the needs of the hearer in mind, an assumption which is prevailing in accounts of definiteness (cf. §4.2.1) and which is well in accordance with Grice's "cooperative principle" and theories of "mutual knowledge" (e.g. Clark and Marshall 1981). As, however, for example argued by Brown (1995), this may well be too strong and idealized a point of view, and there can be mismatches between what the speaker intends to say and what the listener believes the speaker is conveying to him. And Kuteva (2001) regards precisely such speaker-hearer mismatches as one source for the emergence of novel meanings in the process of grammaticalization. In the psycholinguistic literature it is still a controversial question whether the systems underlying speech production and perception should be regarded the same or not (cf. e.g. Schwarz 1992: 190-191). Bock (1991: 143-145) observes that speakers are amazingly good at getting the right form but, strangely, often fail to communicate the appropriate message. She calls this phenomenon the "full-deck-of-cards paradoxon". Since the speaker already knows what he is going to say he will most likely sacrifice communicative explicitness to formal correctness for reasons of economy:

... "playing with a full deck" may not be an especially good thing for a speaker who is forced by the constraints of the vocal-auditory channel to say one thing at a time. If one knows, at some level, much more than one can convey at a given moment, a great deal of work must go into not saying a lot of things, in order to say the right things at the right time.

(Bock 1991: 144)

Here we can already see how and where the economical needs of the speaker and those of the hearer may clash: the speaker wants to get his message across quickly, striving to make the utterance as short and implicit as possible; in contrast, the hearer wants to get every piece of information he can to encode the – for him still unknown – intended message, i.e. the hearer wants the utterance to be as explicit as possible (cf. also Gundel, Houlihan, and Sanders 1988, cf. also §5.2.1.1.1; Hopper and Traugott 1993: 63-65; Krug 1997: 299-302). In the next section, I will further discuss in which respect considerations of speaker versus hearer economy have figured in accounts of grammatical variation.

8.3   Cognitive economy and grammatical variation

In some approaches to grammatical variation considerations of cognitive economy are incorporated. Given two structural alternatives, the option demanding less mental effort is more likely to be chosen than that option requiring more mental effort. Note that such approaches certainly deal with what has been labeled "choice" in chapter 5 above. While all these approaches proceed from the assumption that the easier-to-process option will always be preferred, they differ as to where to place the locus of more efficient language processing – is it within the production system (i.e. the speaker) or the parser (i.e. the hearer)?

One of the most prominent recent approaches to grammatical variation which uses considerations of language processing to account for word order preferences is Hawkins (1994). The basic idea underlying his elaborate "performance theory" is that those constructions are chosen in performance from the available set provided by the grammar of a language which are easiest to process. Ease of processing, in this account, is defined via syntactic complexity, which Hawkins (1994) regards in fact as the major word order determinant (cf. also §3.3.2.2.4).[186] In languages such as English, syntactically more complex constituents tend to be placed rather towards the end of the utterance. While Hawkins (1994) argues from the point of view of the hearer,[187] Wasow (1997a, 1997b) maintains that it is, after all, the speaker who creates the utterance and that speakers are selfish enough not to choose a particular construction to make parsing easier for the hearer but rather to facilitate their own utterance planning. Placing constructions which are simpler and easier to process at the beginning of utterances will not only save time for the planning and production of more complex – and more difficult to process – constituents but also keep the options open for the speaker. As Wasow (1997a, 1997b) argues, speakers very often do not know how to finish their utterances once they have started them and therefore prefer to commit themselves to a particular construction as late as possible (cf. also Arnold et al. 2000).

Bock (1982, and subsequent, partly co-authored, work), proposes yet another cognitive account of linguistic choices. In her account, the language system provides choices to make it possible for the speaker to accommodate information and lexical material in the order in which it becomes available to the mind and/or the lexicon. That is, in this account the availability of alternative structural realizations of a speaker's intention is regarded to be functional in that, given the requirements of speech production, that construction can be chosen which can ensure the quickest, i.e. most efficient and therefore most economical speech processing.

8.4   The role of cognitive economy in language change

Given that cognitive economy plays a role when choosing between alternative constructions synchronically, the question arises how such economically motivated choices might affect a language in the long run. Following from the preceding discussion of cognitive economy, and for the present purpose, I will focus here on two aspects of how cognitive economy can influence language change: (i) How can the asymmetry between speaker- and hearer optimality affect language change? (ii) And how can (synchronic) grammatical variation develop diachronically, driven by cognitive economy?

Given the different needs of speaker and hearer as outlined in §8.2 it is not difficult to see how these should affect language diachronically. Since speakers prefer short and implicit constructions, speaker-economy will naturally tend towards formal reduction.[188] In contrast, hearers need as much information as possible and will therefore demand longer and more explicit constructions. The dualism between these two opposing forces is well-captured by Lüdtke's (1980) cyclical language change theory, where he assumes that phonetic reduction (on the side of the speaker) needs eventually to be compensated by lexical enrichment (– which may then lead to further semantic-syntactic change –) to satisfy the needs of the hearer and guarantee successful communication. This new material will eventually be reduced again phonetically, and a new cycle will begin.

Ronneberger-Sibold (1980) has explicitly elaborated on the role of economy in language change. She distinguishes different types of economy operating on the different linguistic levels and, most importantly, differently for speakers and hearers, which may well be in conflict and constantly need to be balanced out. Thereby she accounts for the fact that languages as such do not become more economical, as one might expect if some unique type of economy was the driving force in language change, but that also uneconomical structures are emerging.

Ever since the work of Labov it has been well-known that grammatical variation and change often go hand in hand – albeit not necessarily so (cf. also discussion of variation and change in chapter 5). The approaches to grammatical variation which use considerations of cognitive economy are, however, essentially synchronic. Although Hawkins (1994) assumes that the patterns of grammar are in fact due to the grammaticalization of the most optimal performance structures, he does not provide any mechanism by which he could explain how this should come about in diachrony. That is, the crucial question is: how do user-optimal constructions become diachronically grammaticalized? This daring question has recently been approached by Haspelmath (1999b), who proposes that – in analogy to evolutionary biology – a mechanism of "diachronic adaptation" can be taken to be responsible for the fact that optimal word order preferences or constructions become fixed in diachronic change. Although the analogy between language and biological systems is not without problems and is, in fact, highly controversial (see e.g. the peer commentaries by Croft 1999, Dahl 1999, Itkonen 1999) the underlying idea seems nonetheless intuitively plausible. The rationale of Haspelmath's (1999b) argumentation is summarized in the following quote:

> In language change, variants are created from which speakers may choose. Being subject to various constraints on language use, speakers tend to choose those variants that suit them best. These variants then become increasingly frequent and entrenched in speakers' minds, and at some point they may become obligatory parts of grammar. In this way grammars come to be adapted to speakers' needs, although speakers cannot shape language actively and voluntarily. Grammatical constraints are thus the way they are because they have arisen from user constraints in a diachronic process of adaptation.   (Haspelmath 1999b: 203-204)

Structural variation is seen as the precondition for selection and adaptation. Like the approaches referred to in §8.3, Haspelmath (1999b) assumes that a user-optimal construction – for reasons of cognitive economy – will be preferred to a non-optimal construction, resulting in a higher frequency of the optimal construction. The higher frequency of the optimal construction will then, in turn, lead to its grammaticalization, in the sense that it eventually becomes obligatory and the exclusive construction (see also Haspelmath 1999a). The latter process is, according to Haspelmath (1999b: 191), akin to a process know in Cognitive Grammar as "entrenchment" (cf. e.g. Langacker 1983: 58; see also Deane 1992), but can also easily be accommodated under Givón's (1979) notion of "syntactization" or the term of "grammaticalization" as defined in §8.6.3.1 (i.e. as automatization).

Haspelmath's (1999b) scenario of diachronic adaptation offers one possible solution to the old and nagging problem of how language change can come about the way it does; it is not language as a system that changes but individual language users that do. Although the role of the individual speaker in language change was already pointed out and stressed by Hermann Paul (1909), it has otherwise long been ignored in modern linguistics. And although functional approaches to language change in principle commonly refer to cognitive arguments, only rarely is it explicated by which mechanism such cognitive factors should in fact be embedded in grammar over time. In his case study on the development of the English *do*-periphrasis Stein (1990) offers a possible user-based scenario, drawing on considerations of cognitive economy in the sense of articulatory ease for the speaker as one of the (many) driving forces in this development. Keller's (1994) "invisible-hand theory" is a plausible meta-framework of how language change may, as a cumulative effect of many intentional actions of speakers, come about although the outcome is not intended, thereby accounting for the amazing fact that speakers, although they do not actively conspire to change language in a certain predetermined way, nonetheless contribute to such a development. Interestingly, Haspelmath (1999b) also refers to Keller's (1994) invisible-hand theory in his scenario of diachronic adaptation. [189] In Haspelmath's account, intentionality – albeit only indirectly – comes into play when a speaker has the choice between a more and less optimal construction at a certain synchronic stage; [190] yet the result of the overall diachronic adaptive process, i.e. the entrenched/grammaticalized form, is certainly not intended by the single speaker in the particular situation of choosing the construction. I will briefly come back to the question of intentionality in my final discussion in chapter 9.

8.5   "Economy" in the present study

In the next section, a diachronic scenario based on considerations of cognitive economy as outlined in §8.1 will be suggested, which directly links to the choice-based approach introduced in §5.3. Synchronically, in accordance to Bock (1982), grammatical variation is conceived of as serving different needs of the human processing system in that either the *s*-genitive or the *of*-genitive is the construction easier to process, i.e. the optimal variant, given a particular context. Note that it is precisely this kind of reasoning which underlies the predictions for the factors animacy and topicality for choosing the *s*-genitive in the present study, and it has already been discussed in §§6.2.1-2 how these two factors can influence the accessibility of concepts, which, in turn, determines the order of processing and linearization. Note also, that the present study focuses on speaker optimality, although, as I will argue in §8.6.3.2, the choice between the *s*-genitive and the *of*-genitive may well serve both the needs of the speaker and the hearer.

For the diachronic argument, I will follow the general spirit of Haspelmath's (1999b) concept of diachronic adaptation – without necessarily adopting his assumption that languages are comparable to biological systems. I will propose a possible scenario of how different types of economy may have interacted, leading to the diachronic extension of the *s*-genitive along the preference structure proposed in chapters 6 and 7 (and see §8.6.1 below). I will not – and do not have to – assume that the innovation, i.e. the actuation of a construction needs to be functionally adaptive in that only user-optimal constructions are innovated in the first place; my concern in the present study is primarily with the diachronic spread of the *s*-genitive, thereby assuming that the type of functional adaptation Haspelmath sketches may be responsible for the transmission of change through a speech community once the form has been innovated, i.e. is already there.

In addition to Haspelmath's (1999b) account, I believe that in general such adaptive diachronic processes can only be safely assumed if what is user-optimal in the present has also been user-optimal in the past (cf. also Minkova 1999: 228). That is, we need, for heuristic reasons, to introduce a uniformitarian principle for cognitive processes, in the same way that such a principle has been introduced into the study of geology (Lyell 1830-33, as cited in Lass 1997: 28) and transferred from there by Labov into his sociolinguistic studies (Labov 1972) (see also §5.1.2).[191] Lass (1997: 29) defines the uniformitarian principle in linguistics as follows: "The (global, cross-linguistic) likelihood of any linguistic state of affairs (structure, inventory, process, etc.) has always been roughly the same as it is now." For the purpose of this study it is sufficient to assume that the cognitive processes have been the same; besides I concur with Deutscher (1999) that a uniformitarian principle can only be safely assumed for processes but not for states (see also Fischer and Rosenbach 2000: 21-22 for discussion).

8.6   The explanandum: the diachronic extension of the *s*-genitive from late Middle English to Modern English

The results of the experimental study in chapter 6 and the EModE corpus analysis in §7.4 have both revealed aspects of stability and change in the diachronic development of the genitive alternation. While the relative importance of the factors animacy, topicality, and possessive relation seems to have remained rather stable from late Middle English to Present-day English, the contexts in which the *s*-genitive can occur and its relative frequency within these contexts have changed considerably. For the sake of exposition and oversimplifying somewhat, the systematic extension of the *s*-genitive can now be summarized and illustrated on the basis of the following unified preference structure for early Modern English until Modern English (cf. figure 44 below).[192]

8.6.1   *Preference structure: late Middle/early Modern English to Present-day English*

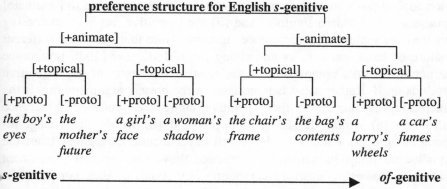

Figure 44.   Preference structure for the English *s*-genitive (late Middle/early Modern English to Present-day English)

This preference structure entails the following information:

(1)   It shows the possible contexts for the occurrence of the *s*-genitive, decreasing in preference from left to right.

(2)   It illustrates in which contexts – if at all – the *s*-genitive is more frequent than the *of*-genitive (= prediction I), with a decreasing likelihood from left to right.

(3)   It also sketches the relative frequency of the *s*-genitive (= prediction II), decreasing from left to right.

(4)   Finally, it outlines the direction of the diachronic extension of the *s*-genitive, context-wise and frequency-wise, again from left to right.

As shown in §7.4, the new productivity of the *s*-genitive seems to have started in the early fifteenth century. If the *s*-genitive could occur at all at that time – then in the most optimal context, i.e. with [+animate] and [+topical] – especially highly topical – possessors with a preference for prototypical possessive relations. But even in this context the *of*-genitive was the more frequent option at that time. During the sixteenth century the *s*-genitive extends along this preference structure, both in contexts and in frequency, and in the early seventeenth century it is almost always the more frequent option with [+animate] [+topical] possessors. Yet note, that the *s*-genitive remains being restricted to the [+animate] domain in late Middle and early Modern English; the extension of the *s*-genitive to [-animate] possessors – again along the preference structure – is a ModE development, a process which, as has been shown in §6.4.3.2, is still ongoing.

To sum up, two kinds of extensions can be observed in the development of the *s*-genitive from late Middle to Modern English. (i) The contexts in which the *s*-genitive can occur have shifted from highly topical to less and non-topical possessors; most notable is the ongoing extension to [-animate] possessors in Modern English. And (ii) the *s*-genitive has been increasing in frequency along this preference structure. Note that given the different nature of empirical data as underlying the EModE and ModE preference structure a direct comparison of the relative frequency of the *s*-genitive forbids itself. Rather, what is important for the present argumentation is the increasing frequency of the *s*-genitive along the proposed preference structure (a) *within* the EModE corpus and (b) *within* the change-in-progress process evident in the ModE experimental data, apart from the qualitative 'jump' to inanimates mentioned above. One frequency argument that can, however, be made comparing both types of data concerns the frequency of the *s*-genitive in the optimal context on ([+animate] [+topical] possessor, [+prototypical] possessive relation). Here it could be shown that the s-genitive is almost obligatory today (in otherwise neutral contexts). Given that the conditions were operationalized in such a way as to represent the worst possible contexts for the occurrence of the s-genitive in order to test its productivity, the almost obligatoriness of the s-genitive, which will be interpreted in §8.6.2.2 below as evidence for its automatization in this context, seems legitimate.[193]

8.6.2 *The role of cognitive economy in the diachronic extension of the* s-*genitive*

To offer a possible account of the diachronic spread of the s-genitive I will in the following distinguish between three different economical principles here: (i) synchronic user-optimality, (ii) automatization, and (iii) analogical/metaphorical extension.

8.6.2.1 Synchronic user-optimality

It has been shown throughout this study that the s-genitive is more likely to occur with a [+animate] possessor, a [+topical] possessor and in a [+prototypical] possessive relation. In §6.2.1.2 I have argued in detail that the preference for [+animate] and [+topical] possessors in the s-genitive is due to the iconic/natural principle according to which it is more efficient for the language processor to process and subsequently linearize animate and topical concepts, since this conforms to the order of how these concepts are conceptualized by the speaker. Therefore, it is quite obvious that for a [+animate] and a [+topical] possessor the s-genitive represents the synchronically more economical option. Moreover, the s-genitive with [+prototypical] possessive relation has been argued to reflect the iconic principle of conceptual distance (cf. §6.2.2.2). Yet why should this also be a synchronically economical choice? As argued by Croft (1990: 254), what is iconic can also be considered to be easier to process. It can also be assumed that it is economical for the speaker to use the more implicit structure for what is the more prototypical possessive relation. As argued above, for the speaker the shorter option should always be the preferred option. Yet he may not always be able to use it without risking being misunderstood. For [+prototypical] possessive relations, such as kin terms, body parts and legal ownership, however, the meaning of the s-genitive is largely predictable, and the speaker can therefore afford to use the s-genitive as the shorter genitive construction. In the ideal case, all three contexts (= [+animate], [+topical], [+prototypical]) go together, resulting in the optimal, i.e. the most economical context for the occurrence of the *s*-genitive in a concrete speech situation for the speaker, as represented by the leftmost side of the preference structure. Note that when the *s*-genitive became increasingly replaced by the *of*-genitive throughout the Middle English period, it became more and more restricted to this optimal context, and it is precisely in this very context that the new productivity of the *s*-genitive in the fifteenth century starts again. As argued above, one possible reason to explain why the synchronic economical potential of the *s*-genitive becomes more productive again may have been its structural change from inflection to clitic, combined with an increasing shift towards determiner function. Yet note, that in the early fifteenth century the *s*-genitive is still a less frequent option than the *of*-genitive even in this optimal context.

8.6.2.2 Automatization

Having established why the [+animate] [+topical] [+prototypical] context is, synchronically, the most economical context for the occurrence of the *s*-genitive, we now, in a second step, need to explain why the *s*-genitive is becoming, diachronically, more frequent than the *of*-genitive and eventually almost obligatory in this context. For this reason, I will now turn to the process of automatization. As argued above (§8.4) the term automatization corresponds largely to the processes of syntactization, entrenchment, and grammaticalization, i.e. they all refer to a process by which a form or construction is becoming increasingly obligatory.[194] In this process, frequency plays a major role in a twofold sense. On the one hand, it should come as no surprise that the *s*-genitive is being used more frequently in the optimal context, since, as argued, it represents the more economical choice in the concrete speech situation. On the other hand, being more frequently used, the *s*-genitive is becoming increasingly entrenched in this context, it has virtually become the routine or default choice in this optimal context, i.e. it has almost become automatized. Note that this is now a type of economy which, although still operating synchronically (> frequent use), already has some diachrony built in (> process of automatization). That is, in accordance with Haspelmath's concept of diachronic adaptation as outlined above, what is most optimal for the language user synchronically, will, diachronically, become more frequent in a kind of adaptive process. And it has indeed been shown that, clearly, by the early seventeenth century the *s*-genitive had ousted the *of*-genitive as the preferred option in the most optimal [+animate] [+topical] [+prototypical] context. And, as the results for the ModE experimental study show, the *s*-genitive is today almost obligatory in this context, with a likelihood of 89.3% for the British subjects and 85.8% for the American subjects (see §6.4.3.1.2), even though proper-noun possessors were not considered in the ModE data, which would have certainly further increased the chance for the s-genitive to occur. Needless to say, this optimal context can easily be counter-balanced by other factors which may bias the choice towards the *of*-genitive (as e.g. a right-branching possessor). That frequent exposure should make a particular construction obligatory over time can be seen as the diachronic (adaptive) shift from the domain of controlled processing to the mode of automatic processing, and hence a shift towards a more economical processing mode, requiring less processing resources (cf. also §8.1).

Frequency, as used in the present study, therefore produces a kind of snowball effect on the increasing use of the s-genitive.There is (i) a higher frequency of usage as induced by synchronic user-optimality, and, following from this, (ii) high frequency in turn leads to the increasing entrenchment and automatization of the s-genitive in the user-optimal context. Thus, while in the first case frequency follows naturally from user-optimality, in the second case it leads to change, resulting in yet another type of user-optimality, i.e. a shift towards the more economical automatic processing mode.

However, precisely by which mechanism frequency leads to automatization is yet not well understood (cf. also Haspelmath 1999b: 191). One possibility may be to regard the child being sensitive to input-frequencies. In such a scenario the increased use of a variant due to synchronic optimality for language users serves as the input for the language-acquiring child. Supposing that grammars do contain information about the probability of a variant (as, for example, underlying Bresnan's Stochastic OT account, cf. §5.1.1.2), the child does not only acquire the variant but also a certain probability attached to it. This dialectics between language usage and language acquisition in diachronic change, as for example recently modeled and formalized in simulation studies by Briscoe (2000a, 2000b) for larger-scale evolutionary processes, may be understood as a kind of algorithmic process eventually leading to the automatization of a construction, or, as in the case of the genitive variation, to the near-automatization of one variant in certain contexts. It may be assumed that once a certain threshold within the input frequency is reached, variability no longer exists for the child. Such an algorithm is probably best understood in terms of "positive feedback", a well-known process underlying the development of biological systems in general (cf. e.g. the excellent discussion in Dawkins 1986: chapter 8). Dawkins (1986: 244) cites St Matthew's Gospel to grasp the general idea of positive feedback: "'Unto everyone that hath shall be given, and he shall have abundance: but from him that hath not shall be taken away even that which he hath.'" Given the effect of frequency so commonly noticed for automatization, it seems very plausible, in my view, to assume the mechanism of positive feedback being at the bottom of this process, as it has already been assumed and implemented in simulation studies, such as Briscoe (2000a, 2000b).

8.6.2.3 Analogical/metaphorical extension

While the two economical principles discussed so far may account for why the *s*-genitive is becoming more frequent in the user-optimal context, i.e. the [+animate] [+topical] [+prototypical] context, it is not at all clear why it should also extend to less optimal contexts, i.e. to [-topical], [-prototypical] and particularly to [-animate] contexts and even become more frequent in these contexts; should this not be an altogether counter-economical process? Not necessarily so. It is just yet another type of economy that comes into play, i.e. the fact that the same linguistic strategy is eventually applied to similar contexts, a process also found under the name "analogical extension", and which is regarded by Ronneberger-Sibold (1980) as an economical meta-principle. The formal process of analogical extension, in turn, is closely linked to the cognitive process of metaphorical change (cf. e.g. Hopper and Traugott 1993: 87; see also Fischer and Rosenbach 2000: §4.1), which describes the process by which a form or construction used for one concept comes to be used for another one because the two have some element in common. Metaphor is to be distinguished from metonymy. While metaphor is "a way of conceiving of one thing in terms of another" (Lakoff and Johnson 1980: 36), metonymy "allows us to use one entity to stand for another" (Lakoff and Johnson 1980: 36). Both metaphor and metonymy are regarded by Lakoff and Johnson (1980) first and foremost as devices of our conceptual system (and not language itself) that operate to a large extent subconsciously, being a basic way of conceptualizing (and understanding) reality.

Applying the concept of analogical/metaphorical extension to the extension of the *s*-genitive presupposes that the whole process does not operate in a blind way but that there is some kind of order and system in it. This is indeed the case. When looking at the process as a whole we can observe that the diachronic extension of the *s*-genitive is by no means arbitrary but runs systematically along the preference structure proposed. When looking at this process in even more detail, the following observations can be made, focusing on the most striking – and still ongoing

– extension of the *s*-genitive to [-animate] possessors. It has already been argued in §4.1.1 and §6.2.1.2 that animacy as a factor influencing language cannot be defined in absolute terms, i.e. in terms of a (biological) opposition between living and non-living kinds, but seems to be susceptible to the way of human being conceive of as being (more or less) animate. This gradient and subjective character of animacy in human conceptualization makes it particularly prone to the process of metaphorical extension from [+animate] to [-animate]. In general, we may observe two points of departure from which the *s*-genitive may have been used with [-animate] possessors.

First, even in early Modern English, where the *s*-genitive is only productive with [+animate] possessors, some residual expressions with [-animate] possessors are still to be found, most notably in compound-like expressions, such as e.g. *a day's journey* or *new yere's eve,* which in general seem to be less sensitive to the animacy constraint (see also §7.3 and §7.4.4.1 above). In addition, Svartengren (1949: 146) points out that *s*-genitives with *end* or *edge* as a possessum noun (e.g. *land's end, finger's end, the water's edge*) are "idiomatic survivals that have proved most fruitful in giving rise to analogical formations" (cf. also Zachrisson 1920: 46).

Second, the *s*-genitive may have spread from [+animate] possessors by way of metaphorical extension to [-animate] ones in the following ways. Within the animate domain we could observe an extension from highly topical proper-noun possessors (*Simon's father*) and extra-contextually-given possessors (*God's love*) to common human nouns (*my father's book*), indicating how the *s*-genitive has shifted from highly into less topical contexts. Metaphorical extensions could also have started from proper nouns denoting persons to proper nouns denoting things. Such an extension would indeed account for the surprising prevalence of *s*-genitives with geographical names that we find today (e.g. *Europe's future, London's suburbs, India's soil*), as for example observed by Jahr Sorheim (1980), Quirk et al. (1985: §5.118), Siemund (1993) or Jucker (1993). From there, the *s*-genitive may have spread to geographical nouns in general (*the county's population, the world's worst coffee,* cf. Jahr Sorheim 1980: 46). According to den Breejen (1937: 55) words belonging to nautical language, such as *ship* or *boat,* may occasionally occur with the *s*-genitive in his late sixteenth-century prose corpus. Note that ships and boats were – and are – usually named as well, and this might then account for the disposition of the *s*-genitive to occur with means of locomotion (e.g. *train, plane*), (cf. also Svartengren 1949: 167-170; Dahl 1971: 154-156). It appears therefore that the potential of things to be named may have played a crucial role in the metaphorical transfer from animates to inanimates, be it resulting from the transfer of higher topical to less highly topical possessors (proper nouns & extra-contextually known referents → common nouns) or due to the fact that things that can be named also allow for some kind of personification. Note that his shows how much topicality and animacy are interacting precisely along the preference structure in the metaphorical extension of the *s*-genitive. Another possible pathway from animate to inanimate, also noted by Zachrisson (1920: 46) is that from personal nouns to collective nouns, which are somehow intermediate between inanimate and animate (e.g. *her friends' notion > her class's notion; the editor's criticism > the paper's criticism*), although this might be rather an instance of metonymy with an inanimate collective noun such as *paper* coming to stand for the journalist(s) and/or editor(s). Personification as a possible bridge from animates to inanimates is mentioned by Zachrisson (1920: 46), in that abstract or concrete nouns involving some personification may eventually come to be used with the *s*-genitive without such a sense of personification (e.g. *love's cruelty > her love's disaster; the abandoned room's appeal > the guest-room's luxurious chill*). As the study by Dabrowska (1998), briefly discussed in §4.1.2, has shown, inanimate possessors, which are metaphorically conceptualized as animate (in her study computer nouns), can much more easily occur with the *s*-genitive than other inanimate nouns. Likewise, in the discussion of the experimental data, we have seen that the possessor *car*, being probably inherently more apt to be conceived of as animate than other concrete nouns, can serve as a good bridging context for the use of the *s*-genitive with [-animate], [-topical] possessors, which are otherwise the least favored contexts of all for the occurrence of the *s*-genitive.

Although much more detailed analysis of this analogical/metaphorical process is certainly in order, particularly for the time span between the eighteenth and the early twentieth century, for which period we do not know much about the distribution of the two genitive constructions, it appears that this process proceeded in a fairly orderly fashion. We may assume that those inanimate possessors allowed the *s*-genitive first, which could be perceived of as animate, which were highly topical and/or in a prototypical possessive relation, besides the fact that always some residues of the *s*-genitive with inanimate possessors have remained in the language.

What still needs to be explained though is why temporal possessors so easily occur with the *s*-genitive today in expressions such as *today's weather, yesterday's news, last week's work.* This noun class does not seem to fit in the general route of metaphorical extension discussed above. It may, however, be that the use of the s-genitive with such temporal possessors is simply a continuation of the residual pattern with compound-like expressions mentioned above (e.g. *a day's work*). What may also have contributed to the spread of the s-genitive with this lexical class is the fact that temporal nouns and adverbs(!) also stand out in that they can occur as subjects in English (e.g. **Today** *is a better day than yesterday.*). As shown in Rosenbach, Stein, and Vezzosi (2000) possessors in an agent relation to the possessum noun, i.e. subjective genitives (*Peter's going to the market*) become extraordinarily more productive in early Modern English. Another possibility is that such temporal nouns can serve as a good anchor for certain possessum nouns. Note that *weather* and *news* are somehow relational, they need to be temporally located in order to identify which weather and which news are referred to.

Note finally, that during early Modern English another development concerning inanimate possessors took place in that a new possessive form for the third person neuter pronoun, i.e. *its*, started emerging in the seventeenth century, replacing the older form *his* (cf. Jespersen 1961: 307; Nevalainen and Raumolin-Brunberg 1994). This development is particularly striking for two reasons. On the one hand, *its* is being composed as a productive pattern, in analogy to the s-genitive (*it* + possessive -s). On the other hand, it is interesting to observe that the third person inanimate personal pronoun (*it*) is the last pronoun to develop a genuine possessive pronoun (*its*) in English, and, once established, becomes increasingly used as the almost exclusive pronominal possessive form,[195] quickly replacing its periphrastic and adverbial alternates, such as *of it* or *thereof*. That is, the evolution – and spread – of *its* also follows the animacy hierarchy ($1^{st}/2^{nd}$ person > 3rd person). We may speculate that the development of *its* is somehow linked to the extension of the s-genitive with lexical inanimate possessors if not contributing to it.

8.6.3 Grammaticalization at work?

The term "grammaticalization" can in principle be used in two ways. In a rather broad sense, it refers to a process by which a form or construction is becoming more and more fixed. In a more strict sense and as traditionally introduced and used by Meillet ([1912] 1951), it refers to the process by which a lexical, less bound element eventually acquires a grammatical meaning, becoming more bound. In the following I will argue that the scenario proposed in the previous section suggests that there are grammaticalization processes at work, in both senses of the term.[196]

8.6.3.1 Grammaticalization as automatization

The process of automatization as outlined in §8.6.2.2, by which the *s*-genitive, as the more preferred choice in its most optimal context (i.e. [+animate] [+topical] [+prototypical]), is becoming more and more frequent until it almost becomes obligatory in this context, is indicative of the first type of grammaticalization, as illustrated in figure 45 below.

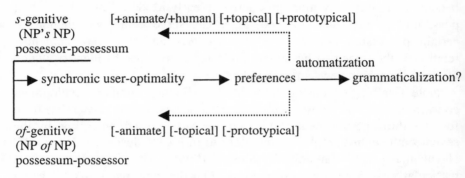

Figure 45. Grammaticalization (as automatization) of the *s*-genitive?

It is also in this sense of automatization that the term "grammaticalization" is used by Haspelmath (1999a) when he accounts for article-possessor complementarity by assuming that a once economically motivated preference eventually becomes the only option and part of grammar. A similar use of "grammaticalization" can be found in Hawkins (1994: 92), when he talks of "grammaticalized basic orders as conventionalizations of the most optimal and most frequent orders in performance." This process can also be captured in Haiman's framework by the process of "routinization" (Haiman 1994b: 1634):

> A linguistic form ... is motivated in certain specified contexts. By 'routinization,' its distribution is generalized so that it occurs independently of the environment which originally motivated its appearance.

Note that in this respect routinization goes well beyond grammaticalization-as-automatization as outlined above in that it also subsumes the shift to non-motivated, i.e. non-optimal, contexts. Accordingly, we can then view the diachronic extension of the *s*-genitive as a shift from what has been shown to be iconically motivated contexts ([+animate], [+topical],

[+prototypical]) towards non-motivated contexts ([-animate], [-topical], [-prototypical]).

Therefore, strictly speaking, grammaticalization in the sense of automatization can only capture the development of the *s*-genitive for the optimal context on the very left of the preference structure in §8.6.1. And even in this optimal context, we cannot really observe full grammaticalization, only a very strong preference.[197]

8.6.3.2 Grammaticalization in the traditional sense

In addition to this first type of grammaticalization (as automatization), there also seem to be grammaticalization processes of the second, more traditional, type at work in the development of the *s*-genitive. Grammaticalization defined as the gradual shift of a lexical item to a more grammatical item typically involves both formal and semantic changes. Some characteristic formal processes are, for example, phonetic reduction, increase in bondedness and reduction of scope, to name the most relevant for the present argumentation (cf. also Lehmann 1995 for diagnostics of grammaticalization). It is generally assumed that such formal change goes hand in hand with semantic change, in particular a loss of lexical referential meaning, resulting in a more abstract, grammatical meaning of the grammaticalized item.[198]

In general, grammaticalization is supposed to proceed along structural clines, such as the one suggested by Hopper and Traugott (1993: 7):

content item > grammatical word > clitic > inflectional affix > zero

In which respect can we identify any grammaticalization processes in this traditional sense in the development of the *s*-genitive? Usually, it is the development of POSS '*s* from inflection to clitic, described and discussed in §7.5 that is discussed in the grammaticalization literature (e.g. Janda 1980, 2001; Plank 1995; Newmeyer 1998: §5.3.4; Tabor and Traugott 1998; Norde 1998, 2001), focusing on the question whether the *s*-genitive is indeed, as seems at first glance, a development back down the structural cline given above from an inflectional affix (= more bound) to a clitic (= less bound). If POSS '*s* is seen as a direct continuation of the OE inflectional genitive (as is implicit in Carstairs' 1987 and Allen's 1997a account), then the evidence speaks certainly for a *de*grammaticalization along the grammaticalization cline above (inflectional affix > clitic). POSS '*s* has certainly *in*creased – and not *de*creased – in scope, as is evident from the fact that it can today attach to whole phrases, as e.g. in the group genitive (see also discussion in §1.2).[199] Such a development would not only be extremely rare but also run counter to the presumed unidirectionality of grammaticalization processes, which are typically believed to be irreversible. It seems, however, to depend on how to interpret the development of POSS *'s* and how to define the constituting criteria for grammaticalization as well as degrammaticalization as to which viewpoint is taken.

Several interpretations are possible. If we adopt Janda's (1980) viewpoint that the inflectional *s*-genitive was first analyzed as the *his*-genitive, which then developed into the ModE clitic *s*-genitive (cf. §7.5.2.3), then both degrammaticalization as well as grammaticalization in the development of POSS *'s* can be argued for, as illustrated below, although Janda (1980, 2001) himself only discusses it as a case of degrammaticalization.

degrammaticalization	**grammaticalization**

inflectional *s*-genitive ———▶ *his*-genitive ———▶ ModE (clitic) *s*-genitive

Degrammaticalization, i.e. an upgrading from more grammatical (i.e. more bound) to less grammatical (i.e. less bound) can be observed in the sense that the old inflectional *s*-genitive was reanalyzed as the *his*-genitive, i.e. a linking possessive pronoun construction, that is, an inflectional ending turns into a possessive pronoun. Once this reanalysis has taken place, however, and the *his*-genitive has turned into ModE clitic POSS *'s*, grammaticalization follows its usual pathway, from less grammatical/bound (a possessive pronoun) to more grammatical/bound (a clitic). Not only is the clitic *'s* phonetically more reduced than the possessive pronoun *his*, but it is also a structurally more bonded element (and for yet further arguments in favor of a grammaticalization of the clitic/determiner *s*-genitive, see also below). That is, strictly speaking, in Janda's (1980, 2001) account we need to carefully distinguish the proximate and the ultimate origin of ModE POSS *'s*. It is only when considering its ultimate origin that degrammaticalization comes into play; looking at its proximate origin, i.e. the *his*-genitive, speaks for a regular case of grammaticalization.

However, it may be difficult in practice to determine the ultimate origin of POSS *'s*. Norde (2001) discusses the ModE *s*-genitive under a section on exaptation without, however, being very explicit precisely in which way the *s*-genitive should be regarded as an exaptated construction. Exaptation is a concept from evolutionary biology, which has been transferred by Lass (1990, 1997: 316-324) to the domain of language. Lass (1997: 316) describes it as "a kind of conceptual renovation, as it were, of material that is already there, but either serving some other purpose, or serving no purpose at all." So, what is crucial is that an older construction, which is either fully functional or already 'junk', gets re-used for another functional purpose. Defined like this, is the ModE s-genitive really a case of exaptation, and if so, in which way should that matter for the question of (de)grammaticalization at all? At first sight, the s-genitive indeed seems to qualify as a case of exaptation. There is a contingency in terms of formal (phonological) substance, i.e. -(e)s,[200] that gets reallocated a new function, i.e. a determiner function (or referential anchoring function), although there is also to a large degree an overlap of the functions of genitive (possessive) case and a definite determiner, due to the inherently anchoring function of possessives. What seems to be important with respect to the question of (de)grammaticalization is that the development of POSS 's towards a clitic determiner in English would not be a case of a construction simply reversing itself along a structural cline, dropping back into some older state. That is, under such a strict reading of degrammaticalization the s-genitive would not qualify as a case of degrammaticalization (whatever the ultimate cause for this development is) because there is no attested previous determiner function of POSS 's in the history of English. Only insofar as – on a more abstract level – the grammatical *status* of the same relational marker, i.e. -(e)s, is concerned (affix > clitic), can a reversal along the structural cline given above be observed.

Yet another possible way at looking at the question of (de)grammaticalization of POSS 's is to regard the prevalence of s-less genitives (*the butcher wyff, the man name*) in early Modern English. According to Altenberg (1982: 13) s-less genitives were used so extensively in early Modern English that the s-genitive was almost threatened by extinction (cf. also §7.5.1.1). So, we may even hypothesize that the OE inflectional genitive had run the full course of grammaticalization, by then exhibiting a zero form (inflectional affix > zero), and that, by means of the possessive pronoun *his*, a new grammaticalization cycle has begun (possessive pronoun > clitic); in this case both developments (i.e. the end of the old cycle and the beginning of the new one) would be fully consistent with typical grammaticalization pathways. Note, however, that there is no evidence that the s-genitive was ever reduced completely to zero; besides an increasing number of s-less genitives the old inflectional s-genitive always persisted too, if very restricted in use.[201]

Taken together, the discussion concerning the (possible) degrammaticalization of the s-genitive is first and foremost a theoretical battlefield within grammaticalization theory, centering on the hypothesis of unidirectionality. Yet, unidirectionality itself has recently come under considerable attack and is increasingly questioned as a 'law' underlying grammaticalization processes. Currently the strongest viewpoint is certainly maintained by Haspelmath (1999c), who argues that grammaticalization processes are always irreversible and unidirectionality is exceptionless. The opponents to unidirectionality usually put forward the following arguments. Some argue that unidirectionality is conceptually irrelevant, because it is already a definitional property built into the very notion of grammaticalization itself; that is, grammaticalization is defined *qua* unidirectionality and therefore, by definition, all grammaticalization processes must be unidirectional (for this view see e.g. Campbell (2001); see also Cowie 1995: 188-189). Moreover, as argued by Janda (2001), if the locus of language lies ultimately within the individual speaker (cf. also §5.2.1.2), it is difficult to conceive of how unidirectionality should come about. Although the historical record may indeed suggest transmissional continuity, speakers do not have any awareness of past stages of their language and therefore "there can be no cross-generational 'diachronic constraints' prohibiting such analyses" (Janda 2001: 267), except of course in the form that speakers necessarily build their language on the basis of the current, historically-evolved grammar. Essentially the same argument – though from a very different ontological position – has been put forward by Lass (2000: 223), who states that "*[i]nformation loss processes have no memory*"; that is, there is nothing inherent in any single stage on a cline which would necessarily lead to another one (besides, Lass 2000: 223-224 rejects clines as unnecessary predefinitions of the development).[202] Other scholars argue that unidirectionality as an empirical claim is simply wrong because counter-examples do exist, so unidirectionality is either rejected completely (cf. e.g. Newmeyer 1998: chapter 5) or only admitted in a weak version (to which there are counter-examples, if few of them), cf. e.g. Lass (2000).

So, while it looks as if degrammaticalization of the *s*-genitive as such, i.e. a development back down the cline from affix to clitic is theoretically possible (given only a weak version of unidirectionality), there is as yet, to complicate matters even further, no unified way of defining what would indeed constitute degrammaticalization – does a morpheme literally has to be reversed into a prior state, or is degrammaticalization rather to be understood more abstractly in the sense that the status of a morpheme reverses along a structural cline (cf. also Norde 2001: 236-238)? As discussed above, it is only in the latter case that the development of POSS '*s* can possibly be regarded a case of degrammaticalization. Also, not yet knowing the ultimate origin of the ModE *s*-genitive (is it a continuation of the old inflectional genitive or is it due to a reanalysis of the *his*-genitive?), the question of the (possible) *de*grammaticalization of the *s*-genitive must, for the time being, remain unsettled.

Yet, we certainly need to distinguish between the structural change of POSS *'s* from an inflectional affix to a clitic on the one hand, and the diachronic extension of the *s*-genitive once POSS *'s* has become a clitic, on the other, as illustrated in figure 46 below. It is for the latter that I would like to suggest in the following some possible grammaticalization processes.

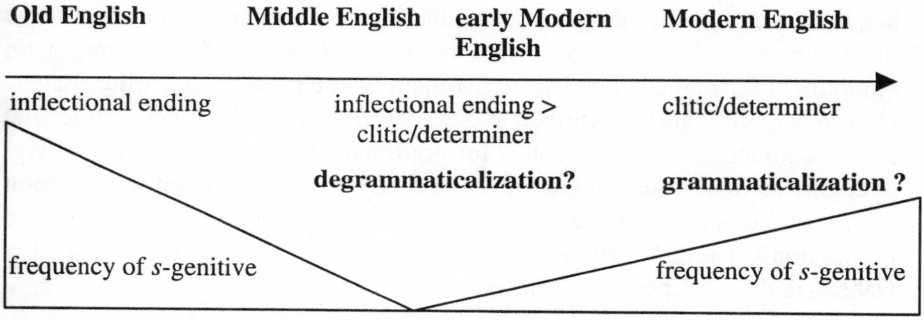

Figure 46.   Degrammaticalization and grammaticalization processes in the development of the *s*-genitive

In the diachronic extension of the *s*-genitive it is the process of analogical/metaphorical extension as outlined in §8.6.2.3 in particular that is a mechanism typical of a grammaticalization process in the framework of grammaticalization theory (cf. e.g. Hopper and Traugott 1993: 77-87). As, for example, argued by Heine (1997), a particularly common extension to be observed in grammaticalization is the one from animate to inanimate:

> An important shift to be encountered in many instances of grammaticalization is in fact one according to which expressions for human concepts come to be used also for concepts that are inanimate. This shift is described by Heine, Claudi, and Hünnemeyer (1991) with reference to what they call the PERSON-TO-OBJECT metaphor.   (Heine 1997: 87-88)

Heine (1997: 85-89) explicitly refers to grammaticalization processes from permanent possession to inanimate possession, i.e. the shift from a human possessor to a non-human possessor, which can, for example, be observed in Estonian. In fact, it is one of the main findings of the present study that such an extension from animate to inanimate possessors has taken place from early Modern English to Present-day English, and it is particularly in this respect that the development of the English *s*-genitive from early Modern English onwards shows traces of grammaticalization at work. Yet it is not exactly clear, which other processes typically involved in grammaticalization (as briefly laid out above) can also be discerned. In which respect should, for example, semantic bleaching have taken place in this process? While the *s*-genitive has certainly become restricted in the functions/meanings it could express from Old English to Modern English (cf. also Tabor and Traugott 1998: 238), it has also been shown in §7.4 how the *s*-genitive has extended to less prototypical possessive relations from late Middle English onwards. Yet it is possible that the *s*-genitive may have acquired some additional pragmatic function and that hence the diachronic development of the *s*-genitive involves some kind of pragmatic strengthening, namely a subjective function not present in earlier stages. Note that such a shift towards a subjective meaning, which goes under the name "subjectification", is typical for grammaticalization processes (cf. e.g. Traugott 1995).[203] As argued by Taylor (1996: 348) "the reference point function involves subjectification of some aspects of paradigmatic possession". Taylor's (1996) use of "subjectification" draws on Langacker (1990), and he defines it as follows:

> An entity is construed objectively if it is the 'object' of conception, while subjective construal obtains when an entity is an inherent (though unprofiled) aspect of the conceptualization process itself.
>
> (Taylor 1996: 348)

According to Taylor (1996), the *s*-genitive as a reference point or anchoring device subjectively construes the route the hearer needs to take when identifying the intended referent of the possessum, i.e. in Taylor's account it is the accessibility of the possessor in relation to the possessum that is (subjectively) invoked and not the relation itself, which would be the corresponding objective construal of the possessive relation. According to Taylor (1996: 351) it is this subjectification, which makes it possible for the *s*-genitive to extend beyond what he calls "paradigmatic possession". Note that if the pathway I suggested in §7.5.2.4.2 for POSS '*s*, from (possessive) compound, i.e. classifier, to determiner proves to be correct, then this would also constitute a change from less to more grammatical and would therefore also possibly qualify as a case of grammaticalization.[204] And, given that the *s*-genitive has indeed undergone subjectification, this would also involve a shift to a more leftward position within the NP (Classifier → Determiner) including subjectification, very much in the sense as outlined by Adamson (2000) for the development of *lovely* from a descriptive adjective to an affective adjective and an intensifier (cf. also §7.5.2.4.2).

The strong effect of topicality in the development of the English s-genitive points also to a grammaticalization process along the Topic Schema, which has already briefly been discussed in §7.5.3.2 when connecting it to the new function of POSS 's as a determiner. In this section I will refer to the Topic Schema in the context of grammaticalization. The Topic Schema (*As for X, X's Y*) as one of the eight event schemas for the grammaticalization of possession proposed by Heine (1997) predicts that the possessor is a topic which precedes the possessum (cf. Heine 1997: 148). As already pointed out in §7.5.3.2, the Topic Schema usually results in possessor specification, i.e. it seems that it naturally develops some kind of determiner function. Heine (1997: 160-161) describes possessor specification as follows:

> The use of possessor specification has a number of implications for the resulting possessive construction. First, it introduces a word order structure where the possessor precedes the possessee. Second, it is typically confined to human possessors. Only at a more advanced stage of grammaticalization, to be observed in relatively few languages, non-human possessors are admitted. (Heine 1997: 160-161)

Note that all specifying genitives, which were focused on in the present study, are by definition anchoring constructions, while classifying genitives can be regarded as non-anchoring. Since topicality has been shown to play a crucial role in the choice of the s-genitive – albeit not the most important one – it is indeed possible that the ModE s-genitive originates from the Topic Schema, with the possessor as a topic preceding the possessum, resulting in possessor specification and having undergone a process of grammaticalization typical for such constructions from human to non-human possessors.

Viewing the s-genitive as an anchoring device we can also see how – in the development of the s-genitive – the needs of the speaker and the hearer go together. As an anchoring device, the s-genitive facilitates the identification of the intended referent of the possessum for the hearer, while the types of economy outlined above operate on the level of the speaker (as illustrated in table 51 below). Note that it is only for the factor possessive relation that speaker economy clashes with hearer economy: while it is economical for the speaker to use the shorter and more implicit construction, the hearer would prefer the longer and more explicit construction.

Table 51. Speaker versus hearer economy in the choice of genitive construction

morphosyntactic properties of the *s*-genitive	economical principles	effect
word order	[+animate] & [+topical] first in linear order	easier to process for speaker
determiner function	anchoring function of possessor	highly accessible possessor facilitates referent identification for hearer
relational marker POSS *'s*	conceptual distance (implicit meaning → more bonded construction)	preference for the shorter construction for the speaker

To conclude, in this section I have discussed the development of the *s*-genitive in the context of grammaticalization theory. I have distinguished two aspects within the history of the *s*-genitive, i.e. (i) the structural development of POSS *'s* from inflection to clitic, and (ii) the re-rise of the *s*-genitive. While these two processes are certainly interdependent, in that the change of POSS *'s* has been regarded in this study as the structural precondition for the new productivity of the *s*-genitive, in terms of grammaticalization these two need to be kept distinct. As far as the former is concerned, it is discussed as a potential case of *de*grammaticalization; as far as the latter is concerned, i.e. once POSS *'s* got reanalyzed, I have pointed out several ways in which processes typical for the grammaticalization of possessives, such as the extension to inanimate possessors, subjectification and grammaticalization along the Topic Schema, can be discerned. I am aware of the fact that I have only scratched the surface of what can possibly be at stake, and some scenarios suggested may fail to stand up to closer scrutiny. Yet it has not been the aim of this discussion to reveal the ultimate grammaticalization processes involved in the development of the *s*-genitive but rather to point out possible interpretations as a suggestion for further research in this area.

8.6.4   *Possible other factors involved in the diachronic extension of the* s-*genitive*

In the present study I have focused on the role of some conceptual factors which, as I have argued, point to a cognitive motivation when choosing between the two genitive constructions. I have also stressed the role of the grammar in that the change of POSS '*s* from an inflection to a clitic and a determiner has been regarded as the structural precondition for the forces of cognitive economy to unfold more strongly from late Middle English onwards. In no way, however, do I intend to imply that these are the sole mechanisms involved in the diachronic extension of the *s*-genitive. Rather, I wanted to show that both the structural state of the grammar and cognitive economy as evident in the three factors investigated have certainly played *some* role in this development. That both these aspects must be taken into account when considering language change has recently also been argued in Fischer and Rosenbach (2000), and I will briefly come back to the general question of where to place the locus of language change – the grammatical system or language usage – in the final conclusion in chapter 9. In the following I will briefly point to some other factors, which also seem likely to have contributed to this development.

8.6.4.1 Stylistic factors

There are two notable stylistic changes which have taken place between early Modern English and Modern English and which may have affected the preference of a particular genitive construction.

First, as shown by Biber and Finegan (1989), there has been a general increase towards more oral styles, i.e. a trend towards more informality, within English written genres from the seventeenth century to Modern English. As has been argued by some scholars, the *s*-genitive is to a large extent stylistically conditioned, occurring more frequently in informal than in formal styles (cf. e.g. Jahr Sorheim 1980; Altenberg 1982; Jucker 1993; see also §3.3.2.2.4). Admittedly, the revival of the *s*-genitive as witnessed in our studies can only be constituted within our corpus (1400 – 1630), which covers a time span not included in Biber and Finegan's (1989) study, and it remains an empirical question whether the drift towards a more oral style holds true for the fifteenth to sixteenth centuries as well. If so, however, the increasing use of the *s*-genitive may not be an exclusively cognitively motivated development in the sense outlined above but could also be due to (i) a change in style or style conventions, or, (ii) in case that the choice of the *s*-genitive creates rather than is affected by a certain style, a change in the speakers/writers' strategies underlying the creation of such styles (see also discussion in §3.3.2.2.4).

In a way connected to the affinity of the *s*-genitive to occur more often in informal than in formal styles is the study by Kohnen (2001), who shows how some selected Latinate constructions in English have spread from more formal, prestigious text types to informal text types. Kohnen's (2001) study shows that while the former become affected first, the latter contribute more to the diachronic spread of the constructions. It is therefore also possible that the *s*-genitive may have resided longest and started to become productive again in a more formal setting, and that only the subsequent spread of the *s*-genitive took place within more informal settings. A scenario that would indeed support such a view is suggested by Bergs and Stein (2001), who show that the *wh*-relativizers entered the linguistic system first as marked forms with deity expressions (e.g. *God, Christ*) as highly marked contexts. Only subsequently, Bergs and Stein (2001) argue, do these relativizers spread to other contexts as well. These findings are well compatible with the historical genitive data investigated in Rosenbach, Stein, and Vezzosi (2000) (see also §7.4 above); here also the *s*-genitive initially is most common with deity possessors. Such deity expressions are naturally most common in religious texts, i.e. a fairly formal text type, shown by Jahr Sorheim (1980) and Altenberg (1982) to take the lowest frequency of the *s*-genitive. We may also speculate that the modern (clitic) *s*-genitive owes its maintenance partly to the fact that it is a more synthetic construction, looking more inflectional than the *of*-genitive, which, in a period when Latin grammar as a model became particularly important (cf. e.g. Görlach 1993: 36; Stein 1997), may also have contributed to its spread. Taken together, the *s*-genitive as an (at least superficially) inflectional form, conforming more to the at that time prestigious model of Latin, may have spread from formal to more informal text types in a similar way as the Latinate constructions described by Kohnen (2001).

Second, also an increasing tendency towards a more nominal style has been observed for Modern English. According to Biber and Finegan's (1989: 491) table of linguistic features nominalizations are, however, indicative of a more literate rather than an oral style. Given the evidence from Biber and Finegan (1989), should it not be somewhat contradictory that nominalization as a more literal and formal feature becomes more common while at the same time a drift towards higher orality can be observed? There is yet another development taking place within the realm of nominalizations, which may possibly account for this seeming contradiction, namely an increasing tendency towards higher premodification rather than postmodification from early Modern English onwards.

8.6.4.2 Premodification versus postmodification

Barber (1964: 142-143) mentions an increasing preference towards adding modifiers to nouns (*Birmingham housewife Mrs Smith*), rather than putting them in apposition after the noun (*Mrs Smith, a Birmingham housewife*). Diachronically, a shift towards syntactically complex nominal premodifiers (e.g. *English-as-a-second-language programme*) from early Modern English onwards has been observed (cf. Mutt 1967; Raumolin-Brunberg 1991: 275), as already discussed in §7.5.2.4 above. This increasing shift towards more nominal premodification may be partly accounted for by a change in the general style conventions in the course of the nineteenth century. As argued by Varantola (1993: 78), from the mid-nineteenth century onwards the style used in scientific writings changed from a personal and narrative style to a more distinct, information-condensed, i.e. shorter style, as it is typical for nominal premodifiers. Note that it is also exactly these properties, which make the *s*-genitive most apt in journalism. Interestingly, Varantola (1993: 76) also draws attention to the fact that premodification, because far less explicit than its postmodifying counterpart, relies much more on shared extralinguistic knowledge and can also serve as a textual device to link already introduced referents or events more cohesively with what follows. It is also in this very respect that nominal premodification resembles the *s*-genitive. As has been shown in the present study the *s*-genitive is much more likely to be used, if the first element, i.e. the possessor, is known (i.e. topical).

Note that there are also other close correlations between nominal pre- and postmodification on the one hand and the genitive variation on the other. As pointed out by Bolinger (1967), premodification in general tends to express rather permanent and inherent states while postmodification is more temporary. So, for example, *a happy man* refers to a man who is characterized by typically being happy. Used predicatively (*The man is happy*) or postnominally (*a man happy*) the adjective rather refers to happiness as a temporary state of the man and not as a characterizing timeless attribute. As has been shown in the present study, prototypical possessive relations, which express a more permanent relation between possessor and possessum, tend rather to occur with the *s*-genitive, while non-prototypical possessive relations are more likely to be realized as an *of*-genitive. So both nominal premodification and possessive constructions are subject to the same iconic/economical principle of conceptual distance.

Moreover, as argued in §2.3.1 and §7.5.2.4, nominal premodification correlates to a great extent with nominal compounding, both of which have been regarded to form a kind of bridging context for the occurrence of the *s*-genitive, (i) due to the general affinities, or gradience, between the *s*-genitive and nominal premodification/compounding, and, more specifically, (ii) due to the inherent ambiguity of indefinite possessors between a referential and a non-referential reading. Moreover, the very fact that nominal premodifiers and (possessive) compounds/classifying genitives more easily permit inanimate premodifiers/possessors may be one crucial link for specifying *s*-genitives to occur with inanimate possessors as well. Another striking parallel between nominal premodification on the one hand and the *s*-genitive on the other is the observation that the tendency towards prenominal modifiers is – very similar to the spread of the *s*-genitive with inanimate possessors – a development which begins, under American influence, in British newspaper language (cf. e.g. Barber 1964).

We may therefore speculate that the development towards higher nominal premodification is in some way connected with – or even contributed to – the diachronic extension of the *s*-genitive, be it for internal structural reasons (gradience between determiners and modifiers), for discourse-pragmatic ones (e.g. textual cohesion) or for stylistic reasons (shift towards a short and explicit style). Comparing in detail the development of adnominal possessive constructions, nominal premodification and compounding certainly looks like a highly promising line for further research.

Chapter 9
Summary and conclusion

The present study is an empirical study of a particular type of grammatical variation, i.e. the genitive variation in English, and set out with the following methodological and theoretical objectives.

Methodologically, special emphasis was paid to the identification of those contexts in which the two variants, the *s*-genitive and the *of*-genitive can, at least potentially, both be realized (= choice contexts). While it is certainly not only a legitimate but also intriguing question to look at which factors make one construction the only possible choice in certain contexts, to include such categorical or knock-out factors in a quantitative analysis would be very misleading, if not utterly misconceived. In addition, even if we narrow down our quantitative analysis to potential choice-contexts we must be aware of the fact that the choice of genitive construction is anything but simple, quite the contrary. Numerous factors conspire to determine which genitive construction is more likely to be used. For the empirical analysis, this has two major implications. First, when investigating a single factor, other intervening (both reinforcing or inhibiting) factors should be controlled to ensure that the effect of this one factor will not be confounded by the effect of others. And second, our study should not only be directed towards the identification of certain factors but go beyond, and attempt to pinpoint more closely how various factors impinge on each other. Both these objectives have been considered in this study in the following way. This study has focused on the effect of some selected conceptual factors, i.e. animacy, topicality, and the type of possessive relation, while other factors, also known to influence the genitive variation, were identified in chapter 3 as non-comparable contexts and subsequently controlled in this study. Since the factors animacy, topicality, and possessive relation could be shown to overlap to quite an extent with each other, their effect had to be kept separate in the empirical analysis. For this reason, these factors as investigated in the present study were defined in such a way as to only test the effect of one single factor and not, as an epiphenomenon, the effect of others. Moreover, all logically possible combinations of these factors were tested, which allowed for an evaluation of their interaction. In particular, it could be shown that – although these factors generally interact with each other – none of them can be completely reduced to the other(s). The results of the present study therefore speak against a category topicworthiness in which animacy and topicality are subsumed as a uniform category (cf. e.g. Deane 1987; 1992; Taylor 1996). Moreover, and more importantly for the present study, the relative effect of these three factors could be identified (i.e. animacy > topicality > possessive relation), with animacy turning out to be the most important factor, followed by topicality, and with the possessive relation exerting the lowest constraint on the choice of genitive construction. Further research is certainly needed to evaluate the interplay of the conceptual factors investigated in this study with other factors, such as phonological and syntactic factors. One factor which has certainly been neglected so far is the relative weight of possessor and possessum as defined phonologically (i.e. in terms of number of syllables). As the discussion in §6.5 has shown, word length seems to have at least some effect on the choice of genitive construction.

When trying to evaluate the relative importance of factors in such a way, we are, however, faced with some practical limitations. The more factors we try to investigate simultaneously, the more logically possible combinations, i.e. conditions to be tested, we get, which may be hard to cope with in an experimental study or for which it would be difficult to find a sufficient number of tokens in a corpus analysis. Even if we can, interpreting the results of such an analysis will become more and more complex, which makes it increasingly difficult to evaluate the interaction of the many factors investigated in an appropriate way.

Theoretically, the present study proceeded from an understanding of grammatical variation in which the locus of choice is supposed to take place in the mind of individual language users, i.e. from a cognitive point of view, and the underlying question was what makes a language user choose one genitive construction rather than the other, and why. The conceptual factors investigated (animacy, topicality, possessive relation) were linked to general cognitive principles, which we know to operate in other areas of English grammar as well and for which there is some independent, i.e. extra-linguistic, motivation. In particular, I have argued that animate and topical entities tend to be conceptualized and accordingly be processed early, which in turn results in early position in linear order, predicting that the *s*-genitive is more likely to be found with [+animate] and [+topical] possessors. Moreover, that which is conceptually in close proximity has been predicted to be expressed by more bound linguistic means (cf. principle of conceptual distance, as in Haiman 1985a), by which we would expect to find the *s*-genitive more frequently realized in closer, or, as I call them, [+prototypical] possessive relations. These general predictions for the factors animacy, topicality, and possessive relation could be confirmed in the empirical analyses.

Moreover, this study is not restricted to the synchronic Modern English situation. I have looked also at how the factors animacy, topicality, and possessive relation were operative in the past when choosing between the two genitive constructions. In particular, two different types of diachronic data have been included: (i) within the Modern English experimental data an apparent-time approach with British and American subjects was taken, and (ii) the results from this ModE experimental study were, in turn, compared with the results of an EModE corpus study, covering the period between the fifteenth and the early seventeenth centuries, in which the same factors were investigated.

Taking such a long-term diachronic look at the genitive variation, a diachronic extension of the *s*-genitive could be observed along the following preference structure based on the relative importance of these three factors (animacy > topicality > possessive relation), cf. figure 44 above (repeated here as figure 47):

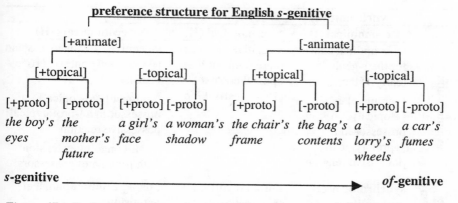

Figure 47. Preference structure for the English *s*-genitive (late Middle/early Modern English to Present-day English)

Synchronically, this preference structure specifies both the preferred contexts and the likelihood for the *s*-genitive to occur in these contexts. Diachronically, the *s*-genitive could be shown to extend along this preference structure from left to right, (i) becoming more frequent and (ii) extending in contexts. The preference structure as such, i.e. the relative importance of the factors animacy, topicality, and possessive relation on the choice of genitive construction, has proved to be stable, remaining basically the same from late Middle to Present-day English, and, within Modern English, the same for British and American English. What is subject to variation and what has changed, however, are the contexts in which the *s*-genitive can occur and its relative frequency in these contexts. While the *s*-genitive was basically restricted to [+animate] possessors throughout the early Modern English period, in Modern English it has extended to [-animate] possessors, a development which has been shown to be more advanced in American English than in British English, and which, in both varieties, is still going on.

Yet to describe how this change has taken place is one thing; to interpret and account for it, however, is another. Evoking three different types of cognitive economy, I have proposed a diachronic scenario which suggests how different types of user-optimality interact, leading to a greater preference for the *s*-genitive, and which can be summarized as follows.

Table 52. The diachronic extension of the s-genitive: synchronic and diachronic economical principles

	synchronically	diachronically	
	economical (I)	**economical (II)**	**economical (III)**
explanandum	most optimal context for the *s*-genitive (early 15thc): [+animate] & [+topical] possessor in a [+prototypical] possessive relation	*s*-genitive becomes more frequent in optimal context (15thc – early 17thc)	*s*-genitive extends to less and less optimal contexts (16thc – PrdE): [-animate] & [-topical] possessor in a [-prototypical] possessive relation → still ongoing extension with [-animate] possessors!
explanation: cognitive economy	**synchronic user-optimality**	**automatization:** (automatic processing) of cognitively most optimal and efficient context	**analogical/metaphorical extension:** same strategy becomes eventually applied to similar contexts

(1) *Economical (I):* The first type of economy discussed concerns synchronic user-optimality accounting for the fact that choosing the *s*-genitive with a [+animate], [+topical] possessor in a [+prototypical]

possessive relation is the most efficient choice for the language user in performance.

(2) *Economical (II)*: Since this context on the leftmost side of the preference structure is the most optimal and efficient context for the *s*-genitive, speakers will use it more frequently. This will, in turn, result, diachronically, in a shift towards the more economical automatic processing mode, i.e. the increasing automatization of the *s*-genitive as the default choice in this context.

(3) *Economical (III):* The concepts of analogical and metaphorical extension can then account for the fact that the *s*-genitive is also extending to less and less optimal contexts systematically along this preference structure. The single contexts on the preference structure have been argued to be gradient, forming potential bridging contexts for the metaphorical jump from one context to the next one.

This scenario proceeds from a choice-based approach to grammatical variation, i.e. an understanding of synchronic variation as the choice of individual language users, and, accordingly, draws on an understanding of language change as occurring within the mind of individual language users when making these choices. One may ask now how we can possibly investigate linguistic change as occurring in speakers' minds? We barely understand what is going on in the mind of present speakers and certainly much less so what is going on in past speakers' minds. So, the argument must necessarily be much more indirect. In fact there are basically two ways in which the 'mind-argument' can be used diachronically. First, we can argue that the very fact that a speaker produces a certain utterance, i.e. use in itself, is self-evident. Since everything that is uttered must in some way be compatible with language as it is represented in the mind (unless, of course, one subscribes to an anti-mentalist conception of language), we can deduce from the occurrence of a linguistic form/construction its mental representation, as e.g. suggested by Kiparsky (1968). In this respect we can then also view language change as a "window to the mind" (cf. e.g. also Mayerthaler 1981; Stein 1988). Whatever changed must in some way, or at some level, also be psychologically real (if not exclusively so). Note that in this kind of argumentation the perspective is from language change to the mind, and not vice versa. That is, psycholinguistic factors can be deduced only *posthoc* from a change but not really be invoked independently and predict the choice among variants and the direction of (possible) changes. It is only when we make appeal to cognitive-psychological factors on independent grounds (i.e. not deduced from the change itself) that such factors can become predictive. In the present case I have shown in chapter 6 how the factors animacy, topicality, and possessive relation, given human conceptualization and the (alleged) make-up of the human processing system, bias the choice of genitive construction. What we need now to connect this essentially synchronic argument to diachrony is the application of the Uniformitarian Principle. Adopting an uniformitarian perspective we can assume that all cognitive and psycholinguistic processes currently at work must also have been operative in the past. And it is precisely in this way that we may account for completed changes. Specifically, if it can be shown that the choice of the *s*-genitive is subject to certain cognitive pressures synchronically, it may be deduced that these pressures were also relevant to past speakers, and, in so doing, even provide some explanation why a certain change has progressed in a particular way (and not in another). And, given that we may assume that all speakers are subject to essentially the same cognitive pressures this, I think, can also cast some light on the old puzzle of how speakers can possibly 'conspire' towards certain directions in change, thereby pursuing an individualist account of language change and yet avoiding a teleological interpretation so often attached to it.

To sum up, there are two ways in which psycholinguistic considerations can be linked to language change: (i) viewing completed changes as a "window to the mind", and (ii) proceeding from a uniformitarian perspective by making reference to psycholinguistic processes to account for completed changes. In the present study both these perspectives play a role, though in different types of empirical data and with stronger emphasis on (ii). While the synchronic approach in the analysis of the experimental data in chapter 6 makes use of the second mind-argument perspective as outlined above, testing first in which way the choice of genitive construction is synchronically determined by cognitive-psycholinguistic factors, the historical evidence rather supports the view that these factors have also been operative in the past, and in so doing, also confirms the applicability of the Uniformitarian Principle. So, in a way, these two perspectives do mutually complement each other in the present study.

In spirit, such a cognitive user-account of language change is close to recent proposals of language change as seen as a kind of adaptive process, in which those constructions become more frequent which are more optimal for the language user. Formally, optimality has been expressed within the recent framework of Optimality Theory (OT), and the findings of the present study, in particular the interaction and ranking of factors along the proposed preference structure, can probably also be modeled within those OT approaches which incorporate probabilities into constraints. In this respect, Bresnan's (and associates') Stochastic OT approach looks to me to be the most apt approach on the OT market to capture a development such as the one laid out in the present study. Besides its probabilistic component, the Stochastic OT approach also proceeds from the assumption that categorical differences among some languages can show up as statistical preferences in other languages. This is precisely the situation to be observed for the genitive variation. While animacy/referentiality and (in)alienability splits are reported in several languages of the world, where the choice of possessive constructions is grammaticalized along the factors animacy and topicality on the one side, and the factor possessive relation on the other, in English, as has been shown in the present study, the choice between the two genitive variants according to these three factors is not a matter of categoriality but of preference, and this preference follows cross-linguistic (grammaticalized) patterns.

In the present study the three factors investigated have been linked to a extralinguistic, cognitive/psycholinguistic basis, which can motivate why the factors exert their effect on the choice of genitive construction in precisely the way they do, arguing how speakers conceptualize and process language in real-time usage. By looking at what makes speakers choose one construction rather than the other instead of looking at how constraints are (unmotivatedly) represented in speakers' grammars (as in classical OT approaches), the observed direction in the extension of the *s*-genitive makes sense too. Speakers more often do what is more useful, i.e. cognitively more efficient, for them (though no agency is involved here, since such cognitive pressures are assumed to operate on a subconscious level; see also below). Such an essentially functional interpretation of user-optimality has recently been introduced by Functional OT (see Bresnan and Aissen 2002), which, however, so far has predominantly been restricted to synchronic analysis. In contrast, a diachronic dimension of user optimality has been repeatedly put forward by Haspelmath (1999a, 1999b, 1999c). Yet while the present study is conceptually very close to Haspelmath's approach of economically-driven language change, it differs and goes, I think, beyond it in several ways. First, Haspelmath's concern is primarily to show how grammaticalized structures come about, i.e. with grammaticalization as automatization, i.e. the fact that a certain construction becomes, over time, more frequent and eventually the sole expression. The present study, however, does not deal with variation as a transitory stage towards grammaticalization of one variant but rather as a shift of the two genitive variants in (a) their respective domains and (b) their distribution within these domains. Second, while Haspelmath primarily postulates user-optimality on general functional principles, I try to trace user-optimality more directly to extralinguistic cognitive and psycholinguistic evidence. Note also, that the present study clearly argues from the speaker's perspective, while Haspelmath does not commit himself to one perspective. Of course, both the perspectives of the speaker and the hearer do play a role when arguing in terms of user-optimality. Since, however, as argued, speaker-optimality may well clash with hearer-optimality, it seems advisable to keep the two apart in argumentation, or make explicit their respective roles. Finally, there is not yet, to my knowledge, any large-scale empirical, statistical study on grammatical variation within such an approach towards economically-driven language change, showing precisely how such an extension due to considerations of user-optimality could take place.

However, probably not everybody would agree with the view that language change should be driven by considerations of user-optimality. As, for example, maintained by Lass (1997) it is not the mind that should be the object of our study when accounting for language change but rather the historically-evolved language system.

> At the moment the best we can say is that the 'causal' role of the speaker or the speaker's 'actions' in certain major and field-defining kinds of change is not proved; we can and indeed ought to talk as we always have ... about 'languages' and the things that they do or that happen to them over time.
>
> (Lass 1997: 385)

Moreover, assuming considerations of user-optimality does in a certain way imply that language change should be geared towards optimization, which is certainly not the case: languages do not become 'better' (cf. also Lass 1997: §7.3.2). Taking a closer look, however, it seems as if the approaches are not as incompatible as they may appear at first glance. Although this study offers a cognitive-psychological account to explain why the *s*-genitive has been spreading, this is not the whole story. There is nothing inherent in the conceptual factors investigated which would indeed predict (in the strong sense of this word) that a change necessarily has to take place, i.e. in the present case, that the *s*-genitive *should* become more frequent in certain contexts. The synchronic user-optimality for having animates and topics first in linear order and for formally expressing in closer proximity what is conceptually closer, can, adopting a uniformitarian perspective, be regarded as timeless (at least within the historical time span we are talking about here). And, as the discussion of the historical development of the genitive variation in chapter 7 has shown, this has indeed been the case: already in Old English and later also in Middle English these factors are found to be operative when choosing between genitive constructions (although the set of variants from which to choose has certainly changed from Old English to Modern English); i.e. it looks as if throughout the history of English animate and topical possessors in particular tended to be realized first in a possessive construction, sometimes more, sometimes less. And it is exactly this latter question, i.e. how these factors affect the frequency of the genitive construction that has been addressed in this study; this study did not set out to account for the question of what made these constructions materialize in the English language in the first place. In this sense, I would certainly agree with Lass (1997) in that the language user can only exploit what is already there in the system, historically evolved, for whatever reason. In the present case, a purely cognitively-based account cannot really explain why, if language users are always subject to the same cognitive pressures, these pressures should suddenly become more effective only from a certain point, i.e. from late Middle English onwards. We can predict *how* such cognitive needs should affect the choice of genitive construction, but we cannot predict what should make them more pressing, or, what should make them be taken into account more. Therefore, an exclusively user-based approach certainly fails to answer the question of *when* such a change should take place; it can only predict the directionality of a change.

What I would like to suggest in this study is that the *s*-genitive could only creep through the English language the way it did – and still does – *under certain favorable circumstances*. I have mainly focused on one such favorable circumstance, i.e. the shape of the grammar, arguing that it is first and foremost the structural change of POSS '*s* from an inflection to a clitic and a determiner that has paved the way for the *s*-genitive to become more productive; other factors certainly still need to be looked at in more detail, such as e.g. the whole socio-cultural setting, in which this change is embedded. It is, for example, to be expected that the process of standardization, which starts about the same time as the *s*-genitive begins to become more frequent, i.e. in the fifteenth century, has contributed in some way to the development of the *s*-genitive.

So, yes, in fact, the kind of scenario I have suggested in this study draws upon the idea that language does change in the mind of speakers but only in a certain way: it is not the structural change (inflection > clitic & determiner) that is accounted for but rather the (increasing) use of the end-product of this change, i.e. the 'new' *s*-genitive (as a clitic & determiner), i.e. in my account it is the frequency of this construction that may – or may not – be captured by such a user-based account and not the structural system as such. Whatever may have caused the latter is still an open empirical question. While so far primarily the "macro-story" (to use Lass' 1997: 288 terms) of POSS '*s* (inflection > clitic) has been looked at, I have suggested some further promising lines for future research which should focus rather on the "micro-story" – or "micro-*stories*", for that matter – looking more closely at the 'small steps' which have led from the inflected *s*-genitive to the ModE clitic one. Particularly promising, in this respect, seems to be an approach which takes into account what happened within the whole English NP. As far as the new determiner function of the *s*-genitive is concerned, it is certainly worthwhile to look more deeply at the evolution of the definite article in English. As far as the new clitic status of POSS '*s* is concerned, some further research into deflexion and the fading of agreement within the English NP as well as (phrasal) compounding and nominal premodification might cast more light on the course and structure of this process. There is, moreover, good reason to assume that the development of the specifying and the classifying genitive should have gone hand in hand. As has been argued throughout this study, there is an intersection between these two genitive types in that indefinite possessors (e.g. *a driver*) in particular are inherently ambiguous, being open for both referential and non-referential interpretation, i.e. they can – potentially, at least – materialize as both a specifying ([*a driver's*] *license*) or a classifying genitive (i.e. *a* [*driver's license*]). Such ambiguity seems to me a very promising starting point for further research on the development of POSS '*s*, and in §7.5.2.4.2 I have offered a tentative, hypothetical proposal of how this may have affected its structural change from inflection to clitic.

Furthermore, arguing in terms of economically-driven language change, as I do, does not necessarily imply that the result should be more economical, i.e. that the English language should become more optimal. Rather, the various economical principles proposed must be held distinct, operating at different stages affecting different contexts and expressing different needs. While the notion of synchronic user-optimality, by which a [+animate] and [+topical] possessor in a [+prototypical] possessive relation favors the *s*-genitive, is the overall starting point for the increasing frequency of the *s*-genitive, another development, i.e. its analogical/metaphorical extension along the proposed preference structure, particularly to inanimate possessors, is – though still economical – diametrically opposed to the synchronic user-optimality type. According to the latter, choosing the *s*-genitive in non-motivated, i.e. non-optimal contexts, is an *un*economical state of affairs. Moreover, there are different economical needs according to the language user: while speakers prefer utterances to be as short as possible, for the hearer a more explicit, i.e. longer construction is more economical, and language change would be expected to compromise in some way between these different needs (cf. e.g. Ronneberger-Sibold 1980). That is, *overall* the English language has not become more optimal in the use of genitive constructions. While looking at every single economical principle in isolation, there certainly is some kind of optimization, looking at it in a broader context, this may not necessarily be the case, with different economical principles operating in different domains neutralizing each other, making the end-product of change no more optimal than its starting point.

This brings us directly to another question, often controversially discussed in accounts of language change, i.e. the question in which way, if at all, language change can be taken to be a conscious, intentional process. Opinions are, as usual, divided, ranging from the idea of the language user as a language builder who consciously shapes a language to his needs (e.g. Hagège 1993) to other accounts in which "the speaker engaged in a change is not an agent but a victim" (Lass 1997: 367), with notions such as "unconscious rationality" (Itkonen 1983) or Keller's (1994) invisible-hand approach somehow in between these two extreme positions. For the present study, the crucial question in this context to be asked is, whether speakers respond consciously or not to the factors investigated. The choice-based approach to grammatical variation employed in the present study proceeds from the assumption that the choice between the *s*-genitive and the *of*-genitive is essentially subconscious and unintentional in nature; the effect of the three conceptual factors investigated is to be understood as cognitive pressures to which the speaker responds but which he does not employ consciously or intentionally. Synchronic user-optimality, defined in terms of a preference towards the easier-to-process construction, and even more so automatization are processes influenced by the needs of real-time on-line processing and therefore run to a great extent subconsciously. It is, however, less clear how the analogical/metaphorical extension of the *s*-genitive should be interpreted since in this case real-time processing pressures cannot be evoked. Metaphor and accordingly metaphorical extension are, however, well-known processes within the human conceptual system, and such conceptualization processes are generally regarded to operate predominantly subconsciously (cf. e.g. Lakoff and Johnson 1980). Hopper and Traugott (1993: 77) describe metaphorical processes as "processes of inference across conceptual boundaries" as "'mappings', or 'associative leaps', from one domain to another", and they consider these mappings as "motivated by analogy and iconic relationships".

It must also be stressed that the results of the present study are not at all incompatible with Taylor's (1996) cognitive account of the *s*-genitive, which regards it as a reference-point (or anchoring) construction in which the speaker subjectively instructs the hearer how to identify the intended referent of the NP. Taylor's (1996) account predicts, like the present one, that the *s*-genitive should be more likely the more accessible (i.e. the more animate and topical) the possessor is, and presupposes that the speaker takes the needs of the hearer into consideration; in fact, facilitation of referent identification is basically a hearer-oriented explanation. While Taylor (1996) is not really explicit about the degree of intentionality involved in what may be called a conceptualization strategy, presupposing that the speaker takes the needs of the hearer into account seems at least to imply a certain amount of consciousness. In general, we need, however, to conclude that we do not know enough yet about conceptualization processes as well as human consciousness, and that we therefore cannot settle the question of how conscious the choice of genitive construction is; we can only speculate on it.

In this study I have also pointed out several ways in which the development of the *s*-genitive points to grammaticalization processes at work, distinguishing between the degrammaticalization of the *s*-genitive (affix > clitic) and its grammaticalization once it has been reanalyzed as a clitic and determiner, as evident from its extension along the proposed preference structure. Note that the question of intentionality also connects to the relation of adaptive, user-optimizing processes on the one side and grammaticalization processes on the other in two ways. First, in his account of adaptive change Haspelmath (1999b), referring to Dahl (1999), mentions that grammaticalization processes seem to be counter-adaptive, in that originally motivated forms tend to lose their original function in this development. This is exactly what we can observe in the development of the *s*-genitive as well. Due to analogical/metaphorical extension the *s*-genitive occurs in less and less 'motivated' contexts in which the synchronic motivation for optimal real-time processing is no longer present. So what is the gain, then, if there is one at all? That is to say, what is the status of analogy as an economical principle in the first place? Ronneberger-Sibold (1980: §2.2) describes analogy very generally as a *Metabedürfnis* in language performance, i.e. as a need to regard more and more contexts as comparable. In the case of the *s*-genitive we might, however, as well ask why, taken by itself, this need for uniformity should necessarily lead to a preference for the *s*-genitive and not the *of*-genitive? Maybe simply because it is shorter, which, at least for the speaker, from whose perspective this study has been arguing, is certainly more optimal. Thus, in the case of analogical/metaphorical extension synchronic user-optimality comes in again through the back door, so to speak.

Let me finally stress again that I do not believe that – in spite of the fact that the *s*-genitive has been gaining ground in Present-day English along the preference structure, showing certain aspects of grammaticalization – it will ever run the full course of grammaticalization in the sense that it will become fixed to certain environments, let alone become the sole genitive construction in English. Although I have somewhat overemphasized the role of the *s*-genitive in the present study – and accordingly neglected that of the *of*-genitive – the choice between the two genitive constructions has always been a matter of preference rather than a choice that becomes grammaticalized towards one option only or to the extent that both constructions become restricted to fixed contexts. That is, in the case of the genitive variation the availability of two options is not an uneconomical, 'pathological' state of affairs. The two constructions are not synonymous but rather serve different functional and cognitive needs. While each construction certainly has its typical applications, there is still enough flexibility left for the two genitive constructions to respond to the many factors which affect the choice between them, making it possible to tip the scales in whichever construction, the *s*-genitive or the *of*-genitive, is needed, i.e. the more 'useful' one in a particular situation or context. What has changed in the history of English and which may (or may not) well further change are the particular domains that are covered by the two constructions and their frequency within these domains. It remains to be seen where the English *s*-genitive will be heading in the future.

Chapter 10
Appendix

10.1 Experimental study

Conditions and items

| | [+animate] | | | | [-animate] | | | |
| | [+topical] | | [-topical] | | [+topical] | | [-topical] | |
	[+prototyp.]	[-prototyp.]	[+prototyp.]	[-prototyp.]	[+prototyp.]	[-prototyp.]	[+prototyp.]	[-prototyp.]
	the girl's cheeks/ the cheeks of the girl	my mother's purview/ the purview of my mother	a bobby's helmet/ the helmet of a bobby	a batsman's career/ the career of a batsman	the bottle's base/ the base of the bottle	the drive's gate/ the gate of the drive	a finger's knuckle/ the knuckle of a finger	a door's shoosh/ the shoosh of a door
	the boy's eyes/ the eyes of the boy	the mother's future/ the future of the mother	a mate's house/ the house of a mate	some composer's greatest hits/ the greatest hits of some composer	the chair's frame/ the frame of the chair	the pit's grime/ the grime of the pit	a cage's bar/ the bar of a cage	a yew hedge's shelter/ the shelter of a yew hedge
	the boy's face/ the face of the boy	the batsman's career/ the career of the batsman	a girl's face/ the face of a girl	an innocent boy's reputation/ the reputation of an innocent boy	her notebook's pages/ the pages of her notebook	the body's transport/ the transport of the body	a bed's side/ the side of a bed	a body's soft thud/ the soft thud of a body

| [+animate] | | | | [-animate] | | | |
| [+topical] | | [-topical] | | [+topical] | | [-topical] | |
[+prototyp.]	[-prototyp.]	[+prototyp.]	[-prototyp.]	[+prototyp.]	[-prototyp.]	[+prototyp.]	[-prototyp.]
his father's body/ the body of his father	*the young girl's height/ the height of the young girl*	*a man's eyes/ the eyes of a man*	*a stranger's presence/ the presence of a stranger*	*the table's drawer/ the drawer of the table*	*the room's darkness/ the darkness of the room*	*a car's headlamps/ the headlamps of a car*	*a car's fumes/ the fumes of a car*
the man's hand/ the hand of the man	*her teenage son's surface/ the surface of her teenage son*	*a man's body/ body of a man*	*a woman's shadow/ the shadow of a woman*	*her car's wings/ the wings of her car*	*her bag's contents/ the contents of her bag*	*a newspaper pages/ the pages of a newspaper*	*a boat's low horn/ the low horn of a boat*
the boy's mother/ the mother of the boy	*your wife's affair/ the affair of your wife*	*a man's bare bones/ the bare bones of a man*	*some pirate's joy and pride/ the joy and pride of some pirate*	*the chair's right side/ the right side of the chair*	*the smoke's acrid sting/ the acrid sting of the smoke*	*a photograph's corner/ the corner of a photograph*	*a tree's shadow/ the shadow of a tree*
the boy's brother/ the brother of the boy	*the boy's exhaustion/ the exhaustion of the boy*	*a girl's body/ the body of a girl*	*a woman's photograph/ the photograph of a woman*	*the chair's stuffing/ the stuffing of chair*	*the fire's speed/ the speed of the fire*	*a lorry's wheels/ the wheels of a lorry*	*a car's driver/ the driver of a car*

| [+animate] | | | | [-animate] | | | |
| [+topical] | | [-topical] | | [+topical] | | [-topical] | |
[+prototyp.]	[-prototyp.]	[+prototyp.]	[-prototyp.]	[+prototyp.]	[-prototyp.]	[+prototyp.]	[-prototyp.]
the small girl's eyes/ the eyes of the small girl	*your wife's infidelity/ the infidelity of your wife*	*a fisherman's widow/ the widow of a fisherman*	*a baby's scent/ the scent of a baby*	*the car's bonnet/ the bonnet of the car*	*the fabric's weave/ the weave of the fabric*	*a silver fir's base/ the base of a silver fir*	*a flat's renovation/ the renovation of a flat*
her husband's hair/ the hair of her husband	*the man's final moments/ the final moments of the man*	*a small boy's voice/ the voice of a small boy*	*a motor-bike's sound/ the sound of a motor-bike*	*the V's tip/ the tip of the V* *the helicopter's doors/the doors of the helicopter*	*the stuffing's age/ the age of the stuffing*	*a cart's creaking wheels/ the wheels of a creaking cart*	*a car's silhouette/ the silhouette of a car*
the masseur's hands/ the hands of the masseur	*the factory workman's talents/ the talents of the factory workman*	*an opposing player's waistband/ the waistband of an opposing player*	*a sixteen-year-old boy's future/ the future of a sixteen-year-old boy*	*the article's headline/ the headline of the article*	*the car's condition/the condition of the car*	*a book's sharp corner/ the sharp corner of a book*	*a perfume's delicate fragrance/the delicate fragrance of a perfume*
the tenor's voice/ the voice of the tenor	*her mother's small world/ the small world of her mother*		*one man's ambition/ the ambition of one man*	*the rucksack's flap/ the flap of the rucksack*			*a motor-bike's sound/the sound of a motor-bike*

| [+animate] | | | | [-animate] | | | |
| [+topical] | | [-topical] | | [+topical] | | [-topical] | |
[+prototyp.]	[-prototyp.]	[+prototyp.]	[-prototyp.]	[+prototyp.]	[-prototyp.]	[+prototyp.]	[-prototyp.]
the Detective Sergeant's hand/ the hand of the Detective Sergeant				*the building's door/ the door of the building*			
his sister-in-law's shoulder/ the shoulder of his sister-in-law				*the milk-float's rear-view mirror/ the rear-view mirror of the milk-float*			
the young woman's arm/ the arm of the young woman				*the car's security system/ the security system of the car*			
				the tree's furrowed bark/the furrowed bark of the tree			

Frequencies

Table 1. British subjects (n=56): relative frequency of the *s*-genitive and the *of*-genitive for the factors animacy [±animate], topicality [±topical], and possessive relation [±prototypical]

British subjects	[+animate]		[-animate]		[+topical]		[-topical]		[+prototypical]		[-prototypical]	
	's	*of*	*'s*	*of*	*'s*	*of*	*'s*	*of*	*'s*	*of*	*'s*	*of*
n	1748	812	574	2043	1586	1256	736	1599	1414	1368	908	1487
%	68.3	31.7	21.9	78.1	55.8	44.2	31.5	68.5	50.8	49.2	37.9	62.1

Table 2. American subjects (n=48): relative frequency of the *s*-genitive and the *of*-genitive for the factors animacy [±animate], topicality [±topical], and possessive relation [±prototypical]

American subjects	[+animate]		[-animate]		[+topical]		[-topical]		[+prototypical]		[-prototypical]	
	's	*of*	*'s*	*of*	*'s*	*of*	*'s*	*of*	*'s*	*of*	*'s*	*of*
n	1435	749	590	1639	1359	1063	666	1325	1218	1153	807	1235
%	65.7	34.3	26.5	73.5	56.1	43.9	33.5	66.5	51.4	48.6	39.5	60.5

Table 3. British subjects (n=56) – interaction of factors: relative frequency of the *s*-genitive versus the *of*-genitive according to the 8 conditions ([±a] = [±animate], [±t] = [±topical], [±p] = [±prototypical])

	[+a/+t/+p]		[+a/+t/-p]		[+a/-t/+p]		[+a/-t/-p]		[-a/+t/+p]		[-a/+t/-p]		[-a/-t/+p]		[-a/-t/-p]	
	's	of	's	of	's	of	's	of	's	of	's	of	's	of	's	of
n	696	83	448	166	341	215	263	348	318	573	124	434	59	497	73	539
%	89.3	10.7	73	27	61.3	38.7	43	57	35.7	64.3	22.2	77.8	10.6	89.4	11.9	88.1

Table 4. American subjects (n=48) – interaction of factors: relative frequency of the *s*-genitive versus the *of*-genitive according to the 8 conditions ([±a] = [±animate], [±t] = [±topical], [±p] = [±prototypical])

	[+a/+t/+p]		[+a/+t/-p]		[+a/-t/+p]		[+a/-t/-p]		[-a/+t/+p]		[-a/+t/-p]		[-a/-t/+p]		[-a/-t/-p]	
	's	of	's	of	's	of	's	of	's	of	's	of	's	of	's	of
n	574	95	363	159	270	202	228	293	291	464	131	345	83	392	85	438
%	85.8	14.2	69.5	30.5	57.2	42.8	43.8	56.2	38.5	61.5	27.5	72.5	17.5	82.5	16.3	83.7

Table 5. British and American subjects: younger versus older subjects: frequency of the *s*-genitive and the *of*-genitive

age group	British subjects				American subjects			
	s-genitive		of-genitive		s-genitive		of-genitive	
	n	%	n	%	n	%	n	%
younger subjects	1579	47.5	1742	52.5	1133	47.4	1259	52.6
older subjects	743	40	1113	60	892	44.1	1129	55.9

Table 6.   British subjects – younger versus older subjects: frequency of the *s*-genitive and the *of*-genitive for single factors

factor	younger subjects (n=36)				older subjects (n=20)			
	s-genitive		of-genitive		s-genitive		of-genitive	
	n	%	n	%	n	%	n	%
[+animate]	1138	69.4	502	30.6	610	66.3	310	33.7
[-animate]	441	26.2	1240	73.8	133	14.2	803	85.8
[+topical]	1072	58.7	754	41.3	514	50.6	502	49.4
[-topical]	507	33.9	988	66.1	229	27.3	611	72.7
[+prototypical]	957	53.6	827	46.4	457	45.8	541	54.2
[-prototypical]	622	40.5	915	59.5	286	33.3	572	66.7

Table 7.   American subjects – younger versus older subjects: frequency of the *s*-genitive and the *of*-genitive for single factors

factor	younger subjects (n=26)				older subjects (n=22)			
	s-genitive		of-genitive		s-genitive		of-genitive	
	n	%	n	%	n	%	n	%
[+animate]	775	65.3	411	34.7	660	66.1	338	33.9
[-animate]	358	29.7	848	70.3	232	22.7	791	77.3
[+topical]	758	57.7	555	42.3	601	54.2	508	45.8
[-topical]	375	34.8	704	65.2	291	31.9	621	68.1
[+prototypical]	685	53.3	599	46.7	533	49	554	51
[-prototypical]	448	40.4	660	59.6	359	38.4	575	61.6

Table 8. Younger British subjects (n=36) – interaction of factors: relative frequency of the *s*-genitive versus the *of*-genitive according to the 8 conditions ([±a] = [±animate], [±t] = [±topical], [±p] = [±prototypical])

	[+a/+t/+p]		[+a/+t/-p]		[+a/-t/+p]		[+a/-t/-p]		[-a/+t/+p]		[-a/+t/-p]		[-a/-t/+p]		[-a/-t/-p]	
	's	*of*	*'s*	*of*	*'s*	*of*	*'s*	*of*	*'s*	*of*	*'s*	*of*	*'s*	*of*	*'s*	*of*
n	449	50	293	101	231	125	165	226	232	341	98	262	45	311	66	326
%	90	10	74.4	25.6	64.9	35.1	42.2	57.8	40.5	59.5	27.2	72.8	12.6	87.4	16.8	83.6

Table 9. Older British subjects (n=20) – interaction of factors: relative frequency of the *s*-genitive versus the *of*-genitive according to the 8 conditions ([±a] = [±animate], [±t] = [±topical], [±p] = [±prototypical])

	[+a/+t/+p]		[+a/+t/-p]		[+a/-t/+p]		[+a/-t/-p]		[-a/+t/+p]		[-a/+t/-p]		[-a/-t/+p]		[-a/-t/-p]	
	's	*of*	*'s*	*of*	*'s*	*of*	*'s*	*of*	*'s*	*of*	*'s*	*of*	*'s*	*of*	*'s*	*of*
n	247	33	155	65	110	90	98	122	86	232	26	172	14	186	7	213
%	88.2	11.8	70.5	29.5	55	45	44.5	5.5	27	73	13.1	86.9	7	93	3.2	96.8

Table 10. Younger American subjects (n=26) – interaction of factors: relative frequency of the *s*-genitive versus the *of*-genitive according to the 8 conditions ([±a] = [±animate], [±t] = [±topical], [±p] = [±prototypical])

	[+a/+t/+p]		[+a/+t/-p]		[+a/-t/+p]		[+a/-t/-p]		[-a/+t/+p]		[-a/+t/-p]		[-a/-t/+p]		[-a/-t/-p]	
	's	*of*	*'s*	*of*	*'s*	*of*	*'s*	*of*	*'s*	*of*	*'s*	*of*	*'s*	*of*	*'s*	*of*
n	309	54	198	87	149	107	119	163	170	237	81	177	57	201	50	233
%	85.1	14.9	69.5	30.5	58.2	41.8	42.2	57.8	41.8	58.2	31.4	68.6	22.1	77.9	17.7	82.3

Table 11. Older American subjects (n=22) – interaction of factors: relative frequency of the *s*-genitive versus the *of*-genitive according to the 8 conditions ([±a] = [±animate], [±t] = [±topical], [±p] = [±prototypical])

	[+a/+t/+p]		[+a/+t/-p]		[+a/-t/+p]		[+a/-t/-p]		[-a/+t/+p]		[-a/+t/-p]		[-a/-t/+p]		[-a/-t/-p]	
	's	*of*	*'s*	*of*	*'s*	*of*	*'s*	*of*	*'s*	*of*	*'s*	*of*	*'s*	*of*	*'s*	*of*
n	265	41	165	72	121	95	109	130	121	227	50	168	26	191	35	205
%	86.6	13.4	69.6	30.4	56	44	45.6	54.4	34.8	65.2	22.9	77.1	12	88	14.6	85.4

Table 12. British subjects (n=56) – word length: frequency of the *s*-genitive and the *of*-genitive in [+animate] conditions

word length conditions	[+animate] conditions															
	[+a/+t/+p]				[+a/+t/-p]				[+a/-t/+p]				[+a/-t/-p]			
	's		of		's		of		's		of		's		of	
	n	%	n	%	n	%	n	%	n	%	n	%	n	%	n	%
neutral condition	556	90.6	58	9.4	263	67.8	125	32.2	289	64.9	156	35.1	187	42.1	257	57.9
short > long					143	85.1	25	14.9								
long > short	140	84.8	25	15.2					53	52.2	58	47.7	46	41.4	65	58.6

Table 13. British subjects (n=56) – word length: frequency of the *s*-genitive and the *of*-genitive in [-animate] conditions

word length conditions	[-animate] conditions															
	[-a/+t/+p]				[-a/+t/-p]				[-a/-t/+p]				[-a/-t/-p]			
	's		of		's		of		's		of		's		of	
	n	%	n	%	n	%	n	%	n	%	n	%	n	%	n	%
neutral condition	185	27.7	483	72.3	102	20.3	400	79.7	41	10.5	351	89.5	42	10.8	348	89.2
short > long	113	67.3	55	32.7												
long > short									16	14.5	94	85.5	31	18.7	135	81.3

Table 14. American subjects (n=48) – word length: frequency of the *s*-genitive and the *of*-genitive in [+animate] conditions

[+animate] conditions

word length conditions	[+a/+t/+p]				[+a/+t/-p]				[+a/-t/+p]				[+a/-t/-p]			
	's n	's %	of n	of %	's n	's %	of n	of %	's n	's %	of n	of %	's n	's %	of n	of %
neutral condition	459	87.3	67	12.7	212	64	119	36	238	63.3	138	36.7	168	44.4	210	55.6
short > long	120	83.9	23	16.1					32	33.3	64	66.7	34	35.8	61	64.2
long > short	115	80.4	28	19.6												

Table 15. American subjects (n=48) – word length: frequency of the *s*-genitive and the *of*-genitive in [-animate] conditions

[-animate] conditions

word length conditions	[-a/+t/+p]				[-a/+t/-p]				[-a/-t/+p]				[-a/-t/-p]			
	's n	's %	of n	of %	's n	's %	of n	of %	's n	's %	of n	of %	's n	's %	of n	of %
neutral condition	187	33.2	376	66.8	116	27.1	312	72.9	57	17.1	277	82.9	58	17.5	274	82.5
short > long	84	58.3	60	41.7					22	23.2	73	76.8	26	18.1	118	81.9
long > short																

10.2   Corpus analysis (1400 – 1630)

Table 16.   Frequency of the *s*-genitive versus the *of*-genitive in [+animate] sub-corpus

1400 – 1449 (I)				1450 – 1499 (II)				1500 – 1559 (III)				1560 – 1630 (IV)			
'*s*		*of*		'*s*		*of*		'*s*		*of*		'*s*		*of*	
n	%	n	%	n	%	n	%	n	%	n	%	n	%	n	%
59	27.8	153	72.2	189	38.7	300	61.3	205	46.9	232	53.1	275	64	155	36

Table 17a.   1400 – 1499: Topicality of possessor: frequency of the *s*-genitive versus the *of*-genitive within [+animate] sub-corpus

topicality	1400 – 1449 (I)				1450 – 1499 (II)			
	s-genitive		*of*-genitive		*s*-genitive		*of*-genitive	
	n	%	n	%	n	%	n	%
[++topical]	57	30.5	130	69.5	176	41.9	244	58.1
[+topical]	2	8	23	92	13	18.8	56	81.2
total	59		153		189		300	

Table 17b.   1500 – 1630: Topicality of possessor: frequency of the *s*-genitive versus the *of*-genitive within [+animate] sub-corpus

topicality	1500 – 1559 (III)				1560 – 1630 (IV)			
	s-genitive		*of*-genitive		*s*-genitive		*of*-genitive	
	n	%	n	%	n	%	n	%
[++topical]	174	51	167	49	196	63.6	112	36.4
[+topical]	27	38	44	62	69	69.7	30	30.3
[-topical]	4	16	21	84	10	43.5	13	56.5
total	205		232		275		155	

Table 18a.   1400 – 1499: Possessive relation: frequency of the *s*-genitive versus the *of*-genitive within [+animate] sub-corpus

possessive relation	1400 – 1449 (I)				1450 – 1499 (II)			
	s-genitive		*of*-genitive		*s*-genitive		*of*-genitive	
	n	%	n	%	n	%	n	%
[+prototyp.]	22	31.4	48	68.6	92	50.5	90	49.5
[-prototyp.]	37	26.1	105	73.9	97	31.6	210	68.4
total	59		153		189		300	

Table 18b.   1500 – 1630: Possessive relation: frequency of the *s*-genitive versus the *of*-genitive within [+animate] sub-corpus

possessive relation	1500 – 1559 (III)				1560 – 1630 (IV)			
	s-genitive		*of*-genitive		*s*-genitive		*of*-genitive	
	n	%	n	%	n	%	n	%
[+prototyp.]	90	50	90	50	152	69.4	67	30.6
[-prototyp.]	115	44.7	142	54.5	125	58.3	88	41.7
total	205		232		275		155	

Table 19a.   1400 – 1449: Interaction of factors topicality and possessive relation within [+animate] sub-corpus: frequency of the *s*-genitive versus the *of*-genitive

1400 – 1449 (I)	[+animate] [++topical]				[+animate] [+topical]				[+animate] [-topical]			
	s-genitive		*of*-genitive		*s*-genitive		*of*-genitive		*s*-genitive		*of*-genitive	
possessive relation	n	%	n	%	n	%	n	%	n	%	n	%
[+prototyp.]	20	33.9	39	66.1	2	18.2	9	91.8	*not enough tokens			
[-prototyp.]	37	28.9	91	71.1	-	-	14	100				

Table 19b.   1450 – 1499: Interaction of factors topicality and possessive relation within [+animate] sub-corpus: frequency of the *s*-genitive versus the *of*-genitive

1450 – 1499 (II)	[+animate] [++topical]				[+animate] [+topical]				[+animate] [-topical]			
	s-genitive		*of*-genitive		*s*-genitive		*of*-genitive		*s*-genitive		*of*-genitive	
possessive relation	n	%	n	%	n	%	n	%	n	%	n	%
[+prototyp.]	84	52.8	75	47.2	8	34.8	15	65.2	*not enough tokens			
[-prototyp.]	92	35.2	169	64.8	5	10.9	41	89.1				

Table 19c.   1500 – 1559: Interaction of factors topicality and possessive relation within [+animate] sub-corpus: frequency of the *s*-genitive versus the *of*-genitive

1500 – 1559 (III)	[+animate] [++topical]				[+animate] [+topical]				[+animate] [-topical]			
	s-genitive		*of*-genitive		*s*-genitive		*of*-genitive		*s*-genitive		*of*-genitive	
possessive relation	n	%	n	%	n	%	n	%	n	%	n	%
[+prototyp.]	72	50.7	70	49.3	15	53.6	13	46.4	3	30	7	70
[-prototyp.]	102	51.3	97	48.7	12	27.9	31	72.1	1	6.7	14	93.3

Table 19d.   1560 – 1630: Interaction of factors topicality and possessive relation within [+animate] sub-corpus: frequency of the *s*-genitive versus the *of*-genitive

1560 – 1630 (IV)	[+animate] [++topical]				[+animate] [+topical]				[+animate] [-topical]			
	s-genitive		*of*-genitive		*s*-genitive		*of*-genitive		*s*-genitive		*of*-genitive	
possessive relation	n	%	n	%	n	%	n	%	n	%	n	%
[+prototyp.]	91	63.6	52	36.4	52	81.3	12	18.7	9	75	3	25
[-prototyp.]	105	63.6	60	36.4	17	48.6	18	51.4	1	9.1	10	90.9

Table 20a.   1400 – 1499: Interaction of factor topicality and possessive relation within [+animate] sub-corpus (II): frequency of the *s*-genitive versus the *of*-genitive, (*including categories [++topical] and [+topical] from tables 19a-b above)

Interaction of factors (II)	[+topical]*							
	1400 – 1449 (I)				1450 – 1499 (II)			
	s-genitive		*of*-genitive		*s*-genitive		*of*-genitve	
	n	%	n	%	n	%	n	%
[+prototypical]	22	31.4	48	68.6	92	50.5	90	49.5
[-prototypical]	37	26.1	105	73.9	97	31.6	210	68.4

Table 20b. 1500 – 1630: Interaction of factor topicality and possessive relation within [+animate] sub-corpus (II): frequency of the *s*-genitive versus the *of*-genitive, (*including categories [++topical] and [+topical] from tables 19c-d above)

Interaction of factors (II)	[+topical]*							
	1500 – 1559 (III)				1560 – 1630 (IV)			
	s-genitive		*of*-genitive		*s*-genitive		*of*-genitve	
	n	%	n	%	n	%	n	%
[+prototypical]	87	51.2	83	48.8	143	69.1	64	30.9
[-prototypical]	114	47.1	128	52.9	122	61	78	39

Notes

1. For more detailed discussion on the nature of POSS *'s* I refer to Zwicky (1987); Bauer (1988); Plank (1992a, 1995); Taylor (1996: §5.2), and Seppänen (1997b).
2. Alternatively one can equally well say, as Jespersen (1961: 300) does, that POSS *'s* needs to immediately precede the possessum rather than immediately being attached to the possessor head.
3. Quirk et al. (1985: §5.123, §17.119) also subsume conjoined NPs and appositions under the term "group genitive"; I prefer to discuss them separately, since these types may well have a different history in that some became possible earlier and some later, see also §7.5.2.4 for discussion.
4. I owe this example to Monika Schmid, who, in turn, got it from JC Smith.
5. Note that the attachment of POSS *'s* to conjoined NPs is only possible if the possessum is indeed conceived of as belonging to both possessors; if not, both possessors need to be marked separately by POSS *'s*. In the present example it is clear from the context that the window belongs to a house owned by both Melody and Henry; if the genitive construction did refer to two windows, one owned by Melody and one owned by Henry, then it should be: *Melody's and Henry's window*.
6. This interpretation rests on the assumption that there is only one basic stem for both singular and plural and that the variant forms are due to conditioned allomorphy. Note, however, that there are also analyses which assume two equally basic stem allomorphs (i.e. /waif – waiv/); for a discussion of the various analyses, see Plank (1985: 213-214).
7. See also Mondorf (2000) for showing that synthetic adjectives do appear in compounds (e.g. *older-fashioned, fuller-flavoured*), which – similar to the case of POSS *'s* discussed above – either calls for a re-evaluation of the theoretical status of English adjective comparison as inflectional or otherwise falsifies models (such as Kiparsky's) which claim that regular inflection should follow compounding.
8. Note that the difference between English and German in this respect may be due to agreement in the German NP which is absent in English. The ungrammaticality of (8b) may result from examples such as **meine Frau und Sohn* ('my wife and son'), in which agreement requirements between the possessive pronoun and the nouns referred to are violated.
9. Note that POSS *'s* after non-morphemic /s z/ is, according to Stemberger (1981: 793), not affected by haplology (*the cheese's flavour – *the cheese' flavour*); the exception is proper names, where haplology may occur (*Gus' house – Gus's house*).
10. For the same reason Seppänen (1997b: 206-207) also rejects the word/phrase distinction as a good criterion for distinguishing between inflectional affixes and clitics.
11. For an opposite view see, however, Lieber (1988).

12.   Quirk et al. (1985: §I.52) regard these phrasal nouns as conversions from phrases to nouns rather than genuine (phrasal) compounds.

13.   Note that instead of treating expressions such as *mother-in-law* invariably as a phrasal lexical unit, plural inflection could equally well be taken as a *test* for phrase- versus wordhood. In this case we may argue that in such cases where the plural *-s* attaches to the first element (*mothers-in-law*) the expression is interpreted as a phrase, while in those cases where it attaches to the last element (*mother-in-laws*) it must be analyzed as a word. In any case, the interesting fact that plural inflection is variable in such cases remains.

14.   As yet another case in point speaking against morphological processes being restricted to words, Seppänen (1997b: 206) also mentions derivational processes in which the derivational affix may be attached to phrases, as in *penny-a-liner* or *old-maidish*. Interestingly, Quirk et al. (1985: §I.18, footnote) draw a direct parallel between such derivational processes and inflection. If the derivational affix attaches to the first element (e.g. *passer-by*), the inflectional plural also occurs in the first element (*passers-by*). As the grammatical alternative pattern to phrasal compounds where the derivational affix is attached to the last element (i.e. the phrase), as in *The window was unget-at-able* (which, again, is regarded as informal), Quirk et al. (1985: §I.18, footnote) mention the group genitive (*Elizabeth the Second's heir*).

15.   On the definiteness of *s*-genitives with indefinite possessors (*a king's daughter, an old man's book*), see Woisetschlaeger (1983) and Lyons, C. (1999: 22-23, see especially fn. 12). Note, however, that the assumption that these *s*-genitives are indeed definite is not uncontroversial, see e.g. Taylor (1996: §7.3).

16.   Note that the concept of definiteness of possessive constructions is closely connected with topicality; it will be of particular interest in the present study and discussed in more detail in §4.2 and §6.2.1.1.2 below. For the general rationale of Haspelmath's (1999a) argumentation see also §8.4 – §8.5 below.

17.   For referentiality and definiteness and particularly the ambiguity of indefinite expressions between a referential and generic interpretation, see also §4.2.1 below.

18.   According to Marchand (1969: 20-29) stress contour is probably the best test for distinguishing between syntactic phrases (i.e. specifying genitives) and compounds (i.e. classifying genitives). As recently argued by Olsen (2000), however, (possessive) compounds can have stress both on the first and the last element (*CROW'S nest* versus *fool's ERRAND*), with different stress patterns not reflecting differences in the underlying structure but rather in the semantic relation expressed. See, e.g., (a) *TOY factory* (= a factory that produces toys) versus (b) *toy FACtory* (= a toy & a factory), cf. Olsen (2000: 64).

19.   See also Taylor (1996: 313) for a more detailed distinction.

20.   On the problems of distinguishing syntactic phrases from compounds see also note 18, §7.5.1.1 and §7.5.2.4.

21.   Note that Quirk et al. (1985) reserve the concept of complementation exclusively for verbal and adjectival parts but not for nominal structures. They regard the possessor in the *of*-genitive uniformly as a postmodifier

(1276). Although Quirk et al. (1985) do not explicitly recognize the structural difference between the two types of *of*-genitives, the modifier-type of the *of*-genitive is identified and distinguished from the complement-type via its function and called "descriptive genitive".

22. The precise analysis of possessive constructions may differ considerably in the various DP analyses proposed. For an overview of recent DP analyses, see e.g. Lyons, C. (1999: §§8.2 – 8.3).

23. A notable exception is the work by Herman Paul; see also §8.4.

24. Cf. Halliday (1970) for distinguishing three functions of language: the "ideational" function, which refers to the propositional or cognitive meaning of sentences, the "interpersonal" function, relating to the interaction between interlocutors, and the "textual" function, referring to the organization of texts.

25. Note that the use of the terms "context-free" and "context-bound" are not to be confounded with the use of a similar terminology in the formal literature, where it refers to the classification of grammars within a theory of formal languages (i.e. context-free versus context-sensitive grammars).

26. With "appositive" genitives I refer to such constructions in which the possessor and the possessum are co-referential. Note, however, that under this definition there is a type of appositive genitive which can be realized by the *s*-genitive: *St. Peter's (church)* and elliptic genitives, such as *Let's meet at John's*; see e.g. van der Gaaf (1932) or Rosenbach and Vezzosi (2000) and §3.3.2.2.2 below for discussion.

27. Note also, that Jespersen (1961: 321) observes that the alternative use of a possessive pronoun versus an *of*-genitive in examples such as (31) points to a difference in meaning: a possessive pronoun (*his thought*) has a subjective reading (= 'the thought he has'), while an *of*-genitive (*the thought of him*) is objective. The phrase *the death of him* is explicitly interpreted as objective by Jespersen (1961: 321), having the reading 'what killed him'.

28. This structural explanation for article-possessor complementary is the traditional one and it is sufficient for the present argumentation; for an alternative view see discussion of Haspelmath (1999a) in §2.3.1.

29. For the historical development of such ellipted genitive constructions see also §7.4.5.1.1 below.

30. It is important to note, though, that the conceptual factors discussed and the economical principles evoked in this study (see especially chapter 8 below) cannot only be assumed to be at work in non-Standard language as well but even be considered to operate much more freely in varieties not as much affected by the norms underlying the Standard language.

31. The fact that phonological factors can affect the choice of genitive construction has, however, interesting implications for the theoretical controversy as to whether phonology can affect syntax. Within the modular architecture of the formal/generative paradigm it is generally assumed that syntactic processes operate completely unaffected by phonological ones (cf. e.g. Chomsky 1980), although in recent years the relation between phonology and syntax has begun to be rethought (cf. e.g. Zec and Inkelas 1990; Golston 1995).

32. It is interesting to note that Plank (1985: 223) concludes that "it is the plural marking of the nouns that happens to precede the attributive marker, rather than that of the internal head noun of complex attributive phrases, which conditions the choice of zero."

33. In the light of these findings it is, however, somewhat surprising that the "group genitive" (*the king of England's daughter*), i.e. an *s*-genitive with a right-branching possessor, could evolve in English in the first place (cf. §7.5). Also, it is striking that although such group genitives are rarely attested in written language, they seem to be more freely used in colloquial and dialectal language (cf. Jespersen 1960: 296-297; Carstairs 1987: 152), as are morphological processes operating over phrases, such as plurals to lexicalized syntactic phrases (*mother-in-laws*) and words resulting from derivation to phrases (*unget-at-able*), as mentioned by Quirk et al. (1985: §5.102, §I.18, footnote); cf. also §2.2. This indicates that right-branching possessors may be dispreferred for stylistic rather than for cognitive reasons.

34. Altenberg (1982: §3.2) does consider the relative distribution of weight within left-branching genitive constructions (i.e. of premodifiers) in his seventeenth-century corpus. He concludes that "the relative distribution of premodifiers has little influence on the choice of construction" (Altenberg 1982: 81). This negative conclusion may, however, be due to the overall low frequency of data with more than one premodifier in his corpus.

35. For a discussion of the different notions and definitions of "weight" see e.g. Hawkins (1994: 117-120) and Wasow (1997a, 1997b).

36. Cf. also (cf. Zachrisson 1920: 46) for arguing that consecutive *of*-genitives are avoided for stylistic reasons; but see also Svartengren (1949: 174) for the opposite view, maintaining that "no tendency to avoid prepositional groups can be observed in present-day English".

37. There are various notions of "focus" in the literature, some of which are diametrically opposed to the one discussed here; for a good discussion and overview of such notions, see e.g. Dorgeloh (1997: 10-11). Note also, that there are accounts of information structure which proceed from the assumption that the communicatively most important element should occur *first* in the sentence; for this, see e.g. Givón's principle of "task urgency" (e.g. Givón 1988: 252); see also §4.2.1 below.

38. For a more detailed discussion of givenness, see §4.2 below.

39. See, for example, Bell (1984) for arguing that speakers deliberately *design* their utterance for their audience. See also Dorgeloh (2000), who calls for a more dynamic text typology, suggesting that it is the way language is perspectualized that can induce a certain text-type (in her case narratives).

40. A general problem in Hundt's (1998) study is, however, that she does not consider the *relative* frequency of the *s*-genitive as opposed to the *of*-genitive (see also discussion in §3.1.2 below, the results obtained may therefore not be a reliable indicator for the differences found between the different Standard varieties.

41. Although subjective and objective genitives have been identified in §3.3.2.1.1 as potential choice contexts they are excluded in the present study for reasons to be briefly discussed in §6.2.2.1.

42. Note that this use of the *s*-genitive seems to have been rather objected to and stigmatized, cf. e.g. Jespersen (1961: 329); Moss (1968: 19-20, as quoted in Hawkins 1981: 255), and Copperud (1980: 298, as quoted in Hundt 1998: 43).

43. In contrast to Quirk et al.'s (1985: §5.118) classification, geographical names and locational nouns are subsumed under a single category "geographical nouns"; the same classification is used in studies by Raab-Fischer (1995) and Hundt (1998), both discussed below.

44. But see also §8.2 below for arguing that the speaker does not necessarily and always have the interests of the hearer in mind.

45. In the following discussion I will roughly equate referentiality and specificity, although, strictly speaking, they are usually held to be distinct. For a good discussion of the subtle relation between specificity and referentiality, I refer to Lyons, C. (1999: §4.2).

46. For the concept of "individuation" see further §4.4.4.

47. Although, superficially, both *the car's windscreen* (= "functional") and *a glass of wine* (= "instance") encode a part/whole relation, they are distinct categories. In *a car's windscreen* the possessor (*car*) is the anchor that narrows down the referent of the whole NP, while in *a glass of wine* it is rather the possessum (*a glass*) that helps to individuate the possessor noun (*wine*); for the *s*-genitive as an anchoring construction, see also §4.4.3; for a brief discussion of the classification of partitives, see §4.3.1.

48. See examples (3) – (5) given in Altenberg (1980: 155), in which proper nouns have obviously been classified as new.

49. See also Jahr Sorheim (1980) and Altenberg (1980, 1982) for showing that new possessors do occur with the *s*-genitive.

50. However, in Altenberg (1982) this distinction is inherent in his analysis of the various noun classes with which the possessor can occur, i.e. what he labels the "lexical factor".

51. See the following example given by Jahr Sorheim (1980: 141) as conveying new information: *The pulse beat at the side of the neck just where a man's collar is.* In this example, the possessor *a man* does not refer to a specific man but rather specifies the type of collar, i.e. that of men.

52. Biber et al. (1999) are not very explicit about their inclusion and exclusion criteria, so this question is difficult to evaluate in their case; Anschutz (1997) seems to have excluded possessive compounds from her analysis; yet it is not clear whether also non-referential possessors in an *of*-genitive have been included or not.

53. A notable exception is Altenberg (1982), who classifies his data according to Fillmore's (1968) framework of "case grammar". The fine-grained taxonomy Altenberg establishes may be able to handle some of the inconsistencies prevailing in other taxonomies, it does, however, – like the traditional approaches – not entail any predictions.

54. Note also, that it is not implicit in Löbner's (1985) account in which respect his taxonomy should be relevant for the choice between the *s*-genitive and the *of*-genitive. While it is crucial in this account that the internal argument of a functional possessum (*wife*) is bound and identified by a possessor noun (*the*

man) thereby receiving a definite interpretation, it seems to be rather irrelevant by which morphosyntactic means this is achieved, by the *s*-genitive (*the man's wife*) or the *of*-genitive (*the wife of the man*). It is only when we link the semantics of functional nouns to the semantics of the *s*-genitive, assuming that the *s*-genitive as an inherently definite construction should be favored for functional nouns that this taxonomy becomes predictive. The problems for the empirical investigation of sortal possessum nouns, however, still remain.

55. Discussing a unified concept of "topicworthiness", Comrie (1989), however, argues that it is not possible to define topicality independently of animacy (as cited in Dahl and Fraurud 1996: 59).

56. Note that such an interpretation is also implicit in the accounts of Fraurud (1996) and Löbner (1985), see also discussion in §4.2.1 and §4.3.1 above, although these do not explicitly deal with the English possessives.

57. For a discussion of individuation, see Fraurud (1996: 79-80) and Yamamoto (1999: §4). See also Hopper and Thompson (1980: 252-253) who show that individuation is one component contributing to "transitivity".

58. See also Jucker (1993: 124) for a similar argumentation, quoting also Altenberg (1982: 303).

59. Taylor (1996: 293) also analyzes possessive compounds as reference point constructions, the difference to specifying genitives ascribing to the status of the reference point, i.e. the possessor. In specifying genitives the possessor denotes an instance, in possessive compounds it denotes a type. This instance-type distinction in the status of the possessor is essentially the same as the [±referential] distinction drawn in §2.3.1 to distinguish between specifying and classifying genitives.

60. For an exhaustive summary of the generative literature on the *s*-genitive, see Taylor (1996: chapter 6).

61. For another – and more up-to-date – generative analysis of the *s*-genitive, see also §2.3.2 (DP-analysis). The aim of this section is, however, to show how the variation between the *s*-genitive and the *of*-genitive is captured by various linguistic approaches. In this respect, DP-analysis has nothing essentially new to offer.

62. While not denying that adults' speech can and does change, in the generative conception of language and change, it is mental grammars that matter. And since these grammars are considered to be biologically endowed entities, acquired and fixed during language acquisition, these are, to put it more carefully, highly unlikely to change in a speaker's lifetime, though this possibility cannot absolutely be ruled out (see e.g. Lightfoot 1999: 80). Note that the assumption of language changing during language acquisition is not an exclusively generative position but can also be found within non-generative work; for this, see most prominently the concept of "abduction" as proposed by Andersen (1973). For a recent critique of child-based theories of language change, see particularly Croft (2000: §3.2).

63. Note that this is not the exclusive approach taken by Lightfoot; in Lightfoot (1991: 136-138), he also proposes one intraspeaker variation scenario as described below (cf. also Croft 2000: 52). Note that the assumption of

invariant synchronic grammars and overlapping generations also underlies Briscoe's (2000b) computer simulation of diachronic syntax.

64. The assumption of several grammars within one speaker is highly controversial though, mainly for alleged problems in the learnability of such grammars; see the discussion in Lightfoot (1999: §4.5, and particularly p.109, fn 6); see also Guy (1997b: 138) for a negative evaluation.

65. What remains, however, unclear is how we should imagine this Constant Rate effect to come about. First, why is it that one option wins while the other loses (and why this option and not the other?), and second, given this 'winner', which mechanism makes speakers eventually use this option more and more, and how is this transmitted over generations, which it must do given the time span of such changes? That is, do speakers of the new generation inherit both grammars plus an internal kind of 'tag' which takes chart of the frequency attached to the variants? And by which mechanism does frequency of usage increase at all? These questions are, I must add, extremely difficult ones and to my knowledge they have not been answered by any approach. Computer simulations modeling the diffusion of change within a language community over several generations and sensitive to changing frequency such as Briscoe (2000a, 2000b) seem to be one promising step towards first answers to those questions (though see also McMahon 2000: 161 for raising some doubts as to the validity of such simulations in that "the programmer's control over the initial conditions means simulations are doomed to success."). I will get back to the question of frequency in diachronic change in §8.6.2.2 below.

66. I am grateful to Janet Grijzenhout for very helpful discussions on OT, and to Joan Bresnan for clarifying some general issues concerning her Functional OT account for me. All remaining misunderstandings are of course my own responsibility.

67. And see also, for example, Hurch (1998: 121), who argues that OT is not falsifiable. Since it is output-oriented any OT analysis must necessarily arrive at the correct output.

68. For some first attempts to find some extragrammatical basis for OT constraints see, however, Hayes (1999) for proposing phonetic grounding of phonological constraints and Haspelmath (1999b) for looking for a functional motivation of OT constraints in general, though these are still the exception rather than the rule. While it is relatively unproblematic to find an extragrammatical motivation for constraints in the field of phonology (in terms of perceptual and/or articulatory ease), recently also an attempt has been made to link morphosyntactic constraints to some underlying functional motivation, an approach, which has become known as "Functional Optimality Theory" (see e.g. Bresnan 2001; Bresnan, Dingare, and Manning 2001; and particularly Bresnan and Aissen 2002). In this line of research, markedness hierarchies are not only invoked on the basis of typological evidence but tried to be linked to underlying functional principles, thereby providing a very promising bridge between formal and functional approaches.

69. As Guy (1997a: 336) has aptly put it: "…: generative theories before OT are categorical and deterministic; OT is non-categorical and deterministic,…"

70. For a more differentiated discussion of various ways of coping, more or less successfully, with optionality in OT, see Müller (1999).

71. But see Anttila and Cho (1998: 40) for arguing that "the distinction between competence and performance is clearly independent of the question whether models of competence are categorical or not".

72. For a discussion of yet other approaches to variation in OT, see for example Anttila (1997); Anttila and Cho (1998); Guy (1997a, b) or McMahon (2000: §3.4). In general, it must be noted that it is somewhat difficult to follow all recent developments of OT coherently since it often appears that a great deal of the works cited are unpublished manuscripts, drafts or handouts not available to the linguist not into OT; this is, for example, the case in most of the literature on the modeling of variation in OT cited in Anttila (1997) and Cho (1998) to give only two examples. If not published yet, at best one can hope to track relevant literature in some of the Internet archives.

73. There is another potential problem I see in matching quantitative OT predictions with actual performance/corpus data: Since variation derives from grammar, and grammar is acquired during language acquisition and presumably remains in the same state throughout adulthood (see discussion in §5.1.1.1 above), variation in a speech community and hence in a corpus will always reflect to some degree interspeaker variation due to a generational overlap between younger speakers already having acquired a new(er) grammar and older speakers still using the old(er) grammar, unless the corpus is controlled for speaker age.

74. As the authors note, their account of Stochastic OT is based on the work in Boersma (1997).

75. For a general learning algorithm on the basis of constraint demotion see also Tesar and Smolensky (2000). The learning algorithm underlying Bresnan and Deo's (2001) stochastic OT account is the "Gradual Learning Algorithm" (GLA), cf. Boersma (1998) and see also recently Boersma and Hayes (2001).

76. Anttila (1997: 49), however, argues that it is well possible that variation is exclusively grammar-driven, i.e. not determined by any extra-grammatical factors and that the question "[t]o what extent extragrammatical factors are needed in deriving accurate statistics remains an empirical question." This is certainly correct. But is it likely? I do not think so. Assuming that there is completely grammar-driven variation means that a language has two (or more) structural realizations for the same propositional meaning and would not distinguish between these according to some non-propositional (such as social or affective) meaning or on other functional grounds. That is, this would assume a strictly context-free version of grammatical variation, which, as argued in §3.2.1 above is just not realistic. Languages hardly ever have absolute synonymy. Note that the ban of absolute synonymy has also a formal correlate, i.e. the "blocking effect", "a global principle of economy that applies to the lexicon and rules out functionally equivalent items" (cf. Kroch 1994: 188). The only way to account for apparent variation by both acknowledging the blocking effect and at the same time keeping within a

grammar-internal approach, seems to be Kroch's (1994) Competing Grammar approach, where diachronic variation is accounted for by the very fact that over a certain period of time speakers may have more than one internal grammar, although even in this scenario variation is a pathological state eventually leading to the elimination of alternative variants, as discussed above. If variation persists, this must then be due to meaning differentiation according to Kroch (1994: 196).

77.   Cf. also McMahon (2000: 115).

78.   There are important differences between *langue* in the Saussurean sense and the generative notion of competence (see e.g. Lyons, J. 1981: 233-234; Sampson 1980: chapter 2). While the former is a static concept, looking at language as an inventory of signs and relations, the latter is "generative" in the sense that language is not a finite set of linguistic elements but rather a generative device, which is able to produce an infinite number of sentences. One important implication of this is that syntax belongs to *parole* in the structuralist terminology (because sentences are not an inventory but created in concrete situations), while it is in the realm (in fact, in the very heart!) of competence within the generative model. Besides the locus of syntax, another important difference is the locus of language itself. While there is quite some debate as to the question of how social Saussure's notion of *langue* is (see e.g. discussion in Botha 1992: §5.2), the term *langue* at least allows for a social reading, i.e. as being situated within a speech community, while the generative notion of competence certainly does not, referring instead to an individual speaker's internalized knowledge of language. It is not exactly clear whether Labov refers to *langue* or competence, or whether in fact he does not discriminate between the two concepts. Conceptually, the concept of *langue* adheres much better to the sociolinguistic conception since (at least possibly) residing within society. As will be argued below, practically, though, Labov seems to place himself within the context of generative grammar by trying to incorporate Variable Rules into generative grammar, assuming them to be part of speakers' competence (for a very good discussion on this, see Romaine 1981: 94-97). See also Guy (1997b: 125) for an undiscriminating use of *langue* versus competence with respect to Variable Rules.

79.   For linguistic factors this should not pose a serious problem; neither for those external factors which operate within speakers, such as style. Any factor determining variation across speakers (as e.g. age, social class or sex), however, seems problematic in this approach.

80.   But see Guy (1997) for arguing that the strength of single factors is the same for all speakers; what seems to be variable between speakers is the overall rate of frequency/probability. This, however, seems to me an empirical question to be decided in every single case of study.

81.   The same has been claimed for Labovian quantitative sociolinguistics. See for example Romaine (1984a) for arguing that the mere correlation between linguistic variation and factors is not explanatory. In a very similar spirit, Cameron (1997: 59-62) refers to this as the "correlational fallacy".

82. For the logical relation between variation and change see Weinreich, Labov, and Herzog (1968: 188): "Not all variability and heterogeneity in language structure involves change; but all change involves variability and heterogeneity."

83. But see Sornicola, Poppe, and Shisha-Halevy (2000) for providing evidence that variation can also be stable or have a stabilizing effect.

84. See also Croft (2000: 53-59) for discussing such "utterance-based" theories of language change.

85. It must be noted though that approaches to linguistic change rarely deal with the innovation of variants (for exceptions see e.g. Milroy 1992); usually investigation starts when a change is already under way through the speech community, i.e. when it has already spread from the ultimately first innovation to other speakers, most probably for the very reason that a change only becomes visible to the researcher once it has spread. For a good discussion on the distinction between innovation and propagation see e.g. Croft (2000); he in fact argues that while innovation is functionally motivated, the propagation of variants is essentially social.

86. For an attempt to classify functionalist approaches, see e.g. Bates and MacWhinney (1982) and Nichols (1984).

87. Note that here I am exclusively dealing with a broad definition of the concept of markedness within functional approaches and that I am altogether ignoring the notion of markedness as used in generative grammar.

88. For discussions on the notion of "basic word order", see e.g. Siewierska (1988: 8-14) or Mithun (1987).

89. Note also, that these diagnostics contain assumptions which may not be empirically correct. For example, taking both what is acquired last in language acquisition and what is lost first in aphasia as indicative for a marked form/construction, presupposes that in fact both correlate. While this has indeed been proposed by Jakobson ([1941] 1971) and ever since long been maintained as received wisdom, there are also studies which provide empirical evidence against the view that aphasia is just a mirror image of language acquisition (see e.g. Penke 2001).

90. Strictly speaking, Haiman (1985a) distinguishes between "isomorphism" and "motivation" as the two main principles of (structural) diagrammatic iconicity, principles (2-4) mentioned below would – according to Haiman's (1985a) terminology – be cases of motivation (cf. also Fischer and Nänny 1999: xxii); on the problems involved in this terminology, see e.g. Croft (1990: §7.3.2) and Hiraga (1994).

91. On the 22nd Annual Meeting of the *Deutsche Gesellschaft für Sprachwissenschaft* (*DGFS*) in Marburg, March 2000, for example, a whole workshop ("Conceptualization and Grammaticalization in Speech Production") was devoted to this very question. Nüse (2000), for example, showed on the basis of an experimental study in which German, English and Arabic subjects had to describe events depicted in a video film, how language-specific structures influence the way these events are construed. In contrast, Nuyts (2000) made a case for the independence of conceptualization from linguistic structure.

92. Note that in this line of research there are interesting links between sociolinguistic approaches to variation and change and grammaticalization theory. See for example the work by Tagliamonte, who, working within the sociolinguist framework, analyses synchronic variation and from this deduces past stages of forms or constructions, a kind of reconstructing past grammaticalization, so to speak (for this, see e.g. Tagliamonte 2000).

93. See for example Hopper and Traugott (1993: 33): "Language does not exist separate from its speakers." Also, focusing on the semantic-pragmatic aspects of grammaticalization, as e.g. Hopper and Traugott (1993) do, necessarily implies speaker-hearer interaction on the level of communication.

94. For a similar argument see Newmeyer (1998: 238-239); for a critical response to Newmeyer in that linguists within grammaticalization research are certainly aware of the terminology being no more than metaphors see Haspelmath (2000: 248, footnote 6). For a good and critical discussion of the use of metaphor in historical linguistics in general see also Lass (1997: §§1.6-1.7, forthcoming).

95. Pinker (1997: 134-145) distinguishes three components of consciousness: (i) self-knowledge, (ii) access-to-information, and (iii) sentience. It is the second aspect of consciousness, access-to-information, which will be most relevant here, and which underlies the definition of "economy" used in this study (see particularly §8.1 and §8.5 below).

96. Note that under such a perspective iconicity and economy are not two distinct forces as is usually assumed (cf. e.g. Haiman 1983) but in fact only two sides of the same coin. In this respect I am following Givón (1985: 198) who states that "[t]he whole raison d'être for iconicity in language is thus grounded in the need to facilitate processing in real time".

97. For further references see particularly Wurzel (1999: 249, footnote 7). For a diachronic case study showing how such conflicts of naturalness can be discerned in the evolution of *do*-periphrasis, see e.g. Stein (1990).

98. Admittedly, in the recent functional OT approach as advocated by Bresnan and Aissen (2002) OT constraints *are* linked to functional motivations. A stochastic (functional) OT analysis, while possible, cannot however really *add* anything to the analysis offered in the present study, except for formalizing the results within a current theoretical approach, which is, however, not my concern here. Note that this not only would to commit (and restrict) myself to the technical apparatus of OT, but also to its general ontological positions, both of which are not my concern here, either. See also Ritt (2001) for arguing that OT "constraints" and "preferences" within Naturalness theory, though "functional counterparts of each other" (291), are proceeding from very different ontological positions.

99. The animacy of the possessum is not investigated here; as argued above it correlates to a great extent with the type of possessive relation (cf. §4.4.2; see also §6.2.2.1 below).

100. For the items to be classed as concrete nouns it was sufficient that they are tangible and visible things; additionally, for the vast majority of items the distinction drawn between concrete and abstract nouns follows the criterion

of countability given by Quirk et al. (1985: §5.2), with concrete nouns being countable and abstract nouns not being countable.

101. For a good overview and summary of the relevant literature, see Hagoort (1998: 240-242).

102. Bock and Warren (1985) adopt the hierarchy of grammatical functions as proposed by Keenan and Comrie (1977) on the basis of the ability of NPs to be relativized: subject > direct object > indirect object > ....

103. Cf. e.g. Bock and Levelt (1994: 965-966) for arguing that topicality in the sense of givenness can be taken to increase the conceptual accessibility of referents by increasing their definiteness; see also Bock and Irwin (1980).

104. See also §5.2.1.1.1, §8.2 and §8.4 for making a systematic distinction between the role of the speaker as opposed the role of the hearer.

105. See also Hiraga (1994: 9) for treating the Me-First principle as a case of "linear iconicity".

106. Note that also in Nichols' (1988) implicational hierarchy part/whole relations rank directly below body parts.

107. Seiler (1983: 5), for example, argues for "a gradient difference between substantival POSSESSION and verbal VALENCE".

108. There are only two items used in this study expressing legal ownership in the [+prototypical] category of animate/human possession; for a list of items used in the respective categories, see Appendix §10.1.

109. In German the ungrammaticality of sentences such as (53b) are due to a more general restriction in that ellipsis is generally prohibited for postmodifying constructions (premodifying: *Ich mag keine roten Blumen sondern nur gelbe _* 'I don't like red flowers but only yellow (flowers)' versus postmodifying: **Ich komme aus Deutschland und nicht _ England* '*I come from Germany and not _ England'. Note, however, that in English probably this restriction cannot hold true to the same extent. While ellipsis from postmodifying constructions seems indeed generally blocked, ellipsis from certain premodifying constructions, i.e. adjectival premodification, is not as free as in German but, as for postmodified constructions, requires a resumptive pronoun: *I don't like red flowers but only yellow ones* versus **I don't like red flowers but only yellow _*.

110. For the typological classification between "head-marking" and "dependent-marking", see Nichols (1986).

111. On the question of what is analyzed as the head of construction and its implication for typological prediction, see also §7.4.3 below.

112. By "monolingual" I mean that the subject should have acquired only one mother tongue, i.e. English, during first language acquisition, and not proficiency in one language only.

113. The maximum number of items left out in a questionnaire that was still included was 11.

114. For example, Pinker and Birdsong (1979) collected preference judgments for alternative word orders of nonsense binominal NPs, and this experiment is generally discussed within the context of language production (see e.g. Bock 1982: 18).

115. The novels used were: Elizabeth George: *Playing for the Ashes*, Elisabeth George: *Missing Joseph*, Elizabeth George: *In the Presence of the Enemy*, and Patricia Cornwell: *The Body Farm*, all crime fiction, and Terry Pratchett: *The Colour of Magic*; see Bibliography (Texts) for complete reference.

116. For a discussion of such excluded items see further §6.5.

117. The relative importance of several factors can also be assessed by multivariate analysis as very commonly applied in sociolinguistic studies. It was not used in the present analysis because (i) multivariate analysis is designed to cope with spontaneous data, i.e. it is not a necessary statistical procedure for experimentally controlled and balanced data, and (ii) in the present case I consider the interdependencies between the three factors animacy, topicality, and possessive relation from the beginning by controlling and neutralizing them as far as possible. In this respect, I am approaching the question of assessing the relative importance of factors from a different vantage point here.

118. I will regard findings which are at least at the $p<0.05$ level as significant; findings below the $p<0.10$ level are not significant but will be referred to as showing a strong tendency.

119. As said in §6.4.2, throughout the analyses in this study it is always the relative frequency of the *s*-genitive as calculated as opposed that of the *of*-genitive that is given and never the frequency of the *s*-genitive alone; i.e. even if only the relative frequency of the *s*-genitive is given the corresponding frequency of the *of*-genitive is implicit as well.

120. Note that all chi-square values referred to in the following are Yates corrected, with df 1.

121. Note that in this table – by way of illustration – only the first two conditions are compared, i.e. ([+a/+t/+p] versus [+a/+t/-p]); the procedure is exactly the same for further comparing [+a/+t/-p] and [+a/-t/+p], [+a/-t/+p] and [+a/-t/-p] and so forth; for the exact results, see table 38 below).

122. For the relevant *t* values throughout this study the default assumption was that the variances are not equal.

123. For a brief discussion of the difficulties involved in real-time and apparent-time studies, see e.g. McMahon (1994: 239-240).

124. Note, however, that for the other [-animate], [-topical] condition, i.e. [-a/-t/-p], there is no significant difference in the frequency of the *s*-genitive between the younger American and British subjects, which is somewhat surprising if the higher use of *s*-genitives with [-animate] [-topical] possessors is considered to be a recent American development. So, maybe this point should not be emphasized too much.

125. This item was part of a running text in which *fire* had already been introduced and was thus topical. Here only the relevant part is reproduced.

126. The fact that the [-a/+t/+p] condition contains more *car* items than the respective [-prototypical] condition did probably not bias the results since in the [-a/+t/+p] condition overall more items were included (16) than in the [-a/+t/-p] condition (10) so that the effect should level out.

127. I am using the term "bridging context" deliberately in a rather non-technical way here to refer to possible contexts in which a metaphorical transfer from

one context to another is possible. I am not sure whether this notion of bridging context as described here fulfils all criteria for the technical use of the term as described in Heine (2002).

128. Cf. also §6.2.2.1.1 above, where word length has been mentioned as one factor contributing to the Lexical Accessibility in speech production.

129. Since the possessor in the *s*-genitive functions as a determiner and is therefore incompatible with any further determiners, a natural imbalance in the number of syllable is inherent in the two genitive constructions. Therefore, when counting the number of syllables only lexical, open-class elements have been considered but not determiners.

130. Note that the [-a/+t/-p] condition is the only condition with less than two items in one of the word-length varying conditions; for this contexts therefore only the "neutral" condition is given in figure 27 and figure 28.

131. See e.g. Brunner (1962: 28) or Mustanoja (1960: 79-80). It is interesting to note that these handbooks primarily give as examples such partitive uses of the *of*-genitive cases in which the possessor stands for the whole and the possessum for the part (cf. also §4.3.1; see also §7.5.3.1 below) and not body parts or other part/whole relations where the partitive relation is exactly the other way, i.e. the possessor represents the whole and the possessum the part.

132. Stahl (1927: 15) notes that the basic meaning of the preposition *of* is partitive. In §7.5.3.1 below I will briefly offer another possible explanation of why partitives are not only the first to be replaced, but also why they are completely supplanted by the *of*-genitive.

133. Note, however, that the fact that the *s*-less and the *his*-genitive occur at all in a corpus of written English is remarkable in itself. In Present-day English these genitive constructions do – if at all – only occur in dialects or in very colloquial language (cf. e.g. Klemola 1997; Seppänen 1997a). This indicates that these constructions are not yet stigmatized as much in early Modern English as they are in Modern English.

134. As "zero-genitive" those *s*-less genitives were classified in which the possessor ended in a regular plural ending (-*s*); in some of these cases a genitive marking is orthographically indicated by an apostrophe (') as in Present-day English, but this orthographical convention had not yet been fully established in the period investigated.

135. Note, however, that some productive uses of the *s*-genitive certainly remained, even in this period, e.g. *Thomas Cotes ymagenyng, the same Tebaldes hows, the kynges aduersairs.*

136. See Rosenbach and Vezzosi (2000) and also Rosenbach, Stein, and Vezzosi (2000: 185).

137. From 1500 onwards the *Helsinki Corpus* presumes all texts to reflect Standard English.

138. But see also Allen (1997a: 115, fn 5) for arguing that English still retains case distinctions in the pronouns, which does not necessarily render the genitive inflection a marked device on typological grounds. Note that such argumentation crucially depends on how to define the existence of inflectional paradigms – is case within the pronouns sufficient to establish an

inflectional category within a language, or is it necessary that case applies more productively to full lexical elements as well?

139. Lehmann (1986: 668) also acknowledges that nominal syntax differs from verbal syntax, suggesting a modified version of the NP accessibility hierarchy in which adnominal syntactic functions, such as the genitive, form an independent subhierarchy to the classic adverbial syntactic functions (such as subject, object, etc.). He also notes that in some languages (e.g. Indonesian, Dagbani) the genitive is apparently as high on the hierarchy as the subject. Note also, that for second language learners Gass (1979) reports an unusually high number of relativizations of the genitive in contrast to the other grammatical functions, which also contradicts Keenan and Comrie's (1977) NP accessibility hierarchy.

140. Harris and Campbell (1995: §8.2.2) generally discuss the question of whether word order in compounds can reflect word order in phrases, and they raise the question whether word order in compounds reflects an older language state, i.e. the word order at that stage of the language when the compound was formed. They conclude that this may be the case but not always, and that in general, there is at present neither sufficient evidence for taking word order in compounds as representative for word order in phrases in general nor for the assumption that word order in compounds reflects previous word order patterns, thereby ruling out word order in compounds as reliable guides to reconstruction.

141. See e.g. Givón (1984: 221): "The position of genitive/possessive modifiers vis-à-vis the head noun is the most consistent correlation between VP and NP word-order..."

142. See also Deutscher (2000) for showing how Akkadian not only is consistently verb-final (OV) while on the phrasal level corresponding entirely to VO-patterns, but also "remains stubbornly attached to its 'problematic' word order" (55) over a period of 2000 years.

143. Strictly speaking, Vennemann (1974) with his "principle of natural serialization" uses formulas of predicate logic distinguishing between an "operator" (i.e. "function", corresponds to "modifier") and "operand" (i.e. "argument", corresponds to "modified"). Such function-argument relations are independent of the syntactic notion of head; on the other hand, not all genitive constructions may be captured by function-arguments relations as argued in §4.3.1 above.

144. Note that for reasons mentioned in §6.2.2.1 the sub-corpus used in the present study is also restricted to possessive meanings only, not including subjective and objective genitives.

145. See also the discussion of topicality in §4.2.1.

146. It is extremely difficult to distinguish within [-definite] expressions between [+referential] and [-referential] ones. This is due to the inherent ambiguity of these constructions which very often give rise to both interpretations (§2.3.1 and §4.2.1). For the Rosenbach, Stein, and Vezzosi (2000) data a fairly strict and straightforward criterion for distinguishing [+referential] from [-referential] indefinite expressions was adopted, counting only such [-definite] possessors which contained a quantifying or quantifiable

expression, such as *any*, *some*, a few, *two*, or, otherwise, where the context was such that it clearly allowed for a [+referential] reading (cf. also Löbner 1985: 287-289).

147. Note that [++topical] corresponds to the category "globally-given" and [+topical] to the category "locally given" in Rosenbach, Stein, and Vezzosi (2000).

148. For the first two intervals there is no data given for [-topical] possessors, since only those contexts are quantified for which there were at least 10 obligatory contexts for the occurrence of a genitive construction.

149. It is only for interval II (1450 – 1499) that the difference in the relative frequency of the *s*-genitive between [++topical] and [+topical] is statistically significant (chi-square, df 1, $p<0.001$); for interval III (1500 – 1559) there was a strong tendency (chi-square, df 1, $p<0.10$). A statistical comparison of the relative frequency of the *s*-genitive between [+topical] and [-topical] was not possible, since the number of tokens in the [-topical] category is too low for the chi-square test to apply.

150. For the [+topical] context in interval (I) there were not enough token to conduct a chi-square test.

151. For the classification and examples from the corpus, see also Rosenbach, Stein, and Vezzosi (2000: 191). Note that additionally social relations (e.g. *Saint Paul's teacher, the friend of Hamlet*) were included under [-prototypical] possessive relations.

152. The examples are all taken from the corpus, adapted to ModE spelling for the sake of illustration.

153. Only the following differences in the relative frequency of the *s*-genitive turned out to be statistically significant: [+a/++t/+p] versus [+a/++t/-p] in interval (II) (chi-square, df 1, $p<0.001$); [+a/+t/+p] versus [+a/+t/-p] in interval (II) (chi-square, df 1, $p < 0.05$) and [+a/+t/+p] versus [+a/+t/-p] in interval (IV) (chi-square, df 1, $p<0.01$); the last context showed a strong tendency in interval (III) (chi-square, df 1, $p<0.10$). For [+a/++t/-p] versus [+a/+t/+p] and [+a/+t/+p] versus [+a/+t/-p] there were not enough tokens to apply the chi-sqare test; likewise any difference implying the [-topical] context did not enter the statistical analysis because of the too low number of tokens.

154. Quoted from Fischer (1992: 227).

155. Altenberg (1982: § 2.8.2) refers here to a particular subgroup of genitives, the postmodified group (e.g. *the king of England's son*); for other group genitives discussed in Altenberg (1982), see also this section below.

156. For the motivation of such criteria distinguishing between an inflectional versus a clitic status of POSS *'s* see also Allen (1997a) and the discussion in §1.2.

157. For more examples indicating the clitic versus inflectional status of POSS *'s* in the EModE corpus as well as in a corpus of Middle Scots, see Rosenbach and Vezzosi (1999).

158. It is possible that this non-occurrence of group genitive in which POSS *'s* is attached to a relative clause (as in *the man I met yesterday's daughter*) is an artefact of the textual evidence. As noted by Jespersen (1961: 296-297) these

are generally avoided in literary language, though widely spread in English dialects.

159. See also Koptjevskaja-Tamm (2002: §3.4) for arguing that "[i]n the Brythonic languages and in Maltese, juxtaposition within PNPs [=possessive noun phrases] is a consequence of losing the entire nominal case paradigm."

160. It is somehow striking that in a non-northern text such as *The Diary of Henry Machyn* the *s*-less genitive is relatively productive. Yet note, that Klemola (1997: 351-352, fn. 5) mentions the possibility that Machyn came from south-east Yorkshire, in which case the frequent use of the *s*-less genitive would not be that surprising.

161. According to Seppänen (1997b: 196) and Allen (1998) independent genitives occur only with the *s*-genitives (e.g. *the palace is the king's*); for absolute genitives van der Gaaf (1932: 50), however, gives some examples for *s*-less genitives (e.g. *at Saynt Peter kirke*), which suggests that the *s*-less genitive was not in general impossible with an omitted possessum noun.

162. It is also interesting to note that the pronominal variant of an independent *s*-genitive is a new type of possessive pronoun (*her(e)s, your(e)s, our(e)s,* etc.) emerging in the course of Middle English derived from the genitive form of the personal pronoun with suffixed *-es* (cf. e.g. Lass 1992: 119-120); according to Seppänen (1997b: 198-199) in analogy to POSS *'s*. That is, the genitive for personal pronouns is ever since divided into two distinct groups: (a) possessive pronouns in pronominal determiner function (e.g. *my house*), and (b) possessive pronouns used predicatively (e.g. *this house is mine*).

163. Interestingly, Seppänen (1997b: 201) also provides a possible explanation why POSS *'s* could become a phrase-marker but the plural *-s* inflection remained attached to the nominal head: while plural is inherently a property of (countable) nouns, case is a property of NPs.

164. And note that Norde (2001: 249) analyzes POSS *'s* as a clitic and not as a phrasal inflection as Seppänen (1997b) does.

165. Cf. Mustanoja (1960: 160) for examples of *his*-genitives after nominative possessors (*Asia and Europe hiera land-gemircu,* 'Asia and Africa their boundary'; *Nilus seo ea hire æwielme,* 'the river Nile her source') in Old English besides the "possessive dative" (*þa Gode his naman neode cigdan,* '[they] called then God his name'). See, however, Allen (1997a: 125-126) for arguing that the examples given in Mustanoja (1960) are not genuine cases of *his*-genitives but can equally well be interpreted as left-dislocations. See also Jespersen (1961: 308-309) for discussing the syntactic ambiguity of *his*-genitives. So *Heer beginnith the Chanouns yeman his tale* in Chaucer could be both interpreted as (i) 'Here begins the Canon's Yeoman his tale' (= *his*-genitive), or (ii) 'Here the Canon's Yeoman begins his tale' (*his tale* = accusative object to *begin*). However, Jespersen (1961: 309) also gives a clear example from Chaucer showing that there were (at least at Chaucer's time) also unambiguous cases of *his*-genitives, as in: *Here endith the man of lawe his tale. And next folwith the shipman his prolog.* While *his tale* might be interpreted as an object to *end*, a reading such as 'And next the shipman follows his prologue' is clearly out.

166. The *his*-genitive was, however, already criticized by grammarians in early Modern English (cf. Görlach 1993: 82), probably because of its close connection to vernacular language. Graband (1965:116) actually regards the *his*-genitive as the hypercorrect variant of the inflected *s*-genitive in vernacular language.

167. A somewhat earlier timing, however, is suggestive from example (87) quoted from Wyld (1936), where a *his*-genitive occurs as a group genitive in the first half of the fifteenth century.

168. There are a few examples in Middle English in which another than a masculine singular possessive pronoun does occur. Allen (1997a: 126-127), however, shows that these are all no genuine cases of possessive linking pronouns but can all be interpreted otherwise as well. So, for example, *Felice hir fairnesse fel hire al to slaundre* 'Felice her fairness became a source of shame to her' (Piers Plowman XII.58) should rather be regarded as a case of left-dislocation.

169. It is not at all clear how these linking possessive pronouns in Scandinavian dialects should be interpreted with respect to the upgrading of the *-s* to a clitic. See for example Norde (2001: 255-256) for rejecting any causal role of possessive pronouns in this process, partly because of the timing (such constructions are attested considerably later than the first examples for the clitic status of *-s*), partly because of the possible loan status of such constructions (from Low German).

170. See also Seppänen (1997a) for a fuller account of such genitive relative pronouns.

171. Going a step further back and looking at strictly word-internal morphological processes we may speculate whether the change from stem-based to word-based inflection and derivation from Old English to early Modern English (cf. e.g. Kastovsky 1992: §5.4.7, 1994) constitutes the first step towards a broader scope of morphological processes in English. Note that in Old English *a*-stems (i.e. those nouns which originally had the *-(e)s* genitive ending) tended towards word-based formation (cf. Kastovsky 1992: 398; Kastovsky 1994: 23).

172. Jespersen (1961: 283) notes, however, that expressions such as *father-in-law* or *the Queen of England* were "not felt as inseparable units", quoting Chaucer (*fader thyn in lawe*); also split constructions such as *the kynges sone of Ireland* (Malory) show that the name-unit was probably not yet as close as today. Important for the present argumentation, however, is that there is something inherent in these units which eventually made them to be perceived as a single expression.

173. Note, for example, that the scenario suggested here would go against the general diachronic cline proposed by Givón (1984: 433): quantification → ref-indef → generics.

174. As Plank (1992b: 445) points out this construction is used by some speakers only, a famous one being the German ex-Chancellor Kohl, and he argues that such constructions "ought to be past their prime rather than on the up-and-up" (463).

175. Note that the descriptive meaning of *lovely* still persists. According to Adamson (2000: 54) the "synchronic alternations ... are the residue of a historical process".

176. Depending on the structural analysis of the English *s*-genitive, strictly speaking, two interpretations are possible. It could be either POSS '*s* that fills the Determiner position, or the whole possessor NP. This is basically a theoretical issue. What is important for the present argumentation is that POSS '*s* no longer functions as a genitive case ending but enters into a determiner construction (whatever the details of analysis may be precisely).

177. Alternatively, it could also be argued that Old English was an "adjectival-genitive" (AG) language, in which the possessive pronoun is an adjective and not a determiner as in "determiner-genitive" (DG) languages, according to the classification given in Lyons, C. (1986).

178. Rissanen (1999:206) notes, however, that in religious (i.e. archaic) language such constructions still persisted after the seventeenth century; he gives the following quotation from the Bible: *these thy servants*.

179. Denison (2001: §6.1) discusses the controversial structural analysis for such partitives in Present-day English. (1) On syntactic grounds an NP such as *a group of students* can be analyzed as the head (possessum) group being postmodified by a prepositional phrase *of students*. (2) On semantic grounds, *a group of* functions as a complex determiner to the head noun *students*. Denison (2001) argues that the first analysis is the historically older, later giving also rise to the second one. The Present-day English situation is supposed to reflect the historically transient stage, as apparent when looking which of the nouns is sensitive to Subject-Verb agreement, thereby determining which is to be considered the head of construction. Today, agreement is possible with both *a group* and *students* (*A group of students is/are waiting outside*), though according to Denison the singular variant by now is probably obsolete, pointing to the second analysis which has *students* as a head noun. Of course, this interpretation hinges on the underlying theoretical framework; within a DP-approach, the question of what is the head of construction and the question of S-V agreement may be an entirely different matter.

180. Weerman and de Wit (1999: 1179) suggest that the German postnominal genitive is no longer a genuine case inflection either or at least is on the way out of the language. As evidence they cite German L1 data which show that while the prenominal -*s* is acquired relatively early by children, the postnominal inflectional genitive is absent from child German, even when accusative and dative have been mastered (cf. Clahsen, Eisenbeiß, and Vainikka 1994 and Eisenbeiß 1994). Referring to the phenomenon of *Genitivschwund* they argue that the postnominal genitive even in adult speech is considered to be stylistically marked and archaic.

181. Examples such as *des Königs Krone* ('the king's crown') are considered to be archaic and no longer really productive.

182 Note, however, that Plank (1992a: 42-47) points out some marginal cases where the German genitive can attach to certain phrases, too, i.e. complex

names, both prenominally (GN, as in a) and postnominally (NG, as in b), see the following examples given by Plank (1992a: 45):

(a)   *(August(*-s)*   *Wilhelm(*-s)*   *Schlegel-s*   *Freunde*
        August(*-GEN)   Wilhelm(*-GEN)   Schlegel-GEN   friends
        'August Wilhelm Schlegel's friends'

(b)   *die Freunde August(*-s)*   *Wilhelm(*-s)*   *Schlegel-s*
        the friends August(*-GEN)   Wilhelm(*-GEN)Schlegel-GEN

Plank (1992a: 46) notes, however, that postnominal genitives (d) are somewhat more restrictive in this respect than prenominal genitives (c):

(c)   *König*   *Michael*   *von*   *Rumänien-s*   *Rückkehr*
        king   Michael   of   Rumania-GEN   return
        'king Michael of Rumania's return'

(d) ??   *die*   *Rückkehr*   *König*   *Michael*   *von*   *Rumänien-s*
        the   return   king   Michael   of   Rumania-GEN
        'king Michael of Rumania's return'

Moreover, Plank (1992a: 47) observes that in appositional phrases genitive marking might be omitted in prenominal genitives:

??*Karl*   *d-es*   *Groß-en*   *Söhne*
   Karl   the-GEN   Great-GEN   sons
   'Karl the Great's sons'

All this indicates that German might be on the way of developing a phrasal genitive as well, or, to put it more cautiously, at least becomes less hesitant to treat complex names, and in particular appositive constructions, as one lexical unit. Note that in English this probably was the first step towards POSS '*s* as a phrase marker, too (cf. §7.5.2.4.1).

183. If OT constraints get defined in terms of cognitive constraints imposed on language users, as recently called for by Haspelmath (1999b) and already exercised in Hayes (1999) or in Functional OT (e.g. Bresnan and Aissen 2002), "optimality" within OT would also be defined in terms of economy in the second sense, i.e. cognitive economy (see also §5.1.1.2).

184. Such an economy principle is, for example, assumed in Relevance Theory (Sperber and Wilson 1986), Fodor's (1983) modularity hypothesis and Chomsky's (1995) Minimalist Program to name just a few.

185. See also Krug (1998) for providing empirical evidence for the impact of frequency in syntagmatic coalescence.

186. Very close in spirit to Hawkins' (1994) approach is Rohdenburg (1996), who also proposes that processing complexity affects the choice of competing constructions. Unlike Hawkins (1994), however, Rohdenburg is more open in allowing further factors, such as semantic, phonological and stylistic to interact with the complexity principle.

187. It is not clear whether Hawkins' (1994) commitment towards a hearer-based approach has primarily methodological reasons or whether he wants to maintain that optimal communication is biased towards the hearer rather than

the speaker (cf. e.g. Siewierska 1996: 374 for expressing such a view). Note that speech production is much less well-understood than speech perception (parsing), and that, for reasons already discussed in §6.4.1.2, an investigation of the processes underlying production poses much more difficulty for the researcher.

188. Note that 'shortness' is to be understood as a relative and not as an absolute term here. Strictly speaking, the economical principle for the speaker is 'as short as possible and as long as necessary to achieve the communicative intention'; cf. also Ronneberger-Sibold (1980: §3.3) for making a similar point.

189. See also Haspelmath (1999a, 1999c) for applying Keller's (1994) invisible-hand account to grammaticalization processes.

190. Haspelmath (1999b: 192) refers to Itkonen's (1983: 185ff.) concept of "unconscious rationality" to regard these speakers' choices as intentional, although they certainly operate automatically on an unconscious level.

191. See e.g. Berg (1998: 284) for assuming that processing principles are to a very large extent diachronically stable.

192. Note that in contrast to the preference structure in §7.4.5, in the following unified preference structure no distinction is made between highly and less highly topical possessors; these are, for reasons of comparison with the ModE data, both subsumed here under [+topical].

193. We may ask, of course, whether such diverse types of data can be legitimately compared at all? I do think so, in this case. Since we already know from empirical corpus studies that the factors animacy, topicality, and possessive relation influence the choice of genitive construction in Present-day English, for the present purpose it was not that important to identify these factors but to scope out the potential of the *s*-genitive (as opposed to the *of*-genitive) for which a controlled experimental design is the optimal tool for the Present-day English situation. As far as the historical situation is concerned, a corpus-driven approach is naturally the only feasible approach. Moreover, comparing EModE with ModE corpus data is not unproblematic either. Note, for example, that the text types most prone to show the *s*-genitives with inanimate possessors today are newspaper and fiction. While newspapers themselves are a new text type not present yet in early Modern English, fiction today certainly exhibits so many features different from fiction, or rather narratives, in early Modern English, that on these grounds a direct comparison of textual data appears to be at least as problematic. I would rather claim that, on the contrary, the very fact that two such different types of empirical data yield essentially the same preference structure and the same direction of diachronic extension (within the EModE corpus data and within the apparent-time approach taken in the ModE data) strengthen in fact the overall result of this study.

194. Haiman's (1994a) notion of "ritualization" does also capture this process. He even explicitly refers to automatization "as the result of repetition" (Haiman 1994a: 10).

195. But see §3.3.2.1.2 for contexts in which periphrastic constructions such as *of it* can be used.

196. There is currently quite a controversy over the question whether the framework of grammaticalization should be given the status of a theory and whether it is an independent process or rather derivative of general mechanisms of change. For particularly critical assessments see Newmeyer (1998: chapter 5) and Campbell (2001).

197. Note that I am referring here to a specific type of automatization, which can be interpreted both synchronically and diachronically. Synchronically, according to the psychological notion of "automatic processing" given in §8.1, it means that a construction is used automatically (i.e. subconsciously), without drawing on working memory resources. Diachronically, it defines the process by which, given two structural alternatives, optionality decreases, and one variant eventually wins, i.e. becomes the only choice left (in this case: the *s*-genitive). In terms of the parameters for grammaticalization as given by Lehmann ([1982] 1995: chapter 4) this corresponds roughly with decrease in paradigmatic variability, and in this sense also the notion of "obligatoriness" as proposed by Lehmann (1995: §4.2.3) is similar to the notion of obligatoriness as used here. Note, however, that routinization as a process does not necessarily have to imply obligatoriness in this paradigmatic sense; considering, for example, the development of idioms there is still paradigmatic variability (e.g. *in fact* versus *in matter of fact*), although routinization (on the syntagmatic axis) certainly occurred. I am grateful to Elizabeth Traugott for drawing my attention to this.

198. It is still controversial what the logical relation between formal and semantic changes is, i.e. whether semantic change follows from formal change, or whether formal change is triggered by semantic change (cf. also Fischer and Rosenbach 2000).

199. As recently argued, however, by Tabor and Traugott (1998), Lehmann's (1995) notion of structural scope is not well enough defined, suggesting instead a "C-command Scope Increase Hypothesis", showing that grammaticalization typically involves an increase rather than a decrease in scope, which again makes the development of POSS '*s* fully conform to the unidirectionality claims of grammaticalization theory, at least as far as the criterion of structural scope is concerned.

200. It may depend, however, precisely how identity in form is defined. If morphosyntactic properties are to be included here, then there is certainly a change in formal substance within POSS '*s*, i.e. from inflection to clitic and determiner.

201. Note that, strictly speaking, we would not really expect a form/construction to become completely reduced to zero and get lost completely when beginning a new cycle (cf. also Traugott 1999: 241).

202. Both Janda (2001) and Lass (2000) do, however, acknowledge unidirectionality as a striking phenomenon to be accounted for, though their accounts differ considerably. While Janda (2001) in his speaker-based approach uses sociolinguistic considerations to account for unidirectionality in spite of the discontinuous transmission of language, Lass (2000), viewing language as an abstract system just as other systems, refers to general physico-mathematical laws such as positive feedback

203. And see also Rosenbach, Stein, and Vezzosi (2000: 198) for suggesting that the *s*-genitive may have undergone subjectification.
204. Note, however, that Heine (1997: 155) seems to suggest that in general the development is rather the other way round, i.e. towards the classifier construction. For the English *s*-genitive this remains an empirical question, yet to be looked at in more detail.

Bibliography

Texts

Cornwell, Patricia
    1994   *The Body Farm*. London: Warner Books (paperback edition).
Doyle, Roddy
    1999   *A Star Called Henry*. London: Jonathan Cape.
George, Elizabeth
    1994   *Playing for the Ashes*. London: Bantam Books (paperback edition).
    1994   *Missing Joseph*. London: Bantam Books (paperback edition).
    1996   *In the Presence of the Enemy*. Bantam Books (paperback edition).
Pinker, Steven and Paul Bloom
    1990   Natural language and natural selection. *Behavioral and Brain Sciences* 13: 707-727.
Pratchett, Terry
    1983   *The Colour of Magic*. Reading, Berkhsire: Cox & Wyman (reprinted paperback edition 1996).
Swift, Graham
    1984   *Waterland*. London: Macmillan (revised Picador edition, 1992).

References

Adamson, Sylvia
    2000   A lovely little example – word order options and category shift in the premodifying string. In: Olga Fischer, Anette Rosenbach, and Dieter Stein (eds.). *Pathways of Change. Grammaticalization in English* (Studies in Language Companion Series 53), 39-66. Amsterdam/ Philadelphia: John Benjamins.
Allan, Keith
    1987   Hierarchies and the choice of left conjuncts (with particular attention to English). *Journal of Linguistics* 23: 51-77.
Allen, Cynthia
    1997a   The origins of the 'group genitive' in English. *Transactions of the Philological Society* 95: 111-131.
    1997b   Middle English case loss and the 'creolization' hypothesis. *English Language and Linguistics* 1: 63-89.
    1998   Genitives and the creolization question. *English Language and Linguistics* 2: 129-134.

Altenberg, Bengt
  1980   Binominal NP's in a thematic perspective: Genitive vs. of-construction in 17th century English: In: Sven Jacobson (ed.). *Papers from the Scandinavian Symposium on Syntactic Variation, Stockholm, May 18-19, 1979, 149-172*. Stockholm: Almqvist & Wiksell.
  1982   *The Genitive v. the Of-Construction. A Study of Syntactic Variation in 17th Century English*. Malmö: CWK Gleerup.
Andersen, Henning
  1973   Abductive and deductive change. *Language* 49: 765-793.
Anttila, Arto
  1997   Deriving variation from grammar. In: Frans Hinskens, Roeland van Hout, and Leo Wetzels (eds.). *Variation, Change, and Phonological Theory*, 35-68. Amsterdam/Philadelphia: John Benjamins.
Anttila, Arto and Young-mee Yu Cho
  1998   Variation and change in Optimality Theory. *Lingua* 104: 31-56.
Anschutz, Arlea
  1997   How to choose a possessive noun phrase construction in four easy steps. *Studies in Language* 21 (1): 1-35.
Arnold, Jennifer E., Thomas Wasow, Anthony Losongco, and Ryan Ginstrom
  2000   Heaviness vs. newness: The effects of structural complexity and discourse status on constituent ordering. *Language* 76 (1): 28-55.
Barber, Charles
  1964   *Linguistic Change in Present-day English*. Edinburgh: Oliver and Boyd.
Bates, Elizabeth and Brian MacWhinney
  1982   Functionalist approaches to grammar. In: Eric Wanner and Lila R. Gleitman (eds.). *Language Acquisition: The State of the Art*, 173-218. Cambridge: Cambridge University Press.
Bauer, Laurie
  1988   *Introducing Linguistic Morphology*. Edinburgh: Edinburgh University Press (corrected 1992, reprinted 1994).
  1998   When is a sequence of two nouns a compound in English? *English Language and Linguistics* 2 (1): 87-119.
Behaghel, Otto
  1932   *Deutsche Syntax: Eine geschichtliche Darstellung, Vol. IV, Wortstellung. Periodenbau*. Heidelberg: Carl Winters Universitätsbuchhandlung.
Bell, Allan
  1984   Language style as audience design. *Language in Society* 13: 145-204.
Berg, Thomas
  1998   *Linguistic Structure and Change*. Oxford: Clarendon Press.

Bergs, Alexander T. and Dieter Stein
   2001   The role of markedness in the actuation and actualization of linguistic change. In: Henning Andersen (ed.). *Actualization: Linguistic Change in Progress*, 79-94. Amsterdam/Philadelphia: John Benjamins.
Biber, Douglas and Edward Finegan
   1989   Drift and the evolution of English style: A history of three genres. *Language* 65: 487-517.
Biber, Douglas, Stig Johansson, Geoffrey Leech, Susan Conrad, and Edward Finegan
   1999   *Longman Grammar of Spoken and Written English*. London/New York: Longman.
Blake, Barry J.
   1977   *Case Marking in Australian Languages*. Canberra: Australian Institute of Aboriginal Studies.
Bock, J. Kathryn
   1982   Toward a cognitive psychology of syntax: Information processing contributions to sentence formulation. *Psychological Review* 89: 1-47.
   1986   Syntactic persistence in language production. *Cognitive Psychology* 18: 355-387.
   1987a   An effect of the accessibility of word forms on sentence structures. *Journal of Memory and Language* 26: 119-137.
   1987b   Coordinating words and syntax in speech plans. In: Andrew W. Ellis (ed.). *Progress in the Psychology of Language*, 337-390. London: Erlbaum.
   1991   A sketchbook of production problems. *Journal of Psycholinguistic Research* 20 (3): 141-160.
   1996   Language production: Methods and methodologies. *Psychonomic Bulletin & Review* 3 (4): 395-421.
Bock, J. Kathryn and David E. Irwin
   1980   Syntactic effects of information availability in sentence production. *Journal of Verbal Learning and Verbal Behavior* 19: 467-484.
Bock, J. Kathryn and Willem Levelt
   1994   Language production: Grammatical encoding. In: Morton Ann Gernsbacher (ed.). *Handbook of Psycholinguistics*, 945-984. San Diego: Academic Press.
Bock, J. Kathryn and Helga Loebell
   1990   Framing sentences. *Cognition* 35: 1-39.
Bock, J. Kathryn and Richard K. Warren
   1985   Conceptual accessibility and syntactic structure in sentence formulation. *Cognition* 21: 47-67.

Boersma, Paul
  1997   How we learn variation, optionality, and probability. *Proceedings of the Institute of Phonetic Sciences* 21: 43-58. University of Amsterdam. (also available on-line: http://ruccs.rutgers.edu/roa.html.)
  1998   Functional phonology. Formalizing the interaction between articulatory and perceptual drives. Amsterdam: University of Amsterdam Ph.D thesis.
Boersma, Paul and Bruce Hayes
  2001   Empirical tests of the gradual learning algorithm. *Linguistic Inquiry* 32: 45-86.
Bolinger, Dwight
  1967   Adjectives in English: Attribution and predication. *Lingua* 18: 1-34.
  1977   *Meaning and Form.* 3rd impression 1983. London/New York: Longman.
Botha, Rudolf P.
  1992   *Twentieth Century Conceptions of Language.* Oxford: Blackwell.
Bowerman, Melissa and Stephen Levinson (eds.)
  2001   *Language Acquisition and Conceptual Development* (Language, Culture and Cognition 3). Cambridge: Cambridge University Press.
Breejen, Bastiaan den
  1937   The Genitive Case and its 'Of'-Equivalent in the Latter Half of the 16th Century. Amsterdam dissertation.
Bresnan, Joan
  2001   Typology in variation: A Stochastic Optimality Theoretic approach to person/voice interactions in English and Lummi (Straits Salish). Paper presented at The Lexicon in Linguistic Theory, 22-23 August 2001, University of Duesseldorf.
Bresnan, Joan and Judith Aissen
  2001   Optimality and functionality: Objections and refutations. *Natural Language and Linguistic Theory* 20 (1): 81-95.
Bresnan, Joan, Shipra Dingare, and Christopher Manning
  forthc. Soft constraints mirror hard constraints: Voice and person in English and Lummi. In: Miriam Butt and Tracy H. King (eds.). *Proceedings of the LFG 01 Conference*, University of Hong Kong, on-line proceedings. Stanford: CSLI Publicatons (http://csli-publications.stanford.edu/).
Bresnan, Joan and Ashwini Deo
  2001   Grammatical constraints on variation: 'Be' in the Survey of English Dialects and (Stochastic) Optimality Theory. Draft of May 7, 2001 (http://www-lfg.stanford.edu/bresnan/download.html).
Briscoe, Ted
  2000a   Grammatical acquisition: Inductive bias and coevolution of language and the language acquisition device. *Language* 76: 245-296.

2000b   Evolutionary perspectives on diachronic syntax. In: Susan Pintzuk, George Tsoulas, and Anthony Warner (eds.). *Diachronic Syntax. Models and Mechanisms*, 75-105. Oxford: Oxford University Press.

Brown, Gillian
1995   *Speakers, Listeners and Communication*. Cambridge: Cambridge University Press.

Brown, William H., Jr.
1970   *A Syntax of King Alfred's Pastoral Care*. The Hague: Mouton.

Brunner, Karl
1962   *Die englische Sprache. Ihre geschichtliche Entwicklung*, vol. 2. 2nd revised edition 1984. Tübingen: Niemeyer.

Butterworth, Brian
1980   Introduction: A brief review of methods of studying language production. In: Brian Butterworth (ed.). *Language Production*: Volume 1, 1-17. London: Academic Press.

Cameron, Deborah
1997   *Demythologizing sociolinguistics*. In: Nikolas Coupland and Adam Jaworski (eds.). *Sociolinguistics*, 55-67. Houndsmill: Macmillan.

Campbell, Lyle
2001   What's wrong with grammaticalization? Language Sciences 23 (2-3): 113-161.

Carstairs, Andrew
1987   Diachronic evidence and the affix-clitic distinction. In: Anna G. Ramat, Onofrio Carruby, and Giuliano Bernini (eds.). *Papers from the 7th International Conference on Historical Linguistics*, 151-162. Amsterdam/Philadelphia: John Benjamins.

Chafe, Wallace
1976   Givenness, contrastiveness, definiteness, subjects, topics and point of view. In: Charles N. Li. (ed.). *Subject and Topic*, 25-56, New York: Academic Press.
1987   Cognitive constraints on information flow. In: Russell Tomlin (ed.). *Coherence and Grounding in Discourse*, 21-52, Amsterdam/Philadelphia: John Benjamins.

Chapell, Hilary and William McGregor
1996   Prolegomena to a theory of inalienability. In: Hilary Chapell and William McGregor (eds.). *The Grammar of Inalienability. A Typological Perspective on Body Part Terms and the Part-Whole Relation*, 3-30. Berlin/New York: Mouton de Gruyter.

Cheshire, Jenny
1987   Syntactic variation, the linguistic variable, and sociolinguistic theory. *Linguistics* 25: 257-282.

Cho, Young-mee Yu
1998   Language change as reranking of constraints. In: Richard M. Hogg

and Linda van den Bergen (eds.). *Historical Linguistics*. Vol. 2: *Germanic Linguistics*, 45-62, Amsterdam/Philadelphia: John Benjamins.

Chomsky, Noam
1965 *Aspects of the Theory of Syntax*. Cambridge, Mass.: MIT Press.
1970 Remarks on nominalization. In: Roderick A. Jacobs and Peter S. Rosenbaum (eds.). *Readings in English Transformational Grammar*, 184-221. Waltham, Mass.: Ginn.
1980 *Rules and Representations*. New York: Columbia Press.
1995 *The Minimalist Program*. Cambridge, Mass.: MIT Press.

Christophersen, Paul
1939 *The Articles. A Study of their Theory and Use in English*. Copenhagen: Munksgaard.

Clahsen, Harald, Sonja Eisenbeiß, and Anne Vainikka
1994 The seeds of structure. In: Teun Hoekstra and Bonnie Schwartz (eds.). *Language Acquisition Studies in Generative Grammar*, 85-118. Amsterdam/Philadelphia: John Benjamins.

Clark, Herbert H. and Catherine R. Marshall
1981 Definite reference and mutual knowledge. In: Aravind K. Joshi, Bonnie L. Webber, and Ivan Sag (eds.). *Elements of Discourse Understanding*, 10-64. Cambridge: Cambridge University Press.

Comrie, Bernard
1989 *Language Universals and Linguistic Typology*. 2nd edition. Oxford: Blackwell.

Coombs, Clyde, Robyn Dawes, and Amos Tversky
1970 *Mathematical Psychology: An Elementary Introduction*. Englewood Cliffs, New Jersey: Prentice Hall.

Cooper, William E. and Gayle V. Klouda
1995 The psychological basis of syntactic iconicity. In: Marge E. Landsberg (ed.). *Syntactic Iconicity and Linguistic Freezes. The Human Dimension*, 331-341. Berlin/New York: Mouton de Gruyter.

Cooper, William E. and John Robert Ross
1975 World order. In: Robin Grossman, L. James San, and Timothy J. Vance (eds.). *Papers from the Parasession on Functionalism*, 63-111. Chicago: Chicago Linguistic Society.

Copperud, Roy H.
1980 *American Usage and Style: The Consensus*. New York/London: Van Nostrand Reinhold.

Corbett, Greville G.
2000 *Number*. Cambridge: Cambridge University Press.

Cowie, Claire
1995 Grammaticalization and the snowball effect. *Language & Communication* 15 (2): 181-193.

Croft, William
    1990   *Typology and Universals.* Cambridge: Cambridge University Press.
    1999   Adaptation, optimality and diachrony. *Zeitschrift für Sprachwissenschaft* 18 (2): 206-208.
    2000   *Explaining Language Change.* London/New York: Longman.
Dabrowska, Ewa
    1998   How metaphors affect grammatical coding: The Saxon genitive in computer manuals. *English Language and Linguistics* 2 (1): 121-127.
Dahl, Liisa
    1971   The *s*-genitive with non-personal nouns in modern English journalistic style. *Neuphilologische Mitteilungen* 72: 140-172.
Dahl, Östen
    1999   Does adaptation really helps us to explain language change? *Zeitschrift für Sprachwissenschaft* 18 (2): 209-211.
Dahl, Östen and Kari Fraurud
    1996   Animacy in grammar and discourse. In: Thorstein Fretheim and Jeanette K. Gundel (eds.). *Reference and Referent Accessibility,* 47-64, Amsterdam/Philadelphia: John Benjamins.
Dawkins, Richard
    1986   *The Blind Watchmaker.* Harmondsworth: Penguin (reissued paperback edition 2000).
Deacon, Terrence W.
    2000   The primacy of symbolic reference. Lecture given at the Nijmwegen Lectures Beneath linguistics: language as a complex coevolutionary phenomenon, December 18-20, 2000.
Deane, Paul Douglas
    1987   English possessives, topicality, and the Silverstein hierarchy. *Proceedings of the Annual Meeting of the Berkeley Linguistics Society* 13: 65-76.
    1992   *Grammar in Mind and Brain: Explorations in Cognitive Syntax.* Berlin/New York: Mouton de Gruyter.
Dell, Gary S.
    1986   A spreading-activation theory of retrieval in sentence production. *Psychological Review* 93: 283-321.
Demske, Ulrike
    2001   *Merkmale und Relationen. Diachrone Studien zur Nominalphrase des Deutschen.* Berlin/New York: Mouton de Gruyter.
Denison, David
    1998   Syntax. In: Suzanne Romaine (ed.). *The Cambridge History of the English Language,* vol. IV, 1776-1997, 92-329. Cambridge: Cambridge University Press.
    2001   Gradience and linguistic change. In: Laurel Brinton (ed.). *Historical*

Linguistics 1999: Selected Papers from the 14th International Conference on Historical Linguistics, Vancouver, 9-13 August 1999, 119-144. Amsterdam/Philadelphia: John Benjamins.

Deutscher, Guy

1999   The different faces of uniformitarianism. Paper given at the XIVth International Conference on Historical Linguistics, August 1999, Vancouver.

2000   Stability against the odds? The survival of verb final order in Akkadian. In: Rosanna Sornicola, Erich Poppe, and Ariel Shisha-Halevy (eds.), 55-69.

de Wit, Petra

1997   *Genitive Case and Genitive Constructions.* Utrecht: UiL OTS Dissertation Series.

Dietrich, Rainer and Kathy Y. van Nice

forthc.   What production data can tell us about a theory of word order. In: Holden Härtl, Susan Olsen, and Heike Tappe (eds.). *The Syntax-Semantics-Interface: Linguistic Structures and Processes* (Trends in Linguistics). Berlin/New York: Mouton de Gruyter.

Dorgeloh, Heidrun

1997   *Inversion in Modern English. Form and Function.* Amsterdam/ Philadelphia: John Benjamins.

2000   Between story and history: Narrativisation in three English genres. In: Alexander Bergs and Dieter Stein (eds.). *LANA – Düsseldorf Working Papers on Linguistics* 2: 1-15 (http://ang3-11.phil-fak.uni.duesseldorf.de/~ang3/LANA/LANA.html).

Dotter, Franz

1990   *Nichtarbitrarität und Ikonizität in der Syntax.* Hamburg: Helmut Buske.

Doyle, Aidan and Bogdan Szymanek

1997   Inalienable possession in English, Irish and Polish morphology. In: Raymond Hickey and Stanislaw Puppel (eds.). *Language History and Linguistic Modelling. A Festschrift for Jacek Fisiak on his 60th Birthday*, vol. II: *Linguistic Modelling*, 1379-1397, Berlin/New York: Mouton de Gruyter.

Dressler, Wolfgang U., Willi Mayerthaler, Oswald Panagl, and Wolfgang U. Wurzel

1987   *Leitmotifs in Natural Morphology.* Amsterdam/Philadelphia: John Benjamins.

DuBois, John W.

1985   Competing motivations. In: John Haiman (ed.), 343-366.

Eisenbeiß, Sonja

1994   Kasus und Wortstellungsvariation im deutschen Mittelfeld. Theoretische Überlegungen und Untersuchungen zum

Erstspracherwerb. In: Brigitta Haftka (ed.). *Was determiniert Wortstellungsvariationen?*, 277-298. Opladen: Westdeutscher Verlag.

Erteschik-Shir, Nomi
1979   Discourse constraints on dative movement. In: Talmy Givón (ed.). *Discourse and Syntax* (Syntax and Semantics, 12), 441-467. New York: Academic Press.

Faiß, Klaus
1989   *Englische Sprachgeschichte.* Tübingen: Francke.

Farah, Martha J., Michael M. Meyer, and Patricia A. McMullen
1996   The living/nonliving dissociation is not an artifact: Giving an a priori implausible hypothesis a strong test. *Cognitive Neuropsychology* 13 (1): 137-154.

Fenk-Oczlon, Gertraud
1983   Ist die SVO-Wortfolge die 'natürlichste'? *Papiere zur Linguistik* 29: 23-32.
1989   Word frequency and word order in freezes. *Linguistics* 27: 517-556.

Ferreira, Fernanda
1994   Choice of passive voice is affected by verb type and animacy. *Journal of Memory and Language* 33: 715-736.

Fillmore, Charles J.
1968   The case for case. In: Emmon Bach and Robert T. Harms (eds.). *Universals in Linguistic Theory*, 1-88. New York: Holt, Rinehart and Winston.

Firbas, Jan
1964   On defining the theme in functional sentence analysis. *Travaux Linguistiques de Prague* 2: 267-280.
1992   *Functional Sentence Perspective in Written and Spoken Communication.* Cambridge: Cambridge University Press.

Fischer, Olga
1992   Syntax. In: Norman Blake (ed.) *The Cambridge History of the English Language*, vol. II, *1066-1476*, 207-408. Cambridge: Cambridge University Press.

Fischer, Olga and Max Nänny
1999   Introduction. In: Max Nänny and Olga Fischer (eds.). *Form Miming Meaning. Iconicity in Language and Literature*, xv-xxxvi. Amsterdam/Philadelphia: John Benjamins.

Fischer, Olga and Anette Rosenbach
2000   Introduction. In: Olga Fischer, Anette Rosenbach, and Dieter Stein (eds.). *Pathways of Change. Grammaticalization in English* (Studies in Language Companion Series 53), 1-37. Amsterdam/Philadelphia: John Benjamins.

Fodor, Jerry A.
    1983   *The Modularity of Mind.* Cambridge, Mass.: MIT Press.
Fraurud, Kari
    1990   Definiteness and the processing of noun phrases in natural discourse.
                Journal of Semantics 7: 395-433.
    1996   Cognitive ontology and NP form. In: Thorstein Fretheim and
                Jeanette K. Gundel (eds.). *Reference and Referent Accessibility*, 65-
                87. Amsterdam/Philadelphia: John Benjamins.
van der Gaaf, W.
    1932   The absolute genitive. *English Studies* 14: 49-65.
Garrett, Merrill
    1992   Disorders of lexical selection. In: Willem J. M. Levelt (ed.). *Lexical
                Access in Speech Production*, 143-180. Oxford: Blackwell.
Gass, Susan
    1979   Language transfer and universal grammatical relation. *Language
                Learning* 29 (2): 327-344.
Givón, Talmy
    1979   *On Understanding Grammar.* New York: Academic Press.
    1983 (ed.) *Topic Continuity in Discourse.* Amsterdam/Philadelphia: John
                Benjamins.
    1984   *Syntax. A Functional-Typological Introduction.* Volume I.
                Amsterdam/Philadelphia: John Benjamins.
    1988   The pragmatics of word order: Predictability, importance and
                attention. In: Michael Hammond, Edith Moravcsik, and Jessica
                Wirth (eds.). *Studies in Syntactic Typology*, 243-284.
                Amsterdam/Philadelphia: John Benjamins.
    1995   *Functionalism and Grammar.* Amsterdam/Philadelphia: John
                Benjamins.
Gnanadesikan, Amalia E.
    forthc.   Markedness and faithfulness constraints in child phonology. In: René
                Kager, Joe Pater, and Wim Zonneveld (eds.). *Fixing Priorities:
                Constraints in Phonological Acquisition.* Cambridge: Cambridge
                University Press.
Golston, Chris
    1995   Syntax outranks phonology: Evidence from Ancient Greek.
                Phonology 12: 1-26.
Görlach, Manfred
    1993   *Introduction to Early Modern English.* Cambridge: Cambridge
                University Press.
Graband, Gerhard
    1965   *Die Entwicklung der frühneuenglischen Nominalflexion.* Tübingen:
                Niemeyer.

Green, Anthony Dubach
  1997   The Prosodic Structure of Irish, Scots Gaelix, and Manx. Doctoral
          dissertation, Ithaka, NY: Cornell University, CLC Publications.
Greenbaum, Sidney and Randolph Quirk
  1970   *Elicitation Experiments in English. Linguistic Studies in Use and
          Attitude.* London/New York: Longman.
Greenberg, Joseph H.
  1963   Some universals of grammar with particular reference to the order of
          meaningful elements. In: Joseph Greenberg (ed.). *Universals of
          Language,* 73-113. Cambridge, Mass.: MIT Press.
  1966   *Language Universals.* The Hague: Mouton.
Gumperz, John F. and Stephen C. Levinson (eds.).
  1996   *Rethinking Linguistic Relativity.* Cambridge: Cambridge University
          Press.
Gundel, Jeanette K.
  1988   Universals of topic-comment structure. In: Michael Hammond, Edith
          Moravcsik, and Jessica Wirth (eds.). *Studies in Syntactic Typology,*
          209-239. Amsterdam/Philadelphia: John Benjamins.
Gundel, Jeanette K., Nancy Hedberg, and Ron Zacharski
  1993   Cognitive status and the form of referring expressions in discourse.
          Language 69: 274-307.
Gundel, Jeanette K., Kathleen Houlihan, and Gerald Sanders
  1988   On the function of marked and unmarked terms. In: Michael
          Hammond, Edith Moravcsik, and Jessica Wirth (eds.). *Studies in
          Syntactic Typology,* 285-301. Amsterdam/Philadelphia: John
          Benjamins.
Guy, Gregory R.
  1997a   Violable is variable: Optimality Theory and linguistic variation.
          Language Variation and Change 9: 333-347.
  1997b   Competence, performance, and the generative grammar of variation.
          In: Frans Hinskens, Roeland van Hout, and Leo Wetzels (eds.).
          Variation, Change, and Phonological Theory, 125-143.
          Amsterdam/Philadelphia: John Benjamins.
Hagège, Claude
  1993   *The Language Builder* (Current Issues in Linguistic Theory, 94).
          Amsterdam/Philadelphia: John Benjamins.
Hagoort, Peter
  1998   The shadows of lexical meaning in patients with semantic
          impairments. In: Brigitte Stemmer and Harry A. Whitaker (eds.).
          Handbook of Neurolinguistics, 235-248. San Diego/London:
          Academic Press.
Haiman, John
  1983   Iconic and economic motivation. *Language* 59: 781-819.

1985a   *Natural Syntax. Iconicity and Erosion*. Cambridge: Cambridge University Press.

1985b   *Iconicity in Syntax*. Amsterdam/Philadelphia: John Benjamins.
(ed.)

1994a   Ritualization and the development of language. In: William Pagliuca (ed.). *Perspectives on Grammaticalization*, 3-28. Amsterdam/ Philadelphia: John Benjamins.

1994b   Iconicity. In: R. E. Asher and J. M. Y. Simpson (eds.). *The Encyclopedia of Language and Linguistics*, 1629-1637. Oxford: Pergamon.

Halliday, Michael K. A.

1967   Notes on transitivity and theme in English. *Journal of Linguistics* 3: 199-244.

1970   Language structure and language function. In: John Lyons (ed.). *New Horizons in Linguistics*, 140-165. Harmondsworth/ Baltimore/ Ringwood: Penguin Books.

Harris, Alice C. and Lyle Campbell

1995   *Historical Syntax in Cross-Linguistic Perspective*. Cambridge: Cambridge University Press.

Haspelmath, Martin

1999a   Explaining article-possessor complementarity: Economic motivation in noun phrase syntax. *Language* 75 (2): 227-243.

1999b   Optimality and diachronic adaptation. *Zeitschrift für Sprachwissenschaft* 18 (2): 180-205.

1999c   Why is grammaticalization irreversible? *Linguistics* 37: 1043-1068.

2000   Why can't we talk to each other? *Lingua* 110: 235-255.

Hawkins, John A.

1978   *Definiteness and Indefiniteness: A Study in Reference and Grammaticality Prediction*. London: Croom Helm.

1983   *Word Order Universals*. New York: Academic Press.

1994   *A Performance Theory of Order and Constituency*. Cambridge: Cambridge University Press.

Hawkins, Roger

1981   Towards an account of the possessive constructions: NP's N and the N of NP. *Journal of Linguistics* 17: 179-392.

Hayes, Bruce

1999   Phonetically driven phonology: The role of Optimality Theory and inductive grounding. In: Michael Darnell, Edith Moravcsik, Michael Noonan, Frederick Newmeyer, and Kathleen Wheatly (eds.). *Functionalism and Formalism. in Linguistics*, vol.1: *General Papers*, 243-285. Amsterdam/Philadelphia: John Benjamins.

Heine, Bernd

1997   *Possession. Cognitive Sources, Forces and Grammaticalization*.

Cambridge: Cambridge University Press.

2002   On the role of context in grammaticalization. In: Ilse Wischer and Gabriele Diewald (eds.). *New Reflections on Grammaticalization* (Typological Studies in Language 49), 83-101. Amsterdam/ Philadelphia: John Benjamins.

Heine, Bernd and Tania Kuteva
2001   Attributive possession in Creoles. Manuscript, Universities of Cologne and Duesseldorf.

Hiraga, Masako K.
1994   Diagrams and metaphors: Iconic aspects in language. *Journal of Pragmatics* 22: 5-21.

Hopper, Paul
1991   On some principles in grammaticalization. In: Elizabeth C. Traugott and Bernd Heine (eds.). *Approaches to Grammaticalization*, vol. 1, 17-35. Amsterdam/Philadelphia: John Benjamins.

Hopper, Paul J. and Sandra A. Thompson
1980   Transitivity in grammar and discourse. *Language* 56 (2): 251-299.

Hopper, Paul and Elizabeth C. Traugott
1993   *Grammaticalization*. Cambridge: Cambridge University Press.

van Hout, Roeland
1984   The need for a theory of choice in sociolinguistics, *Linguistische Berichte* 90: 39-57.

Huddleston, Rodney
1984   *Introduction to the Grammar of English*. Cambridge: Cambridge University Press.

Hundt, Marianne
1997   Has BrE been catching up with AmE over the past thirty years? In: Magnus Ljung (ed.). *Corpus-based Studies in English: Papers from the 17th International Conference on English Language Research on Computerized Corpora (ICAME 17), Stockholm, May 15-19, 1996,* 135-151. Amsterdam/Atlanta: Rodopi.

1998   *New Zealand English Grammar. Fact or Fiction. A Corpus-Based Study in Morphosyntactic Variation.* Amsterdam/Philadelphia: John Benjamins.

Hurch, Bernhard
1998   Optimalität und Natürlichkeit. *ZAS Papers in Linguistics* 13: 115-130.

Itkonen, Esa
1983   *Causality in Linguistic Theory: A Critical Investigation into the Philosophical and Methodological Foundations of 'Non-Autonomous' Linguistics.* London: Croom Helm.

1999   Functionalism yes, biologism no. *Zeitschrift für Sprachwissenschaft* 18 (2): 219-221.

Jacobson, Sven
 1980   Issues in the study of syntactic variation. In: Sven Jacobson (ed.).
          Papers from the Scandinavian Symposium on Syntactic Variation,
          Stockholm, May 18-19, 1979, 23-36. Stockholm: Almqvist &
          Wiksell.
Jahr Sorheim, Mette-Catherine
 1980   The s-genitive in Present-day English. Thesis, Department of
          English, University of Oslo.
Jakobson, Roman
 1971   Kindersprache, Aphasie und allgemeine Lautgesetze. In: *Selected*
          Writings I, 328-401. The Hague: Mouton [1941].
Janda, Richard D.
 1980   On the decline of declensional systems: The overall loss of OE
          nominal case inflections and the ME reanalysis of -es as his. In:
          Elizabeth C. Traugott, Rebecca Labrum, and Susan Shepherd (eds.).
          Papers from the 4th International Conference on Historical
          Linguistics, 243-253. Amsterdam/Philadelphia: John Benjamins.
 2001   Beyond 'pathways' and 'unidirectionality': On the discontinuity of
          language transmission and the counterability of grammaticalization.
          Language Sciences 23 (2-3): 265-340.
Jespersen, Otto
 1960   Chapters on English, reprinted in *Selected Writings of Otto*
          Jespersen, 153-345. London: Allen & Unwin [1918].
 1961   *A Modern English Grammar on Historical Principles.* Part VII:
          Syntax. London: Allen & Unwin [1949].
Johnson, David and Shalom Lappin
 1997   A critique of the minimalist program. *Linguistics and Philosophy* 20:
          273-333.
Jucker, Andreas
 1993   The genitive versus the of-construction in newspaper language. In:
          Andreas Jucker (ed.). *The Noun Phrase in English. Its Structure and*
          Variability, 121-136. Heidelberg: Carl Winter.
Kager, René
 1999   *Optimality Theory.* Cambridge: Cambridge University Press.
Kastovsky, Dieter
 1992   Semantics and vocabulary. In: Richard Hogg (ed.) *The Cambridge*
          History of the English Language, vol. I, *The Beginnings–1066,* 290-
          408. Cambridge: Cambridge University Press.
 1994   Historical English word-formation. From a monostratal to a
          polystratal system. In: Rolando Bacchielli (ed.). *Historical English*
          Word-Formation. Papers read at the Sixth National Conference of
          the History of English, University of Urbino, 24th and 25th
          September 1993, 17-31. Urbino: QuattroVenti.

Katamba, Francis
  1993   *Morphology*. London: Macmillan.
Keenan, Edward L. and Bernard Comrie
  1977   Noun phrase accessibility and universal grammar. *Linguistic Inquiry* 8: 63-99.
Keller, Rudi
  1994   *On Language Change. The Invisible Hand in Language*. London: Routledge.
Kempson, Ruth
  1977   *Semantic Theory*. Cambridge: Cambridge University Press.
Kiparsky, Paul
  1968   Linguistic universals and linguistic change. In: Emmon Bach and Robert T. Harms (eds.). *Universals in Linguistic Theory*, 171-210. London: Holt, Rinehart and Winston.
  1982   Lexical morphology and phonology. In: The Linguistic Society of Korea (ed.). *Linguistics in the Morning Calm*, 3-91. Seoul: Hanshin Publishing Co.
Klemola, Juhani
  1997   Dialect evidence for the loss of genitive inflection in English. *English Language and Linguistics* 1 (2): 350-353.
Kohnen, Thomas
  2001   The influence of 'Latinate' constructions in Early Modern English: Orality and literacy as complementary forces. In: Dieter Kastovsky and Andreas Mettinger (eds.). *Language Contact in the History of English*, 171-194. Frankfurt a.M.: Peter Lang.
Koptjevskaja-Tamm, Maria
  2001   Adnominal possession. In: Martin Haspelmath, Ekkehard König, Wulf Oesterreicher, and Wolfgang Raichle (eds.). *Language Typology and Language Universals* (Handbooks of Linguistics and Communication Science 20.1,2). Vol. II, 960-970. Berlin/New York: Mouton de Gruyter.
  2002   Possessive NPs in the languages of Europe. In: Frans Plank (ed.). *The Noun Phrase in the Languages of Europe*. Berlin/New York: Mouton de Gruyter.
  forthc. Adnominal possesion in the European languages. In: Thomas Stolz (ed.). *Inalienable possession in the European languages, STUF: Sprachtypologie und Universalienforschung*, special issue.
Kortmann, Bernd
  1999   Typology and dialectology. In: Bernard Caron (ed.). *Proceedings of the 16th International Congress of Linguists, Paris 1997*. CD-ROM. Amsterdam: Elsevier Science.

Koziol, Herbert
1972   *Handbuch der englischen Wortbildungslehre.* Heidelberg: Carl Winter.

Kroch, Anthony
1994   Morphosyntactic variation. In: Katharine Beals, Jeanette Denton, Robert Knippen, Lynette Melnar, Hisami Suzuki, and Erica Zeinfeld (eds.). *Papers from the 30th Regional Meeting of the Chicago Linguistic Society,* Vol. 2: *The Parasession on Variation in Linguistic Theory* (CLS 30), 180-201. Chicago: Chicago Linguistics Society.
1997   Comments on 'Syntax Shinding' papers. *Transactions of the Philological Society* 95 (1): 133-147.

Krug, Manfred
1998   String frequency. A cognitive motivating factor in coalescence, language processing, and linguistic change. *Journal of English Linguistics* 26 (4): 286-320.

Kuno, Susumu and Etsuko Kaburaki
1977   Empathy and syntax. *Linguistic Inquiry* 8 (4): 627-672.

Kuteva, Tania
2001   *Auxiliation. An Enquiry into the Nature of Grammaticalization.* Oxford: Oxford University Press.

Labov, William
1969   Contraction, deletion and inherent variability of the English copula. *Language* 45: 715-762.
1972   *Sociolinguistic Patterns.* Philadelphia: University of Philadelphia Press.

Lakoff, George
1987   *Women, Fire, and Dangerous Things.* Chicago: The University of Chicago Press.

Lakoff, George and Mark Johnson
1980   *Metaphors we live by.* Chicago: The University of Chicago Press.

Lambrecht, Knud
1994   *Information Structure and Sentence Form.* Cambridge: Cambridge University Press.

Langacker, Ronald W.
1983   *Foundations of Cognitive Grammar,* vol. 1. Bloomington: Indiana Universty Linguistics Club.
1990   Subjectification. *Cognitive Linguistics* 1: 5-38.
1991   *Foundations of Cognitive Grammar,* vol. 2. Stanford: Stanford University Press.
1995   Possession and possessive constructions. In: John R. Taylor and Robert E. MacLaury (eds.). *Language and the Cognitive Construal of the World,* 51-79. Berlin/New York: Mouton de Gruyter.

Lass, Roger

1980   *On Explaining Language Change.* Cambridge: Cambridge University Press.

1990   How to do things with junk: Exaptation in language evolution. *Journal of Linguistics* 26: 79-102.

1992   Phonology and morphology. In: Norman Blake (ed.) *The Cambridge History of the English Language*, vol. II, *1066-1476*, 23-155. Cambridge: Cambridge University Press.

1994   *Old English.* Cambridge: Cambridge University Press.

1997   *Historical Linguistics and Language Change.* Cambridge: Cambridge University Press.

1999   Phonology and morphology. In: Roger Lass (ed.). *The Cambridge History of the English Language*, vol. III, *1476-1776*, 56-186. Cambridge: Cambridge University Press.

2000   Remarks on (uni)directionality. In: Olga Fischer, Anette Rosenbach, and Dieter Stein (eds.). *Pathways of Change. Grammaticalization in English* (Studies in Language Companion Series 53), 207-227. Amsterdam/ Philadelphia: John Benjamins.

forthc. Genetic metaphor in historical linguistics. In: April M. and Robert McMahon (eds.). *Proceedings of Conference on Genes, Languages and Peoples.*

Lavandera, Beatriz R.

1978   Where does the sociolinguistic variable stop? *Language in Society* 7: 171-182.

Leech, Geoffrey

1966   *English in Advertising. A Linguistic Study of Advertising in Great Britain.* London/New York: Longman.

Leech, Geoffrey, Brian Francis, and Xunfeng Xu

1994   The use of computer corpora in the textual demonstrability of gradience in linguistic categories. In: Catherine Fuchs and Bernard Victorri (eds.). *Continuity in Linguistic Semantics*, 57-76. Amsterdam/Philadelphia: John Benjamins.

Lehmann, Christian

1986   On the typology of relative clauses. *Linguistics* 24: 663-680.

1995   *Thoughts on Grammaticalization. A Programmatic Sketch.* University of Cologne. Revised and expanded version (LINCOM Studies in Theoretical Linguistics 01). München/Newcastle: Lincom [1982].

Levelt, Willem J.M.

1989   *Speaking. From Intention to Articulation.* Cambridge, Mass.: MIT Press.

Lieber, Rochelle

1988   Phrasal compounds in English and the morphology-syntax interface.

Papers from the Regional Meeting of the Chicago Linguistic Society 24 (2): 202-222.

Lightfoot, David

1991   *How to Set Parameters: Arguments from Language Change,* Cambridge, Mass.: MIT Press.

1999   *The Development of Language. Acquisition, Change, and Evolution.* Oxford: Blackwell.

Ljung, Magnus

1997   The *s*-genitive and the *of*-construction in different types of English texts. In: Udo Fried, Viviane Müller, and Peter Schneider (eds.). *From Ælfric to the New York Times. Studies in English Corpus Linguistics,* 21-32. Amsterdam/Atlanta: Rodopi.

Löbner, Sebastian

1985   Definites. *Journal of Semantics* 4: 279-326.

Lüdtke, Helmut

1980   Auf dem Wege zu einer Theorie des Sprachwandels. In: Helmut Lüdtke (ed.). *Kommunikationstheoretische Grundlagen des Sprachwandels,* 182-252. Berlin/New York: Mouton de Gruyter.

Lyell, Charles

1830-1833   *Principles of Geology: Being an Atempt to Explain the Former Changes to the Earth's Surface by Reference to Causes Now in Operation.* 3 vls. London: John Murray.

Lyons, Christopher

1986   The syntax of English genitive constructions. *Journal of Linguistics* 22: 123-143.

1989   Phrase structure, possessives and definiteness. *York Papers in Linguistics* 14: 221-228.

1999   *Definiteness.* Cambridge: Cambridge University Press.

Lyons, John

1977   *Semantics,* volume 1. Cambridge: Cambridge University Press.

1981   *Language and Linguistics: An Introduction.* Cambridge: Cambridge University Press.

MacKay, Donald

1987   *The Organization of Perception and Action: A Theory for Language and other Cognitive Skills.* New York: Springer.

Maes, Alfons

1997   Referent ontology and centering in discourse. *Journal of Semantics* 14: 207-235.

Marchand, Hans

1969   *The Categories and Types of Present-Day English Word-Formation.* München: C.H. Beck.

Martin, A., L.L. Wiggs, L.G. Ungerleider, and J.V. Haxby
1996   Neural correlates of category-specific knowledge. *Nature* 379: 649-
         652.
Mayerthaler, Willi
1981   *Morphologische Natürlichkeit*. Wiesbaden: Athenaion.
Mayerthaler, Willi and Günter Fliedl
1993   Syntaktische Präferenztheorie. In: Hugo Steger and Herbert Ernst
         Wiegand (eds.). *Syntax: Ein internationales Handbuch
         zeitgenössischer Forschung*, vol. 9.1 (1) (Handbücher zur Sprach-
         und Kommunikationswissenschaft), 610-635. Berlin/New York:
         Walter de Gruyter.
McDonald, Janet L., Kathryn Bock, and Michael Kelly
1993   Word and world order: Semantic, phonological, and metrical
         determinants of serial position. *Cognitive Psychology* 25: 188-230.
McMahon, April M.S.
1994   *Understanding Language Change*. Cambridge: Cambridge
         University Press.
2000   *Change, Chance, and Optimality*. Oxford: Oxford University Press.
Meillet, Antoine
1951   L'évolution des formes grammaticales. *Scientia* (Rivista di Scienza)
         12, no. 26, 6. Reprinted in: *Linuistique historique et linguistique
         générale*, 130-148. Paris: Klingensieck [1912].
Milroy, James
1992   *Linguistic Variation and Change*. Oxford: Blackwell.
Minkova, Donka
1999   Proximate mechanisms vs. causal explanations. *Zeitschrift für
         Sprachwissenschaft* 18 (2): 226-229.
Mitchell, Bruce
1985   *Old English Syntax*. Vol. I. Oxford: Clarendon Press.
Mithun, Marianne
1987   Is basic word order universal? In: Russell Tomlin (ed.) *Coherence
         and Grounding in Discourse*, 281-328. Amsterdam/Philadelphia:
         John Benjamins.
Mondorf, Britta
2000   Wider-ranging vs. more old-fashioned views on comparative
         formation in adjectival compounds/derivatives. In: Bernhard Reitz
         and Sigrid Rieuwerts (eds.). *Proceedings of the Anglistentag 1999,
         Mainz*, 35-44. Trier: Wissenschaftlicher Verlag.
Moss, P.
1968   *Today's English*. London: John Murray.
Müller, Gereon
1999   Optionality in Optimality-Theoretic Syntax. *Glot International* 4 (5):
         3-8.

Mulkern, Ann E.
1996   The game of the name. In: Thorstein Fretheim and Jeanette K.
            Gundel (eds.). *Reference and Referent Accessibility*, 235-250.
            Amsterdam/Philadelphia: John Benjamins.
Mustanoja, Tauno
1960   *A Midlde English Syntax*. Helsinki: Société Néophilologique.
Mutt, O.
1967   On some recent developments in the use nouns as premodifiers in
            English. *Zeitschrift für Anglistik und Amerikanistik* 4: 401-408.
Nevalainen, Terttu and Helena Raumolin-Brunberg
1994   *Its* strength and the beauty *of it*: The standardization of the third
            person neuter possessive in Early Modern English. In: Dieter Stein
            and Ingrid Tieken-Boon van Ostade (eds.). *Towards a Standard
            English, 1600-1800*, 171-215. Berlin/New York: Mouton de Gruyter.
Newmeyer, Frederick
1998   *Language Form and Language Function*. Cambridge, Mass.: MIT
            Press.
Nichols, Johanna
1984   Functional theories of grammar. *Annual Review of Anthropology* 13:
            97-117.
1986   Head-marking and dependent-marking grammar. *Language* 62 (1):
            56-119.
1988   On alienable and inalienable possession. In: William Shipley (ed.).
            *In Honor of Mary Haas: From the Haas Festival Conference on
            Native American Linguistics*, 557-609. Berlin/New York: Mouton de
            Gruyter.
1992   *Linguistic Diversity in Space and Time*. Chicago: University of
            Chicago Press.
Nicolle, Steve
1998   A relevance theory perspective on grammaticalization. *Cognitive
            Linguistics* 9 (1); 1-35.
Nikiforidou, Kiki
1991   The meanings of the genitive: A case study in semantic structure and
            semantic change. *Cognitive Linguistics* 2: 149-205.
Norde, Muriel
1998   Grammaticalization versus reanalysis: The case of possessive
            constructions in Germanic. In: Richard M. Hogg and Linda van
            Bergen (eds.). *Historical Linguistics 1995*, vol. 2: *Germanic
            Linguistics*, 211-222. Amsterdam/Philadelphia: John Benjamins.
2001   Deflexion as a counterdirectional factor in grammatical change.
            Language Sciences 23 (2-3): 231-264.
Nüse, Ralf
2000   Language-specific effects in the construction of events. Paper given

at the 22nd Annual Meeting of the Deutsche Gesellschaft für Sprachwissenschaft (DGFS), Marburg, March 1-3, 2000.

Nuyts, Jan
2000 Semantic paradigms and the nature and organization of the conceptual systems underlying language use. Paper given at the 22nd Annual Meeting of the Deutsche Gesellschaft für Sprachwissenschaft (DGFS), Marburg, March 1-3, 2000.

Olsen, Susan
2000 Compounding and stress in English: a closer look at the boundary between morphology and syntax. Linguistische Berichte 18: 55-69.

Ortmann, Albert
1998 The role of [± animate] in inflection. In: Ray Fabry, Albert Ortmann, and Teresa Parodi (eds.). Models of Inflection, 60-84. Tübingen: Niemeyer.

Paul, Hermann
1909 *Prinzipien der Sprachgeschichte.* Halle: Niemeyer.

Pechmann, Thomas
1994 *Sprachproduktion: Zur Generierung komplexer Nominalphrasen.* Opladen: Westdeutscher Verlag.

Penke, Martina
2001 Controversies about CP: A comparison of language acquisition and language impairments in Broca's aphasia. *Brain and Language* 77: 351-363.

Pinker, Steven
1994 *The Language Instinct. How the Mind Creates Language.* New York: William Morrow.
1997 *How the Mind Works.* Harmondsworth: Penguin.

Pinker, Steven and David Birdsong
1979 Speakers' sensitivity to rules of frozen word order. *Journal of Verbal Learning and Verbal Behavior* 18: 497-508.

Pintzuk, Susan, George Tsoulas, and Anthony Warner
2000 Syntactic change: Theory and method. In: Susan Pintzuk, George Tsoulas, and Anthony Warner (eds.) *Diachronic Syntax. Models and Mechanisms*, 1-22. Oxford: Oxford University Press.

Plank, Frans
1985 The interpretation and development of form alternations conditioned across word boundaries. The case of *wife's*, *wives*, and *wives*. In: Roger Eaton, Olga Fischer, Willem Koopman, and Friederike van der Leek (eds.). *Papers from the 4th International Conference on English Historical Linguistics*, 205-233. Amsterdam/Philadelphia: John Benjamins.
1992a From cases to adpositions. In: Nicola Pantaleo (ed.). *Aspects of English Diachronic Linguistics: Papers read at the Second National*

Conference of History of English, Naples, 28-29 April 1989, 19-61. Fasano: Schena.

1992b   Possessives and the distinction between determiners and modifiers (with special reference to German). *Journal of Linguistics* 28: 453-468.

1995   Entgrammatisierung – Spiegelbild der Grammatisierung? In: Norbert Boretzky, Wolfgang Dressler, Janez Orešnik, Karmen Terzan, and Wolfgang Wurzel (eds.). *Natürlichkeitstheorie und Sprachwandel,* 199-219. Bochum: Universitätsverlag Dr. N. Brockmeyer.

Potter, Simeon

1969   *Changing English.* 2nd revised edition 1975. London: Deutsch.

Poutsma, Hendrik

1914-1916 *A Grammar of Late Modern English, for Use of Continental, especially Dutch, Students.* Part II: *The Parts of Speech.* Groningen: Noordhoff.

Prince, Alan and Paul Smolensky

1993   *Optimality Theory: Constraint Interaction in Generative Grammar.* RuCCS Technical Report #2. Piscateway, NJ: Rutgers University Center for Cognitive Science.

Prince, Ellen

1981   Toward a taxonomy of given-new information. In: Peter Cole (ed.). *Radical Pragmatics,* 223-255. New York: Academic Press.

Quirk, Randolph, Sidney Greenbaum, Geoffrey Leechm, and Jan Svartvik

1985   *A Comprehensive Grammar of the English Language.* London/New York: Longman.

Raab-Fischer, Roswitha

1995   Löst der Genitiv die of-Phrase ab? Eine korpusgestützte Studie zum Sprachwandel im heutigen Englisch. *Zeitschrift für Anglistik und Amerikanistik* 43 (2): 123-132.

Radford, Andrew

1990   *Syntactic Theory and the Acquisition of Syntax.* Oxford: Blackwell.

Radford, Andrew, Martin Atkinson, David Britain, Harald Clahsen, and Andrew Spencer

1999   *Linguistics: An Introduction.* Cambridge: Cambridge University Press.

Raumolin-Brunberg, Helena

1991   *The Noun Phrase in Early Sixteenth-Century English. A Study based on Sir Thomas More's Writings.* Helsinki: Société Néophilologique.

Rissanen, Matti

1999   Syntax. In: Roger Lass (ed.). *The Cambridge History of the English Language,* vol. III, *1476-1776,* 187-331. Cambridge: Cambridge University Press.

Ritt, Nikolaus
  2001   Are optimality theoretic 'constraints' the same as natural linguistic
            'preferences'? In: Katarzyna Dziubalska-Kołaczyk (ed.). *Constraints
            and Preferences*, 291-310. Berlin/New York: Mouton de Gruyter.
Rohdenburg, Günter
  1996   Cognitive complexity and increased grammatical explicitness in
            English. *Cognitive Linguistics* 7: 149-182.
  forthc.   Cognitive complexity and *horror aequi* as factors determining the
            use of competing clause linkers in English. In: Günter Rohdenburg
            and Britta Mondorf (eds.). *Determinants of Grammatical Variation
            in English*. Berlin/New York: Mouton de Gruyter.
Romaine, Suzanne
  1981   The status of variable rules in sociolinguistic theory. *Journal of
            Linguistics* 17: 93-119.
  1984a   The status of sociological models and categories in explaining
            language variation. *Linguistische Berichte* 90: 25-38.
  1984b   On the problem of syntactic variation and pragmatic meaning in
            sociolinguistic theory. *Folia Linguistica* 18 (3-4): 409-437.
  1994   Sociolinguistics. In: R.E. Asher (ed.). *The Encyclopedia of Language
            and Linguistics*. Vol. 7, 4005-4014. Oxford: Pergamon Press.
Ronneberger-Sibold, Elke
  1980   *Sprachverwendung – Sprachsystem. Ökonomie und Wandel.*
            Tübingen: Niemeyer.
Rosenbach, Anette, Dieter Stein, and Letizia Vezzosi
  2000   On the history of the *s*-genitive. In: Ricardo Bermúdez-Otero, David
            Denison, Richard M. Hogg, and C.B. McCully (eds.). *Generative
            Theory and Corpus Study: A Dialogue from 10ICEH* (Topics in
            English Linguistics 31), 183-210. Berlin/New York: Mouton de
            Gruyter.
Rosenbach, Anette and Letizia Vezzosi
  1999   Was the *s*-genitive a traveller through England? In: Alexander Bergs
            and Dieter Stein (eds.). *LANA – Düsseldorf Working Papers on
            Linguistics* 1: 35-55 (http://ang3-11.phil-fak.uni.duesseldorf.de/
            ~ang3/LANA/LANA.html).
Rosenbach, Anette and Letizia Vezzosi
  2000   Genitive constructions in Early Modern English: New evidence from
            a corpus analysis. In: Rosanna Sornicola, Erich Poppe and Ariel
            Shisha-Halevy (eds.), 285-307.
Rumelhart, David E. and James L. McClelland
  1982   An interactive activation model of context effects in letter
            perception: Part 2. The contextual enhancement effect and some tests
            and extensions of the model. *Psychological Review* 89: 60-94.

Sampson, Geoffrey
1980   *Schools of Linguistics*. London: Hutchinson.
Sankoff, David and Pascale Rousseau
1980   Categorical contexts and variable rules. In: Sven Jacobson (ed.). *Papers from the Scandinavian Symposium on Syntactic Variation, Stockholm, May 18-19, 1979*, 7-22. Stockholm: Almqvist & Wiksell.
Sapir, Edward
1921   *Language: An Introduction to the Study of Speech*. New York: Harcourt, Brace & World.
Schneider, Walter and Richard M. Shiffrin
1977   Controlled and automatic human information processing: I. Detection, search and attention. *Psychological Review* 84: 1-66.
Schulze, Rainer
1998   Preface. In: Rainer Schulze (ed.). *Making Meaningful Choices in English*, 8-10. Tübingen: Gunter Narr.
Schwarz, Monika
1992   *Einführung in die Kognitive Linguistik*. Tübingen: Francke.
Seiler, HansJakob
1983   *Possession as an Operational Dimension of Language*. Tübingen: Gunter Narr Verlag.
Seppänen, Aimo
1997a   The genitives of the relative pronouns in present-day English. In: Jenny Cheshire and Dieter Stein (eds.). *Taming the Vernacular. From Dialect to Written Standard* Language, 152-169. London/New York: Longman.
1997b   The genitive and the category of case in the history of English. In: Raymond Hickey and Stanislaw Puppel (eds.). *Language History and Linguistic Modelling. A Festschrift for Jacek Fisiak on his 60th Birthday, Vol. 1*, 193-214. Berlin/New York: Mouton de Gruyter.
Siemund, Rainer
1993   Aspect of language change in progress: A corpus-based study of British Newspaper English in 1961 and 1991. M.A. thesis, University of Freiburg.
Siewierska, Anna
1988   *Word Order Rules*. London: Croom Helm.
1996   Word order and linearization. In: Keith Brown and Jim Miller (eds.). *Concise Encylcopedia of Syntactic Theories*, 372-378. Oxford: Pergamon.
Silva-Corvalán, Carmen
1986   On the problem of meaning in sociolinguistic studies of syntactic variation. In: Dieter Kastovsky and Aleksander Swedek (eds.). *Linguistics and Historical and Geographical Boundaries: In Honour of Jacek Fisiak on the Occasion of his fiftieth Birthday, I: Linguistic*

Theory and Historical Linguistics, 111-123. Berlin/New York: Mouton de Gruyter.

Silverstein, Michael
1976   Hierarchy of features and ergativity. In: Robert M.W. Dixon (ed.). *Grammatical Categories in Australian Languages*, 112-171. Canberra: Australian Institute of Aboriginal Studies.

Slobin, Dan I.
1996   From 'thought and language' to 'thinking for speaking'. In: John Gumperz and Stephen Levinson (eds.). *Rethinking Linguistic Relativity*, 70-96. Cambridge: Cambridge University Press.

Sornicola, Rosanna, Erich Poppe, and Ariel Shisha-Halevy (eds.)
2000   *Stability, Variation and Change of Word-Order Patterns over Time.* Amsterdam/Philadelphia: John Benjamins.

Spencer, Andrew
1991   *Morphological Theory.* Oxford: Blackwell.

Sperber, Dan
1996   *Explaining Culture. A Naturalistic Approach.* Oxford: Blackwell.

Sperber, Deirdre and Dan Wilson
1986   *Relevance.* Oxford: Blackwell.

Stahl, Leon
1927   Der adnominale Genitiv und sein Ersatz im Mittelenglischen und frühneuenglischen. *Giessener Beiträge* 3: 1-35.

Stampe, David
1972   How I spent my summer vacation. Ph.D. thesis, Ohio State University.

Stein, Dieter
1988   Psycholinguistic issues and determinants of syntactic change. *Papiere zur Linguistik* 39 (2): 31-48.
1990   *The Semantics of Syntactic Change. Aspects of the Evolution of* Do *in English.* Berlin/New York: Mouton de Gruyter.
1997   Syntax and varieties. In: Jenny Cheshire and Dieter Stein (eds.). *Taming the Vernacular. From Dialect to Written Standard Language*, 35-50. London/New York: Longman.

Stemberger, Joseph Paul
1981   Morphological haplology. *Language* 57 (4): 791-817.
1985   An interactive activation model of language production. In: Andrew Ellis (ed.). *Progress in the Psychology of Language*, 143-186. London: Erlbaum.

Stiebels, Barbara
2000   *Typologie des Argumentlinkings: Ökonomie und Expressivität.* Habilitation thesis, University of Düsseldorf.

Svartengren, Hilding
1949   The *'s*-genitive of non-personal nouns in present-day English.

Studier i Modern Spraekvetenskap [Stockholm studies in modern philology] 17: 139-180.

Tabor, Whitney
1994 Syntactic innovation: A connectionist model. Stanford University dissertation (http://www.sp.uconn.edu/~ps300vl/papers.html).

Tabor, Whitney and Elizabeth C. Traugott
1998 Structural scope expansion and grammaticalization. In: Anna G. Ramat and Paul Hopper (eds.). *The Limits of Grammaticalization*, 229-272. Amsterdam/Philadelphia: John Benjamins.

Tagliamonte, Sali
2000 The grammaticalization of the present perfect in English: Tracks of change and continuity in a linguistic enclave. In: Olga Fischer, Anette Rosenbach, and Dieter Stein (eds.). *Pathways of Change. Grammaticalization in English* (Studies in Language Companion Series 53), 329-354. Amsterdam/Philadelphia: John Benjamins.

Taylor, John
1989 Possessive genitives in English. *Linguistics* 27: 663-686.
1995 *Linguistic Categorization: Prototypes in Linguistic Theory*. 2nd edition. Oxford: Clarendon Press [1989].
1996 *Possessives in English*. Oxford: Clarendon.
1999 Possession. In: Keith Brown and Jim Miller (eds.). *Concise Encyclopedia of Grammatical Categories*, 300-303. Amsterdam: Elsevier.

Tesar, Bruce and Paul Smolensky
2000 *Learnability in Optimality Theory*. Cambridge, Mass.: MIT Press.

Thomas, Russel
1931 Syntactical processes involved in the development of the adnominal periphrastic genitive in the English language. Ann Arbor: University of Michigan, unpublished Ph. D. dissertation.
1953 Notes on the inflected genitive in modern American prose. *College English* XIV: 236-239.

Thompson, Sandra A.
1990 Information flow and dative shift in English discourse. In: Jerold A. Edmondson, Crawford Feagin, and Peter Muhlhausler (eds.). *Development and Diversity: Language Variation across Time and Space*, 239-253. Dallas: Summer Institue of Linguistics and University of Texas at Arlington.

Timberlake, Alan
1977 Reanalysis and actualization in syntactic change. In Charles N. Li (ed.). *Mechanisms of Syntactic Change*, 141-177. Austin (Texas)/London: University of Texas Press.

Timmer, B. J.
    1939   The place of the attributive noun-genitive in Anglo-Saxon. *English Studies* 21: 49-72.
Traugott, Elizabeth C.
    1992   Syntax. In: Richard Hogg (ed.) *The Cambridge History of the English Language,* vol. I, *The Beginnings – 1066,* 168-289. Cambridge: Cambridge University Press.
    1995   Subjectification in grammaticalization. In: Dieter Stein and Susan Wright (eds.). *Subjectivity and Subjectivisation,* 31-54. Cambridge: Cambridge University Press.
    1999   From a diachronic perspective. *Zeitschrift für Sprachwissenschaft* 18 (2): 238-241.
Tyler, L. K., H. E. Moss, M. R Durant-Peatfield, and J. P. Levy
    2000   Conceptual structure and the structure of concepts: A distributed account of category-specific deficits. *Brain and Language* 75: 195-231.
Varantola, Krista
    1993   Modification of nouns by nouns – bad by definition? In: Andreas Jucker (ed.). *The Noun Phrase in English: Its Structure and Variability,* 69-83. Heidelberg: Carl Winter.
Vennemann, Theo
    1974   Topics, subjects and word order: From SXV to SVX via TVX. In: John M. Anderson and Charles Jones (eds.). *Historical Linguistics.* Volume 1: *Syntax, Morphology, Internal and Comparative Reconstruction,* 339-376. Amsterdam: North Holland.
Vincent, Nigel
    2000   Competition and correspondence in syntactic change: Null arguments in Latin and Romance. In: Susan Pintzuk, George Tsoulas, and Anthony Warner (eds.). *Diachronic Syntax. Models and Mechanisms,* 25-50. Oxford: Oxford University Press.
Warrington, E. and T. Shallice
    1984   Category specific semantic impairments. *Brain* 107: 829-854.
Wasow, Thomas
    1997a   End-weight from the speaker's perspective. *Journal of Psycholinguistic Research* 26 (3): 347-361.
    1997b   Remarks on grammatical weight. *Language Variation and Change* 9: 81-105.
Weerman, Fred and Petra de Wit
    1999   The decline of the genitive in Dutch. *Linguistics* 37 (6): 1155-1192.
Weiner, E. Judith and William Labov
    1983   Constraints on the agentless passive. *Journal of Linguistics* 19: 29-58.

Weinreich, Uriel, William Labov, and Marvin Herzog
  1968   Empirical foundations for a theory of language change. In: Winfrid
            Lehmann and Yakov Malkiel (eds.). *Directions for Historical
            Linguistics*, 95-188. Austin: University of Texas Press.
Wilder, Chris and Hans-Martin Gärtner
  1997   Introduction. In: Chris Wilder, Hans-Martin Gärtner, and Manfred
            Bierwisch (eds.). *The Role of Economic Principles in Linguistic
            Theory*, 1-35. Berlin: Adademie Verlag.
Woisetschlaeger, Ernst
  1983   On the question of definiteness in 'an old man's book'. *Linguistic
            Inquiry* 14 (1): 137-154.
Wolff, Dieter
  1975   *Grundzüge der diachronischen Morphologie des Englischen.*
            Tübingen: Niemeyer.
Wurzel, Wolfgang
  1989   *Inflectional Morphology and Naturalness.* Kluwer: Dordrecht.
  1997   Natürlicher grammatischer Wandel, unsichtbare Hand' und
            Sprachökonomie – Wollen wir wirklich so Grundverschiedenes? In:
            Thomas Birkmann, Heinz Klingenberg, Damaris Nübling, and Elke
            Ronneberger-Sibold (eds.). *Vergleichende germanische Philologie
            und Skandinavistik. Festschrift für Otmar Werner*, 295-308.
            Tübingen: Niemeyer.
  1999   Principles of evaluation, change an related issues. *Zeitschrift für
            Sprachwissenschaft* 18 (2): 242-250.
Wyld, Henry Cecil
  1936   *A History of Modern Colloquial English.* 3rd edition. Oxford: Basil
            Blackwell.
Yamamoto, Mutsumi
  1999   *Animacy and Reference.* Amsterdam/Philadelphia: John Benjamins.
Zachrisson, R. E.
  1920   Grammatical changes in present-day English. *Studier i Modern
            Spraekvetsenskap* [Stockholm Studies in Modern Philology] 7: 19-
            61.
Zec, Draga and Sharon Incelas
  1990   Prosodically constrained syntax. In: Sharon Inkelas and Draga Zec
            (eds.). *The Phonology-Syntax Connection*, 365-378. Chicago: The
            University of Chicago Press.
Zwicky, Arnold M.
  1987   Suppressing the Zs. *Journal of Linguistics* 23: 133-148.
  1994   Clitics. In: R. E. Asher and J. M. Y. Simpson (eds.). *The
            Encyclopedia of Language and Linguistics*, 571-576. Oxford:
            Pergamon Press.

Name index

Subject index